AN AUTOBIOGRAPHY BY

JOAN

Past Imperfect

COLLINS

SIMON AND SCHUSTER · NEW YORK

Library of Congress Cataloging in Publication Data
Collins, Joan
  Past imperfect.

  Filmography: p.
  1. Collins, Joan   2. Moving-picture
actors and actresses—Great Britain—Biography.   I. Title.
PN2598.C66A36   1984   791.43'028'0924   84-1263
ISBN 0-671-47360-3

For permission to reprint lyrics, the author is grateful to the following:

"Why Do You Try and Change Me?" Words and music by Anthony Newley. Copyright © 1968 Cynara Music Ltd., London, England. TRO—Musical Comedy Productions, Inc., New York, controls all publication rights for the U.S.A. and Canada. Used by permission.

"What Kind of Fool Am I?" From the musical production *Stop the World—I Want to Get Off.* Words and music by Leslie Bricusse and Anthony Newley. Copyright © 1961 TRO Essex Music Ltd., London, England. TRO—Ludlow Music, Inc., New York, controls all publication rights for the U.S.A. and Canada. Used by permission.

"I Wanna Be Rich." From the musical production *Stop the World—I Want to Get Off.* Words and music by Leslie Bricusse and Anthony Newley. Copyright © 1961 and 1978 TRO Essex Music Ltd., London, England. TRO—Ludlow Music, Inc., New York, controls all publication rights for the U.S.A. and Canada. Used by permission.

"Chalk and Cheese." Words by Herbert Kretzmer. Music by Anthony Newley. Copyright © 1968 by Duchess Music Corporation, New York, N.Y. Rights administered by MCA Music, a division of MCA, Inc., New York, N.Y. Used by permission. All rights reserved.

"I'm All I Need." Words by Herbert Kretzmer. Music by Anthony Newley. Copyright © 1968, 1969 by Duchess Music Corporation, New York, N.Y. Rights administered by MCA Music, a division of MCA, Inc., New York, N.Y. Used by permission. All rights reserved.

For my beautiful children, Tara, Sacha and Katyana. They are the past, the present and, especially, the future. And for my mother, Elsa. I wish she could be here to share it all with me.

ACKNOWLEDGMENTS

Grateful thanks to Judy Bryer and Barry Langford, who painstakingly deciphered the hieroglyphics; Michael Korda, my editor, and Dan Green, for giving me the carrot and the stick; George Christy, who insisted I should publish it in America.

Prologue

THERE ARE A LOT OF REASONS FOR writing this book, but the major one is my desire to "get the record straight." I want to describe my life as it's *really* been—not as the gossip columns reported it (though they were not always wrong).

I'm a very positive and frank person. I have lived through some bad patches in my life as a woman, an actress and a mother. It has usually been my positive attitude, stamina, optimism and sense of humor that have not only made me survive, but have brought me success again as Alexis Carrington Colby in "Dynasty," in a profession where I've been down for the ten count more than once. Although I was a celebrity, a "star" (a term I hate) before "Dynasty," it is with this television series that I have come into my own.

But perhaps the strongest reason for the book is this: I feel in some small way that I have been a pioneer in the cause of women's sexual equality, and also in overcoming the age barrier that sets a cruel double standard for so many women in every walk of life.

If I had been a man and had lived my life as I did, I don't think I would have shocked anybody. As a woman I have come in for more than my share of brickbats, criticism and public and professional flak.

I am fortunate in having a core of good friends and close family who love and support me, who know my flaws and weaknesses,

9

and who have helped me to try and overcome them, to grow, to change and to improve.

I'm still growing up. This may sound ridiculous from a woman who has lived so much, but I have much to learn. I want to broaden my horizons and to stretch myself to my utmost capabilities because I believe that change is the only constant in life.

And I truly believe that the best is yet to come!

California, December 1983.

MY FIRST RECORDED PUBLIC AP-
pearance is a photograph of my mother and father and Lew
Grade at a charity ball seven hours before I was born.

Apart from a slightly panicky look in my mother's eyes, no one
could ever tell that she was about to deliver her firstborn. She is
smoothly blond, soignée and flanked by the two young dinner-
jacketed men.

My father, Joe Collins, and Lew Grade were at that time part-
ners in the theatrical agency Collins and Grade. They had the
suitably smug expressions of men about to become father and godfather for the first time. Although Lord Lew Grade (as he is today) never became my official godfather, he and my parents were
then, and for many years to come, so close, both in business and
in their personal lives, that he was "Uncle Lew" to me, and he
took a personal interest in me when I was a child. Mummy and
Daddy were bridesmaid and best man when he married a lovely
young singer, Kathleen Moody, during the war—and until Mummy's death in 1962, she and Kathy were the closest of friends, although the business relationship between my father and Lew had
long been dissolved.

I was in awe of my father for so many years that it is even now
hard to write about him without the feeling he may get cross with
me. Throughout years of analysis and soul-searching, with intellectual and emotional knowledge of myself and my relationships, Daddy had always been a frightening figure rather than a

11

father figure. There is no doubt that some of my quests for the eternal love of impossible men were to capture Daddy, for there is no doubt that I had his love for at least the first five or six years of my life.

I was born in a Bayswater nursing home in north London on May 23, sometime between the end of the Great Depression and the beginning of the war. "Any woman who would reveal her age would reveal anything." Thus spake Oscar Wilde. And I agree with him.

According to my parents and relatives I was the world's most adorable-looking baby—but lacked the personality to match. Gemini children are mercurial and moody, charming and delightful one minute, totally impossible the next . . . and I was a typical Gemini. My baby looks were so appealing that my ever vigilant mother had a printed sign, "Please Do Not Kiss Me" displayed in my pram whenever we took our morning strolls.

Beautiful bonny babies must have been rare in north London then, for Mummy was often fighting off women begging to kiss, hold or adopt me. I was so overprotected that my mother even put ice cream in the oven for a few minutes before I ate it so the chill should be off!

It was an idyllic infancy and early childhood. We lived in a flat in Maida Vale three or four blocks from Regent's Park. Daddy worked at the agency with Lew, and adored Baby Joan and Mummy. One of the reasons I was called Joan was because they had wanted a boy, to have been called Joe, Jr., no doubt, and my name was the closest feminine equivalent. Throughout my first fifteen years, whenever my mother called out "Joe," I would often answer.

My adoration for my father was intense. At nursery school I told the other kids that my father was the tallest and handsomest man in the world. Handsome he was, with jet-black curly hair, which he would slick flat to his head with three layers of Brylcreem, dark-brown flashing eyes and a finely chiseled profile. Tall? Well, hardly. One day I realized to my disappointment that my father was only about five feet ten. There is a yellowing photograph in an old family album that epitomizes for me the idealistic father-daughter relationship and is my favorite picture of him and me.

12

I am four or five years old, gap-toothed, large bow in hair and wearing a pretty sunsuit. We are in some faraway summer vacationland. I am sitting on the grass, legs neatly crossed, and smiling fit to burst. He is suntanned, curly-haired and smiling, gray-flanneled and sports-coated, holding in his hand a huge fishing net with which he is about to "catch" the little girl who sits trusting and happy, secure in the love of her handsome father.

My mother was gorgeous too. Blond and blue-eyed, she had the perfect Anglo-Saxon looks to complement my father's darkly Jewish ones. She was as fair as he was dark, and as gentle and kind as he could be stern and strict; my memories of my mother have become fonder through the years. I was always stronger than she and it irritated me that she seemed to adore being a slave to my father. When Joe became angry, we all fled. His raised voice made us nervous. But on looking back, I can see that one of the many qualities that made my mother love him so much was his outrageous sense of humor. He was always cracking jokes, and with his many friends often around, the flat would echo with their laughter.

I was sent to dancing school before I was three. Throughout the rest of my childhood I attended nine or ten different dancing academies as well as thirteen different schools. Before I was even old enough to go to kindergarten I would spend part of each morning listening avidly to the radio, dancing and whirling and humming to the early morning radio programs, while my mother did the housework. In the days before the radio became one continuous DJ program, the variety was infinite, and I would dance spiritedly to marches, classical music, brass bands, Strauss waltzes and, best of all, jazz. And sing too. I had aspirations as a singer, as well as an actress and I knew most of the words to every popular song ever written until the advent of Beatlemania.

Each Sunday we would get into the car and go for a long drive. There was usually a new car each year—impeccably tuned. The boredom of those endless drives lives with me still. To this day, I'd rather go on a plane, train or helicopter than drive anywhere for longer than two hours. We would drive through the unspoiled English countryside to Brighton, where Daddy's mother lived, or to Bognor, where Mummy's mother lived, or to Devon or Sussex or Kent, where nobody we even knew lived, and to relieve the boredom of the drives, I would sing and sing and sing.

Even as a tiny girl my interest in movies, dancing and theater was enormous. My fantasies took over completely, giving me fodder for my bedtime thoughts.

My father was second-generation show business. He was born in Port Elizabeth, South Africa, in 1902, to a successful theatrical agent, Will Collins, and a saucy soubrette and dancer, Henrietta Collins. Hetty must have been an early emancipated woman since she continued dancing with her sister act "The Three Cape Girls" until a month or so before Joe's birth. Considering it was still the Victorian Age, this showed a remarkable lack of concern for convention, something I obviously inherited from her. Photographs of her—hand on hip or posed in a daring cancan costume—show a beautiful, strong-featured young brunette with a willful look about her and a twinkle in her eye.

I remember Grandma Hetty as a lovely, effervescent gutsy lady, who taught me to dance and do the "splits" and high kicks, and was always full of life, laughter and fun up until her death. She encouraged me in my youthful aspirations as singer-dancer-actress. She regaled me with stories of backstage life, and made it sound wonderfully exciting—a world peopled with clowns, dancing and make-believe. I could almost smell the greasepaint and the musty, dank backstage odor of the scenery when she talked.

She had two other children, Lalla and Pauline. My father, the only boy, was spoiled rotten as a child. Both his sisters adored him, as did Hetty, as subsequently did my mother, Elsa, and eventually, of course, me and my sister, Jackie, and my half-sister, Natasha. He had a long line of women all competing for his favors. And there's no doubt about it, he was a handsome devil whom women found irresistible.

Both of Hetty's daughters went into the theatrical world— Pauline became a theatrical agent and Lalla, the blond beauty of the family, became a dancer and one of "Cochran's Young Ladies."

Our apartment was always full of amusing and gregarious people whom Daddy represented—comedians, singers, dancers, conjurers and ventriloquists. A veritable procession of outgoing personalities congregated there. Daddy often played cards with them until the early hours; he played a formidable game of poker, which I learned from "kibitzing" over his shoulder.

All of these fascinating people, perhaps to ingratiate themselves with my father to get more work, or maybe because they believed it, would compliment me on my cute little nose, eyes or personal ity, and usually ended their remarks with "Of course you really *must* go on the stage."

So the seed was planted, and I started to dream my dreams of becoming an actress.

Daddy was proud of me then, there was no doubt of that. He liked the fact that I was cute, bubbly and captivating, and he agreed with his friends that I did indeed have the makings of an actress, although he himself did not advocate the theater as a suitable profession for young girls, knowing the difficulties and rejection so many of them suffered.

I can't pinpoint exactly when I stopped being Daddy's little darling. It could have been when little baby Jackie arrived to take some of the attention away from me. It could have been that with the coming of the London blitz we were speedily packed off to safer pastures in Brighton, Ilfracombe or Bognor, leaving Daddy alone in London to fend for himself. Oh, how my mother worried about him! But he had to stay in the city. There was a huge demand for variety shows and entertainment during the war, and he was putting his comedians, ventriloquists and dancers to work.

The war years are a hazy blur of evacuation to new places—boarding with strange people in even stranger houses and, horror of horrors, *constant* new schools. Shyness, something I had never suffered from previously, suddenly descended on me along with insecurities and doubts. New children at school whispering and giggling in the corner at the nervous new girl made me feel an outsider. I retreated more and more into a fantasy world of dolls, cinema, books and film magazines. Over all of it was a nagging feeling of rejection. I felt that if Daddy *really* loved me he would be with me in all those unfamiliar places.

It was a gypsylike existence. When the blitz and the bombings eased up, we returned to London for a few weeks or months. When the air raids started again, we were awakened in the middle of the night by Mummy and our nanny, bundled into "siren suits" and down to the basement of our block of flats, where we fitfully slept the night away, the sounds of distant exploding bombs and antiaircraft fire echoing through the dark and smelly air-raid shelter.

I was too young to understand how dangerous it really was, or how terrified was my poor mother. With a baby and a small girl to contend with, she was petrified that anything would befall us. Her ambivalent feelings of wanting to be with my father, and yet having to expose her children to peril to do so, must have caused her anguish. So after a short or a long time in London, off we'd go again, to yet another sanctuary, and another new school, and another painful time of trying to make new friends again. And that was the beginning of my gypsy life.

At the age of thirteen I was awkward, spotty, gawky, shy, boy-hating and introverted.

Convinced I didn't have any charms to capture my father's affection as I had when I was a toddler, and with the added horror of a baby brother, Bill, the family's new darling, I decided that there was only one way to regain his affection and make things the way they were: I decided to try as hard as possible to act and look like a boy! The imminent onset of puberty was a disaster I was convinced couldn't *possibly* happen to me. Girls at school would discuss in hushed tones the horrors of the "curse." I searched the library in vain for an explanation of this, but with nothing forthcoming from my parents, my vivid imagination could only fear the worst.

I accompanied my father to his favorite football games every Saturday afternoon, freezing bravely in boyish corduroy trousers, jumper and brightly striped football scarf, waving my ratchet and jumping up in hysterical joy every time somebody scored a goal, trying hard to please him.

I actually loathed football. I couldn't comprehend the fascination of twenty-two unkempt, dirty men kicking a ball around a muddy field, while thousands of raucous blokes in caps and mufflers cheered and screamed. My hatred of football also extended to other active sports, with the exception of swimming, at which

I was fair. My performance at netball, lacrosse and tennis was atrocious. However, I feigned enormous enthusiasm for soccer and listened with phony fascination to the Saturday evening football results, hoping to impress my father.

Of course it didn't work. Bill, at two or three, was far more fascinating than gawky me. He pushed his toy cars and trucks happily around on the carpet, watched fondly by my parents, while I glowered jealously at him, stuffed myself frustratedly with sausage rolls and biscuits, and reaffirmed silently to myself my vow to become an actress.

The word "love" was an enigma to me for many years. In spite of two years of analysis and a weekend session at Actualizations, a workshop to explore human potential, my quests for love, although seemingly successful at the time, would leave me two or three years later with the question in my mind as to whether or not I had really loved that man as much as I thought I had at the time.

In the time that I spent at the Royal Academy of Dramatic Art, between the ages of fifteen and a half and sixteen and a half, I discovered the opposite sex for the first time and fell "in love" many times. Much of the time I should have spent studying was squandered in dithering daydreams about the current beloved. Some of these flirtations lasted as long as three or four months, some only three or four days—but they were all platonic. For this was the flirty fifties and God forbid a well brought up half-Jewish girl would do anything as gravely taboo as "go all the way." There were only stolen kisses under the lamppost, furtive hand-holding at the movies, and whispered undying protestations of love in the austere corridors of the Royal Academy.

It was unthinkable for a young girl to sleep with a boy then. General knowledge of sexual practices, not to mention birth control, was skimpy and vague. It was an accepted fact between both sexes that you petted and necked, kissed and cuddled, but, as far as the girls were concerned, you saved your virginity for the marital bed.

I was popular. David McCallum, who was in my class, told me that I was the first girl he and the other boys in class noticed. I suddenly became aware of my sex appeal. It was a novelty to be able to attract young men. However, my interest in them bloomed and faded as fast as the summer flowers; when I lost interest in one, I immediately focused my attention on another. This little game continued in different fashion for many years. It was a classic. A girl with a father complex, looking for affirmation of her desirability by enticing hard-to-get males.

The ones who flocked after *me* were of no interest, and this pattern continued more or less for years. I have always, with few exceptions, chosen the "love object," been the pursuer, won the heart and ended the game. My span of interest and involvement lengthened as I became more mature, and from the brief mad weekly crushes at RADA to my seven-month first marriage to Maxwell Reed, and thence to deeper and more involved affairs, they have successively lasted for longer and longer periods of time.

Most of the men and boys I chose were difficult, unattainable, moody, unpredictable, sometimes unable to love or to be giving and that was *always* what intrigued me. Not for me to be wooed and won; I was the wooer, and in being so I was wounded many times.

But I also was working hard at RADA. Determined to succeed in my profession, I had already been discovered. A modeling agency came to RADA to choose a girl for photographic modeling in women's magazines. I was the lucky one, and even with the miserly salaries paid to a model, I was then able to buy better tickets to the theater and movies, to which I went two or three times a week, to buy some new clothes and occasionally even take a taxi.

I modeled for the illustrations of love stories in women's magazines. In one I was a terrified teenager in a yellow turtleneck about to be raped by a madman in a haunted house. In another, a heartbroken teenager sobbing into her pillow when she discovers she is pregnant. Although not exactly svelte, I modeled teenage clothes for the pages of *Woman* and *Woman's Own*. There was no such thing as a totally teen-oriented market in the early 1950s. Mass-market jeans and casual wear were not the vogue, so the clothes I wore in the photos were frumpy and unflattering. My usual attire was tight jeans and workmen's plaid shirts bought from men's stores. With these I featured giant gypsy gold earrings, flat ballet shoes and a black polo-necked sweater, a hand-me-down from my sophisticated Aunt Lalla. This was an avant-garde costume then. With my exotic makeup—eyes rimmed with black pencil à la the top models of the day—two-inch-thick black eyebrows à la Elizabeth Taylor, my favorite actress, and long, straight bangs and a ponytail, I was the focus of attention wherever I went. Leslie Bricusse—then a student at Cambridge—remembers seeing me at a pub in King's Road, and although he didn't meet me, my outré image stuck with him.

A national magazine did a photo story on jazz clubs, and my picture appeared in print with my partner, with the caption "The couple who dress 'très Jazz.' " I was unnamed and unknown in the photo. It was only my outrageous outfit that caused me to be noticed.

Jazz clubs and dancing were now my favorite relaxation. Three nights a week, two or three girlfriends and I would sit in smoky dives and listen ecstatically to "Humph," Humphrey Lyttleton's Dixieland Band, which played at 100 Oxford Street, or would go to outlying suburbs to catch other of our favorites: George Melly, Sidney Bechet and Claude Luter. "Humph" was my favorite, and I sat mesmerized for hours as his trumpet played ragtime and jazz from an era that fascinated me—the twenties—"When the Saints Go Marching In," "Jelly Roll Blues," "Hotter Than That," and dozens of others. I danced nonstop for endless hours in the steamy cellar on Oxford Street.

Suddenly my career started to happen. One day the phone rang and someone with a charming voice introduced himself as Bill Watts, a well-known agent, whose specialty was representing pretty young girls. He had seen my pictures in *Woman's Own* and thought that I was a possibility for films.

I met him at his office in Mayfair. The walls were completely covered with photos of starlets in bathing suits and various stages of undress. He took me to lunch at a four-star restaurant, and over the shrimp cocktail and chicken vol-au-vent told me that I had "definite film potential." "But I want to be a *serious* actress," I said seriously. "Film stars can't act. They are just discovered behind soda fountains or cosmetic counters. I want to finish my next year at RADA, do several seasons in rep, and then, hopefully, get to the West End. Films are not for me." I sipped some white wine, gazing at him challengingly.

My views were heavily colored by RADA's attitude toward the movie medium. They thought that art was possible only in the theater, and the emphasis was heavily on having a melodic voice, the correct vowels and articulation, wonderfully theatrical gestures and the proper classical attitudes. I quote one of my report cards from RADA: "With so much in her favor this student is hampered by the weakness of her voice. She seems to lack the confidence to project and make use of the amount of voice she does possess. If she will make up her mind to cast away all fear and self-consciousness and *speak out* she will find her confidence increasing, and the unsure element in her acting will disappear. Otherwise it is 'the Films' for her and that would be such a pity." Oh what irony!

Although I worked at it diligently, my voice production and projection were constantly criticized by the teachers at RADA, and instead of gaining confidence and improving I became even more inhibited. We had endless elocution classes. Any dialect was taboo. An Albert Finney or a Michael Caine wouldn't have stood a chance to grow as an actor until he learned to speak with a conformist, aristocratic accent. We were supposed to speak and act as though we were from the same cookie cutter; consequently our true personalities and abilities were never really able to unfold. I was trying to talk and behave on stage like someone else—Claire Bloom or Vivien Leigh.

So I was snobbish about "the films" and it was only the persuasiveness of Bill Watts and his insistence that doing a few movie roles would only enhance my ability and not hinder it that made me sign with his agency.

He worked fast. Within a week I was being considered for the leading role in a film called *Lady Godiva Rides Again*, about the rise and fall of a beauty queen. I tested at Shepperton with several up-and-coming starlets. The makeup man and the hairdresser who painted and coiffed me for Lady Godiva had learned their craft in the dark ages. A thick layer of orange pancake was applied to my cherubic face. "She's moon-faced," they said to each other laconically. Dark-brown shading was plastered on my cheeks, pale-blue eyeshadow on my lids, and away with the doe eyes and the two-inch eyebrows. Carmine lipstick completed the look. A cross between a teenage Joan Crawford and an albino.

No wonder I didn't get the lead. For consolation, I was awarded a supporting role as one of the contestants and spent three freezing days in a black, boned bathing suit shivering in Folkestone Town Hall, along with other runners up, among them Jean Marsh, who went on to bigger and better things with her portrayal of the maid Rose in "Upstairs Downstairs" and the TV series "Nine to Five."

Filming was uncomfortable and boring. Up at 5 A.M. in the pitch-dark, herded around like cattle by a harassed assistant director, either freezing to death or boiling under the arc lights and listening to an incomprehensible jargon from the crew: "It's a dolly shot," "Save the baby," "Trim the arc," "Where's the Chippy?" "Turn over," "Action" . . . little did I realize that this was the dialogue I was destined to hear throughout my career.

Two weeks later, Bill got me a slightly better role as a Greek maid in a forgettable film called *The Woman's Angle* starring Lois Maxwell, later Miss Moneypenny in the James Bond films. The money was princely—fifty pounds. It helped me buy more imitation-gold earrings and polo-neck sweaters, and the publicity helped me become even more of a minor celebrity at RADA, where my amorous adventures were gossiped about.

I now had a double life: aspiring film starlet and dedicated drama student, and the British press were cottoning on to me fast: "Britain's Best Bet Since Jean Simmons" . . . "She has the come-hither eyes of Ava Gardner, the sultry look of Lauren Bacall, a Jane Russell figure, and more sex appeal at her age than any other film actress I've met," raved *Reveille*, the workingman's favorite paper.

But RADA did not approve. "What's all this filming nonsense?" boomed Sir Kenneth Barnes, the austere and forbidding principal, as he blocked my way one morning with his Hitchcockian build. "It's nothing serious, sir," I ventured timidly, trying to get by his bulk. "I'm just doing it to make some extra pocket money." "Well

21

just don't get carried away by it, my dear," he said pontifically. "When all is said and done there is only one thing that matters, and that's the *theatah*." "Right, sir," I agreed and scampered away to cut a class in favor of a photo session at the *Daily Mirror*. RADA was becoming a drag. I was fed up with being told my voice was too small and breathy, my performances dull, and my projection too inhibited. In the plays we performed I was being given the roles of the sixty-year-old aunt or the crazy Scandinavian maid—a form of revenge by the teachers who disliked my everything, I thought.

At the film studios they told me I was gorgeous and sexy. Actors and crew flirted with me and made me feel that I was talented and wonderful. Bill Watts was my strongest supporter. Of all the agents I have had, he is without a doubt the one who not only believed in my ability, but went out on a limb to tell everyone how much potential I had. It was his gutsy belief in me that got me over my debilitating self-consciousness about my voice and personality and made me realize that I had much more to offer than the teachers at RADA believed.

I took stock of myself. I couldn't possibly believe the "Baby Ava Gardner" nonsense that the newspapers were spouting. I looked in the mirror and saw a big-eyed, round-faced, slightly spotty young girl, with long, thin brownish hair—the bane of my life—and eight pounds overweight. And still a virgin. "Life is a constant diet," I groaned, pushing away the potatoes and reaching for the Lucky Strikes. I drank too much—straight gin usually— smoked too much to look sophisticated, and stayed up too late. I either read avidly until three or four in the morning or danced and dated, so I had deep, dark circles under my eyes. I decided to start a beauty regimen from which I have seldom deviated and went on the first of three hundred or so diets. "If I'm England's answer to Marilyn Monroe—" I gritted my teeth as I brushed my hair with a hundred strokes each night—"I might as well start trying to act the part. And if I get rid of my virginity, that may get rid of my spots too."

I was enjoying my days at the studio—the camaraderie and rapport that exists among the members of a film unit. I usually gravitated to the crew. Their humor and wit appealed to me far more than the boring talk of box-office grosses and script problems that producers and directors indulged in.

On most of the movies I made on location—*Island in the Sun, Seawife, The Bravados, Our Girl Friday*—I would normally be found sharing my box lunches with the hairdresser and the camera crew rather than with the other actors. Although I like actors, I resented the fact that the leading man in a movie usually took it as his prerogative to try to have an affair with the leading lady, and some became quite offended when their advances were rejected. Basically I am a down-to-earth person who likes to "send things up"—something that film crews, particularly in England, also love to do.

It was time for my first important film role and the beginning of what was to become a series of teenage delinquent and "bad girl" roles. The part of Lil in *Judgment Deferred*, a low-budget thriller made at Southall studios, was described in the script as "an exacting and emotional role of a one-time beautiful young girl, a convict's daughter, ruined by the colorful and dangerous crowd in which she has sought pleasure." The *Evening News* review said, "Although so young for her emotional role, Joan comes through with flying colors!" Apparently Basil Dearden and Michael Relph felt so too—for soon after completing *Judgment Deferred* I went to Ealing Studios, home of the moneymaking comedies starring Alec Guinness, to make a screen test for Norma, the runaway juvenile delinquent in *I Believe in You.*

Dearden and Relph were a hot team as director and producer. They had a string of successful credits, among them *The Blue Lamp* and *Kind Hearts and Coronets*, and whoever got the part of Norma was, according to Bill Watts, bound to become a star.

I had already made some tests for other films, but they were all unsuccessful for me, usually due to my youth or sultry "foreign" looks. English roses were still big in Britain. The test with Dirk Bogarde was the most thrilling. I wore a pink "baby doll" nightgown and Dirk and I slithered around on a vast satin double bed, indulging in much cinematic kissing. Dirk was attractive and fun, but far too old for me. I had become involved with a fellow RADA student, John Turner. It had lasted several months, something of a record for me. Although we spent nights together when circumstances permitted, he was too much of a gentleman to take advantage of my by now encumbering virginity. Since I had no idea how to seduce him, we kept it a little bit less than platonic.

My picture appeared on the front page of *Reveille*—my first cover! I was thrilled, more so when I was recognized while making a tour of the jewelry counter at Woolworth's looking for more plastic bangles to add to my collection. Even though I was becoming known and in demand, I was making not much more than twenty pounds a week. One doesn't shop at Dior on that kind of money.

Although we were well off, Daddy wasn't lavish with money. Mummy had to save out of the housekeeping to buy herself little extras. Although she was always well dressed and bejeweled, I know how persuasive she had to be with my father to get the things she wanted. I vowed at an early age that my desires for material things would never depend on the whims of a man. It was extremely important to me to become financially independent as soon as possible. In fact, throughout my entire life, through three marriages and all my relationships with men, I have always bought all my own clothes, furs, most of my jewelry, and paid my own bills.

Summer vacation started. One of my girlfriends at RADA became pregnant and had the most horrific abortion at the hands of a back-street butcher. My other girlfriends and I thought that was the wages of sin. I made yet a third test for *I Believe in You*. One of the producers was hot and heavy for me. I got the message loud and clear that if I was "nice" to him, the part would be mine. Since I was not about to be "nice" even to those I was madly in love with, the thought of the sweaty embraces of this (to me) elderly gent was quite appalling. He was somewhere between thirty-five and forty-five with long greasy hair, a florid complexion and a tendency to sweat profusely, especially when he came near me. I declined his advances with as much grace as I could while he drove me home in his Jaguar after the test, and I gloomily realized that I had probably blown the part—if not the producer! For the first time the specter of the casting couch started to raise its ugly head—the favors of pretty young things were to be used as barter to help them up the ladder of fame and fortune. If I was not to

24

take advantage of these opportunities there were plenty of other girls who would be only too delighted to oblige.

I had to make a decision, which I made—and I have *never* gone against that original decision. I would not be "nice to," "sleep with" or even kiss anyone for a job or a part no matter how tempting the role that was offered.

Several years later, when Buddy Adler, who was head of 20th Century–Fox, to whom I was under contract, asked me in his own home if I would like to be the biggest star on the lot, I said "Yes, of course." "All you have to do—" and he smiled suavely as he maneuvered me across the lacquered dance floor of his Beverly Hills mansion—"is be nice to me, and the best parts at the studio are yours." "What do you mean exactly by 'be nice,' Mr. Adler?" a worldly and sophisticated twenty-two-year-old Joan asked warily.

"Listen, honey—" he held me closer in the dance and whispered in my ear—"you're a beautiful girl and I'm not exactly an ugly old man—in fact a lot of women find me very attractive!" He smiled conspiratorially. I looked at him. Six feet, mahogany-tanned, silver hair, and at least old enough to be my father. "We'll see each other a couple of times a week, you can still have your own life, and I'll have mine, of course." He glanced over at his attractive blond wife, Anita Louise. "And you'll have your pick of scripts."

"Mr. Adler." I moved away frostily. "I came here with my agent, Jay Kanter. Why don't we discuss the deal with him?" He looked surprised and then he laughed. "Honey, you have quite a sense of humor." "You bet I have," I muttered to myself, as I went to regale Jay with this sweet story, "and my sense of humor is about all you'll ever get from me."

One of the current crop of contractees was very nice to Mr. Adler, and she landed a lot of the roles I really wanted.

But at seventeen I wasn't as sure of myself as at twenty-two. Convinced that by my coolness to the producer I would not get to play Norma, I left for a vacation in Cannes with my sister, Jackie, and my Aunt Lalla and threw myself into getting tanned and terrific in a bikini. Sidney Bechet and Claude Luter were playing in Juan-les-Pins and I was able to continue my favorite sport—dancing—when the telegram arrived. "Dear Joan, thought you would like to know you have got the part signed Basil Dearden." I was ecstatic.

25

This was a major film at a major studio and the chance to play with some fine actors: Celia Johnson, Cecil Parker, Harry Fowler and Laurence Harvey. Bill Watts called me: "Come home, all is forgiven," he joked. "You start shooting in two weeks."

The costumes I wore in *I Believe in You* were shabby and tarty. Anthony Mendleson, the costume designer, believed in realism, so we toured the secondhand clothing shops in the East End until we finally found the appropriate clothes. I was convinced I would pick up a social disease from trying them on. Some of them still bore the distinctive odors of their original owners, but the final effect was splendidly sleazy. For the opening scene I wore a brown sateen dress with a low neck and short puffy sleeves. It was ten years old and had probably been worn by its owner for a great deal of that time. It went to the dry cleaner's three times before we got rid of the fragrance. My long hair, which was drenched with olive oil to make it lank and greasy, flopped sadly on my shoulders. I wore vermilion lipstick, rhinestone earrings and down-at-the-heels ankle-strap shoes. I looked like a pathetic little cockney tart. Dearden and Relph were pleased as punch.

When not on call I posed for innumerable publicity pictures: romping with puppies and kittens, in shortie nighties, in bikinis, in shorts and the ubiquitous black polo-neck shirt. Nobody realizes how exhausting photographic modeling can be. Sitting or standing with a frozen smile or a sultry sulk on one's face for hours and hours under hot uncomfortable lights, wearing ridiculous outfits and trying to look as if this was a joyful or significant experience takes an enormous amount of discipline and concentration. I soon learned how to cope with it, and it became the kind of discipline that has stood me in good stead all my life.

I became a mini-celebrity, opening fetes and attending garden parties and premieres, all for the great God. Publicity!

The first day on *I Believe in You* we shot my most difficult scene. Cecil Parker, as a truant officer, finds me hiding in his apartment, having escaped from reform school. I had to cry hysterically, which I did, over and over and over again. At the end of the day I had cried for sixty different takes. Sometimes the tears were real, and sometimes the makeup man blew crystals in my eyes, which left them red-rimmed for the next twenty-four hours. Basil Dearden seemed satisfied with my performance, but he was somewhat austere, and since I had always had enormous difficulty in communicating with older men, my shyness and nervousness and desire to excel in this film made me a bumbling and respectful servant to him. I could never call him Basil as the crew did. He was, throughout the eight weeks of shooting, "Mr. Dearden."

Celia Johnson was a gifted, sensitive actress whose most memorable film performance was in Noel Coward's *Brief Encounter* with Trevor Howard. She was extremely kind and thoughtful toward me, helpful and patient. She played my probation officer, and our scenes together were really enjoyable and a wonderful learning experience.

And then there was Larry, Laurence Harvey—or to give him his full Lithuanian name, Larushka Skikne. He was flamboyant, eccentric, gifted, extrovert; he swore wittily; smoked endlessly; drank white wine incessantly; drove dashing cars; wore elegant and expensive suits; told fabulously amusing, naughty stories; and I became instantly smitten. He epitomized a lifestyle to which I knew I could become accustomed: the rich, fast life of fine restaurants, international travel, sophisticated parties and scintillating conversation. He took me under his wing. "I'm going to educate you, little girl," he told me, sipping a vintage claret at La Rue, while a tinkling piano in the background played Gershwin medleys. Elegant women in black strapless cocktail dresses flirted delicately with suave, lounge-suited men, and red-coated waiters hovered discreetly.

"Living well is the best revenge" was Larry's policy. And he certainly did. He tried to teach me some dress sense to make the most of my rather gauche appearance. He tried to educate me about wine and the mysteries of a French menu. He taught me to smoke with elan and swear like a trooper and a lady, but he refused to teach me about life's greatest mystery. Sex. He had a zest for living that was unparalleled and thrilling, and I wanted him to be my first lover. I was convinced he was the one I had been saving myself for.

I didn't know it but he was living with Hermione Baddeley, a middle-aged character actress not noted for her beauty. So when

27

he asked me to a party at her house, I innocently and enthusiastically accepted. Immediately we arrived she approached me, saying, "So this is the one you're seeing, Larry, is it? This is 'the new Jean Simmons.'" She gave me a sarcastic look up and down, not missing a detail of my less-than-expert outfit, her red curls bobbing, a cigarette hanging from carmine lips. "Let me tell you something, my dear, Jean has absolutely nothing to worry about. You don't have her looks, you don't have her talent—and you certainly don't have half the overblown things the newspapers have been saying you have." I burst into tears and rushed to the front door to escape her tirade. "That's right, leave," she called. "No guts, that's the trouble with you young ones today—no guts at all!"

Larry caught up with me in Park Lane and tried to smooth things over. "Don't worry, darling, she doesn't mean it. Come back to the party—I really want you two to be friends." "Oh, Larry," I sobbed, "I'm so humiliated—I can't face that woman— please take me home." But the party had more interest for Larry than I did. He quickly plonked me in a cab, gave the driver a pound, me a paternal kiss on the forehead, told me he loved me and scooted back to Totie's.

I should have realized then and there that Larry really loved only himself. But I saw him through rose-colored glasses. I went home and cried myself to sleep. My fragile ego had again been crumpled. If a woman as talented and important as Hermione Baddeley thought I was untalented and unattractive, maybe I really was. I was quick to believe the worst about myself—especially if disapproval came from someone I respected. Highly sensitive to criticism, I seemed to spend my life trying to do everything to please everybody. Consequently, not only did I not please myself, but I was so busy being what the other person wanted me to be that I almost assumed another identity. This was especially true when I was with my more neurotic boyfriends. I became a nonperson, a willing slave—my moods matched theirs. If they wanted to be quiet, I was silent as a mouse. If they wanted to tell funny stories, I would laugh and be a wide-eyed audience. But other than Larry, boys were seldom in my thoughts these days as I plunged into the exciting life of a rising young movie star.

CHAPTER

Two

tion was the most powerful and prolific filmmaker of the 1950s
and 1960s. For several years it had placed young actors and actresses under contract for between twenty and fifty pounds a week
and "groomed" them for stardom. This grooming was somewhat
like going back to drama school but with enormous emphasis on
such important acting assets as charm, posture, elegance and a nice
smile. A "charm school" had been formed but was now disbanded,
and dozens of eager young thespians had received the dubious
benefits of what that had offered. Among them had been Honor
Blackman, Petula Clark and Maxwell Reed.

Maxwell Reed was my childhood fantasy hero. From the time
I first saw him on the screen, smoldering on a Sicilian island with
Patricia Roc in *The Brothers*, to the night that Larry Harvey introduced us at La Rue, I had had a tremendous schoolgirl crush
on him. I had also adored Montgomery Clift, Gene Kelly and
Richard Widmark, but Max epitomized all my adolescent fantasies. He looked divine gazing out of the cover of *Picturegoer* in
1949, black brooding eyes, thick wavy black hair, lips cruel, thick
and wet, in anticipation of Margaret Lockwood or Phyllis Calvert.
"You'll probably marry him one day" said Diana, my closest school
chum, confidently. "He's so gorgeous, almost as handsome as Gregory Peck."

"Oh, he's much better-looking than Gregory Peck," I said, as I
lovingly Scotch-taped his smoldering countenance to the inside of

29

my desk. "But I'm never going to get married, you dope. I'm going to be a famous and brilliantly successful actress and have lots of lovers."

My fascination with Maxwell Reed had never waned. When I looked up at all six feet four and a half of him that autumn night in La Rue, my heart leaped into my mouth and the back of my knees went weak. There he was in a white-on-white shirt, white tie with the biggest knot I'd ever seen outside the Duke of Windsor's, navy blue pinstripe suit with the widest shoulders and the narrowest pegtop trousers—and mirror-polished black "winklepicker" shoes.

He was my schoolgirl dream come to life, and he smiled at me so sexily that I blushed from head to toe. He had an American accent, which was quite odd for a man from South London. He bought me a whiskey and Coke and chatted lightly about Hollywood, from whence he had just returned after starring in a Universal swashbuckler with Ann Blyth, who, he told me, was over the hill now since she was pushing twenty-five.

I was heavily impressed. This was the real thing—a real live handsome famous film star, and he was actually flirting with *me!* I felt inadequate, stupid and badly dressed. I was earning thirty pounds a week on *I Believe in You* and starting to invest some of it in a suitable wardrobe, but my sense of style was still underdeveloped in spite of Larry's tutoring. I was wearing an unflattering green-and-gold brocade dress with puffed sleeves and a Peter Pan collar, black patent high-heeled shoes, and imitation pearl earrings. This was hardly what Ava Gardner would have worn, but dressing well takes time, energy and money, and I had little of any of these. Nevertheless, Max seemed to like what he saw, and after he ditched the girl he had arrived with, he joined us for drinks. He and Larry had recently made a movie together and were friends.

I had an early call at Ealing. Since I didn't drive and couldn't afford to hire a car, I would have to rise at 4:30 A.M. to get to the studio by six-thirty, but this did not detract from my enjoyment of this scintillating evening. I smoked half a pack of Lucky Strikes, drank too many whiskeys and Coke and tried to be witty, pretty and wise. I didn't want him to know I was only seventeen. I thought a thirty-three-year-old man would have no interest in a girl of that age, especially a virgin to boot. How naive.

At seven-thirty the next morning the phone rang in the makeup department. It was he. In a sultry American-cockney accent, he drawled, "Hi, baby, how's it going?" We chatted for a few minutes and then he asked me out. I instantly accepted. I knew it would cause trouble at home if he came to pick me up. Going out with Larry, who was only in his twenties, had driven my parents mad at first until they realized that he was a gentleman and could be trusted with their precious daughter, but a man in his thirties—a man with a reputation as a womanizer (and, as I found out later, a pimp)—this my parents would never accept. I arranged to meet him the following Sunday outside the Bayswater Road tube station.

I was in an agony of indecision for the next two days as to what to wear—casual or formal? Jeans or brocade dress? My choices were limited but going out with such a famous actor and man of the world was a definite sartorial challenge.

I finally chose, for safety, my "uniform" of the day: a tight black gabardine skirt with slits up the side, a sleeveless, low-necked black sweater cinched in by a wide black patent-leather belt that accentuated my twenty-two-inch waist, black stockings, three bangles instead of the usual ten; and my smallest gold gypsy earrings completed what I thought of as a sophisticated look. My toilette took three hours. I was terribly nervous, almost as nervous as I was before the first day's filming of *I Believe in You*.

Would I be interesting enough to hold his attention for the evening? Would he think I was too immature and be bored by my conversation? Where were we going to go? If we went to any restaurant or club in the West End or Soho, someone would be bound to see us together and report back to Daddy, who had friends at every spot in town. Certainly, whenever I had ever gone somewhere with Larry, it had been reported back to them by some spy.

I was so nervous I smoked eight Lucky Strikes just while applying makeup. In any case my hands were shaking so much I could hardly get it on. My mother bade me a fond and approving "Goodnight, have a good time, darling." I had told her I was going to a

31

party with Larry and then to a club so she would not worry. I knew Larry was seeing Totie that evening and I doubted that he would phone. All I had to worry about now were my looks, my personality, my figure and my conversation, all of which I was convinced were way below par.

I took the tube to Bayswater Station—a major mistake, as I got leered at and leched at all the way in my provocative outfit. I arrived at my destination in a frenzy of nerves and fifteen minutes early.

He arrived twenty minutes late, by which time I was convinced he would never appear and I would have to go and drown my sorrows at a nearby pub.

As I peeked in my compact for the three-hundredth time, lo and behold, a gigantic sleek, powder-blue American Buick drew up to the curb, and there he was!

"Get in, baby," he drawled, not bothering to get out to open the door. I had become so used to Larry's impeccable manners that I was slightly taken aback for a second, but I jumped in obediently and we drove off into the London traffic.

He was casually dressed in a black open-necked shirt and black trousers and a belt with an ornate buckle and he wore a massive gold chain around his tanned neck. He seemed friendly and glad to see me. We smoked Chesterfields and drove through Hyde Park. I had never been in an American car before and was interested in the gadgets in the interior. Larry drove an elegant old Bentley, and the other boys I had dated either had no car or drove battered MGs or Triumphs. "Bill would really love this car," I trilled, referring to my seven-year-old brother. "He's mad for cars." I realized how boring that must have sounded and cast desperately around for some wittier dialogue. He gave me a sleepy-eyed Robert Mitchum look. "Oh, yeah, we must give the kid a ride one day." How considerate, I thought, film stars are human beings after all. There was some more silence, and I smoked furiously while thinking of a suitable subject. A tongue-tied, seventeen-year-old virgin, I thought bitterly, he must be so bored.

We had been driving for about twenty minutes and I paid no attention to where we were going, but suddenly I realized that we had just been driving round Hyde Park all the time. "Where are we going?" I ventured to say. He shot me another Mitchum look. "You'll see, baby, it'll be a surprise." I sat back expectantly. I liked surprises and he probably knew some exciting clubs and dives. In the 1950s London had many clubs that were situated in unusual places: lofts, cellars, in apartment buildings and in houses, so when we drew up outside an old Georgian house in Hanover Square, I did not find this strange. "What's this place?" I said gaily. "The Country Club—baby, come on up." We walked up four flights of stairs past empty office suites and at the top came to a door which he unlocked with a key.

I was slightly puzzled because there were no sounds of conversation or music, but when the door opened it all became horribly clear.

Up yet another flight of stairs, these carpeted in thick crimson carpet, and we entered what was obviously somebody's apartment— and when I took a good look through my starry eyes, I realized from the eight-by-ten glossies it was Max's. Instant panic gripped me this was very tricky. This was no fellow drama student. This was not polite, gentlemanly John Turner, who would never take advantage of my innocence; or urbane, sophisticated Larry Harvey, to whom sexual matters were unimportant. We hadn't even had dinner and Max had brought me to his flat already. I tried to hide my panic by examining some of the interesting pieces of furniture and objects scattered around. The flat was decorated in medieval-Spanish-Hollywood style. There was a lot of crimson velvet and gold braid, purple silk lampshades on six-masted schooner lamps, some carved-wood thronelike chairs and three or four Impressionist oil paintings. Oh, my God, there was also, I saw out of the corner of my eye, a sort of sofa bed against the far wall, in front of the TV, which appeared to be covered in a zebra-skin rug and three thousand velvet cushions. My parents' shocked expressions seemed to gaze out at me from the black TV screen.

"I'm going to have a bath," Maxwell Reed said casually, as if this was a perfectly ordinary thing to do on your first date. "Do you want a whiskey and Coke, baby?" I nodded numbly. I needed a drink desperately. His having a bath would give me a chance to think about this situation, which seemed to be fraught with dangerous possibilities. He was obviously going to try and seduce me.

The flat was an absolute love nest. Subdued lighting, sexy paintings, everything seemed designed to set the scene for a spree—which I just might have been ready for after a few days of getting to know each other—but I had only just met this man.

All my mother's dire prophecies came flooding into my mind: "Men only want *one thing*." She had drummed that into me since I was twelve, when I had asked her what the word "fuck" meant. I had seen it written on railway-carriage walls and toilets. I had gone to the Public Library and looked it up in every dictionary I could find, but apparently there was no such word. We were walking down Oxford Street on a Saturday morning when I asked the question and my mother threw a mini-fit, pushed me against the wall of Dolcis' shoe shop and hissed at me vehemently, "Don't you *ever* say that word—that's a *terrible* word. I told your father that if he ever said that word I would *divorce* him." So that was the end of finding out at twelve what the word "fuck" meant.

Maxwell interrupted my thoughts. He pressed into my hand an immense red Venetian goblet full to the brim with my favorite drink, Scotch and Coke, and into the other a slim book in a plain brown cover. "Make yourself at home, baby, and have a read while I have a bath," he said, sitting me down in a purple velvet chair. "I won't be long." He disappeared smoothly, leaving me to my sordid thoughts. I took a huge swallow of the drink, which tasted slightly different from the usual Scotch-and-Coke mix, but different brands of whiskey had different tastes. I didn't worry about it too much. I had other things to think about.

I opened the book and gasped. It was an illustrated volume of extremely explicit and detailed drawings of men and women having sex. I had never seen anything like this before and my mind boggled at some of the different and peculiar positions they were in. I finished the drink and started to feel very strange indeed, and then nothing—total oblivion—I was out.

I came to, to find Max and me entwined on the sofa. I was feeling violently ill. "I'm going to be sick," I gasped. "I'll get the bucket again," he said.

Again! I thought through waves of nausea. "Again—have I been sick before, then?" I lay back, drained, on the zebra-skin rug, with the realization that I had finally "done it" but that I had not even been conscious of it. Max turned on the television set. The screen was dark. "Telly's finished for the night," he said, passing me a Chesterfield. "What do you mean—what time is it?" I cried. If TV had closed down for the night, that meant it was after 11 P.M. and I had been here for over three hours. Doing what? Oh, God, I couldn't even remember.

I passed out again and came to with him trying to kiss me. "I can't! Oh, please stop it!" I tried to say, the nausea rising uncontrollably—"Please, please, don't—I'm going to be sick again." I staggered weakly away from the couch and the debris and tried to find the bathroom.

My favorite black sweater was ripped and lying on the floor, next to a crumpled heap of clothes. My stockings were torn and the clasp had been ripped off my bra. Max turned and smiled at me lazily when I returned from repairing what I could salvage of myself and patted the couch. "Come over here, kid," he said, "and lie down. I think we both got a little more than we expected."

"What did you expect?" I moaned as I fell exhausted onto the couch.

"Well, I gave you a bit of a Mickey Finn to make you feel sexy." He smiled, inhaling deeply. I listened, horrified. "Larry told me that he hadn't had you, and that you were a virgin, but I didn't really believe him—gorgeous little seventeen-year-old birds like you don't stay virgins for long in this business, baby. Did you like it?" He turned to me. I looked at him dumbly. *Like* it? I *hated* it. From what I could remember, it was horrible, degrading and demeaning—and even worse than my mother had led me to expect. Were there actually women who *liked* doing this sort of thing? No wonder some of them got paid for it. It was all too ghastly, and in my weakened state I drifted off into a drugged sleep.

He was starting again, but I felt nothing—not even pain. I just lay there while he continued to—what?—well, no wonder "fuck" was considered a dirty word.

I came to again to find him making me drink some strong coffee. Now I felt awful and used and exhausted.

"Come on, kid," he urged, "gotta get you home to Mummy and Daddy. Are you working tomorrow?" I nodded numbly—I had a 6 A.M. call. Help!

"It's after three," he said. "Come on, girl, up and at 'em." Sheer terror gripped me now. My parents would wait up for me even though they pretended to be asleep. As soon as the clock struck two and I wasn't home, Mummy would be pacing.

Max helped me into my torn and tattered finery. The stockings were a write-off so I didn't even bother to put them back on. My face was a disaster. I stared at it in horror in my compact mirror—mascara-stained cheeks, caked foundation and smeared lipstick. I lurched into the bathroom and washed everything off with soap and water and then shakily applied some lipstick and tried to comb my hair. I couldn't think about what had happened. I still felt incredibly ill and I was petrified thinking about my parents' reactions.

He guided my wobbly legs down the endless flights of stairs. We said little. He kept giving me his laconic Robert Mitchum look as he drove me home to Harley House, which was only about seven minutes' drive from Hanover Square.

"Stop before you come to the entrance," I whispered nervously as we approached the grim Victorian outlines of the flats. "I'll get out here." He leaned over me to open the door. "Will I see you again, baby?" he said, putting his hand on my knee. "Of course," I gulped, nervously pushing his hand away. "I'll give you a ring in a couple of days," he said, kissed me perfunctorily on the cheek and zoomed off into the deserted street.

I staggered into Harley House, hearing voices raised and the phone ringing even before I put my key in the door.

We had lived in this huge basement flat for several years. It looked out on to busy Marylebone Road and got very little daylight, but it was big and spacious enough for three kids and was behind Regent's Park. I opened the heavy oak door and my mother rushed forward and grabbed my arm. "Your father's furious with you!" she cried. "Where have you been? I've called everyone, and *why* are you home so late?" I looked at the grandfather clock in the hall. It was indeed now half-past three and I would have to be up in an hour to take the train to Ealing. "I've been to a party with Larry," I said feebly, trying to muster up some power in my voice.

"Your mother called Laurence Harvey," said my father coming

out of the bedroom and tying the knot in his red-and-blue-striped dressing gown. "He said he had not seen you tonight, and did not know where you were—so where *have* you been?"

When my father shouted at me like that my stomach went cold and I got a weak feeling in the back of my knees. He truly scared me to death when he was so angry. He had never actually hit any of us, or used any physical violence at all, but his temper was so strong and his anger so fierce that when he threatened to "beat the daylights out of you," although he actually never did, it was a threat that we kids thought could come true if we behaved badly enough. I think now that it would have been better if he had occasionally hit us—because it couldn't have hurt us as much as the constant threat that he *might*.

"Larry was terribly worried," said Mummy, trying to smooth things over as usual. "He called some of the people at the studio to see if you were with them, but they didn't know where you were either." "So where were you?" said Daddy. "You'd better tell us, or you'll be standing here all night."

I looked at the clock and for one wild moment felt like shrieking at them, "I've been drugged and raped and abused by a thirty-three-year-old degenerate film star and I *hated* it. You were right, Mummy—it is horrible and vile and I'll never, ever do it again—*ever*. I promise."

But my courage was waning. I tried histrionics and hysterics, which sometimes worked. I needed to lie down, have a bath and collect my thoughts before I left in forty-five minutes for the two-hour trip to the studio. Time was running out. "I went to Beryl's father's pub," I sobbed in my mother's arms. "And we had a few drinks and went over to Wood Green jazz club. We met some friends from RADA and went back to their flat to play some records. I was having so much fun I didn't realize the time. I'm sorry." My shoulders were racked with sobs as my mother rocked me gently. My crying had become real. I was extremely upset, and I felt abused and dirty.

This garbled explanation seemed to satisfy my father. He barked a few more terse sentences about ". . . get to bed—you look like hell" and went back to his own bed. Mummy walked me back to my room. I badly wanted to tell her what had happened. I needed

37

comfort and advice—I needed to be mothered, in fact—but I could never trust my mother completely because she sometimes repeated what I said or did, either to my father or one of her girl-friends. Besides, if I told her, she would be absolutely horrified, and convinced yet again that "Men only want one thing" and would forbid me to ever see Max again. I needed time to think.

I kissed her goodnight and ran a bath. I scrubbed thoroughly, washed my hair, cleaned my teeth for ten minutes, put on jeans, sweater and duffle coat and, after making a strong cup of instant coffee, slipped out of the front door and into the dark and silent streets of Marylebone Road. I walked swiftly for five minutes to Baker Street. In the fifties, a girl could walk around London streets in the dark and not be concerned about muggers or rapists. Since I had been raped once that evening anyway, the odds were against it.

I sat in the railway carriage and looked at my face in the compact mirror. I tried to analyze if I had changed. A workman in paint-stained overalls was staring at me. I wonder if he can tell, I thought to myself, that I'm not a virgin. My face looked the same—the circles under the eyes were darker but that was lack of sleep. I looked young and vulnerable. But I felt I had ended a chapter of my life. I didn't feel like a girl any more. On the other hand, I didn't feel like a woman either.

There was no such thing as "the Pill" yet. I needed to talk to a woman to find out what I had to do. I spoke to Ursula Howells, an actress in *I Believe in You*, about my experience. She was sympathetic and concerned—especially about my becoming pregnant. Horrors! That hadn't even occurred to me. But since it seemed there was nothing I could do about it now, like Scarlett in *Gone With the Wind*, I would have to "think about that tomorrow." Visions of my RADA girlfriend butchered by an abortionist crossed my mind and I shuddered with fear.

I worked hard all day. At the end of the day I went to wardrobe where I was outfitted in a delicious gold lamé dress once worn by Audrey Hepburn, and the publicity boys took me to Ciro's Club, where *Photoplay* magazine was holding its annual Christmas party, although it was still only autumn. Many stars were there, among them Anthony Steel (who had that summer followed my sister,

Jackie, and myself all through the streets of Cannes), Kenneth More and Kay Kendall. I had gone out with Steel a couple of times and he seemed quite nice but drank too much. Besides, I didn't really like older men.

Max was turning out to be the exception, however. He had, to my surprise, called me at the studio in the afternoon and asked if I was free for dinner that night. Confused as ever, I accepted. After the party I went to meet him at the Caprice, an exclusive theatrical restaurant. Why did I go to meet him with the ghastly events of last night still fresh in my mind? I was probably flattered that he still wanted to see me after having "had his way with me," as my mother would have put it. And I wanted to prove to myself that I was not just a sex object to be used and discarded at a man's whim. I didn't want to be rejected by him after he had seduced me and I didn't feel like rejecting him. After all, he was a *star!* The only way to win was to play the game to the hilt, and so I tried to pretend that last night had not really happened.

I also apportioned some of the blame to myself—one of my more naive traits. I shouldn't have dated him in the first place. When I saw I was in his apartment I should have got the hell out of there. I could twist this incident in my mind to such an extent that the whole thing became my fault totally. But most of all I was still curious about him as a person, an actor and someone I had admired for a long time. Since our conversation last night had been negligible, I was determined to start afresh. And I was definitely *not* going to the "Country Club" again.

The studio had given me a special coiffure, and I thought I looked grown-up and glamorous. I was aware we made an arresting couple; many people in the restaurant stared at us. He was witty that evening, telling jokes and anecdotes about his life in the merchant navy, his days with the Rank Organization and his recent trip to Hollywood. There had been some talk of me going there to do a movie with Bob Hope, but unfortunately it didn't happen, as the producers thought I was much too young to play opposite Bob— although I did appear with him and Bing Crosby several years later in the last of the "Road" pictures, *The Road to Hong Kong.*

Max had a good sense of humor—his saving grace and a trait which has always appealed to me strongly—and I was in fits of laughter all night. The previous night was not mentioned. It was almost as though it hadn't happened. I was confused, yet happy. He took me home and acted in a very gentlemanly way as he kissed me chastely goodnight on the cheek. I think he was feeling some self-recriminations but we avoided the subject.

We started seeing each other, and he did not approach me sexually for some time—as though to atone for his fault.

During the next month we dated each other constantly. I became involved—in fact, we fell in love, but it was tough because he was exceedingly moody. We had days of lighthearted fun, boating, going to movies and theaters and dancing all night—and then for three or four days he would be in a black mood, surly and vile, snarling, cruel, sadistic and sarcastic. It was hard for me to understand these sudden changes of mood, but I put up with them, as I had strong guilt feelings about his having "deflowered me." And also because my childhood dream was coming true—I was dating a famous, handsome movie star—Maxwell Reed. As far as sex went in our relationship, I gritted my teeth and tolerated it. In fact, I found it really boring, without a flicker of pleasure, just as I had been warned by my mother.

In the days before *Cosmopolitan* magazine told you how to have the most thrilling sexual adventures, before Masters and Johnson published their theories on multiple orgasm and sexual freedom, before the sexual revolution of the sixties, sex was something a girl just did not discuss or think about too much. I realize now that Max was a far from considerate lover. And since there were certain things he liked to do which hurt and revolted me, I merely tolerated the sex because I thought I was in love with him, and because I genuinely thought that this was the way things were *supposed* to be. It was a man's sport—and a woman's chore. Luckily for me the couch on which we usually made love faced the TV set, which was always turned on—even if I wasn't—so I was able to concentrate on something else. It was ironic that at this time I was being hailed as "Britain's Best Bet for Stardom." I was considered the sexiest girl in England. I was Britain's Marilyn Monroe, Sophia Loren and Brigitte Bardot. But none of this idolatry went to my head. I remained insecure and dumb and frigid.

I was still filming *I Believe in You*, going to jazz clubs, visiting

RADA to see my friends, going to the theater, doing interviews and publicity and seeing Max two or three times a week. I was very busy whirling, with little time to think.

I have always been able to do two or three times the amount of activities the average person can do. I have enormous energy and wake up practically every day excited about just being alive. This was now a frenetic and exciting period for me. J. Arthur Rank was becoming interested in signing me to a seven-year exclusive contract. They had seen the rushes of *I Believe in You* and liked what they saw. Hollywood had made a couple of nibbles—I was getting warm.

Eventually my parents found out that I had been seeing Maxwell Reed; they were appalled. Max smoothly assured them that he was only educating me in the myriad problems of stardom, that he was my mentor, not my lover, and that our relationship was totally platonic. Incredibly, they believed him. He was the most convincing liar I had ever seen.

After a few months he wanted me to move in with him. The idea was rather appealing. His apartment was cozy, and I was fed up with the endless rules and regulations I had to conform to at home. I had to be home at one o'clock every night or there had better be a good reason why not. But living together seemed premature. Although Max had told me he loved me, I knew there was something vitally wrong with the relationship. I didn't know whether I loved *him* or loved the idea of togetherness. I adored his sense of humor, his looks, his fame. But there was a dark side that I feared and loathed. Maybe I can cope with it, I thought confidently.

He started to suffer severe back pains, and sometimes he would be doubled up in agony. For some reason he blamed me for causing this. He had started talking to me about marriage seriously now, since living together was out of the question because of my moralistic parents, but I was still resistant and unsure. And as I learned later, the more resistant and hard to get a woman is, the more a man wants her—something I'm sure my mother did try to tell me.

One day he was in such severe pain that after the doctor examined him he was sent immediately to the hospital. The next day I was told that Max had slipped a disc and would have to have an operation. After the operation he found he had a total loss of feeling in his lower body—the whole area had become completely numb. In a way, this was poetic justice since I always felt the same way.

The doctors assured him it was temporary—that a few nerve endings had been severed during the operation and that in a few months the nerves would heal, but it put him into the blackest and foulest of moods and he consistently accused me of causing his injury. Since I never instigated lovemaking and, in fact, went to lengths to avoid it, this was farcical. But I was the villainess and the cause of his problems. Not to mention his sudden lack of film offers. As I became "hot," he became "cold."

My guilt got worse as he ranted and raved and screamed at me because he had not made a film for several months. He was short of cash. Suddenly, for every possible thing that went wrong, I became the scapegoat.

He definitely wanted to marry me even more now, but I felt more dubious as to the likely longevity of our marriage. I was still only seventeen and extremely immature mentally and emotionally in spite of my physical appearance. My emotions veered between ecstasy and misery, with very little gray area. There is a fine line between love and hate, and I was treading it with Max. Confusion, guilt and uncertainty were my day-to-day companions now. Because of his disability, Max could only get aroused by sadism. I was so frightened of him I went along with the beatings and the perversions he thought up. He insisted I pose for some nude Polaroid photographs which he thought might turn him on. My pity for him was intense—and my guilt—but now a new sinister element entered our relationship. The more he hurt me physically, the more excited he became. I tolerated it because I hoped it would only be temporary and that when he regained his feelings he would stop. He kept telling me how much he desired me and how difficult it was for him and how I must understand his problems. A woman's lot is to suffer. Thus spake my female ancestors.

My contract with the J. Arthur Rank Organization was signed. I was the first actress Rank had put under contract for over a year. They started to build me up. Every day I did some sort of publicity, and every other day the papers had something to say about me, good, bad or sarcastic.

The Rank contract was probably based a lot on my personal reviews for *I Believe in You*. Although some of the critics were lukewarm toward the movie, most of them had high praise for my potential. Jympson Harmon, one of the top critics, wrote in his review, "Joan Collins makes a tremendous impression as the wayward girl. She has a dark luscious kind of beauty which puts her in the Jane Russell class, but Joan already seems to be an actress of greater ability. On the showing of this first big film part, she looks like the most impressive recruit to British films for many a moon." And *News of the World* raved, "A dozen of my darkest red roses to Joan Collins. Fire and spirit in her acting and that odd combination of allure and mystery that spells eventual world stardom."

This was heady stuff for a teenager. It seems ironic that my very earliest reviews were far more favorable than those in my later years. It's as if the critics said later, "Oh, yeah—she looks good but what else is in the package?" Certainly, on viewing again some of my films and remembering the ghastly reviews I got, I felt that in a way I became the critics' whipping boy. Max had started kidding me about how, with my looks and youth, he and his friends could make a fortune if I would become a high-class courtesan. They were constantly cracking lewd jokes about sex. In fact, sex and women made up 90 percent of the subject matter of conversation between Max and his friends, and usually discussed in derogatory fashion. I knew they had little or no respect for women and were the epitome of what my mother had always described— the men who want only "one thing."

Since neither Max nor I had a film at the moment, we decided to appear together at the Q Theatre in *The Seventh Veil* in the roles portrayed on the screen by James Mason and Ann Todd. Max played the part of the sadistically cruel piano teacher. He played it with so much authenticity that in one of the scenes where he is terrorizing me, he threw me across the stage with such violence and ferocity that I was black and blue for three days. The sadomasochism obviously appealed because we immediately started rehearsing yet another similar story: A "young frightened girl, intimidated but mesmerized by an attractive, sadistic older man"—absolutely the basis of *our* relationship. This one was called *Jassy*, freely adapted from the film of the same name with Margaret Lockwood and again, James Mason.

I was mad about the theater and was only regretful that these were only one-week gigs, but my reviews were excellent, and I started looking for a suitable property to do in the West End.

Finally Max went to my parents to ask for my hand in marriage. Although my father had suspected this, I think he was amazed that it was actually happening. The four of us sat self-consciously in the living room of our Harley House flat. Dinner was over. The television sound had been turned down, although the black-and-white picture flickered on. Max and I perched on the green velvet Knowle sofa sipping tea from Mummy's best pink china.

When he wanted to, Max could charm the birds out of the trees. A typical actor. My mother was already won over, but Daddy was a harder nut. He disapproved of Max's flashy West End image, he disapproved of the age difference, he disapproved totally of everything the man represented, and would absolutely not allow me to get married at such a tender age to such an unsuitable man. "Well, then," I said, finally asserting myself in their conversation, "if you won't let me marry him, I'll go and live with him."

My parents stared at me in alarm. "You must be out of your mind," my father said. "What would people think? Can you imagine what our friends would say? It would be the talk of London. You absolutely *cannot* live together, I will not allow it!"

"You can't stop me," I said defiantly. "We love each other, Joe," said Max smoothly. "And we want to be together—what can we do?"

Both my parents looked bemused. I think Mummy was secretly thrilled by the romance of it all, but didn't dare come around until my father did first.

"All right," said Daddy, puffing vehemently on a Player's. "All right, but I'll tell you something—and I mean it." He looked at me and I got that funny feeling in the back of my knees again. "This marriage had better last, because if it doesn't—" he stared at me hard—"I never want to speak to you again." I looked at Mummy. She looked away. I looked at the walls and mantelpiece and sideboard in the room. They were covered with photographs of me and my brother, Bill, and sister, Jackie. They certainly loved their kids, but wasn't this a funny way of showing it? Was my darling Daddy serious about disowning me if my marriage failed?

"That's all. That's it," said my father and he leaned over and turned up the sound on the TV. "Make us another cup of tea, Elsa." End of subject.

Max and I left as soon as possible and went to the Mandrake Club, where we celebrated our engagement with Pimm's Number 1. I was outwardly happy—I would get away from home and have some freedom. But my mind was a turmoil of doubts.

One of Max's favorite slogans was "Hate is akin to love." It seemed weird to me, but maybe it might explain my ambivalent feelings toward him. He was not at all good for my fragile ego. Although he thought I was beautiful, he was consistently belittling my conversation, my acting ability and my personality. He advised me often to "cash in on all you have going for you *now* as by the time you're twenty-three you'll be old and washed up." Twenty-three was apparently the cutoff point for Max and his cronies to be attracted to a girl. Anyone older than that was "an old scrubber" in whom they had no interest whatsoever.

We married the day after my eighteenth birthday, at the registry office, Caxton Hall, in a blaze of publicity. I had spent most of the previous week sobbing myself to sleep each night. The thought of getting married terrified me. Suddenly I didn't want to leave the safety and security of the cozy flat where I had spent so much of my childhood. I was scared of my father but I was even more frightened of Max. I had lost eight pounds, and in my white-and-gold wedding dress I looked tiny. I heard some women in the crowd say I was *too* skinny! I'd achieved something I had been trying to do for years without succeeding. Misery must be good for svelteness.

We drove in the Buick to Cannes for our honcymoon. I always became drowsy on long car trips and wanted to sleep. Max pinched and yelled at me to "wake up!" I tried to keep my eyes open by looking at the pictures and the articles that had appeared about us on our wedding day. How happy we seemed. How grownup

45

and assured I looked, as if I married a film star every year. I read with interest a particular story that was printed in the *Daily Mirror*.

"I shall do no cooking or cleaning!" the headline shrieked, shocked that a young bride should be so untraditional as to not get kicks from wearing a frilly apron and cooking tasty meals for her husband. "Her ideas of marriage are honestly unconventional," scolded the article. "She doesn't want to have children for seven or eight years at least—and she wants to keep on acting all the time."

These were revolutionary ideas for the fifties. Women were made to feel guilty if they did not adore housework and want a houseful of kids. My sights were set a little higher. Even though I had chosen to marry so young, I did not feel I had to conform to the usual patterns a wife was supposed to follow.

The honeymoon was a nightmare. Max suddenly became extraordinarily jealous of any man's notice of me. However, the wealthier a man was, the less jealous he became, and he often suggested that we could make some money by "being nice to that chap." But when a couple of young, obviously not rich French photographers came to take photos of me on the beach, Max took me back to our cramped beach hut on the Carlton Beach and slapped my face so hard I felt my teeth would fall out.

"You belong to me now," he screamed so loudly that I knew the ladies sipping afternoon tea on the Carlton Terrace could hear. "So don't be looking at other men—ever—unless they're the ones I choose!" The veins stood out on his neck and his eyes bulged in a frenzy. He looked mad. I pressed myself against the wall of the hut. In my pink gingham bikini I felt vulnerable and terrified of the man I married. His hair was dyed black and permed. He had shown me how he did it in the sink at his flat. His eyebrows and eyelashes were heavily mascaraed. Today he was not wearing makeup, because we were on the beach—but he often did. He wore a pair of tiny white shorts and black thong sandals that laced up to mid-calf; three large gold medallions hung around his neck. He got more wolf whistles in the South of France than I did.

Thank God I'm going to start work next week, I thought fervently. Rank, having put me under contract for fifty pounds a week, had immediately loaned me out to Columbia to play in Boccaccio's *Decameron Nights*, to be made in Madrid and Segovia. It would be my first American film, and I was full of enthusiasm.

Max decided to stay in Cannes and enjoy himself for another week. He had met a millionaire who was talking movie deals, so he was happy. And when he was happy he was nice to me and didn't hit or otherwise hurt me, and then I was happy.

Decameron Nights starred Joan Fontaine and Louis Jourdan and consisted of three or four episodes of Boccaccio's stories. I played Joan Fontaine's handmaiden in one segment and in another had tender love scenes with Louis Jourdan. This role was much smaller than my role in *I Believe in You*. But Rank had insisted I do the film, otherwise they would release me from my contract. There were not many roles for sexy-looking teenagers, and Rank was getting a good loan-out price for me, too, none of which I received, however. I just got fifty pounds a week, and Rank got about $25,000. The director, Hugo Fregonese, was cold and treated us casually. Segovia was smelly and dirty and the hotel where we stayed a veritable doss house.

As soon as Max arrived, a week later, we started fighting again. I became petulant, bad-tempered, and unpopular, and was glad to return to London and start another movie.

Cosh Boy was the story of a group of youths who spent their time getting their kicks by robbing and beating up people—rather like today's muggers. I played Renee, the innocent young girlfriend of the leading boy, James Kenney. We had a love scene in the garden of a deserted house, which by today's standards was tame enough to be in a Disney film. After the seduction I become pregnant and try to commit suicide. It was a shopgirl's melodrama and the public loved it. But the simulated sex scenes were so steamy that it became Britain's first X-rated film. The director, Lewis Gilbert, who later did many of the James Bond films, was adorable and lovely to work with. And Max finally got a job and left for Jersey to make *Sea Devils* for Raoul Walsh. It was just the sort of pirate potboiler he loved, especially since he played the "heavy" against Rock Hudson.

. . .

We did another play at the Q Theatre, *The Skin of Our Teeth,* by Thornton Wilder, one of the American classics. My part was Sabina, the mischievous vamp, which had originally been played by Vivien Leigh. I was delighted that finally I was going to play a classic role in a great play.

The Q Theatre specialized in revivals. Although it was a small, intimate theater, it nevertheless put on excellent productions and it was considered a coup to play there. Although too young for the role of sixty-year-old Mr. Antrobus, Max put on a ton of makeup, grayed his tinted black hair and played the part quite well. When he stopped posturing, posing and using a phony American accent, he was a reasonable actor. We had just finished a film together for Rank, *The Square Ring,* again directed by Basil Dearden. I played a cameo role as Max's girlfriend, and Max wasted much time accusing me of upstaging him. Since I was still inexperienced in film acting, I had no idea how to do a lot of things, let alone upstage anyone. I became uneasy during our scenes together for fear I was displeasing him.

The reviews for *The Skin of Our Teeth* were excellent and I enjoyed it more than any film I had made so far. I wanted to do more theater, but first I had to make a strong dramatic film for Rank. *Turn the Key Softly* was the tale of one day in the lives of three women just released from prison. It was an authentic, raw film, so authentic, in fact, that the opening scenes of Yvonne Mitchell, Kathleen Harrison and me being released from prison were shot in Holloway Women's Prison.

I played a young prostitute, in the clink for shoplifting, who tries to keep on the straight and narrow but is tempted by the bright lights and glamour of the West End. We shot on actual locations around London in the dead of winter. It was bitterly cold and I was fitted out in my usual sleaze: tight black satin skirt, slit to the thigh, black stockings, ankle-strap shoes, a flimsy, low-cut Lurex sweater and a yellow short-sleeved jacket. I was blue with cold for most of the time and started thinking longingly of sunkissed California, from where Bill Watts was getting regular calls about my availability.

Due to Rank's giving me a tremendous publicity buildup, I

became known as "Britain's Best Bad Girl," and I had hardly any time for myself. At night, exhausted from shooting, I would return to our flat in Hanover Square and attempt to cook dinner and do housework before I flopped exhausted into bed. For, contrary to my brave statements in the *Daily Mirror,* Max was a true male chauvinist and expected his hot dinners every night. My mother had not educated me in the culinary arts because I had always had so many projects going after school that she was loath to take me away from them. Besides my voracious reading (at least seven or eight books a week) I spent a great deal of time writing to film stars for their autographed photos, or cutting and pasting pictures of stars into great scrapbooks. Cooking was too boring to contend with, and besides, I thought I would never need to do it. But Max liked his meat and potatoes, and it was he who taught me the rudiments of cooking. However, if it didn't turn out to his satisfaction, he would sling the whole plate of food across the room.

There was a mirror above the kitchen sink, and sometimes I looked at my bedraggled reflection as I was washing up and compared it with the provocative and alluring face adorning magazines and newspapers. They seemed like two different people—the glamour girl and this pale, pathetic waif. The irony, too, was that Max, due to his work or his disability, didn't want sex very much—a pleasing fact to me—but the public was being fooled when they saw my sexy photos about what I must really be like. I was a celibate sex kitten! My marriage was a fiasco. I lived in fear of Max's moods and rages, but I didn't have the guts to get out. When I wasn't working I rushed to voice classes, dance classes, acting classes—anything to get away from him.

After finishing *Turn the Key Softly* I had several meetings with the Italian film director Renato Castellani. He was about to make a film of *Romeo and Juliet* and the Rank Organization decided that I would be the perfect Juliet! This did not thrill either Signor Castellani or me. I did not think I was the Juliet type—I had always preferred parts with more meat on their bones, such as Sabina in *The Skin of Our Teeth,* or Cleopatra, or Katherine in *Taming of the Shrew.* I did not see myself as an innocent fourteen-year-old virgin, which was how Castellani wanted the part played. Rank was adamant. He must test me, so test me he did. At least two or three times.

The final test at Pinewood was with Laurence Harvey, who had been signed for Romeo. We were still friendly, but even he agreed that I was too sophisticated-looking for their version of Juliet. Signor Castellani came to me before the last test and gave me his ultimatum. "You will havva the nose job," he said in his heavily accented English. "I will havva the what?" I said incredulously. "Giulietta she hassa the Roman nose! You havva the nose it goes up—is not aristocratic—you go to the good plastic surgeon—he make-a the Roman nose—you be Giulietta!"

"Oh *no*—you've got to be kidding," I wailed, then broke into hysterical laughter. A nose job to get a part? No way. Besides, I liked my nose—hadn't one of the papers said that the three prettiest noses in Britain belonged to Vivien Leigh, Jean Simmons and Joan Collins? I drew the line. Bill Watts was summoned, and amidst much Italian screaming and yelling and my hysterics and total refusal to get the nose job, Rank reluctantly backed down and an unknown actress was signed for Juliet.

Although I'd been under contract for some months, Rank still didn't have much idea what to do with me. When in doubt they sent me to the Stills Gallery. So, when Noel Langley and George Minter approached them about a loan-out to star in Langley's own novel, *Our Girl Friday*, they allowed me to do it. It was an absolutely gorgeous part. And funny, too. My yen to play comedy was developing. The script was hilarious and the three actors who were in it were important stars. I played Sadie, a willful, spoiled brat of a girl on a holiday cruise with her parents. Their ship is wrecked and Sadie and the three men manage to reach a deserted island where they live together for many months.

Kenneth More played Pat Plunket, the ship's colorful Irish stoker with a fondness for liquor and an eye for the ladies. Kenneth had recently had a huge success in *Genevieve* and had become a big star. George Cole played Carrol, a cynical journalist who hated Sadie, and Robertson Hare—one of the greatest farce actors in England—played Professor Gibble, a prim and proper old economics professor.

This motley group assemble on the island, realize that it's uninhabited and are appalled—one girl on a desert island with three men! A situation fraught with peril for them all, but with amusement for the audience, we hoped. We shot on the island of Majorca. I was given the opportunity to look desirable and wholesome for a change and to wear some pretty clothes, which became skimpier as time and the ravages of desert-island life progressed. The film was a minor hit in England and then in America, where the title was changed to *The Adventures of Sadie*. My performance started to seriously interest the heads of several studios—among them Darryl Zanuck, the head of production at Fox.

Edward Leggevie, an executive at Fox in London, asked if I would be interested in the idea of going to Hollywood under contract to Fox. Would I? My heart leaped at the idea. I was getting sick of doing endless tests for parts that I didn't get—sick of the snide remarks the press were making about me. "Let's have an end to the puppy fat otaro," said Logan Courtney. "She strains to look like Marilyn Monroe," said Donald Zec (a total lie). "Too much publicity and not enough performances," sneered another. Working nonstop (five films and four plays in one-and-a-half years) I thought this most unfair. But the press always managed to make out that I was a total playgirl even if I was working constantly—possibly because of my later cavalier attitude toward negative media criticism. By this time my marriage was so intolerable that I would do *anything* to get away from London. The location in Majorca was wonderful. I felt 100 percent free for the first time ever. But I needed more freedom. I called on the support of my loyal and trustworthy Bill Watts. He promised to find me a play to go on tour. To escape from Maxwell Reed.

The Praying Mantis was a new play—not a particularly good one, but I didn't care. I had to get away. The Rank Organization gave me a bonus of nine hundred pounds—a fortune! They had probably made over seventy-five thousand pounds on me from the various loan-outs, but I was still making only one hundred pounds a week. In *The Praying Mantis* I played a young Byzantine empress who, after making love to her men, sends them away to be executed. Hence the title, from the insect of the same name.

The director, Esme Percy, was a touch grand. He had been a well-known actor, but now was well over sixty and possibly bitter over the passing of the years. He told me condescendingly that I looked like "an expensive toy," a compliment not guaranteed to bring out the best of one's acting talents, particularly in a less than mediocre play.

We played a week at the Q Theatre to lukewarm reviews and houses, and then went on tour for three weeks to Brighton, Wimbledon and Folkestone. In spite of the lousy play and unenthusiastic audiences, I still completely relished it. For the first time I felt I was achieving what I originally wanted to do—to become an actress and not a movie starlet. I felt tremendous freedom on the stage. The inhibitions I had in front of the camera disappeared. I loved the rapport and jokes among the actors. I loved the old drafty dressing rooms with the musty mothball smells of a thousand ancient costumes and stale greasepaint. Our troupe would sit for hours after the show in seedy pubs and even seedier digs, talking about acting, about our lives and aspirations—gossiping, drinking, playing cards and judging ourselves and each other. I knew I was accepted for what I really was: an immature girl trying to learn to act, to grow up, improve herself, in a glare of publicity, with faults, weaknesses and insecurities about herself. But I also knew I had humor and guts and intelligence. I didn't have to play the sexy starlet with Fanny, Jimmy and Ian. We were family and we formed the closest of bonds—we were all just actors. Although the play flopped, this did not deter me from doing another, and on returning to London, I immediately started rehearsals for *Claudia and David*, a funny, tender romantic American comedy about a slightly scatty child bride and her husband.

During this time Max was traveling to and from Rome trying to get work. On one of his trips back he suggested we go to our favorite restaurant-nightclub in London, Les Ambassadeurs.

Les Ambassadeurs was terribly chic. All the visiting American actors and producers and directors made it their home away from home. The club itself was in a beautiful old Georgian house in Hamilton Terrace. The furnishings were subdued and impeccable, the food excellent, and the music, although slightly tame for my jazz-oriented taste, was gay and danceable.

I sat drinking Pimm's, deep in thought about *Claudia and David;* Max was chatting to an elderly Arabian gentleman on the banquette next to him. I ignored them. Max had a habit of gravitating toward rich, elderly men who usually lusted after me. They talked animatedly for a long time.

I was intrigued watching Linda Christian and Edmund Purdom doing the cha-cha when Max pulled my arm and introduced me to the gentleman. "This is Sheik Abdul Ben Kafir," he said. I nodded coldly to this aged roué, who smiled excitedly and looked me up and down. I was wearing a low-cut white chiffon blouse and a green velvet skirt, and I was starting to get a vague idea of what this was all about from the expectant look on the Arab's fat face.

"Excuse me, Sheik," said Max smoothly. "Back in a minute. Going to take little Joanie for a trot around the dance floor." He pulled me onto the floor and to the strains of "From This Moment On" we danced. "Ten thousand pounds," said Max, his face aglow with pride. "He'll pay you ten thousand pounds for *one night!*—and I can even watch!"

"I beg your pardon, Max," I said as coldly as I could, fear gripping the pit of my stomach. "Are you *seriously* suggesting I go to bed with that disgusting old man for *money?*"

"You bloody little idiot," he snarled, whirling me to the far end of the floor. "Ten grand! Tax free! Do you realize what we can do with that sort of money? We can go to Hollywood. We can have a holiday in Florida. We can even buy a cottage in the country. You better start cashing in on what you've got, girl—doing plays at the Q for ten quid a week is *not* going to make us rich in our old age."

I started to protest but he wouldn't listen and squeezed my arms tighter and tighter, until I felt tears welling up. I forced myself not to cry. "One night, baby—that's all. One night with Abdul and we can say 'Fuck you' to all of 'em, be off to Hollywood— What do you say, baby?"

I looked at Abdul nodding and smiling at me over his champagne goblet. His pendulous jowls were wobbling. I looked at my handsome, *loathsome* husband and the tears flooded. "Never," I screamed, turning the heads of Linda and Edmund, who were dancing right behind us. "I will never, ever, ever do that. Never in

a million years, Max. Take your sheik and go to hell, both of you."
I couldn't control myself any more. The place had become cathe-
dral quiet at my outburst. I rushed from the club, grabbed a cab
and went home. It was the final straw. I couldn't take it for another minute. I didn't care if my father disowned me for not making the marriage work. I didn't care if Max made good his oft
repeated threat to "have some of the *boys* carve your pretty little
face up with a razor if you ever leave me"—nothing mattered any
more except saving my self-respect and my sanity.

I went home to Mummy.

CHAPTER

Three

but it was hopeless. Not only did I not love him any more—I disliked him intensely. His ailment hadn't improved and his sexual tendencies were increasingly sadistic and perverted. My parents were glad to have me home again—my father seemed to have forgotten his promise to disown me—and I moved back happily into the familiar back bedroom.

The meetings between my agent and the Fox representatives had heated up and negotiations began to buy my contract outright from Rank. I left for Rome to play wicked Princess Nellifer in a lavish Biblical epic, *Land of the Pharaohs*. It was my first big American film, with an international cast headed by Jack Hawkins. Directed by Howard Hawks, one of the most famous of the Hollywood directors, it was written by an imposing duo—William Faulkner and Harry Kurnitz. Although they slaved away, writing and rewriting daily, it was, in spite of their efforts, a hokey script with some impossible dialogue, made even worse by the fact that they tried to "Biblicize" it.

I was incredibly lucky to get this break and I knew it. I plunged feverishly into an endless series of photo tests, costume fittings, hair and makeup tests. Nellifer was Egyptian, exotic and simmeringly evil, and a multitude of excitable costume designers, blasé hairdressers and enthusiastic makeup men strove to turn a gauche girl only three years out of school into a sultry, wicked Egyptian goddess. My hair was the despair of the brittle, hawk-eyed American hairdresser. Long, thin and stringy, it conformed not at all to the "luxuriantly cascading abundant tresses" attributed to the princess in the script. After my countless brief encounters with every piece of fake hair in Rome, the hairdresser was by now my least favorite person in the world. She constantly lamented my lack of locks.

"We'll just have to call you old pinhead," she sneered jovially, stabbing my skull once more with her three-inch steel hairpins. She finally found a wig we both liked. Waist-length, it contained the life savings of the hair of twelve Italian nuns. It was so heavy that when I moved my head it was as if in slow motion. To keep it stuck to my scalp we used 47 bobby pins, 92 sharp hairpins and half a bottle of toupee glue.

When, as often happens today, *Land of the Pharaohs* is shown on the late show and I get praise for my appearance, I smile when I think of the agony I endured at the hands of that hairdresser. Not to mention the complex I had for years because of the "old pinhead" line. Although I have a small head, it is not deformed, as I was led to believe then; I thought I was a bit of a freak in the skull department, thanks to her.

Rome was exciting. "La Dolce Vita" was in full swing. Down the Via Veneto strolled household-name American actors and actresses escaping their taxes by taking eighteen months out of the States. Gorgeous raven-haired Italian starlets sat sipping cappuccino at the sidewalk cafés, waiting to be discovered. Everyone was alive and gay. It was summer and I found a new romance.

Sydney Chaplin was the second son of Charlie Chaplin. Twenty-eight years old, he was very tall, very dark and quite handsome, with black curly hair flecked with gray, and amused brown eyes. He had an outrageous and scurrilous wit. He was so originally hilarious that he made me literally weep with laughter.

Every day we started laughing and didn't stop until the early hours of the morning, when we would stagger out of Victor's Club, the Number One, or whatever disco or club we hit upon that night, and giggle all the way back to the sedate Hotel de La Ville, where most of the international cast stayed during the filming of *Land of the Pharaohs*.

There had been an absence of laughter and gaiety in the latter months of my life with Maxwell Reed. Sydney was like ice water in the desert. He filled a tremendous need in my life to have fun; to enjoy my flaming youth and to be nonconformist as far as the "establishment" went. I didn't deliberately set out to shock people, but Syd gave not a single damn about what the world thought of him. Since I was a chameleon where men were concerned, I too adopted his "screw you" attitude toward his fellow man.

After two weeks of staying up till dawn and listening to Sydney enthrall a roomful of people with his crazy monologues and outrageous jokes, we finally laughed our way into bed—where we proceeded to become, if possible, even *more* hysterical. Someone said to me once, after literally chasing me around my living room for half an hour with me evading this humorist's clutches till, weak with laughter, I managed to usher him to the door, "Well, I may not be much of a lover, but I'm a funny fuck!" Although this was not strictly true of Syd, nevertheless we often ended our nights by my breaking up and him doing a comedy routine. *Nothing* was to be taken seriously, and after a year of torment with Max that was OK by me.

His favorite expression was "motherfucker"—usually shortened to "mother," and his vocabulary was so sprinkled with four-letter words that it was always slightly surprising to play in a scene with him and hear normal dialogue come out of his mouth. Sometimes in our scenes together I would have to dig my nails into the palms of my hands to stop giggling. To Syd, life was one great big ball. He loved to drink, to dance, to gamble, to joke and to play. He didn't take acting seriously. It was just a way to make some bread. I had thought that he would surely have been wealthy, as his father was a multimillionaire—but that was not the case. He had a small allowance but not enough to lead the crazy playboy existence he desired. He owned two expensive sports cars, a red Ferrari and a blue Alfa-Romeo, and he lived out of two alligator suitcases.

We would drive back from the beach at Ostia or Fregene in the early hours at 125 miles an hour, the convertible top down, the warm wind whipping my hair wildly, and the trees above us melting into a ceiling of green leaves—laughing all the way. It was a miracle we were never killed. We gave a new meaning to

57

the word reckless. We lived life in the fast lane—Zelda and Scott reincarnated.

The part of Princess Nellifer necessitated many changes of wardrobe, each one more exotic or revealing than the last. The seamstresses at Scalera Studios were hard at it, sewing hundreds of yards of gold lamé, silver brocade, chiffon, silk and gold braid into elaborate costumes that I would wear when I became the Egyptian Queen. My opening outfit was somewhat simpler. I wore a gold mesh bra and a long purple brocade skirt which sat low on my hips. Over this was a velvet cloak in which when I was presented as a gift to the Pharaoh, I would be wrapped.

However, my naked navel presented a problem. It was the mid-fifties. Censorship was severe. If the Hays Office thought a scene or a costume too risqué, it was cut, and thousands of dollars of valuable footage went down the drain.

My outfit was as Egyptian-authentic as the Italian designer could make it, but my navel was a no-no as far as the censor was concerned. "Cover it up," said Howard Hawks testily when I presented myself to him for final approval on this costume. "Find a way to cover it up. The censor thinks navels are obscene," he snorted despairingly, and went back to his scene. The designer, Mayo, an excitable Latin, shrugged. "Il censore è matto—completamente matto—ma cosa facciamo adesso?"

"How about a Band-Aid?" I joked. "Or some Plasticine inside it. We'll get some Plasticine and dye it to match my stomach, and then I'll be navel-less, just like a big doll!"

They looked at me pityingly—English humor does not appeal to Italians. "Aha!" Mayo suddenly shrieked, jumping up and down excitedly. "Mettiamo un bottone in sua piccola bucca!" My Italian was scratchy, but roughly translated this meant "Let's put a button in her little 'hole!" They scurried to their treasure chests and pulled out dozens of buttons—silver, gold, emerald and finally a ruby. Mayo tried to insert the ruby while I squirmed uncomfortably. "Bella!" said Mayo proudly. "Molto bella! Cara—you think so too?"

I looked in the mirror at the little ruby twinkling brightly in the middle of my stomach and burst into laughter. With that the ruby exploded out of its place and disappeared under a sewing machine. *"Chè cosa?"* said Mayo angrily. "We must put the sticky stuff—we stuff it in hard and it stay there. *Bellissimo—un effetto bellissimo."* I endured a tube of Johnson's liquid adhesive poured into my navel, and there the ruby stayed, proud and glistening, defying the censor. I thought it looked infinitely more obscene and erotic with the shiny stone drawing attention to what was meant to be unobtrusive, but everyone seemed satisfied, and shooting commenced.

However, several weeks in Sydney's company, scoffing fettuccine and lasagne at Alfredo's and Il Piccolo Mondo and drinking quantities of red wine and crème de menthe had added about eight pounds to my already voluptuous figure. When it came time to do a retake of the first scene I was embarrassed. *Zaftig* was an understatement. I knew Howard Hawks hated plump ladies (he had discovered, or sponsored, Lauren Bacall, Lizabeth Scott and Angie Dickinson, none of them exactly blimps), I endeavored to hold my stomach in tightly during the scene, but each time I squeezed in my muscles, out plopped the dreaded red stone!

Howard Hawks was going crazy.

"For God's sakes—get some airplane glue. Get anything to keep the damned thing in place." And then accusingly to me: "You've gained weight. I told you last week in the rushes you looked *fat*. Have you been dieting?"

"All I've eaten for two days is three hard-boiled eggs, Mr. Hawks," I lied feverishly, thinking of the vast amount of spaghetti Bolognese and zabaglione I had consumed at Alfredo's last night.

"Well you better cut it down to two hard-boiled eggs," he said crustily. "Princess Nellifer should not look as though she is four months pregnant." He stormed off, leaving me properly chastened. He was right. Here I was playing the best role of my career and I was goofing off. Too many late nights and too much pasta and wine do not a love affair with the camera make. I vowed to discipline myself.

I was playing the role of a lifetime—being directed by one of the world's greatest movie directors, working with some of the finest actors around, and I was acting and behaving like a stupid schoolgirl. I was wrong and knew it. I quit drinking, banished pasta from my mind, and was in bed at ten o'clock each night with a copy of *Land of the Pharaohs* in front of me.

But it was not easy, with Syd. When I stayed in and went to bed early he went out with his gang anyway, and since I was infatuated with him I wanted to be where the action was—and that was with him.

I was staying at the Hotel de la Ville, a popular watering hole for French and Italian actors and directors. On my second day, while enjoying a drink on the terrace with Christian Marquand and Dewey Martin, one of the stars of *Pharaohs*, a vision appeared.

"Who is *that?*" breathed Dewey in awe, as the most gorgeous girl I had ever seen walked to the bar.

"Ah, *elle s'appelle Brigitte Bardot, une nouvelle jeune vedette du cinéma, et une amie de moi,*" said Christian. "*Bonsoir,* Roger."

Bardot's escort, a young intense man with a shock of black hair and sharp features, shook hands with Christian hurriedly, gave me the onceover and hastened to the bar where Bardot, to whom he was then married, was getting more than admiring glances from every man in the place.

She was about my age and was indeed delicious. An enviable, petite beauty wearing her soon-to-be-famous pink-and-white tight-waisted gingham peasant dress with the extremely low neckline, her masses of blond hair looking as if she had just tumbled out of bed, and the eyes and lips that every man desired.

And every woman wanted to look like her. I even whipped over to a dressmaker the very next day to have the pink-and-white gingham dress copied!

Although we never met again I remained a fan of Bardot's. Not particularly for her acting—although I thought she had a lot more talent than her sexuality allowed her to show—but for her free and honest approach to love, men and sex. I was also interested through the years to see her ever changing parade of lovers and husbands, and I admired her self-admitted freedom from sexual taboos. I was shocked, however, to read this quote in a magazine recently from this liberated, emancipated lady:

I have to accept old age, right? It is horrible, you rot, you fall to pieces, you stink. It scares me more than anything else. There's a beach not far away but I never go during the day. I am 48 and not so pretty. I wouldn't inflict this sight on anyone any more.

Sad words from anyone, but particularly sad from such a dazzling woman who, had she only felt more secure about things other than just her physical attributes, should realize she is in her prime.

Sydney had gained a few pounds too, and as the time drew near to start our love scenes together, we both made a concerted effort to cut calories and get in shape. His costumes were even more "kitsch" than mine. He wore a small beige felt skullcap which was cunningly cut out to reveal his ears—not his best feature—a long loincloth of an ornate fabric, and a vast neckpiece of gold and ebony; also curious pointed slippers and two large gold slave bracelets on his upper arms, which, due to the amount of food we were consuming, made the flesh squash out above and below in a most unattractive fashion. I was wearing a pink chiffon gown, low-cut and heavily embroidered with crystals, and on my upper arm a tight silver-and-ruby bracelet, around which flesh also bulged. Thank God I wasn't wearing the ruby in my navel too.

When Sydney and I met at 8:30 A.M. on the sound stage at Scalera Studios, we took one look at each other and burst out laughing. "Is this how Theda Bara started?"

"More like Ma and Pa Kettle meet the motherfucking Pharaoh," said Syd, tripping over his pointed sandals and getting entangled in his maxiskirt.

"Quiet, now hold it down," called the assistant director, and we started blocking the scene when Trenah (Syd) declares his love for Princess Nellifer.

Actors have two dreaded nightmares: One is to appear on stage and forget one's dialogue; the other is to be unable to speak the dialogue because of an uncontrollable urge to laugh. The latter nightmare happened to Sydney and me that day. It was truly ghastly because however hard we forced ourselves not to break up, one or the other of us would at one point or another in the scene start to collapse into giggles. The angrier Howard Hawks became the more we laughed. I was actually terrified and upset after this occurred four or five times, but it didn't help. One look at Syd's earnest face, with his ears sticking out of the weird hat, and I was convulsed. I would try not to break up completely, but Syd saw the strain in my face and that would set him off. It was like an hysterical bad dream. It was also catching. Half the crew were starting to giggle, and it was when we caught sight of the overly serious and cross faces of Howard and the more somber crew members that we all broke up over and over again.

Eventually Howard stopped shooting and bawled Sydney and me out vehemently in front of the entire crew. He sent us home and lectured us sternly to stop behaving like children or our careers would be finished before they got started. He brought us down to earth with a big bang.

This time I really decided to pull myself together—to lose the excess pounds and take my work more seriously. I realized I was losing face and that my behavior was becoming terribly unprofessional.

I had tried to file for a divorce in London before leaving for Rome, but one could not file unless the marriage had existed for three years or more. All I had was an unofficial separation from Max, who was also in Rome at the time working on *Helen of Troy*, another historical and hysterical soap opera.

I was sunbathing on the beach at Fregene one day when I felt a shadow looming over me. I looked up. There he was. Tanned, dyed black hair and small white shorts, and an ominous look on his face. "I want to talk to you." I was surrounded by friends who tried to get rid of him, but he was insistent. "You better come and talk to me now or I'll make a scene right here," he said menacingly. I reluctantly followed him to the beach bar. "Do you remember the photographs I took of you?" he said casually, offering me a cigarette.

I did remember them. It is not an uncommon occurrence for husbands to take nude photos of their wives. Some of our friends did, and although he had coaxed me into posing for them with assurances that he would never show them to a soul, I had been uneasy at the time. The pictures were fairly tame as far as I remembered. I wore the bottom half of a bikini and was posed, bored and sulky, on the zebra-skin sofa. Tame stuff by today's standards. "So what about them?" I said brazening it out.

"I've got a good offer from one of the Italian magazines to buy them from me. They'll pay me a lot of money and I need it." He smiled his Mitchum smile. I looked at him numbly. He surely had to be the lowest form of human life. How could I have ever married such a vile creep? Just looking at him filled me with revulsion.

"So what do you want from me?" I said.

"All the rings I gave you when we were married," he said smoothly. "Wedding, engagement and the topaz."

"You're welcome to them," I said icily. "I'll have someone bring them to your hotel."

"And the check," he said, blocking me as I tried to get back to the beach. "Don't forget to sign it."

I couldn't believe he was serious. In the past month he had sent several crazy letters to me professing his love, and in one of them he had enclosed a blank check from my personal account and asked me to sign it.

"You know I don't have much money," I protested. "There's only a couple of hundred pounds in my account, that's all."

"The check and the rings at my hotel tomorrow night, or the magazine gets the pictures. *Ciao*, kid," and he sauntered off to the bar. I was furious. The man had no ethics at all. He was a street fighter. Maybe I should become one too. I told my mother, who was staying with me. She had grown to hate Max as much as I. I had revealed to her some of the horrors I had been through. We discussed our strategy with Eddie Fowlie, the special-effects man on *Pharaohs* and a friend, who had also been on *Our Girl Friday*. He agreed to take the rings and the blank check to Max at the Residence Palace Hotel the next night.

I didn't have much choice. The money wasn't important and the rings had no sentimental value, but it would have been complete disaster for my career had those nude photos appeared in print. Rumors had been circulating that nude pictures of Marilyn Monroe had been printed some time ago on a girlie calendar.

The world was puritanical and quick to condemn any public figures whose morals were less than faultless. I was worried that if a whiff of this possible scandal reached the ears of 20th Century–Fox, who were in final negotiations with Rank to buy my contract, my Hollywood career would be finished before it had barely begun.

Mummy and I sat in a nearby café compulsively drinking cappuccino and brandy while Eddie went to pick up the photos from Max. He returned triumphantly with a large, sealed manila envelope. I opened the envelope and out fell twelve eight-by-ten glossy pinup pictures from Rank!

"That rotten bastard!" I was so furious I didn't even censor my language in front of my mother. "Of all the lowdown, filthy, lying tricks. He's still got the goddamned pictures." Mummy and Eddie looked at each other helplessly. "I'm going to go and punch him out," said Eddie. But my mother laid a restraining hand on him. "No, let me talk to him first." She strode to the phone. I knocked back a brandy and wondered from where my mother— Mrs. Gentle-Meek-and-Mild, usually—had unearthed this ferocious streak.

When Mummy came back she was trembling with fury. "He told me the photographs are in London in a safety-deposit box," she said, her voice shaking. I was proud of her; she didn't assert herself too often, but there she was—a tigress protecting her cub.

"I called him all the names under the sun, but he said he wants to keep them to remember you by." I passed her my brandy.

"Oh, charming," I said bitterly. "He can show them to all his dirty old Arabian millionaires and tell them what they've missed."

"Anyway," said Mummy, smiling bravely, "he's promised *me* that he will not sell them to any publications, so I suppose we'll just have to take his word for it."

"His *word*—ha!" I threw down another brandy. "He doesn't know the meaning of honor and ethics." Mummy patted my hand comfortingly.

"Never mind, darling. I'm sure we've heard the last of him this time." I nodded weakly but I had a nasty suspicion that the last chapter on Maxwell Reed had yet to be written.

. . .

"Three hundred and fifty dollars a week," announced John Shepbridge, his eyes glowing with excitement. "What do you think of that, Joanie? That is terrific for the first year." "Not much," I said diffidently. I sat across from "Goulash," as he was affectionately known, sitting behind his highly polished walnut desk in his London house at 16 South Audley Street. The weak London sun seeped through the tiny Georgian latticed windows and reflected off the silver and porcelain objects scattered tastefully around his office-living room. We were meeting to discuss my deal with Fox. Rank had accepted the fifteen thousand pounds that Fox had offered to buy my contract from them, and Goulash, who was a senior executive of the Famous Artists Agency, was now negotiating my salary terms.

My dream was about to be realized. I was going to Hollywood under an exclusive seven-year contract with 20th Century–Fox. It was an offer not to be sneezed at, but I was sneezing. The reason for my lack of enthusiasm was at this minute in Paris, probably languishing in some bistro or boîte, consuming quantities of vodka and playing the pinball machines.

Goulash looked at me, a flicker of annoyance crossing his face. "What did you say, dear?"

"Three hundred and fifty dollars a week is not that much money, Goulash. You know that and I know that. Now if Fox is willing to pay Rank so much money for me, I'm quite sure they will be willing to pay me more as a contract player. I was thinking of, say, twelve hundred and fifty a week."

I had read in a magazine that $1,250 a week was a reasonable salary for a young contract player, and if one settled for less than that, the studios thought of you more as a feature or bit player and it was harder to obtain leading roles. Although I would have sold my soul to go to Hollywood, I had ambivalent feelings at the moment because of my crush on Sydney.

"You're crazy," said Goulash angrily, his Hungarian blood rising to the occasion. "They will never go for that. Never. *Never*. You're totally *unknown* in the States. Why should they pay you three times as much as they usually do? Crazy—crazy." He stomped around his desk angrily mumbling to himself.

"What am I going to tell Charlie?" he said. "He's been talking about you to Darryl for three months now. It's because of *him* you're getting this deal. He's going to be furious."

Charlie was Charles K. Feldman, top executive agent at Famous Artists and a wheeler-dealer to be reckoned with. I knew that because of his influence with Darryl Zanuck, head of production at Fox, who trusted Feldman's enthusiasm for me, I was being offered this contract. I also shrewdly realized that the chances of my getting the better roles at Fox and not being just another two-bit contract player would be enhanced by getting a large weekly salary rather than what was virtually a pittance. (Studio grips earned more than $350 a week.) It was a calculated gamble, and if I lost I could always go back to Syd in Paris, or work in Rome, where I had been getting movie offers.

"I'm very appreciative of all that you and Charlie have done for me," I said formally. "But it's my life and my decision. I want twelve hundred and fifty a week, and if I don't get it—forget it." I got up to leave. "Darling Goulash—I'm leaving for Paris tonight. I'll be at the Hotel Trémoille. Let me know what happens." I kissed him goodbye and he raised his eyebrows in a gesture of resignation.

"Crazy little girl," he said. "You can always find a good *shtup*, but a good contract is a once-in-a-lifetime thing. I hope you're not blowing your career, Joanie."

"I'm not," I said confidently. "Let me quote Joan Crawford: 'You can't cuddle up to a career at night.' " (I had just read that in *Photoplay* and thought it quite profound.) "*Ciao*, Goulash." I walked into South Audley Street feeling grownup and confident. I was not yet twenty-one, but I knew what I wanted—and I was *not* going to sell myself short this time.

As soon as I arrived in Paris, Sydney and I took off in the Ferrari with his friend Adolph Green for a trip to Vevey, Switzerland, to visit Syd's father, Charlie Chaplin. Adolph was squashed in the tiny back seat and we had a hair-raising trip over the snowy, winding mountain roads. I was excitedly looking forward to meeting Syd's family and especially the legendary Charlie.

The house was set in a secluded area, just outside the tiny picturesque village of Vevey, which looked like every postcard of

Switzerland. It was an imposing two-story mansion with an apparently endless series of rooms. The rooms were necessary because there seemed to be an endless series of children and nannies, maids, gardeners and secretaries. Although the senior Chaplin had a reputation for being penurious, his lifestyle was lavish. Beyond the rolling green lawns and flower beds was a beautiful lake where all the kids and Charlie and his lovely black-haired, madonnalike wife, Oona, swam and sunbathed. I liked being around this happy family atmosphere, and although Charlie reminded me somewhat of my father, very much the patriarch, strict and authoritarian, he was also warm and human, funny and, strangely, extremely shy.

Although over sixty, Charlie was still busy siring babies. They ranged in age from Charlie, Jr., who was about thirty, to the newest baby of only a few months old. I admired Oona for her lovely maternal calmness, and, playing with her babies, I felt for the very first time a slight flicker of maternal instinct. "What a crazy idea," I said to myself, dismissing it instantly and putting down baby, who was in the process of covering his entire face with nourishing Swiss chocolate. "I've got years to go before I even think about having kids—got my whole life ahead yet. Kids! Ugh! *Quel horreur!*"

Sydney and I stayed with his family for three days, and another side of his personality revealed itself. He was much more subdued around Charlie, not nearly as bawdy, and didn't want any "romantic interludes" in the same house as his father.

"But why?" I whispered. "His room is miles away." "I don't know, for Christ's sake," he whispered angrily. "I just feel funny about it—can't you understand that?" "I guess so," I said, imagining my reactions in the same situation. "But since they know we have the same room, do you think they imagine we're playing gin rummy all night? And from the number of kids they have, I bet *they* don't play cards too often."

I remembered Syd regaling me with stories about him, his brother and his ex-stepmother, Paulette Goddard. Charlie, Jr., and Syd were about thirteen and fourteen years old, Paulette not more than a dozen years older. Sometimes in the morning the boys would jump into Paulette's silken-covered bed with her and share her toast and coffee while she read her mail and talked on the phone. She would tease and cuddle the adolescent boys, and, though Sydney assured me it was all very innocent, it struck me as odd, to say the least.

In any event, I couldn't understand the great unwillingness on Syd's part to sully the Swiss sheets. Maybe he was a genuine prude—people who swore a lot often were.

In Paris, it was a fun time again; up all night at Jimmy's night-club or L'Éléphant Blanc, or our favorite restaurant, Moustache. The owner, a huge man with a fine hairy upper lip, was a friend, and we spent wonderfully convivial evenings there. I took long walks through Paris and along the Seine while Syd played golf. I loved exploring the sophisticated Right Bank boutiques, and the tiny cluttered antique and book shops. We rode on the *bateau mouche* on the Seine, spent a day at the Louvre and fell in love with the city. When we weren't exploring, we played Sinatra records and cards, pinball machines in overheated cafés, and drank Beaujolais and laughed and nightclubbed all night. It was good to be alive, young and carefree.

I was still playing the waiting game with Fox. When Goulash called to tell me not only that Fox had accepted my terms, but that they wanted me in California almost immediately, I was thrilled—but dismayed.

Sydney and I sat in a tiny restaurant in Montmartre. The candlelight flickered on the red-checked tablecloth and the air was thick with the smell of Gauloises and garlic. I was leaving the next day for London to pack and depart for the States. He tried to comfort me as I sobbed into my wine. We thought we loved each other. We would be together soon, he tried to assure me. As soon as he knew about a job that he was hoping for, he would join me in Los Angeles. Not to worry, it would all work out in the end. I hoped he was right.

In London I was surrounded by family and friends, photographers coming over to take pictures, and dressmakers bringing new finery. I was caught up in a whirl of activity and excitement. In the pre-jet days a trip to the States was a major event. To get to New York alone took over ten hours. Today I make a minimum of eight or nine trips a year between L.A. and London and think nothing of it. Finally, amidst tears, laughter and sadness I said goodbye. I hugged my little brother, Bill, whom I felt I hardly knew, kissed my teenage sister, Jackie—we had just started to become close and now I was leaving—a big hug for Daddy and, finally, my darling mother, whom I was beginning to understand and love more and more. She was trying desperately not to cry—and so was I. We were surrounded by reporters and photographers trying to get a human-interest photo story on "Britain's Bad Girl Goes to Hollywood."

Every two or three minutes we heard the sound of a plane taking off. I clutched my brand-new ankle-length mink coat tightly around me and tried to be brave. "I'll write you every week," I said, my voice breaking. "And I'll come and visit as often as I can—it's only a little over five thousand miles from L.A. to London after all." Five thousand miles seemed like a million in the days before transatlantic jets, but I had to say something. The flight was called and I was off, leaving the family and friends I knew and loved, leaving cold, austerity-ridden England: the English country lanes; the pubs; the theater; the jazz clubs; the Sunday papers; everything that was familiar.

My whole life was being left behind and I was going to a strange new country. To a totally different environment. To meet and work with people I didn't know and to start a new life. In Hollywood.

CHAPTER

Four

"THEY'RE GOING TO LOVE YOU IN Hollywood," Goulash had told me confidently. "They love English girls. You'll be a smash."

I thought ruefully about his words as I sat in my hideous orange-and-yellow hotel room in Beverly Hills for the seventh consecutive night, alone, gazing at an unusual personality on television called Liberace. The days were so full I didn't have time to think. 20th Century–Fox was a hive of activity and I was running from wardrobe department to hairdressing to stills gallery for a never-ending succession of photographs and interviews. I met every producer and casting director on the lot and didn't remember any of their names. I sat in the bustling, hustling commissary at lunchtime eating a new delicacy called "tuna salad" and observed, wide-eyed, the comings and goings of the stars.

Fox had a huge list of contract players, all of whom were either working in the many films that were in production or were on the lot doing what I was doing, which was getting their faces in front of as many directors and producers as possible who were preparing projects. They included Susan Hayward, Rita Moreno, Sheree North, Debra Paget, Jeff Hunter, Barbara Rush, Robert Wagner, Gene Tierney, Joanne Woodward, even Clifton Webb—and many more. I hopefully looked each day for Fox's top star, Marilyn Monroe, but she preferred to lunch in the seclusion of her dressing-room.

70

Although Fox was making many movies, its box-office returns for the past couple of years had been less than brilliant. Zanuck did not have as much control as he had had when the studio was making such blockbusters as *Gentleman's Agreement*, *A Letter to Three Wives* and *All About Eve*, and although they had made the first CinemaScope film, *The Robe*, a few years before, things were soggy at the box office. Their films with Marilyn Monroe, queen of the lot and America's number one pinup, usually made a profit, but of late Miss Monroe had been giving them problems by refusing to make such epics as *The Lady in Pink Tights*, and had been going on suspension and to the Actors Studio in New York. Fox was starting to groom two young actresses, Jayne Mansfield and Sheree North, to take her place. They didn't take disobedience from anyone—not even Marilyn.

Goulash's words seemed anything but prophetic as I sat miserably alone night after night. The phone rang with invitations to dinner from men I had heard of but did not know—Nick Hilton, Bob Neal, Greg Bautzer—but I was always a one-man woman. Faithful to Sydney. I waited hopefully for him to arrive.

The vastness and variety of Los Angeles astounded me. The place sprawled on endlessly. Fashionable Beverly Hills, gracious Bel Air, swinging, youthful Westwood, seedy Hollywood, and the endless suburban fringes with quaint names like Pomona, Orange County, West Covina, Redlands, Santa Ana, Anaheim—it seemed bigger than *England!* Each area had a character of its own, and after I rented a car I explored each of them diligently. I had never seen so many drugstores and gas stations in my life—but these all looked alike.

The only people I knew socially were the makeup man from *Land of the Pharaohs* and my agents, and although they were very kind, and I went to dinner at their houses, I was lonely and homesick. I had not yet found friends of my own. The social structure of Hollywood and Beverly Hills was based on dozens of varied cliques. Some people belonged to one clique and some overlapped and belonged to several. Three or four or five hundred people made up the social center of Hollywood then, and I didn't know one of them.

• • •

I was cast in *The Virgin Queen*, a highly colored and fictionalized account of Queen Elizabeth's supposed romance with Sir Walter Raleigh. The redoubtable and legendary Bette Davis played Queen Elizabeth for the second time, as she had had a huge success in *Elizabeth and Essex* some years back with Errol Flynn. Richard Todd played Raleigh and I played Elizabeth's innocent lady-in-waiting Beth Throgmorton, in love with Raleigh and pregnant by him, much to Good Queen Bess's chagrin. Again I seemed to be playing a wayward girl, but instead of having to wear the sleazy costumes of *Cosh Boy* and *I Believe in You*, I was exquisitely dressed in beautiful Elizabethan laces and farthingales.

Painstaking effort and attention to detail went into the design and construction of these costumes. The wardrobe department at Fox was humming day and night with dozens of seamstresses, tailors, milliners and dressmakers making each creation a vision of perfection. I don't think even in the highest-fashion houses of Paris has there ever been so much time and attention to detail lavished on clothing as there was at the major film studios during their heyday. Each costume was a work of art. One dress was completely embroidered in thousands of tiny seed pearls over rare Belgian lace. Each pearl was sewn on by hand. The workmanship that went into inside seams was as careful as that lavished on the visible parts. For some outfits I would have six or seven complete fittings, and I would stand for hours while every seam was measured to an exact eighth of an inch—God help me if I put on a pound or two at lunch. The waist seams would be snipped and unpicked painstakingly and the dress would be refitted all over again. After I endured this agony a couple of times, I bought a scale and started watching my weight like a hawk. I was impatient at fittings and would yawn, stretch, scratch and fidget to the despair of these dedicated seamstresses.

Bette Davis awed me, and I avoided her off the set whenever possible. I had been warned she did not take kindly to young pretty actresses, and she lashed out at me a couple of times. She had a scathing wit and was not known for mincing words, and I thought it best to keep a low profile around her. I was still insecure about my work. My reviews from the British films constantly

72

emphasized my looks and sex appeal, and this seemed the only aspect of me that the magazine writers and reporters were interested in talking about. My measurements, my love life, and what I ate for breakfast were of far more interest to them than my brain, my approach to my craft, and what I thought of the State of the Union.

I had been warned by the vast publicity department that I should not talk about anything controversial (politics, religion, capital punishment, etc.). There was a morals clause in my contract which guaranteed that if I did anything to invoke the wrath of the Daughters of the American Revolution, the members of the John Birch Society or any other of the dozens of anti-anything organizations that proliferated in America at that time, I would be in trouble. America was in a time of prosperity but, living in the aftermath of the Joe McCarthy hearings, everyone attempted to be good, clean, upstanding, patriotic and loyal to America, with no whiff of communist leanings or subversive activities or sexual aberrations to sully their records.

Sydney finally arrived, and we rented a small, antiseptic furnished apartment on Beverly Glen Boulevard, just four minutes from Fox, and set up house together. Living together openly was considered terribly daring, especially since I was still married, so we tried to keep it as quiet as possible, especially from the Snoop Sisters, the gossip columnists Hedda Hopper and Louella Parsons.

I worked hard on *The Virgin Queen*. On my days off I would have to learn horseback riding, a frightening experience, as horses petrified me. There were also constant fittings, lunch interviews with every magazine in the U.S.A., and photo sessions, which went on endlessly.

It couldn't have been easy for Syd. He was living with a girl who not only was paying the rent but also was busy working all the time. He was not. There wasn't much on the horizon for him, so he threw himself into golf, cards and television—in that order. The only thing he didn't throw himself into too often was me.

He'd changed. Maybe it was being away from his beloved Europe and his cronies. America did not suit him. There were no cozy corner cafés to pass the time of day sipping coffee and telling bawdy stories. No friendly neighborhood bistros full of hearty red-faced, black-bereted men knocking back absinthe and playing the pinball machines. No Ferrari. No nightclubs to sit in until five in the morning, with the action still going strong. Add to this no work, and no wonder a sullen despondency suddenly settled on my handsome, usually laughing and happy lover.

All day, if he wasn't at the golf or tennis or bridge clubs, he was glued to The Box. "Milton Berle," "I Love Lucy," "Dragnet," "Ed Sullivan"—he watched them all, even the soap operas and the children's programs. TV bored me stiff. It had been useful to watch in London as an alternative to Max's unromantic interludes, but I would much rather go to a movie and be enveloped in wide-screen, color and CinemaScope than concentrate on a flickering black-and-white screen.

Life was an adventure, and although I was still shy and reticent with people I didn't know, I wanted to live it to the hilt.

Sydney was part of Gene Kelly's set. They were among the more stimulating and intellectual people in Hollywood. They included Harry Kurnitz, one of the writers on *Land of the Pharaohs,* one of the most amusing men who ever lived; Stanley Donen, who had directed many of MGM's more successful musicals; Adolph Green and Betty Comden, playwrights who had had many smash musical successes on Broadway and were now writing musicals at MGM; George Englund, a producer, and his actress wife, Cloris Leachman; Oscar Levant, a great wit and a great pianist; and Betsy Blair, Gene's wife, an actress and a very bright lady indeed. All of these people intimidated the hell out of me and although they couldn't have been more friendly, I felt like an outsider.

It was only three years since I had made my first film in England and now I was part of a Hollywood group, but I felt inferior to them in every way. They played volleyball, which, on the rare occasions when I attempted to play, ended up with me spraining a finger or breaking a nail. They played charades with skill and expertise. And they conversed with wit and wisdom. I loved hanging out at the Kellys' Cape Cod-style house on Rodeo Drive, and I observed and absorbed all I could. I wanted to expand my knowledge, which I felt was limited, having left the last of many schools at fifteen. I wanted to learn, to experience more of the world of art, literature and music, and to be able to converse easily and knowledgeably with this, to me, highly civilized group. I was conscious of my lack of higher education. I wanted to belong, but I felt like a child whose nose was pressed against the candy-store window—a babe in the Hollywoods.

One Saturday night at the Kellys' I noticed a rather nondescript blond girl sitting on the sofa near the bar. Nobody was paying any attention to her so I wandered over and started a conversation. It was unusual for me to find someone shyer than myself. She wore a white knitted silky dress, rather low-cut, and sleeveless, and no bra, which was frightfully daring in the mid-fifties. Her short blond hair was combed carelessly. She had little makeup on her averagely pretty face. It was hard to realize that this was Marilyn Monroe in the flesh! She appeared to be at the party without a date, but her mentor, Milton Greene, was lurking in the background.

She seemed glad that someone was talking to her and we discussed astrology and found out that we were both born under the sign of Gemini—"the terrible twins." She admired my hair, which I wore long and straight, with bangs, to the despair of the hairdressing department at Fox which was always trying to persuade me to cut it in a fashionable bubble cut. It was fascinating to talk to the world-famous Monroe—legendary sex symbol and idol of millions. She seemed a pretty but shy girl, with some complexes and a distrust of people. She left the party early, and I wondered if we would ever bump into each other on the Fox lot. But Marilyn was so insulated from the outside world at the studio that I never did see her again.

She had been supposed to star at Fox in a film about the Stanford White-Harry K. Thaw-Evelyn Nesbit triangle, one of the great scandals of the turn of the century, but she had refused to do it—probably wisely, since Evelyn was supposed to be seventeen or eighteen years old and Marilyn, although marvelous-looking, was around thirty. The studio was going ahead with the movie which was to be called *The Girl in the Red Velvet Swing* and there was much rivalry on the lot as to who would get the plum role of Evelyn Nesbit.

Terry Moore, Debra Paget and several others were tested, and as soon as I completed *The Virgin Queen,* so was I. I didn't hold out much hope of getting the part because it was essential that the girl be American and I still had a strong British accent. I worked on an American accent studiously before the test and waited for the result, which was not long in coming. I read the announcement in the *Hollywood Reporter* one morning and almost choked to death on my bagel. "Collins to play Nesbit" blazed across page one. I was jubilant. To play the leading female role in what was to be one of Fox's most extravagant productions was some achievement for an English girl who had been under contract less than four months.

I was plunged into frantic preparations. Evelyn had started in the chorus at the Floradora Theater so there were two lavish production numbers to learn, and although I had taken dancing classes since childhood, competing with professionals and performing strenuous dances like the cakewalk and cancan were exhausting. We rehearsed the dances in the morning, and after a quick lunch break, I would have to be at wardrobe to fit some of the twenty-seven costumes I was to wear. Then work for two hours on my accent, with Jeff Hunter, a contract actor who had been assigned for some curious reason to be my vocal coach. It was hard to get rid of my clipped British delivery, and I realized that if the accent was going to be authentic at all I would have to adopt it for everyday life too. I started talking with a sort of mid-Atlantic drawl, which reverted to clipped English whenever I returned to England. The word I was never able to master, however, was "girl." The "rl" sound was impossible for me to say with the right drawl. So Jeff and I went through the script substituting whenever possible synonyms for any word ending in "rl"—not an easy task.

Richard Fleischer, a director who had been recently successful at Fox, was directing, and Ray Milland and Farley Granger were to play Stanford White, the architect, and Harry K. Thaw, the dissolute playboy, respectively. If I thought I had been busy before, it was nothing to what happened now. The publicity department had instructions to fill the newspapers and magazines with stories and photos of me. After all, I was still relatively unknown, and Fox wanted to be sure my name was familiar to the American public before *Swing* was released. Now I didn't even have lunch hours to myself. Fox insisted that articles and photos of me were to appear in all the major fan magazines. America was saturated with me.

In print I came out sounding like a cross between Dame Edith Evans and Rita Hayworth. "She thinks America is cool, crazy and jolly good," enthusiastically bannered *Photoplay* and *Modern Screen*; "The Lady Is Dangerous," shrieked *Motion Picture*. Various epithets were attached to me: "Bundle from Britain," "Electric and Elusive," "Cool, Cool Collins," "A Bohemian at Heart," "Global Glamour Girl," and my particular favorite, from the Italian magazine *Oggi*: "The Pouting Panther!"

I was maligned, scorned, criticized, lied about, and my fairly normal mode of living was considered scandalous and disgraceful. All of a sudden I found myself with a reputation as a raving sexpot, swinger and home wrecker, whom Beverly Hills wives were supposed to live in fear of in case I cast my green "orbs" in the direction of their men. Ninety nine percent of this was total fabrication. I was outspoken, yes. Never a diplomat, I have always found it easier to tell the truth than beat around the bush; but the outrageous stories that proliferated about me surprised even the publicity department. I got an instant reputation as a free-living, free-loving rebel, and it was hard for me to handle.

The electric, elusive bundle from Britain, Hollywood's gain and England's loss, bounced into the tiny apartment after work one evening and excitedly started getting dressed for the first press screening of *The Virgin Queen*.

"The bathroom's all yours now," I yelled to Syd, who was lying on the orange living-room couch engrossed in "The Mouseketeers."

"Aw honey, I'm really beat. I don't think I can make it," he called, not raising his eyes from Annette Funicello's ears.

"Beat? Beat from what?" I angrily surveyed myself in the bedroom mirror as I towel-dryed my hair.

He was always beat lately. He played golf from noon till five, hung out and drank with the guys and played poker all night— for stakes he could ill afford. The life and soul of every party we attended, at home he went into a morose depression. Whatever had happened to the jokes and the laughter when we were alone together? "Oh, Sydney must be so much *fun* to be with all the time," trilled a blond starlet as we combed our locks together in the powder room of a Bel Air house, while he was at the bar wowing them with his gags. Sure, I thought bitterly. Only if he has an audience of more than one.

Recently we had adopted a new friend, as bitingly humorous and witty as Sydney but in a slightly more reserved way. Having him around guaranteed that there was never a dull moment, and for the past few weeks the three of us had been inseparable. His name was Arthur Loew, Jr., and he was the scion of one of the royal families of the motion-picture industry. His grandfather, Marcus Loew, had founded Metro-Goldwyn-Mayer studios, and his maternal grandfather, Adolph Zukor, was one of the oldest, most respected and most successful industry figures. Arthur dabbled in writing and producing features at MGM, but his heart was not truly in it, and he was considered to be a rich playboy, squiring beautiful starlets to premieres and parties and living the good life.

I liked him a lot, and so did Sydney, so when Syd suggested that I go to the screening with Arthur, my anger was slightly mollified. Recently I had confided in Arthur some of Syd's and my problems, and he had been a sympathetic listener.

After the screening we went to dinner at a La Cienega steakhouse, and there on the red leather brass-buttoned banquette, drinking whiskey sours and chain-smoking Chesterfields, I started to feel an empathy with Arthur. He was extremely sensitive, an attribute he covered up with his flippant jokes and casual attitudes. He well understood Sydney's dilemma: an out-of-work actor being practically supported by a young, fast-rising actress, and the insurmountable problems we faced.

Sydney and I had never been strong on communicating with each other. Deep feelings were not discussed between us. We never even argued. Our relationship, which had been great fun at the beginning, had disintegrated badly because of a lack of communication. If I found eight pairs of slacks and ten sweaters and dozens of old socks on a chair for weeks, the pile growing and growing, I would not bother to make waves by mentioning it, even if it irritated me. A chasm had developed. I tried to make him hustle to get jobs, but he was self-admittedly bone-lazy and would not go out of his way to grasp opportunities. In a town where opportunities must be grabbed as soon as they appear, this left him sitting by the phone waiting for it to ring—a deadly situation for any actor.

Arthur and I talked on and on. I felt I hadn't really *talked* to anyone for months. I had listened and learned and gossiped and small-talked, but it was unusual to be having a serious conversation about feelings and emotions. Arthur was in analysis and had been for a few years. Although not yet thirty, and wealthy, he had suffered continually during his life. His parents had been divorced several times each, and although close to his mother, Mickey Loew, his great affinity was with his uncle Gerald, who lived in Arizona. "One day I'll give up all this producing bullshit and have a farm in Arizona and raise cattle," he announced prophetically. How boring, I thought to myself. "What fun," I said.

The ending for Syd and me was almost as scruffy as the last part of our relationship had been.

Deep into principal photography on *The Girl in the Red Velvet Swing* I was unable to go with him one Friday to the Racquet Club in Palm Springs where we were spending the weekend. Being of a kind nature, I lent him my car, with the proviso that he meet me at the airport in Palm Springs on Saturday afternoon after I had finished that morning's shooting.

Arriving at Palm Springs airport in sweltering weather, I found no sign of Syd, no messages, no car and no taxis available either. Fuming, I called the Racquet Club. No answer from his room. Eventually a cab appeared, and sweating and hot we drove to the club. The desk clerk informed me that Mr. Chaplin was in the bar. Oh, really, I thought. How typical.

In the bar a pretty sight greeted my eyes. Syd, Gene Kelly, Greg Bautzer, Jack Cushingham and a few other cronies had decided to imbibe after-lunch liquors. They thought it would be fun to sample the bartender's selection alphabetically. Accordingly they had gone from Amaretto to brandy to creme de menthe to Drambuie, and were obviously now on to V for vodka, when I appeared, flushed and furious, in blue jeans.

"Sydney Chaplin," I hissed, "I let you borrow my car, I paid to fly on a bumpy two-engine plane to this godforsaken hole for aging tennis bums to meet you for a relaxing weekend, and you don't even *meet the plane!*" My voice started rising to a crescendo, much to the embarrassment of Greg and Co. Syd, smashed as he was, managed to look sheepish, but, unable to answer me, he picked up his Smirnoff and downed it in a gulp.

"Fuck you, Sydney," I screamed. "Fuck you. Fuck you. Fuck you. Fuck you!"

The select members of the Racquet Club looked aghast at such foul language coming from the lips of such a dainty English girl. Sydney turned slowly on his barstool to face me and staggered to his feet.

"And fuck you too," he blurted out before keeling over, and was only saved from hitting the linoleum by his friend John.

"Well, that," I enunciated clearly in my best Royal Academy of Dramatic Art diction, "will be the last time you will *ever* fuck me again, Sydney." And it was.

Arthur Loew and I fell in love—or did we fall in "like"? It seems to me that in the halcyon days of youth, saying "I love you" was akin to saying "Pass the salt." The feelings I had had for Syd for nearly a year were transferred to Arthur.

I am a strong advocate of monogamy—sequentially, that is. I think it is very hard to stay madly in love for any length of time, be it three months, three years or fifteen years. Eventually a time will come when the thrill is gone, and if there is not something infinitely stronger than romantic sexual attraction, the relationship will flounder. Only a true basis of compatibility can surmount the vagaries of a fickle heart.

With Arthur's encouragement I threw myself into thrice-weekly analysis to try and find out what and who I was. At the same time I was trying to fulfill myself as an actress and was caught up in the merry-go-round of being made into a "star." I started to hate the word "star." It denoted being untouchable. Stars are perfect.

They are revered and worshipped. They must always look and act and dress as if they are not mortal. Watching the careers of Elizabeth Taylor and Brigitte Bardot, I have felt pity and sympathy for women who cannot even go to the corner drugstore without causing a riot, whose every move is tabloid fodder. Who can live a normal life with the harness of stardom around her neck? To have the constant pressure of having to live up to the box-office returns of your last picture? To have every line and wrinkle in your face eagerly awaited by avid gossip columnists? To be surrounded by yes-men and pressures that a "civilian" would find hard to understand is unhealthy and poisonous to the mind and spirit.

It takes a very strong character indeed to become a star, remain a star, and still be a real person. Paul Newman is one of the few people I know who is unaffected by his nearly thirty years of stardom. But there are dozens, believing in their invulnerability and their publicity, who have fallen from the grace of the public to become bitter, sad and pathetic people seeking solace in drink, drugs or frantic sexual activity.

I realized in analysis that that was not my goal. Above the title—below the title—it wasn't important. I wanted to work, I wanted to *live*, and I wanted to enjoy my life and my work without obligations to a public whose fickleness stars lived in fear of.

I took a small apartment on Olive Drive off the Sunset Strip, conveniently located. It was close to Ciro's and the Mocambo nightclubs, our stomping grounds, and a stone's throw from Arthur Loew's house on Miller Drive. I worked practically every day and every Saturday morning on *Swing*, so there was no time to play. I was determined to give a good performance as Evelyn Nesbit, but I found that a great deal more emphasis than I wanted was being attached to my physical appearance. Granted, Evelyn was the original "Gibson Girl" and one of the great beauties from an age in which great beauties abounded, but I felt that the constant scrutiny of a corps of makeup men, hairdressers, costume designers, lighting directors, cameramen and even the director, Richard Fleischer, was beginning to inhibit me.

I was supposed to look exquisite in every frame of the film, which entailed being combed, sprayed, kiss-curled, powdered and lip-glossed before and after every single take. If I moved too violently and a stray lock fell out of place I would hear "Cut" and the wrecking crew would leap to my person. If my smile became too broad, there would be the dreaded word again: "Cut. Joanie, baby, don't smile so wide, you're showing your gums," or "The light's reflecting off her teeth." "Joanie, a little less *grin*, sweetheart—you look like you're catching flies with that smirk." If I did not hit my mark *exactly*, the key light would be a millimeter off, meaning my face would not be perfectly lit. "Cut. Let's go again." I was frightened to breathe too hard in case they complained about my chest moving too much.

Added to this were the costumes, which, although breathtakingly gorgeous to look at, were agony to wear. I wore an authentic corset that laced my waist into the fashionable hourglass figure of the 1900s. On top of this went several lace petticoats with millions of ruffles, a camisole and then one of the twenty-seven gowns, all of which had more tiny bones in them than a sardine. The collars had little bones or stays in them so that if I moved my head at too much of an angle I would get stabbed in the throat. On my head sat an enormous black wig, beautiful but heavy, secured with ninety hairpins and stuck to my forehead and the side of my face with glue. Sometimes on top of this hair would rest a gigantic hat covered with peacock or ostrich feathers, or an abundance of flowers on trailing ribbons, and the hat was secured to the wig with several lethal hatpins. To dress and arrange the wig alone took an hour and a half each morning—and then another forty-five minutes for makeup and body makeup, which was applied to every inch of skin the camera might possibly glimpse. Add to this the extremely hot lights, and the presence of the *real* Evelyn Nesbit Thaw on the set, watching me like a hawk, and I was understandably a nervous wreck.

Mrs. Thaw was a lady in her seventies, and any vestige of the great beauty she had once possessed was long gone, except for her luxuriant gray hair. I scrutinized her features to find some residue of her looks but to no avail. She was fond of the gin bottle and ate violet-scented cashews to disguise the smell. They didn't. Closer than a foot from her face, and I became dizzy from the fumes.

She constantly told me how much I reminded her of herself when she was a young girl and the toast of New York. She showed me fabulous paintings and photographs of herself from that era. I found this extremely depressing. To have been one of the world's great beauties and to end one's days a penniless, garrulous old woman was a horrible twist of fate. To be born physically perfect is akin to being born rich and then to gradually become poorer with age. I felt thankful that I did not think myself particularly beautiful, and would, perhaps, with maturity, be able to develop the inner me rather than the exterior which was currently being so overemphasized.

On days when I was not on call I threw on old jeans and a shirt, left off the makeup completely, and, in fact, barely bothered to brush my hair, and I wandered around the supermarkets, the five-and-tens and the drugstores—places I loved. England had been so austere; America was like a great candy store. The studio was not thrilled to see their rising glamour girl looking like a fugitive from Bucks County, and the awesome Hedda Hopper severely censured me in print for "looking like she combs her hair with an egg-beater." Dick Fleischer, coming across me lolling with a group of girlfriends in the commissary one day in blue jeans and makeupless, threw up his hands in mock horror, exclaiming, "My God, I didn't recognize you. You look so ugly!" This caused me in my oversensitive state to cry. I seemed to be going from the sublime to the ridiculous. I achieved the dubious reputation of being a rebel, a swinger and a nonconformist in the days before it was fashionable to be so. I couldn't get it together to look chic and smart when I wasn't working—I just wanted to be me.

Anyone whose mode of dress was in any way unkempt was considered bohemian and a bit strange. Marlon Brando and James Dean were the foremost exponents of the new antiestablishment attitude. Both were greatly admired on the one hand, but on the other they contended with much disapproval.

Jimmy Dean was a fascinating young man who had become a giant star with his first movie, *East of Eden*. He played to perfection the brooding troubled boy in competition with his more favored brother, and questing for the truth about his relationship with his mother. The young people of the fifties immediately adopted him as their symbol, and his star ascended rapidly. He made *Rebel Without a Cause*, which was written by Arthur's cousin, Stewart Stern, and immediately after that was completed, starred in the mammoth production of *Giant*.

It was during the filming of *Giant* that I first met him. It was a brief meeting at a small dinner party in the Valley. I was particularly mesmerized by his eyes, which were a deep, piercing blue and could change instantly from a look of sullen brooding to an expression of extreme mischievousness. He was quite short for a film actor and had longish, blond wavy hair. He seemed terribly shy and clutched the hand of his girlfriend, a gorgeous Swiss starlet under contract to Paramount called Ursula Andress. She had a fabulous body and the shortest haircut I had ever seen. They made a striking couple, both wearing white T-shirts and Levi's.

We often saw him at the home of Oscar Levant. On one occasion Oscar remarked after viewing me in a rather low-cut blouse (I was still wearing those bangs that almost covered my eyes), "I have now seen every part of Joan's anatomy except her forehead!"

James Dean and Oscar Levant, although total opposites, got along famously. Each relished the other's unusualness. Arthur and I would drop by the Levants' after dinner and sit until the early hours talking and laughing with them.

A group of us had dinner one night at Don the Beachcomber's, a Polynesian restaurant in Hollywood noted for its incredibly strong rum-based drinks. After three or four Navy Grogs I was feeling daring, so when Jimmy asked who would like a drive in his brand-new silver Porsche I cheerfully volunteered. Arthur, who usually indulged most of my whims with good grace, pulled me aside and told me not to drive with Jimmy. "He drives like a maniac," he said earnestly. "And after four of those Zombies, or whatever the hell it was we've been drinking, it's too dangerous."

"Oh don't be such a stick-in-the-mud," I giggled. "Come on, Jimmy. Let's race them to Oscar's house." We jumped into his shiny new Porsche. The interior was cramped and it smelled of new leather, but it was indeed a beauty. Jimmy threw the shift into first gear and with the gearbox protesting violently we screeched into the Hollywood Boulevard traffic. During the ten minutes it took us to get to Beverly Hills, I sobered up rapidly. He certainly did drive fast, even recklessly, but with the summer wind blowing through the open windows and the radio blaring, it was exhilarating.

"Don't you think we should slow down?" I said nervously, as we sped down the Strip at about seventy miles an hour, dodging in and out of the after-dinner traffic. He gave me one of his mischievous, brooding looks. "Chicken?" he asked. "What, me? Oh, no. I'd just like to live to be twenty-one." I gulped nervously, hoping a cop car would miraculously appear. "The thing about these cars is that they're fail safe," he said, expertly overtaking a bleached blonde in a Cadillac and sliding in just a car's length behind a slow-moving Ford. "These cars are made like tanks. They have the best engine and the best transmission, they're totally safe."

He talked on about the merits of his baby until we screeched to a stop in front of the Levants'. "Well, thanks a lot, Jimmy," I said descending on trembling legs. "If I ever need a quick ride to the airport, I'll call on you."

"Do that." He lit up a cigarette and smiled at me sleepily, amused by my timorousness. "Let's go see Oscar." I followed him into the house, making a mental note never to get in a moving vehicle with him again. When Arthur arrived fifteen minutes later, I told him he was right about Jimmy's driving. "He's going to kill himself one of these days if he continues to drive like that!" he said.

A couple of months later I was in New York at the Plaza Hotel for promotions on *Virgin Queen*. The doorbell rang insistently and woke me up. It was only eight o'clock, and I grumpily trundled to the door. "It's me, Arthur," said a strained voice. I opened up. Ashen-faced, he handed me *The New York Times* and then sat down heavily on the sofa. I read unbelievingly: "James Dean dies in automobile accident." He was killed in the silver Porsche. He was twenty-four.

One Friday night Arthur and I walked into Chasen's, one of my favorite restaurants. No work tomorrow, so I could go on a two-day eating binge. I was looking forward to having the hashed-in-cream potatoes Chasen's is renowned for. Maybe even a soufflé for dessert. A headline caught my eye on the front page of the

Los Angeles Times, stacked neatly on the steps outside the restaurant: "Actor sues actress for $1,250 support per month," screamed the banner.

"Oh, darling, buy the paper. I wonder who it is?" I chirped.

We sat in our booth and I scanned the paper. My face stared out at me smiling broadly from column two.

"Oh, my God!" I howled, to the surprise of the headwaiter, who was smiling and taking our order for drinks. He raised his eyebrows fractionally, ignoring the outburst.

"Christ, that rotten bastard has gone and sued me. What am I going to *do?*"

Arthur grabbed the paper and read the article out loud. "Actor Maxwell Reed announced from London today that he was suing his wife, actress Joan Collins, for $1,250 per month. 'I know this is unusual,' said Reed, 'but I have not worked in over a year and am practically destitute. My wife has been in Hollywood for the past nine months. She is making a lot of money and I think she owes me something.' "

We looked at each other. He smiled and patted my hand.

"Poor baby," he said playfully. "Didn't your mummy tell you that all men are rotten?" When things got rough, Arthur joked, but I was not in the mood for jokes. Being sued for alimony is a fairly common occurrence for men—but I had never heard of a woman being sued before.

My parents had been sending me various stories that had been appearing in the English press about Max. They were all based on the same sniveling premise: "I found her. I made her a success. I loved her. She left me—to go to Hollywood. Now I can't get a job."

One particularly revolting story featured a picture of Max trying to look humble in a forty-five-dollar cashmere sweater and heavily mascaraed eyebrows, clutching a large photo of me to his breast and complaining about his love for me and his poverty—and he wondered why no one would employ him! It was nauseating, but I was so busy, I had no time to think of divorce plans. Again, like Scarlett O'Hara, I decided to "think about that tomorrow."

Nothing, however, could put me off food, and we ate heartily while discussing strategy. At the end of the evening my face felt very hot, and hivelike bumps had broken out over my back and shoulders. Peculiar, I thought, probably nerves—and dismissed it from my mind.

I started shooting what I consider to be my first "grown-up" role. In other films I had played girls—wayward, spoiled, delinquent or sexy. Nevertheless they were juvenile-type parts. But the part of Crystal in *The Opposite Sex*, a remake of *The Women*, was definitely not a girl. She was all woman—and all bitch. Sexy, conniving and shrewd, she was the embryo Alexis.

The Women had been a big success in the 1930s, with Joan Crawford as Crystal. The cast had included Norma Shearer, Paulette Goddard, Joan Fontaine and Rosalind Russell.

MGM, who had borrowed me from Fox for this part, was gathering an equally prestigious cast for the latest version: June Allyson, the darling of the Metro lot; Ann Sheridan, the ex-"Oomph Girl"; Ann Miller; Dolores Gray; Carolyn Jones; and many others were cast in this updated version of ladies in the jungle warfare of sex, men, husband-snatching, gossip, backbiting and bitchery. Crystal is the biggest bitch of them all—and loves it. She is a showgirl who has an affair with June Allyson's husband and flaunts it to the world.

Although the part was not that large, it was flashy and juicy, and I had some good scenes. June confronts me in my dressing room and accuses me of the affair. I nonchalantly continue with removing my brief stage costume and changing into street clothes while she addresses me and progressively becomes more angry. June was a tiny lady, about five feet two in heels. She was famous for her cute blond bob and her Peter Pan collars. She was petite, delicate and ladylike, so I was not concerned about the fact that she had to slap my face after the following dialogue:

JUNE: "By the way, if you're dressing for Steven, I wouldn't wear that. He doesn't like anything quite so obvious."

CRYSTAL: "When Steven doesn't like what I wear I take it off!" . . . And June hauled off and belted me. This little lady with her tiny hands had a punch like Muhammad Ali! I felt as if a steamroller had hit me. Something fell from my face and hit the floor with a loud clatter—my teeth? Oh, God, no. Please don't let her have knocked out my *teeth!* My head was ringing, as the slap had connected with my ears, and I couldn't hear a thing. Stars danced before my eyes and I staggered to a chair and collapsed.

"Cut—cut, for Christ's sake, cut!" screamed director David Miller.

"What the *hell's* going on here?" June burst into tears and collapsed into another chair. Makeup men and dressers rushed to the set with smelling salts and succor.

I put my hands tentatively to my mouth. Thank God, a full set of teeth still, but what flew off me? The wardrobe lady solved the mystery, retrieving the long rhinestone earrings which the force of June's slap had sent spinning. But any more shooting was out of the question. On each of my cheeks was forming the perfect imprint of a tiny hand! Branded, if not for life, for the two or three days it took for the welts to go down. June was desperately sorry, and it took longer to calm her down than it did me. Luckily, when they saw the scene on rushes it was unnecessary to reshoot the slap—it had complete authenticity!

The first day of shooting of *The Opposite Sex* at MGM I sat in the large airy makeup-and-hairdressing room and observed wide-eyed the gossipy bustling scene. Sydney Guilaroff, Metro's reigning hairdresser, was in the process of cutting a shoulder-length wig for me. This necessitated a "test" after each trim to get the right chic-yet-sexy look for Crystal. From a long wig, throughout seven or eight haircuts, Sydney finally ended up with giving me a sleek bob.

Sitting in the makeup chair next to me was June Allyson, having a minimal amount of makeup applied to her retroussé nose and pert features. Next to June sat Elizabeth Taylor. Gorgeous and exotic. She was excitedly showing everyone photos of her children.

The biggest star of the Metro lot sat quietly on the side waiting her turn for the makeup man's magic. Grace Kelly. Exquisite. Breeding and class emanating from her aristocratic face and bearing. She was then twenty-six years old—the Princess of Hollywood. Having made several extremely successful films, she was—oh, foolish girl, thought I—giving it all up for the love of handsome Prince Rainier, monarch of Monaco.

This fairytale wedding, which had captured the imagination of the world, was now imminent. Grace sat quietly in plain gray slacks and nondescript blouse going over lists with her secretary, oblivious to the makeup and hair people who bustled around her. She was truly serene even then, and one of the most ravishing women I had ever seen.

I had a number of physical problems on *The Opposite Sex*. A long bathtub scene entailed Crystal's sitting in an ornate marble bathtub, covered with bubbles, talking on the telephone to her boyfriend, and having a conversation with Dolores Gray and a little girl. David Miller believed in endless rehearsals, and we rehearsed for two days, with me immersed in real bubbles. Since bubbles do not last very long, the prop men had to keep adding to the water a mixture of dishwashing detergent and Lux soap flakes.

At the end of the first day my nether regions were pink and puffy. At the end of the second day they were sore and swollen. On the third day, when we finally started to shoot, I was a mass of tender raw flesh. It was agony to sit down, and when the detergent-filled water touched my body, I felt like Joan of Arc burning at the stake. The misery on my face was evident. Something had to be done. The studio doctor was called to give me pain-killing injections, and the prop department evolved an ingenious contraption to prevent my delicate blistered body from touching the water. To the onlooker viewing the scene, here was a glamorous creature chatting cattily on the phone, luscious bubbles caressing her body. Underneath the bubbles, however, was a sheet of strong plywood with a hole cut in to fit my body, and the bubbles were on top of the plywood. Underneath the plywood I was encased in Vaseline and bandages, and on top of this an attractive pair of men's long johns from the gentlemen's wardrobe department. Over this was a large rubber sheet in case any sneaky bubbles managed to slither through the armor. I sat on several cushions, and all in all was feeling no pain and relishing the comparative comfort of these appliances.

Then a young man burst onto the set in the middle of a scene. "Joan Collins?" he asked accusingly.

"Er, yes—er, maybe," I said nervously, signaling to the assistant director to remove this madman before he did me some injury.

"Cut—cut," yelled David. "What the hell's going on around here? Who is this jerk?"

"Sign here, please," said the jerk, handing me a summons from my ever-dependable husband, Maxwell Reed. I read it unbelievingly while three assistant directors gave the smirking, successful process server the bum's rush.

Maxwell Reed was taking me to court and insisting that I pay him the $1,250 a month he had demanded for support. It was an injunction from a Los Angeles Court judge. I had to do something. And fast.

Fred Leopold was an attorney who specialized in divorce cases. (He later became Mayor of Beverly Hills.) He advised me to pay up. I had a seven-year contract starting at $1,250 a week for the first year and escalating to $5,000 for the seventh year. He told me that if I did not make a deal with Max now, he could wait two or three years and get even more money from me in the future.

I was furious. His allegation that he had "discovered" me and sent me to Hollywood was totally false. I thought I had escaped his vindictiveness but I still sometimes awoke in the middle of the night with the terrifying nightmare again: "One day you'll think you're safe, baby. But one night you'll walk around a dark corner and one of the 'boys' will come and carve that pretty little face of yours up until no one will ever want to look at you again."

I woke in a cold sweat. It was chilling and not beyond the realm of possibility that he would do this ghastly thing to me. God knows he knew enough petty criminal types around London. And now he had come here, to Los Angeles. To try to find work— and to get money from me.

For safety I moved into Arthur's house on Miller Drive. Fred Leopold advised me strongly against it, but I was scared, and I needed someone to be there when I woke up with nightmares.

The divorce cost me over $10,000—an utter fortune for me. I had to get an advance in salary from Fox, for I did not have that kind of money even though I did not live lavishly. Leopold had

persuaded Max to accept a lump sum of $4,250, after convincing
him and his lawyers that I was not as wealthy as they expected. I
also gave him all the money in our joint bank account in London—
about $1,400—and I had over $4,000 in legal fees to pay—his and
mine. The judge in Los Angeles Superior Court seemed surprised
at this settlement and cross-examined me on the stand for ten
minutes as to why I was paying this supposedly healthy, reasonably
young man such a grand sum. I prayed that the divorce would be
granted and that I would be finished with Maxwell Reed forever.
The judge, reluctantly, it seemed, granted it. I walked out of the
courtroom a free woman—older, wiser, poorer, and with a growing distrust of and hostility toward men.

My mother's words were always in the back of my mind. "Men
only want one thing. Men will use a girl, then toss her away when
they are tired of her."

Although part of me realized that this was ridiculous, another
part of me said, "She's right. Mummy is *right*. Look at how my
father treated her. Look at how Max abused you. Sydney didn't
really care for you—what about *him?*"

I looked at Arthur, sprawled out on the comfortable sofa of his
ranch-style house high in the Hollywood Hills. He was just like
the others. He had me. I lived with him. I bought all my own
clothes (although he had given me a few pieces of jewelry). I
paid for my airfare when I went to London. I was young, beautiful, desirable, successful. Why should he have all of this for nothing? He was young, rich and good-looking, tall, blond, thin, with
an aquiline nose—and a terrific sense of humor. I liked him. We
had fun together. I wasn't "in love," because ours was not a passionate relationship, but I felt great affection for him.

He had recently finished producing a film starring Paul Newman called *The Rack*. Newman was talking to Arthur now. The
two of them lolled on the sofa drinking beer and telling jokes like
schoolboys. The house was full of friends, as it was most nights.
Arthur ran an open house and there were always eight or ten
people for dinner. I was leaving for London in a week to start another film. The gossip columnists had even started hinting that we
were on the verge of matrimony.

After all the guests departed, I broached the subject.

"Do you think we ought to date other people while I'm gone?" I said, casually pouring two cognacs into large snifters and handing him one. He looked at me quizzically. "Whom do you have in mind, Richard Burton?" Burton was to be my co-star in *Seawife*.

"Burton's married," I said briskly. "No, I mean three months is a long time to be apart."

"But I'm going to visit you in Jamaica," he interrupted.

"I know that," I said. "How do you feel about me going out with other men, then?"

"I'd rather you didn't," he said flatly, drinking the cognac and preparing to end the conversation.

"Well, then what are you going to do about it, Arthur? If you don't want me to date other guys?"

"I just don't know if I can be faithful to you for that length of time." The words tumbled unselfconsciously from his lips.

I looked at him with growing consternation. "You mean you want to fuck around?"

"Spoken like the Queen of England," he said dryly. "No, my dear, I don't *want* to fuck around, as you so beautifully put it, but if, in the twelve weeks of our separation, a lady should appear who should—how shall I say—arouse my libido, I might, just might, find the temptation alluring enough to—well, yes, fuck around." He drained his glass and looked at me, his boyish face challenging. "It doesn't mean I don't love you, baby."

"Yeah, what's a fuck between friends," I said sarcastically, pulling my fingers away from his. "Don't you have any *control?*"

"I'll tell you what." He pulled my rigid body toward him and put his arms around my shoulders. "Let's play it by ear. If we can be faithful to each other during the time you're away, then I think we should get engaged when you come back." I moved my face quickly so that his lips connected with my ear.

"OK." I jumped up and ground my cigarette out violently. "That's a terrific idea, Arthur. You try to be faithful to me, and I—" I looked him straight in the eye—"I will *try* to be faithful to you. And now I'm going to bed."

I walked upstairs, seething with rage. How dare he put me on trial. *Men.* Who did he think he *was?* Another phrase of my father's flitted through my thoughts: "Why buy the cake when you can have a slice for free?"

I felt angry. I hurt and I wanted him to hurt too.

Fox was about to film *Seawife*, from a best-selling novel, *Sea Wyf and Biscuit*, about a nun wrecked on a desert island with three men. I had already made *Our Girl Friday*, which also had a girl stuck on an island with three men, but for me to play a nun was not only the biggest acting challenge I had yet faced but also to many people one of the worst pieces of miscasting since Lana Turner played a vestal virgin.

Roberto Rossellini, the volatile and talented Italian film director, famous not only for having directed the touching *Open City*, but also for his volcanic affair and subsequent marriage to Ingrid Bergman, had chosen me as his "face of innocence," after seeing one reel of *The Girl in the Red Velvet Swing*. He obviously realized that, behind the wigs, costumes and plastic facade I presented in that film, there was a naive and vulnerable young girl. Rossellini was a stubborn, opinionated genius who had total autonomy over all his productions. This was to be his first American film and he was determined to do it his way.

Fox was agreeable to practically all his demands except for one thing. They absolutely would not allow Richard Burton, who played "Biscuit," to kiss "Seawife," the nun. Rossellini thought this was an essential part of the story and was insistent on the love scene.

Although Fox, around the same time, was making another nun film with sexual overtones, *Heaven Knows Mr. Allison*, starring Deborah Kerr and Robert Mitchum, nonetheless they were strongly opposed to there being any hint of sex between Burton and me on the screen. For one thing, they would never get a seal of approval from the censor, and for another, every Catholic women's group in America would be up in arms, probably boycotting *all* their movies. So they were understandably worried about Signor Rossellini's preoccupation with the kissing scene.

That was the least of my worries as I arrived in London to face a barrage of press people splitting their sides with laughter at the thought of "Britain's Bad Girl" playing a nun.

"Sister Sizzle," giggled Donald Zee in the *Daily Mirror*.

"Is *this* the face of innocence?" jeered the *Daily Express*, under a two-column picture of me with a ruby in my navel and a come-hither look in my eye. All the old labels were pulled out: "Torrid Baggage"; "Coffee Bar Jezebel"; and the press had a field day with this excruciatingly funny piece of show-biz news. The more I tried to be serious and mature in the countless interviews I gave, the more the press sent me up. It was infuriating because I really did believe that I was good casting for *Seawife*. Without makeup and with my hair cropped short and unstyled, I did have a trusting, innocent look, and I resented the attitude that the newspapers were taking toward me.

Before I left California, Arthur had christened the movie "I Fucked a Nun!"

I spent the two weeks of preproduction in London reading every book on Catholicism I could. I visited a group of nuns in a small convent in Chelsea. I spent many hours talking with them, observing their attitudes, manners and bearing. They were a delightful group of women and girls, with a wonderful inner glow and beauty that emanated from them. Some even had a wicked and wild sense of humor, and many of my preconceived notions of nuns as "holier-than-thou goody-goodies" were shattered. They were real, warm, vibrant human beings who were happier and more at peace with themselves than many of the people I knew. I went to Catholic church and immersed myself in the peace and energy that seemed to glow there.

We made the usual makeup and costume tests. With my scrubbed face, short no-style hair and nun's habit, it looked very much as if Rossellini's intuition had been right and I did have the "face of innocence."

Meanwhile, there were two scripts to study: one, the Fox-approved script, without any intimations of sex and love between Biscuit and Seawife, and the other, Rossellini's infinitely more interesting story of a young novice nun, who had not yet taken her final vows, finding her emotions deeply disturbed by an extended period of time on a deserted island with an attractive and compassionate man. And in the latter script the two do indeed

Miss Hettie Collins — Comedienne & Dancer

Grandmama Henrietta Collins on tour in South Africa. Although already pregnant with my father, this early emancipated woman continued dancing until shortly before his birth in Port Elizabeth.

My father, Joe, and mother, Elsa, and "Godfather" Lord Lew Grade. The reason for my mother's anxious look—I was born seven hours later.

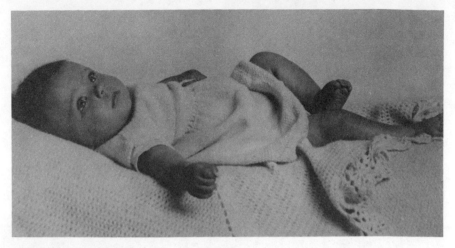

Oh, what a beautiful baby!

My favorite picture of Mummy and me.

My favorite picture of Daddy and me—somewhat Freudian, it appears.

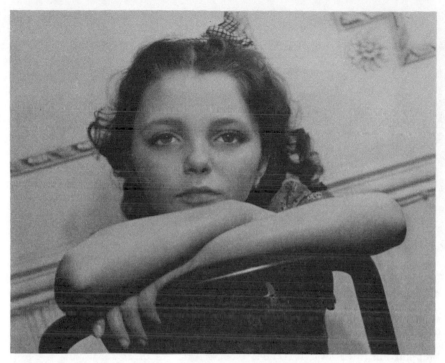

Age 11—I was already dreaming of becoming an actress.

Mummy and her brood: Jackie, Bill and me.

At 15 I was going through an ugly-
duckling stage.

Signed for Rank—my first fan photo.

Stepping out to starlethood in *Lady Godiva Rides Again*. It was my first
movie "bit" part. I had one line.

First husband, Maxwell Reed, had me eating out of his hand. But not for long!

My first starring movie part in *I Believe in You* with Laurence Harvey. I was terribly impressed by him.

Treading the boards on tour in
The Praying Mantis, one of my
first "man-eating" roles.

Called "Britain's answer to Ava
Gardner," I honestly didn't think
she had much to worry about.

GEORGE MINTER presents

The Adventures of Sadie

A DESERT ISLAND COMEDY IN COLOR

JOAN COLLINS · GEORGE COLE · KENNETH MORE · ROBERTSON HARE

GUEST STAR HERMIONE GINGOLD

ADAPTED FOR THE SCREEN AND DIRECTED BY NOEL LANGLEY

My first top billing.

Oh, the embarrassment of this outfit! I was sometimes dressed as the Easter Bunny or the Thanksgiving Turkey.

The "face" of the 50s. Three-inch eyebrows were all the rage.

Darryl F. Zanuck liked what he saw and I was whisked off to Hollywood instantly! Darryl's weakness was women, but luckily I escaped his clutches.

Howard Hawks' *Land of the Pharaohs.* The anguished look comes from holding in my stomach. The ruby was there to satisfy the censor's stringent code.

In Rome and in love with Sydney Chaplin, son of Charlie.

have a "romantic involvement" which would necessitate some torrid love scenes.

Rossellini had left for location scouting in Jamaica after our initial brief meeting and film test in London. There he remained with script number two, which he was now adamant was the only one he would shoot.

When the cast and crew arrived in Jamaica, we found that Signor Rossellini was incommunicado in his suite at the Jamaica Inn. We unpacked and waited for the first day's shooting to commence. We had been hearing rumbles of major rows going on between the Fox brass back in L.A. and Rossellini. The assistant directors kept on saying we would be shooting tomorrow or the day after, but days went by with nothing happening. Everyone sat around swimming, drinking rum punches, playing poker and gossiping about each new event. We were having a relaxing holiday in the sun, all expenses paid by Fox.

Four days later a call sheet was pushed under the door of my suite: "Title of Production 'Seawife'—1st Day's Shooting—Exterior Shipwreck—Director, Bob McNaught."

"Bob McNaught! Who the hell is he?"

I rushed next door to the Burtons' suite to find out what was going on. Richard was sitting with his pretty Welsh wife, Sybil, drinking tea and playing Scrabble. He seemed not at all perturbed by my agitation and confirmed what I and the rest of the crew had feared. Fox would not back down on their watered-down script and Rossellini would not back down on his torrid version. It was a total impasse. Rossellini was fired, and instead of spending the time and money to import another director from London or America, Fox was putting the director's reins in the hands of Bob McNaught, who was listed on the unit list as "Production Manager."

A production manager was going to direct *Seawife*! I was horrified. I had been looking forward to being directed in this role by the fabulous, talented Rossellini, whose ability to get magnificent performances from his cast and to bring magic to the screen was legendary. What a bummer! What chance did I stand now of giving a good performance. Although I was fairly confident of my ability to play the role, I knew that I needed the extra impetus that only a really good director can give to an actor to make my performance come believably alive—particularly because I knew so many people were waiting for me to fall flat on my face. And what of Bob McNaught? The poor man would have so many problems with just the mechanics and technicalities of everyday filming, I felt sure there would be little time to give me the support and help I needed.

Bob turned out to be a nice, stolid, middle-aged Englishman, eminently more suited to dealing with the million and one major and minor details of managing a production than directing one.

The picture thus became just another run-of-the-mill program filler. Burton didn't give a damn. This was the last of his multiple picture deals with Fox, and he didn't particularly like the script or his role. He had a "take the money and run" attitude toward it, which I found depressing. Already a millionaire, he had cleverly set up all sorts of tax havens and was one of the very first actors to take up residence in Switzerland. Although a successful film actor, his true love was still the theater, and he was longing to get back to New York, where he was about to do a play.

Burton was then about thirty-three years old, with thick, light-brown hair, intense, strong features and eyes of a piercingly hypnotic greenish-blue. His voice was magnificent—deep, resonant—a voice made to declaim *Hamlet* and indeed all of Shakespeare's plays. His skin left a lot to be desired, however. Due to years of working in the coal mines of Wales, his back and shoulders were deeply pitted and rutted with pimples, blackheads and what looked like small craters.

I had admired him for years, and as a schoolgirl had stood outside the Queen's Theatre on Shaftesbury Avenue to get his autograph after seeing his performance in Jean Anouilh's *Ring Around the Moon*. I had watched him, mesmerized by his voice and talent, from high up in the "Gods," and thought him so handsome and talented that I wrote off for an autographed photo, which duly arrived personally signed: "Thank you for your letter. Best wishes, Richard Burton." This treasured memento went into my autograph book along with other trusty favorites. And now, here I was acting opposite this paragon of theatrical proficiency.

His reputation as a lady's man had also preceded him. Although married, rumors of his affairs were discussed knowingly and openly, and he lost no time in making known his intentions toward me. A few days after filming had commenced, we took a swim together during the lunch hour to a small diving raft a few hundred yards from shore. I wore a bikini and presented a wholesome and well-scrubbed look. I lay on my back on the raft, eyes closed, and feeling the hot Jamaican sun absorbing the salt water from my skin. I was feeling happy. I was enjoying the film, and Bob Mc-Naught was OK. Not an innovative director, but not too bad either. The crew was fun, mostly English, and I had been spending a lot of time with them playing poker and giggling at their typically English humor. Arthur had written me several letters, professing undying adoration and "fidelity," and missing me madly, and I was in the sun all the time. I was an avid sun worshipper and I was working on my tan when I felt fingers stroking my wet hair.

"Did anyone ever tell you you look pretty with short hair?" he said, casually moving his hand to my neck.

"Yes," I said, firmly removing the roving hand and squinting up at the greenish eyes, now a foot from mine. "Mr. Rossellini thought I looked adorable with short hair. And so does Arthur, my *boyfriend*." That should stop him.

"Ah, yes, of course, you go out with the heir to the Loew millions, don't you?" he said, amused and not at all deterred by my evasive tactics.

"Yes. He's very *jealous*. Gets homicidal if he thinks anyone is messing around with his property." I peeked through my wet lashes to see if he had taken the implication.

"My dear, what the eye does not see the heart does not grieve for," he breathed in his most Shakespearean tones and pressed his salty lips to my firmly closed ones. I gritted my teeth and let him kiss me. There is nothing more off-putting to a man than to kiss a girl who won't respond.

"Why don't you relax?" he whispered, his hand fiddling with the ties on my bikini top. "None of the crew can see us."

"I am relaxed," I said gaily. "Relaxed and lying in the sun and thinking about *Arthur!*"

97

He laughed and lay back on the raft. He was quite attractive . . . if you ignored the spots. But Mrs. Burton was languishing in her suite at the hotel, and I was not interested in an involvement with a married Don Juan.

He looked at me and we both smiled.

"I'll get you yet, Miss Collins," he said lightly, then cleverly realizing that now was not the time, proceeded to tell me in detail about his seductions and conquests of all the actresses he had worked with on stage and screen.

"How fascinating," I breathed during this lengthy saga of lust and intrigue on sets and in dressing rooms and elegant boudoirs. "They *always* succumbed to you finally?"

"Always," he said triumphantly. "Even if—" looking meaningful—"they were not receptive at the outset."

"Well, it should be interesting to see what happens now," I said, noticing that the third assistant was signaling to us frantically from the beach. "You have eight more weeks on location with me, but I never have liked being part of a collection."

I dived into the warm Caribbean ocean and swam rapidly back to where the crew were assembling for the next setup. He followed, joking and talking, until we got to shore. It was amusing. The great Richard Burton, not only a womanizer but a scalp collector to boot! It would give me the greatest pleasure to *not* be another one on his belt.

He soon found other ladies to console himself with. Some were reasonably attractive and some were, to put it bluntly, dogs! I glimpsed an almost toothless and middle-aged Jamaican maid leaving his quarters early one morning with a satisfied gleam in her eye. When I questioned him about her later in the day he freely admitted he had dallied with her. We were lying side by side on our stomachs in the warm sand waiting for the crew to set up.

"Richard, I do believe you would screw a snake if you had the chance." I laughed unbelievingly.

"Only if it was wearing a skirt, darling," he countered smoothly. "It would have to be a female snake."

I still wrote to Arthur and he to me. According to his letters he was a paragon of fidelity and spent all his evenings either watching TV or going to dinner with his friends Stewart Stern, Paul Newman or George Englund. I didn't believe him; I felt it unlikely that he would write and tell me of his affairs if he was having them.

He arrived in a blaze of hilarity and jokes the last week of shooting in Jamaica. The first night we had dinner with a group from the film, and Arthur was so wildly funny and entertaining that he had everyone, including me, in stitches the whole time. During the week he visited we spent very little time alone and had no time to talk about anything.

"Where's Joan?" said Bob McNaught one day.

"She's laying Loew," said the unit wit, and everyone collapsed with laughter.

We were coming to the culmination of the film, which necessitated some difficult and emotional scenes for me. I was involved in my role and concentrating on it. The weather turned rainy and everyone was getting edgy. They wanted to finish the picture and get the hell off this island and back to England. Eight weeks is a long time to be away from home, and the first halcyon weeks of the location had worn off for the crew and the actors. They wanted their fish and chips for lunch and their *Daily Mirror*, their football on the "telly" and their warm beer in the pubs. Bored already with the rum punches and the rice and jumbo shrimp—Englishmen need England—anxious faces scanned the sky each morning for the dreaded drops of rain that might delay our departure for the homeland.

At last we finished, and I bade a tearful goodbye to Arthur. I was going to London for several more weeks of shooting and post-production, and he to Los Angeles. I was genuinely miserable on the plane to London. I cared about him, even if it was not a passionate and exciting romance. We had not communicated any of our private thoughts and feelings during the week we had been together. No deep communication at all. It was just one big laugh all the time, and I felt sad for us.

It was summertime, but England was predictably cold, wet and rainy. I happily moved in again to the back bedroom at Harley House, luxuriating in my mother's attention. On the days when I wasn't shooting she brought me scrambled eggs and tea in bed in the morning and we would sit and gossip. We became closer than we had at any time that I could remember during my childhood. I felt like a child again in those familiar surroundings. Although Jackie had taken my room when I went to Hollywood, my mother had put back many of my possessions, since Jackie was now in Los Angeles, living in my apartment.

All my old scrapbooks of movie stars were still on the bookshelves. I spent hours looking at all the magazine pictures I had painstakingly pasted in so long ago. What was ironic was that so many of the stars I had admired I had now either worked with or had met socially. There was Maxwell Reed, lids lowered, cigarette in hand, glowering sexily. I shuddered and quickly turned the page. There was Richard Burton, young and innocent, in *The Last Days of Dolwyn*, his first film—not so young and innocent now, I thought. There was chirpy cockney schoolboy Anthony Newley (whom I would marry a few years later) in *Oliver Twist* and *Vice Versa* and *The Huggets*. And there were others I had finally met: Elizabeth Taylor, Gene Kelly, Humphrey Bogart, Montgomery Clift—all staring and smiling from my make-believe paper world. It seemed long ago and yet it was only a few short years.

Arthur had written me:

"I wish I were able to tell you and show you how much I really love you but somehow when we are together I have great trouble in letting my hair down and seem to be flip all the time rather than warm. It seems during my stay in Jamaica that my main task was to entertain the crew rather than be close to you. Anyway, from now on I am really going to try and *force* myself to show you how I feel toward you . . ."

I felt sorry that he was unable to show his love for me and sadness that *I* was stupid enough to choose to love a man who had to *force* himself to show his feelings. We were now shooting *Seawife* at Elstree in the huge water-filled tank that was on stage, filming the shipwreck scenes and the night scenes on the raft. It was miserably cold and uncomfortable, but every evening after work I would adjourn with the crew to the pub across the road, drink gin and tonic and eat sausage rolls. It was convivial, and I enjoyed everyone's company and humor a lot. I found myself wanting more and more to stay home at night with my parents.

Although Jackie was in Hollywood, my eleven-year-old brother, Bill, was home, and I suddenly found I really liked family life.

Because I was now a sophisticated divorcee, a well-known actress, and over twenty-one, my father was far more lenient with me, and I was free to come and go as I pleased. For the first time in my life, I had no one to answer to. No more "Where have you been?" "Who with?" "What time will you be home?"

I had my own space—I could think and breathe freely. My parents were so glad to have me back that I could have stayed out all night and they wouldn't have cared.

I borrowed a friend's flat in Eaton Terrace and stayed there sometimes alone, reading, studying my script and thinking about my life. I didn't fancy this life of a "star" much—and I didn't want to marry Arthur either. My one taste of marriage had been such a disaster. I decided to take each day as it came—let the chips fall where they may. The one thing I really loved more than anything else was working; *that* I needed, and after *Seawife* I wanted to do better scripts and get better roles. Men I could live without right now.

I had a few weeks off after *Seawife* and then had to leave again for the West Indies to shoot *Island in the Sun*. Arthur wasn't thrilled with the fact that I was going on location again after nearly three months of being apart. But I had no choice. I was under contract to Fox and they had the right to do with me as they wished for forty weeks of the year.

Island in the Sun was based on a best-selling book by Alec Waugh, with a highly topical theme. Darryl Zanuck himself was going to produce it and had chosen an exciting cast for this story of tension between blacks and whites in the West Indies.

There were fourteen stars, among them James Mason, Joan Fontaine, Harry Belafonte, Dorothy Dandridge, Stephen Boyd and Michael Rennie. It promised to be a highly explosive and controversial film. It would be the first American film to show love scenes between blacks and whites. Already the censor was getting nervous.

I flew back to Los Angeles for a few weeks and picked up several awards for being "The Most Promising Actress," "The Face of the Year" or "Favorite Newcomer" from various exhibitors and magazines, all of which prompted me to comment, "I'm afraid I'll be a has-been before I finish being promising." Then it was back on the plane and off to Barbados in the British West Indies.

The main theme of *Island* was miscegenation. Several interwoven stories all concerned the racial issue, a hot and taboo subject in the late fifties. I played a girl who discovers that her grandmother was black, thus giving her "colored blood," the euphemism then for being one-quarter black. The subject—that of black and white people of both sexes becoming involved with one another and falling in love—was considered so shocking and outrageous that there was a tremendous outcry when Darryl Zanuck announced he was making the novel into a movie. Many states instantly announced that they would never allow it to be shown. Controversy raged, Mr. Zanuck and Robert Rossen were often closeted in their tiny hotel rooms trying to placate some of the more stringent censorship demands.

There was a great similarity between the locations of *Seawife* and *Island in the Sun*—the same tropical days and romantic nights. *Island in the Sun* is still talked about as being one of the most enjoyable locations ever among the British film units. It has become almost legendary. We had an enormous crew, including a second unit. Over one hundred technical men and women converged on the tiny island. Robert Rossen, the American director, working again after years of being on McCarthy's blacklist, and most known for the award-winning *All the King's Men,* was a hard taskmaster and a tough man, but a complete professional, and he expected total support and obedience from his actors and crew. He was such a martinet that one day he called "Action!" while I was still behind a palm tree putting on my gloves. He chastised me strongly for not being ready when he was ready to shoot. This little confrontation has lived with me to this day and is one of the many reasons why I am always on time, know my lines, and am as disciplined professionally as I can be.

The producer, the cigar-chomping, diminutive Darryl Zanuck, had been instrumental in my coming to Fox. An immensely powerful force in motion pictures, his weak spot was women. Throughout the years he had had a series of affairs with some talented, and not so talented, actresses. His present mistress was absent from this location and he had recently cast his eyes in my direction. Giving new meaning to the word "predatory," he had grabbed me one afternoon in the corridor of the hotel, pressed me against the wall, cigar still firmly clamped between his fingers and tried to convince me of his endurance, prowess and endowments as one of the world's best lovers.

"You've had nothing until you've had me," he muttered, his breath reeking of cigar smoke, as he tried to press gray-moustached lips to mine. "I've got the biggest and the best. I can go all night and all day."

I tried to wriggle free. Though shorter than me, he was powerful in body as well as presence, and I was pinned like a beetle to a board. My struggles would not stop his torrent of lust.

"Why do you waste your time with these boys?" he croaked hoarsely as I skewered my face away from his. "These Arthur Loews and Nicky Hiltons don't know how to please you. You need a real man."

Oh, my God. He was actually giving me the oldest line in the business. I wondered how to get out of this without having to knee him in the groin. Luckily Dorothy Dandridge and a makeup man came walking down the corridor and I made my escape, vowing to keep out of Mr. Z's way in the future.

A tight schedule we were not on. Because of the position of the sun, we finished work by four o'clock every day. The rest of the time we did as we pleased. I always liked to play games, and an endless series of card and party games began: charades, Monopoly, Scrabble and, of course, poker—Gin and Liar's Poker Dice. It was an ongoing party. Each night ended with all of us taking a dip in the warm Caribbean after dozens of Planter's Punches and dancing till we dropped, to the music of exciting steel bands. Although we all boozed, none of us ever felt tired or hung over. Cast and crew alike operated at peak proficiency. The crew were like my brothers; I loved them all.

I had noticed Harry Belafonte immediately, of course, admired his stunning physical appearance. Cast and crew had gathered together at the hotel for a cocktail party during the first week of filming. We would all get to know each other, hopefully like each other, and probably form close attachments which would usually last for as long as the shooting of the movie. Actors are fickle folk. Although closeness develops fast when thrown together on location, it does not always linger longer than the final "Cut." D.C.O.L. "Doesn't count on location" was a well-known phrase.

I had been chatting with Joan Fontaine, whom I knew from *Decameron Nights*, and had observed him from afar. Tall, dark and handsome was an understatement. About six feet one, he had black close-cropped hair, and his skin was the color of caramels. His body was slim and muscular, clothed in tight ivory-colored pants and a bright red shirt open to the navel. He laughed a lot, I noticed, as he, James Mason and Dorothy Dandridge were involved in animated discussion—full, deep-throated laughter that seemed to come right from his gut as he threw back his head and guffawed lustily. The West Indian waiters, running about with trays of rum punches and platters of fried shrimp and other delicacies of the island, smiled every time they caught sight of him. To them, he was a local boy who had made good, and even though he was not from Barbados his songs were indigenous to all parts of the West Indies. He was a folk hero.

He caught my eyes, smiled, and wandered over to us.

"Hi!" he said, extending his hand with a lazy smile.

Joan Fontaine said a brisk hello and I stood slightly tongue-tied, unusual for me, while she and he discussed their roles in the movie.

I gazed at his warm brown eyes and aristocratic nose. He was indeed gorgeous—as women from coast to coast had been discovering for the past several years. In concert, nightclubs and records his fame was spreading rapidly. His sex appeal made women of all ages go weak at the knees, and I, never one to let male beauty go unappreciated, got his message. But I was cautious about men who were overly conscious of their sexual power. My strict and old-fashioned upbringing also made me wary of the ramifications that any involvement with a black man could bring. The pages of *Confidential* were filled with innuendos about celebrities involved in relationships with other races. It was not the thing to do. I started to move away, but he took my arm and looked into my eyes.

"Where are you going?" he asked, his eyes shining with interest and amusement.

"Oh—I—said I'd have dinner with some of the camera boys." I stammered, aware of heat from his hand on my bare arm. He glanced over to where three or four of the English camera crew, mates of mine from *Seawife*, were grouped, observing us with amusement and waiting for developments, which from the look of it seemed inevitable. His grip on my arm did not lessen, and he looked at them and then back to me with even more amusement. My, he was sure of himself.

"An appointment you cannot break?" his voice was husky, sexy and confident.

"That's right," I said lightly, my eyes locked in his as I removed his persuasive fingers from my rather too receptive flesh. "We're having dinner and then playing poker."

"Poker—aahh. Of course. You English ladies always like to play games."

The innuendo was there. He knew and I knew. Even Joan Fontaine knew as she drifted away in a sea of chiffon.

"Well, then, I'll let you go—for now," he said meaningfully, bestowing on me a dazzling and promise-filled smile. I felt my face blushing under its suntan. "Since I don't play games—another time, then." And he smoothly glided off, catlike and elegant, leaving the blushing schoolgirl standing somewhat off balance.

I joined my British compatriots, who went to some lengths to let me know that this fabulous man was considered to be a ladies' man par excellence, and gossip had it that one of his ambitions was to be able to make love to as many beautiful women as he could possibly find. Cheap crew talk, I thought. Though my heart beat a little faster when I thought of him, I realized it was a no-no situation.

Although Belafonte and I had no scenes together, everyone was in the same hotel, so our paths crossed often. At breakfast, lunch and dinner—there he was. Smiling, confident—sexy. Throwing me glances and waiting for *me* to make the move.

For a week I kept out of his way, until the following Sunday when Zanuck arranged a festive brunch for the cast and crew. A hundred and fifty of us gathered around the tables groaning with Caribbean goodies, and I was seated next to him. His proximity and poise made me so nervous that I couldn't eat and I started to chain-smoke.

"You've been avoiding me, Joan Collins," he said, nonchalantly spooning up papaya and melon. "Have the poker games been that exciting?"

"I'm on a winning streak," I said offhandedly, lighting yet another cigarette with shaking hands.

"Allow me," he said, removing the cigarette from my lips and dumping it in the ashtray. I realized that I had lit the wrong end and the singed filter was on fire. Not exactly sophisticated behavior.

From an adjoining table the camera boys were enjoying the whole scene. Damn them, I thought. Interfering busybodies. I didn't belong to them. They were looking out for me as if I were Little Red Riding Hood with the Big Bad Wolf. I decided to enjoy Belafonte's engaging company and ignore the boys and their sniggers.

He was a spirited conversationalist. Warm and articulate, funny; and so engrossed were we in talking that the heaping plates of chicken gumbo, fried shrimps, lobsters, brown rice and exotic fruits were barely touched. Although the chat was light, the undercurrent of mutual attraction was heavy. Darryl Zanuck sat opposite us, chomping on an immense cigar, wearing little blue-and-white-striped shorts and matching shirt, open to show a protruding, gray-haired belly. He occasionally shot us penetrating looks as if questioning whether or not this conversation was innocent. But I gave him my sweetest, most innocent smile to assure him that all was aboveboard.

One thing I gathered from lunching with my handsome friend— he was smart and he was cool. He was no Zanuck who had to press his advances on a woman. Why should he? Women flocked to *him*. I watched them in the hotel lobby, going dithery and weak as they gazed at his sensual frame clad as usual in tight pants and shirt open to the waist, and not at all oblivious to the effect he had on them. He also knew that the entire cast and crew were waiting to see what, if any, developments were about to happen between him and me. Since I did not wish to be the object of gossip during the movie, I didn't relish the idea of the whole world's knowing about an event which to me should be private, so I decided that this tropical, romantic island was neither the time nor the place for us. I stopped thinking about him and returned to the poker games. And he, taking my cue, did not pursue it either.

Toward the end of his shooting—he was to be finished before the rest of us as he had a concert tour—we took a walk along the beach one night. There had been yet another party at the hotel and we had both gone outside for some air. It was hot and the moon was silver and full. I was wearing a bare-shouldered white cotton *broderie anglaise* dress that showed off my deep tan. I took off my sandals to walk where the ocean lapped at the sand. He was also in white, trousers and shirt, and in the silvery light shimmering on our faces, we seemed the same color.

I was sad that he was leaving. Although we had spent little time together, it was only because circumstances and morals decreed that it was "wrong" for us to have anything other than the most casual acquaintanceship. He was a sensitive and bright man. What difference did it make if he was black, white or blue?

"I suppose I won't see you again," I said after we had walked silently along the surf for a while. He didn't answer, but he stopped and looked up at the sky for a while with a faraway intense look on his face. I knelt down to pick up some of the little shells that had scattered like uncut gems over the sand. He was still looking out toward the ocean, the moon making his face into a carved bronze statue and the warm wind blowing the white cotton shirt out from his body. There was something so atavistic and powerful about him, and his silence seemed so full of secret meaning that I felt like an intruder. I continued picking up shells until he suddenly turned, his mood changing—laughing, joking—and pulled me up to stand beside him.

"Look." He pointed to the moon. "Two hundred billion years or more it's been there—what does it matter about us?" He turned to look at me and put his hands on each side of my head and said, "I'll be in Los Angeles in April. At the Grove. Come then." It was neither an invitation nor a command. It was a fact. I would be there.

And I was. His opening night at the Coconut Grove was jam-packed. Half the celebrities in Los Angeles had come to see the magnetic personality and performance of this man who was becoming famous throughout America. He was the first man ever to sell over one million LPs. Not for nothing was he called "King of the Calypso." He had recently broken all records at a huge sports stadium in New York and was fast becoming one of the first black film idols. He had been mesmerizing audiences of every type from true folk-music aficionados to smitten teenagers and matrons to music critics and intellectuals with his honey-voiced and spirited renditions of calypso folk songs and spiritual jazz performed with guts, emotion and honesty.

The Coconut Grove had been built during the peak glamour era of the movies, the 1920s. Gable and Lombard had romanced there. Crawford, Harlow, Bogart, all of the great movie stars had wined and dined, brawled and romanced in its splendid environs. It now had the aura of faded glory. If one looked too closely, the paint was peeling off the walls and the fringe was falling off the pink lampshades that cast flattering soft lights on the jaded faces of those who frequented it now. For the age of the nightclub was fast disappearing as the disco started to take hold. But tonight the giant fake palm trees were magnificently flashy and the atmosphere had an electric anticipatory mood. And so did I.

I had been invited by the studio to attend. I had never seen Belafonte perform before more than just a few people, casually, at some of our gatherings in the West Indies. I was eager to see him. And he did not disappoint. As the stage went dark, a spotlight was turned on, and to the calypso rhythm of his theme song he strolled on—casual, confident—singing, dancing, with a slightly arrogant self-assured style—wholly original.

"If you see me you'll love me" seemed to be his attitude, and so certain was he of his sexuality and magnetism that most of the women there were more than overcome. I sat enthralled, in my low-cut black satin dress, my hair a concoction of curls and bows, a white mink stole gracefully slipping off my shoulders to show cleavage, and with my new diamond earrings from Asprey's flashing—a present to myself. I looked fetching and knew it. And he knew it too as our eyes connected during his act.

The show over, the applause and encores still echoing, an elite group of invitees trekked through the corridors of the old Ambassador Hotel to the "star's dressing room," which is really the star's hotel room, since the management was too cheap to supply both. He was lionized. Bouffant-haired matrons gushed and squealed around him, elbowing each other to get closer. Sharply dressed and sharp-talking guys hovered, ready to talk deals if only they could get to him through the throbbing female hordes.

A waiter passed Dom Perignon which I sipped, sitting in the background, not about to join the gushing group around him. He looked over at me and smiled.

I raised my glass in a silent salute. It was obviously going to be a long party and I didn't feel like sticking around for the grand finale. When my group was ready to leave I went over to him for the *de rigueur* kiss on each cheek and the "Goodbye, darling, you were divine" routine, which I sincerely meant. We exchanged a last lingering look. It was only in the eyes, but it was high voltage. I was silent on the way back to my small apartment. My thoughts were of him, and what might have been.

The Arthur Loew relationship had lasted for nearly fifteen months, but was cooling off now. Although we still saw each other we dated others.

I wanted more than a semi-platonic relationship. I realized that sex was quite important to me. Many people thought it was shocking for a woman to admit she enjoyed making love and that she thought it a perfectly natural thing to do.

Jayne Mansfield tried to change that in a somewhat different way. Arriving under contract to Fox around the same time that I did, she plunged into the publicity machine where Marilyn Monroe left off. An unbelievable figure—40–18–36. Long platinum-blond hair, baby-blue eyes and a talent for gathering personal publicity out of practically everything she did. She starred in several forgettable films but became the American workingman's number one turn-on.

Fox had the brilliant idea of co-starring her and me in a film together. It was a serious and seamy John Steinbeck novel called *The Wayward Bus*. For this true slice of Americana in the raw, they unbelievably imported a young French director from Paris.

For the role of the sluttish, nagging, alcoholic wife who runs the tacky diner where the bus makes pit stops, they chose me. I was extremely pleased at the chance to play a character role and not just be the pretty wallpaper. The studio was happy with my performances in *Seawife* and *Island in the Sun* and was giving me a meaty part that showed its confidence in me was growing.

I had to be aged for the role of the drunken wife. Bags and circles were applied under my eyes; my hair, still short from *Seawife*, was a snarled and tangled mess; and I played most of the film in a stained dressing gown. It was challenging to be able to work on a character totally unlike myself. All my personal characteristics, from accent to walk, had to be changed. In *Seawife* I had been able to use parts of myself that were never revealed in films before—innocence and vulnerability, which were in my own makeup. I was surprised Fox had not given this role to Joanne Woodward, their resident young character actress. Surprised, but glad, I threw myself into the movie with tremendous enthusiasm.

Unfortunately, the director, Victor Vicas, was so unfamiliar with the American way of life and so petrified of making mistakes that it was difficult for him to bring Steinbeck's grimly realistic story to life. The film was reviewed unfavorably and it bombed at the box office. I, however, received favorable comments and good reviews. I hoped that this would bring me better and more fulfilling roles and not just "pretty-pretty" ones. Some people seemed amazed at my performance: "But you were *good!*" they would say, the surprise thinly disguised in their voices. Or "I didn't know you could *act*, Joanie baby."

I gritted my teeth, smiling politely. I was gaining more confidence in my ability, but I still constantly had to prove it to others. This continued for several years. Directors, actors or crew members often came up to me with surprised smiles to tell me how good I was, as though they never expected it. I found it galling.

I was still treated by many people like a brainless starlet whose main talent was to go partying and who built a career based on looks and sex appeal. Now I know, since my career has continued for over thirty years, that this isn't true. There are any number of young actresses who flowered and bloomed in the first flush of stardom for a few years only to fall into total obscurity. There are very few so-called beauties or glamour girls who have sustained a career for over three decades. This is a business of survival. To survive you have to work at your craft and become good. You don't get charity jobs.

I was also chastised and criticized for wanting to enjoy my personal life. If I want to go traveling or to parties or discos, who is to say I am inferior to Miss X, who stays at home at night with a boiled egg and a copy of Stanislavsky, and is maybe not a "10"? It has always been easier to be considered a serious actress if you are not good-looking. Beauty is definitely an asset at the beginning of a career. I know it was basically my looks that got me to Hollywood; but after a few years looks are, in fact, a hindrance in advancing a career. It is hard for people to accept beauty and a good actress in the same package.

However, I was not about to go to seed and fall apart physically just to prove I could act, and in fact, I won't ever do that. I enjoy being attractive and dressing well, and it amuses me to see that some people are resentful of how I look.

"How do you *do* it?" they ask bitchily, trying to look behind my ears for some telltale scars; or, "What are you doing to yourself? You've got some magic secret for staying young—tell me what it is."

The truth is, there's no secret. You get the face that you deserve, eventually. I believe in enjoying the life you have as much as possible, in living without envy, frustration and bitterness toward others—and in trying to be happy and worry-free. (Not an easy goal in my life.) A little narcissism is not a bad thing either. It was Gore Vidal who said, "A narcissist is someone better-looking than yourself." True!

I would like to have had some magical prophetic man or woman in my life who became my mentor and helped and guided me through the difficulties of my career. Unfortunately, they did not appear. I went through the jungle alone. Not for me a Carlo Ponti, Roger Vadim or Dino de Laurentiis to help guide me. Not even a trusty agent or manager has gone the distance, with the exception of Bill Watts.

With three films under my belt in less than a year, I took off for Acapulco for a rest. Arthur and I had come to a final parting of the ways on New Year's Eve.

We were dancing at the Charles Lederers' New Year's Eve party. The music was soft and romantic, but we were not. We were having another peevish row, quietly, so that the imposing array of distinguished guests could not overhear our heated discussion. They could not have failed to hear the following dazzling dialogue:

Arthur: "You are a fucking bore."

Me: "And you are a boring fuck." And that was the end of that.

I stayed in Acapulco for four weeks, tanning and learning to water-ski.

I started dating Nicky Hilton, a playboy and first husband of Elizabeth Taylor and the son of Conrad Hilton of the huge hotel chain. Nicky was good-looking in a dissolute and rakish way. Dark hair, dark eyes, he enjoyed a reputation as one of Hollywood's swingingest playboys. Although he had his own office and was assistant to his father in the hotel business, he preferred to spend his time with girls, at the racetrack and nightclubbing. Since I was not in the mood for serious involvement, and neither was he, he divided his time between Natalie Wood and me for several months, which suited me fine.

Nicky was a devout Catholic in spite of his prolific womanizing. He kept a rosary on the bedside table, which featured an amazing array of pill bottles in all shapes and sizes, girlie magazines, pornographic books, bottles of Coca-Cola, a crucifix, and a gun. He enjoyed filling the gun with blanks and firing it repeatedly at the ceiling in the middle of the night, to the horror of his neighbors on Doheny Drive, who would call the police in a frenzy of fear.

Although only in his early thirties, he appeared as if he had seen and done everything. He had been everywhere, could get practically any girl he wanted and was completely jaded. He had a Southern drawl and was racially bigoted.

Rich men's sons have a hard road to hoe. It is almost the equivalent of being a beautiful girl. You are born with everything. You don't have to do a thing for yourself. It's all there: the

112

money, the power, the girls, the fast cars and the fast life. Arthur learned that his money did not make for happiness. He moved to a ranch in Arizona where he completely changed his lifestyle. He raised cattle, married and found himself. And Syd Chaplin got his act together and made a success on Broadway for a few years.

Alas, poor Nicky did not find a way out, and a few years later he was dead from a drug overdose.

CHAPTER

Five

"CAN YOU BE READY TO LEAVE FOR Tokyo in three days?" My agent's voice, crisp and businesslike on the phone, woke me from a dreamless sleep. My cocoon of pillows and sheets was rumpled and my mouth was dry from too many cigarettes.

"Damn." I fumbled for the Visine eyedrops among the bedside-table junk. A glass of water fell off the cluttered table that held scripts, magazines, vitamins, a clock, Kleenex, a photo of my parents in an antique silver frame, diamond earrings and pearls tossed carelessly about, and an overflowing ashtray.

I pushed the ashtray under the pile of magazines—the smell was vile at that time of the morning—I tried to collect my thoughts as the Visine did its job on my eyes.

"Three days—that's impossible. I can't be ready in time," I croaked, pulling the sheet around my shoulders and wishing some-one would bring me some fresh orange juice, coffee and raisin toast. Oh, for a live-in housekeeper. Alas, my business manager convinced me I couldn't really afford one, although I was earning two thousand dollars a week, had starred in half a dozen movies, and appeared regularly on the covers of magazines worldwide. I was a commodity now, a young, sexy, salable commodity, and my studio employers took full advantage of this fact and were pushing me into film after film—movies unfortunately noted more for their visual beauty and scenic splendor than for their integrity or realism.

My agent was sympathetic but firm. I must report to the Fox wardrobe department at eleven, hair department at one-thirty—and visit the insurance doctor at three for whatever shots I might need for Japan and for his verification that I was healthy. Then, in the two and a half days that would be left prior to my departure, I had to organize the bits and pieces of my own life as well as I could. It was par for the course. I didn't have much say in the direction my career went. If I ever rebelled, I was put on suspension. No work. No money. Not even another studio was allowed to employ me. And TV was considered lower than low. I was fairly frugal. The apartment on Shoreham Drive—furnished in white-beige-and-pink Sears Roebuck starlet style—cost two hundred fifty dollars a month. I either ate out or was on a diet so my fridge contained cottage cheese, a few bottles of white wine and little else. The freezer, however, was full of Will Wright's ice cream in every different flavor for the odd afternoons when I threw caution to the wind and indulged in an ice-cream fit. I had a car befitting my starlet status. A flashy pink Thunderbird, which certainly got attention when I zipped along Sunset Boulevard well over the speed limit, with the radio blaring Latin American music. My closet contained a large selection of Saks and Magnin's lowest-cut dresses, a white mink stole, a black mink coat, a white sheared-beaver coat and a blue fox hat which I had bought in an abandoned moment and had never worn. I was sartorially prepared for any eventuality. Of material possessions other than these I had none. No paintings or even lithographs graced my walls—I had not yet discovered my passion for collecting Art Deco and Art Nouveau objects. And of emotional involvements I also had none, although my date book was filled.

I lay back on the Porthault pillows—another indulgence, but I liked to wake up in a field of flowers—and thought about Japan. With the memory of two recent locations still lingering, I was not keen on a trip so soon. But I decided I had better think positively and make the best of it. I had never been to the Orient—it could be an exciting experience.

I had never in my life seen such a horde of fans as greeted Robert Wagner, Edmond O'Brien and myself on our arrival at Tokyo airport. Literally thousands of yelling and screaming excited Japanese of all ages whipped themselves into a frenzy at the sight of us. It was quite overwhelming and rather frightening. Even Robert ("R.J.") Wagner, a movie star since his teens, was bowled over by it. The Japanese have always been eager movie fans, and a million flashbulbs on a million Nikon cameras seemed to explode in front of us as we forced our way through the *extremely* polite throngs. The Japanese are so polite and well-mannered that they apologize profusely while shoving you violently at the same time.

On the way to our hotel in the Ginza district I saw dozens of movie theaters literally festooned with giant multicolored blowups of the stars who were appearing in the movies. John Wayne's face in vivid colors one hundred feet high, with slightly slanted eyes, was some sight to behold. But although I enjoyed the ancient charms of Japan I was lonely and miserable.

The script of the film was really awful. Called *Stopover Tokyo*, I immediately dubbed it *Stop Overacting!* R.J., though friendly and nice, was newly engaged to Natalie Wood and spent most of his off-set time with his parents in his suite or calling Natalie in Los Angeles. His phone bill must have been astronomical since he called at least once a day. The crew, with whom I usually hung out on location, were all men well over fifty, who threw themselves into the male-oriented Japanese society with gusto. They frequented the geisha houses where they were treated like lords, fawned over and adored by the geishas—small-boned, tiny creatures, seemingly from another century in their gorgeous, brightly colored kimonos and obis, their miniature feet padding softly in white cotton tabis, their faces masked by white powder, carmine lips and intricate eye makeup, and their heads crowned with enormously heavy glossy black wigs. I did not envy the life of a Japanese woman. Most were still virtually chattels to their men, men who spent practically every night out with other men frolicking at the baths, the geisha houses and the restaurants, where it was taboo for women to join in the festivities. On the few occasions when I did accompany some of the crew to the restaurants and clubs, I felt gawky and gauche next to these exquisite little women, and the men made no secret of their preference for the Oriental female.

"A bunch of woman haters," I muttered to my companion, the unit hairdresser, as we sat in the hotel dining room eating teriyaki and fried rice unenthusiastically and feeling bored and despondent. One of the camera crew, a huge beefy Southern redneck, middle-aged and dressed in a hideous plaid shirt, Stetson hat and checked trousers, with his gross paunch hanging over his belt, had dropped by our table with his tiny beautiful geisha to lay a bit of his new-found philosophy on us.

"You Western gals should take a few lessons from these Oriental ladies," he said, his saki-drenched breath causing us to stop eating. "Now little Tamiko here—she *really* knows how to treat a man right. Don't you, Tamiko?"

Tamiko nodded and smiled subserviently at this lout, and I felt disgusted that Japanese women thought themselves so inferior to even the most loathsome of the male sex.

Women's liberation was a glimmer on the horizon. But at least that glimmer was becoming stronger. I considered myself by now to be an emancipated and free woman. If I chose to sleep with whom I wanted, and when I wanted, however, I sometimes became the butt of jokes, crude remarks and a general attitude among some people that I was no better than I should be, or a "tramp." It was considered shocking to be free in sexual attitudes. My proclivity for taking as lovers men who were interesting, young and good-looking did not endear me to a whole section of men in the movie business—producers, directors, heads of studios and big-wigs in general—because I would never have anything to do with *them* at all. The thought of going to bed with some old, fat, ugly or rich man for a job or to do myself some good careerwise was revolting. *That* to me was being a tramp. If I wanted to bed down with three men a week whom I genuinely fancied and liked, I would. It was my life and the time had come to get rid of guilts and live it for *myself*.

However, in Japan there was *no one* I felt even faintly attracted to and I spent most of my free time with the hairdresser, reading, trying to study the ghastly script in my hotel room, or sightseeing.

One evening the phone rang. It was a man called Charles. We'd met once in Los Angeles and when he invited me to dinner I accepted. A new face was more than welcome in my life. I had killed more time having an elaborate wardrobe made, choosing from the profusion of glorious fabrics—silks, brocades and chiffon —that Japan had to offer. I had to buy five more suitcases to cart home this loot. There were enough cocktail dresses and evening gowns all copied from Vogue and Harper's Bazaar to keep me dressed differently every night for a year.

For my night out with Charles I wore a pink-and-gold brocade cheongsam—a high-necked Chinese-style dress, tightly fitted, with a skirt slit to the thigh—quite appropriate for anywhere we might go, be it a quiet bistro or a nightclub. However, I was not prepared for what Charles—tall, dark and quite elegant—suggested we do after dinner. We went to what appeared to be an attractive, dimly lit nightclub—small, very small—and we sat on thick soft cushions on the floor close to a stage that was rather too tiny for dancing.

It was a live sex show—an erotic fantasy! To start with, an amazingly beautiful and nubile young girl cavorted naked on stage. She had shaved her pubic hair and spent much time massaging herself with a long rounded object. After a while two equally sexy young men joined her, and the girl, truly one of the greatest contortionists I have ever seen, knelt and arched her back and bent her head to a 90-degree angle while one of the men made love to her with rabbit rapidity and the other had the most expert fellatio performed on him. I sat there stunned. I could not believe the scene before me. All of this was done in silence, except for some mysterious lute music emanating from an unknown source and the irregular breathing of my escort.

"God! Fantastic!" Charles whispered, his hand landing light as a butterfly's wings on my thigh. "What do you think?" he breathed, nuzzling my left ear, obviously getting wildly aroused.

"I wonder if she can cook," I whispered back, gently removing his hand.

"Who cares," he mumbled as another couple joined the threesome on the stage and proceeded to arrange themselves in every conceivable position. They looked like the "Snake Pit" and I started to giggle furiously—especially when I caught sight of all the tourists' rapt horny faces in the audience. The more vigorously the performers writhed the more amused I became. To me there was nothing erotic or exciting in this flagrant exhibitionism. Always romantic, I thought the kiss between Montgomery Clift and Elizabeth Taylor in A *Place in the Sun* infinitely more sexy.

Charles, his ardor whetted by this display, thought otherwise, and I pleaded every known combination of female ailments at the entrance to my hotel room before I gracefully got rid of him. Maybe there was something wrong with me if I found a group-sex scene which people paid money to watch such a turn-*off*. Charles was an attractive man. In my circumstances, stuck in Japan for five weeks, celibate and bored, it was curious that his taking me to a supposedly stimulating show had had the reverse effect on me. Most women would probably have leaped into bed with him and made love imaginatively and passionately for hours, turned on by what they had seen. Somehow I felt that both sexes were demeaning themselves by these acts. They were being used, and their degradation was much more apparent than any enjoyment they were probably simulating.

Sex is certainly not a spectator sport, I thought as I got into my lonely bed for the thirty-fifth consecutive night. Charles probably thinks I'm a total square—and I drifted off into a sleep filled with writhing nests of vipers and boa constrictors.

CHAPTER

Six

IF I THOUGHT I HAD BEEN IN LOVE
before, those feelings paled in comparison with my infatuation
with George Englund. I had known him, his wife and their rapidly
increasing family ever since I had met him at Gene Kelly's house
soon after I arrived in America. He had gone to military academy
with Sydney Chaplin and was a close friend of Arthur Loew's. His
wife, Cloris Leachman, who in the 1970s would become a popular
television star playing the role of Phyllis on "The Mary Tyler
Moore Show," was an actress, pretty, friendly and neurotic, who
dedicated her life and herself to George and the rearing of their
three children.

Our friends were mutual. As a foursome with Sydney we'd gone
to Palm Springs and Tijuana together, and although I knew that
George and Cloris bickered a lot I thought their marriage was OK
as most marriages go—not tremendous but not at breaking point
either. I was aware of him as an intelligent, attractive man with a
fabulous sense of humor—but that was all. Married men were a
no-no in my book, especially if I was pally with their wives. It was
not cricket.

When I mentioned that I was going to Chicago and New York
on promotions for *Stopover Tokyo*, George told me he would be
in New York at the same time and perhaps we'd get together for
dinner one night, our schedules permitting. We were, coinciden-
tally, staying at the same hotel, the Plaza. When he came to pick

120

me up that night I was unaware that I was embarking on one of the most traumatic, emotional and unsettling periods of my life.

In retrospect I don't think the highs balanced the lows, but when one is madly, passionately, blindly in love, all reason evaporates. On our first date we went to the Little Club for dinner. He was dressed impeccably as always in a dark blue suit from a Savile Row tailor, a pale blue Turnbull and Asser silk shirt and a Cardin tie. He had a reputation for being very well dressed, and sartorially he could not be faulted. Aside from his clothes, he was devastatingly good-looking. Six feet two, green-eyed, with light brown hair, going ever so *slightly* thin on top—about the only flaw I noticed as I became increasingly aware of him as more than a friend during dinner. He had a wicked wit and a superb mastery of the English language. Indeed he was the perfect advocate of the adage Why use a short word when a six-syllable one will do? Words and phrases I seldom heard outside the New Oxford Dictionary tumbled effortlessly from his lips. He was smart as a whip, and we seemed to spark each other's funnybone too, for he laughed at me as much as I laughed at him.

Ahhh, laughter—one of the greatest aphrodisiacs in the world! He ordered a Mouton-Rothschild '53 with our beef Wellington, and after dinner we drank Calvados and listened to the 30s-style music as the pianist played a selection of what suddenly became my favorite tunes. It was too romantic to be true. The wine, the superb dinner, the intimate velvet banquette where we sat next to each other, George's hand on mine, the Gershwin and Cole Porter songs, some of which he sang softly (he knew the words to even the most obscure songs—there was no end to his talents).

We walked hand in hand after dinner through the empty New York streets with the steam rising from the sidewalks, back to the Plaza, and as he accompanied me to my room my heart was pounding. Was it possible to fall in love over *dinner* with someone you had thought of only as a friend for two years? Apparently it was, and I was hopelessly—helplessly—hooked.

For three days I thought of nothing else. Every possible moment we could share away from my schedule of TV, radio and newspaper interviews, and he from his business meetings, we spent

121

together. We passed a frosty autumnal Sunday walking starry-eyed through Central Park. I was besotted beyond belief and refused to think of the insurmountable problems of his wife and three boys, aged six, four and two.

He assured me over and over again that the marriage was and had been in deep and serious trouble for several years, and that they were only staying together for the sake of the kids. Despite its being such a cliché, it was said so convincingly that I completely believed him. His influence over me was so strong that he could have demanded I skate naked in Rockefeller Center and I would have happily done so. I became truly the Trilby to his Svengali.

On our last evening in New York we went back to the Little Club, which I would forever think of as "our place." I wore a beige suit and a green felt "Garbo" hat. I had just read *The Green Hat* and rather fancied myself as its star-crossed heroine. I sniffled through cocktails, started to cry during dinner, and wept profusely during dessert and coffee. I was feeling guilty now about our situation but I knew I couldn't and wouldn't give him up. Little did I know I was beginning twenty-one months of the most intense misery of my life.

My best friend was Caprice Caprone Yordan, an exquisitely elegant and witty, sophisticated black-haired beauty, married to Philip Yordan, a prolific writer-producer of epic films, usually set in Spain or Africa. Cappy and I shared practically every intimate secret of our lives with each other, and since Philip was constantly working, she had time to kill. She lived in a rambling old Spanish hacienda on Benedict Canyon, and spent her days entertaining her myriad friends, dispensing advice and worldly wisdom with a strong dose of astrology thrown in.

"Guess who I've fallen in love with," I blurted out. It was the morning after I had arrived in L.A., and I rushed over to her house to find her languishing elegantly in bed surrounded by satin-and-lace pillows, a wicker breakfast tray full of tea and croissants, English jams and marmalade and with eleven books on astrology spread over her pink satin coverlet.

"I hope he's rich," said Cappy. "It's about time you found a rich one."

"Not only is he not rich—but he's married," I despaired. "You know I don't care about money but the wife situation is a disaster." I gloomily devoured a croissant with honey while Cappy surveyed me disapprovingly. She was like my big sister. She knew the way my mind worked.

"Married and *poor*—wonderful. You've done it again, my darling. Enough guessing games—who is he and what's his sign?" She pulled one of the astrology books toward her and looked at me questioningly.

"George Englund," I blurted out. "I'm *madly* in love with him— and he with me, so he says." A wave of doubt engulfed me momentarily. I gave Cappy his birth date and waited expectantly for her verdict.

"Oh, you fool," said Cappy. "Not only is he a Cancer—" she consulted her book and frowned—"but he'll hang on to you *forever* and never let you go. His wife will never let *him* go either. What are you letting yourself in for, Joanie?"

"It's too late now," I groaned, grabbing another croissant for succor. "I can't give him up. It's ghastly. It's as though he's put a spell on me—what am I going to *do*, Cappy? I simply cannot stop thinking about him *all day long!* This has never happened to me before—Oh, God!"

She looked at me pityingly and did some quick calculations on a pad. "He's perfect for you, of course," she said as she finished her calculations and I finished her breakfast. "His moon and his Venus are in the same house as yours, and all your other signs are totally compatible. You're a perfect match for each other. But darling, he will *never* leave the wife and those kids. He's a *Cancer*, for goodness' sake—*the crab*—my God, his claws won't ever release *anything!* And his wife thinks so too," she said, pushing the books away. "You know she worships the ground he walks on. The best thing for you is to get back to work as quickly as possible and forget him."

I tried halfheartedly to heed my learned friend's advice, but now that I wanted and needed to work, suddenly I went through a dry spell. Although Fox paid me handsomely each week, they did not have any properties suitable for me at the moment. However there was a strong rumor on the lot that they were considering making yet another version of *Cleopatra* and that I was being touted as first choice to play the fabled queen.

Meanwhile, George and I saw each other four or five times a week. We lunched at out-of-the-way restaurants—usually near the airport, where the sound of jet engines often drowned our conversation—or he came to my little apartment for dinner. I never really knew until the last minute when or if I would see him, as he had about forty-seven different projects going at the same time and was wheeling and dealing in all channels. Although I went out on "dates," which I kept platonic, I would never commit my evenings until I knew if he was available. It was hell. I was "back street wife" personified. The worst times were when he said he would be over at eight and didn't show up until ten or eleven and sometimes not at all—only a hurried phone call: "Sorry, babe— can't make it tonight. Have to catch you tomorrow."

I would go to bed forlorn and miserable, trying to understand his problems and trying not to become upset. As the weeks passed and his promises of "trial separations" from his wife came to nothing I began to get immensely depressed.

I tried to become interested in other men, much to his chagrin, but no one could hold a candle to his charm, his wit, his looks or his personality, and I never even tried to find out how they compared in the other departments. After the misery of two days of not seeing him, a few hours in his company with his incredible mind bewitching me with his humor—everything seemed worth it.

He was extraordinarily jealous of me. Cancer crab with claws out. Whenever I dated someone he considered a possible rival, he would cross-question me afterwards for hours. We had vicious fights culminating in blissful making-up sessions.

His best friend at the time was Marlon Brando, who was almost as great an admirer of George as I was. George inspired people to worship him. He was confident, clever and so aggressively charming that most people found him irresistible.

Marlon adored him, he emulated his vocabulary and mannerisms, his prowess at storytelling, his slightly superior attitude toward others not on his wavelength. Sometimes I found it hard to tell the difference between the two voices on the telephone. Often Marlon would "beard" for us when we went to restaurants, theaters or screenings. A photograph was taken of the three of us at the theater. When it was printed, luckily only Marlon and I were in it. "Marlon does the town with British actress," crowed the New York tabloids. "Brando and Joan step out together." "We're just extremely good friends," said Miss Collins with originality.

I was conscious of the fact that I had left school at the age of fifteen and that my vocabulary consisted of about twenty thousand words fewer than these two together. They managed to combine the exuberant enthusiasm of two schoolboys at a baseball game with the sophistication of scholarly professors. Their humor and whimsicality fed off each other and they would spark each other to new heights of erudite and enlightening prose.

Marlon had an insatiable curiosity about people. What made them tick? What did they think about the world and other people, what were their feelings, observations, needs? At any gathering Marlon would usually gravitate to the quietest, and what to the unpracticed eye appeared the dullest, person in the room, and engage that person in animated and spirited conversation for hours. He was a master at making the shrinking violet bloom and the wallflower leave the wall. His interest was genuine. He really *was* interested in that pimpled, bespectacled young woman whose manner bespoke the library rather than the boudoir. He would draw her out slowly, painstakingly, with questions asked with intelligence and such obvious concern that the girl would flower before our eyes. He would not, or would rarely, converse with the more secure, flamboyant party-going types—he preferred to find his own party fodder. Deeply engrossed, eyeball to eyeball, hunched in the farthest corner of the room, oblivious to the madding crowd, Marlon and his newfound interest would sit engrossed in each other's company for hours.

This amused George, who would make jokes about Marlon's proclivity for turning on the ugliest girl in the room. "Hey Bud," he teased, as Brando hove into view after a two-hour marathon chat with a mousy little Pasadena housewife type, flustered, breathless and glowing from her encounter with the star—"If you play your cards right I think you may get her!"

Marlon would grin, unable to resist the blandishment of George's forceful personality. His quest was for truth. To find the person behind the mask, the real feelings behind the facade. When he turned his piercing blue eyes on his target, no third degree was necessary. People who had held themselves tightly in check for years would open the floodgates of confession and emotion to Brando. One of the greatest qualities of his acting is that he brings an amazing realism, truth and authenticity to whatever part he plays. In the late 1950s few, if any, actors brought these attributes to their film roles. With the exception of James Dean and Montgomery Clift, intensity and depth of feeling were not inherent in actors of the fifties and sixties—indeed they were almost frowned on as the more fashionable attributes of handsomeness, charm and virility were in favor.

Today Al Pacino, Robert de Niro and Richard Gere carry on where Brando pioneered. The age of the "personality" actor is ending, and a breed of thinking and feeling individuals has appeared, to whom the words "movie star" are anathema, and whose egos are sublimated to the personalities of the characters they are portraying.

Marlon's curiosity extended not only to people he met at parties but also to the content of his friends' refrigerators. To say he was fond of food is an understatement. Food seemed to be sucked down his throat as though by some invisible vacuum. Once we discussed the merits and disadvantages of having a "vomitorium" built into one's house, as in Roman times—a room where after two or three courses of excessive wining and dining, a well-to-do Roman of his day would excuse himself and retire to this quaintly but appropriately named room and relieve his congested stomach by way of an old fashioned vomit. He would then return to the dining room to indulge in another four or five courses—tripping to the vomitorium whenever the need arose.

The advantages of such a custom to those of us (among them me) who like to eat were obvious. Marlon did sometimes practice this odd method of weight watching while dieting for a role to get down to fighting weight, but I never could. Ah, the joys of being able to indulge in a four-course meal with appropriate wines and

126

liqueurs and having no telltale aftereffects to show up on the scales next day.

George and I caught Marlon red-handed one night at my apartment spooning up the last dregs of a quart of Will Wright's peach-vanilla ice cream while two empty quart containers on the side testified to his healthy appetite.

Caught like a seven-year-old, spoon in mouth, his aplomb never faltered and he managed to give the impression of *savoir-faire* with a trickle of ice cream dribbling down his T-shirt.

George was *everything* I had ever wanted in a man. Except for the fact that he was married, he was perfect in every way. Although his treatment of me was often casual indifference, somehow I accepted it. If love is blind, in my case this was utterly true. I saw George through a rich haze of rose-colored spectacles.

"I am divorcing Cloris," he announced definitively one afternoon three or four months after our liaison had begun. "We will still live together for a while for the sake of the children—occupying separate bedrooms, of course," he added hastily, seeing the sparks appearing in my eyes.

At last! Subconsciously my desire to get Daddy away from Mummy was finally being fulfilled in this relationship. To celebrate his new freedom we flew to Eleuthera, one of the most remote and romantic islands in the Caribbean, where there was nothing but green frothy sea, white sand and a cool blue alcove of a suite. But George was unsatisfied—edgy, upset and remote.

"Why?" I wailed, sitting on the gorgeous golden white beach— an uninhabited vista of paradise to the north, south, east and west of us. "*Why* do you have to think of Cloris and the children *now?*" I threw myself onto the powdery sand in my white bikini and started to sob. I wondered *how* he could *possibly*—viewing my lithe, suntanned body, my face recently described as the world's most beautiful, not to mention all the clever things he'd taught me to say and do—could he *possibly* think of wife and kiddies now? What did I *lack* that I seemed to leave him so unfulfilled? Although I was leaning heavily on my shrink three times a week, I was unable to see that the lacks were not in me alone. George's insurmountable guilt at leaving his wife and three children was

127

fueled by his obsession with me. Our island paradise became a disaster area. Feuding and fighting, we flew back to the States after only three days in Heaven, and I commenced living "back street wife" again.

"Dollink, I know a vonderful man who is *mad* about you." Zsa Zsa Gabor bit crisply into a shrimp and surveyed me shrewdly. "Vat you vant with this—this—son of a bitch married idiot. Dollink, vat he give you?" We sat lunching at Romanoff's, Zsa Zsa dispensing her worldly advice, diamonds glinting in the noonday sun, and I, dark glasses covering the ravages of last night's crying, trying to join in the fun and games of a girls' lunch.

Last night I had operated on a hunch. At eleven, as the dreary prime time ended and the news started, it came to me in a blinding flash that there was no "spare bedroom" at the Englunds' house! Without thinking, I jumped into my car and zoomed over to Westwood. I carefully cruised the alley behind the two-story white house and observed the action. The house had three bedrooms and six occupants—George and Cloris, their three sons and a housekeeper. It was so obvious. Their three sons in one room, the housekeeper in another, Mr. and Mrs. in the master bedroom. I knew the lay of the land, and as if to prove me right, I saw the two leading actors in my soap opera enter the bedroom and indulge in animated discussion as they proceeded to disrobe. Horrified, I gunned my engine and hastily turned into Wilshire Boulevard. I made a U-turn, zombielike, from Wilshire and Westwood Boulevard and cruised the alley more slowly and surely, and more observantly. Yes, it was he. No mistaking that six-foot-two tanned and terrific body—clad now only in blue undershorts as he discussed some subject animatedly with her—wearing an expensive orange Juel Park nightgown—which he could ill afford—and, with shoes off, a good ten inches shorter than he. My most ghastly suspicions were verified. He had lied to me. The bastard was cheating on me—with his wife!

There was no "spare bedroom" while they discussed their upcoming divorce. There was a cozy queen-sized bed and a thirty-two-year-old man and woman with three children and seven years of marriage behind them, off to bed together.

I pressed my foot on the accelerator as hard as I could and zoomed off blinded by tears. At Sunset Boulevard the C.H.I.P.S. got me. Leaving the apartment hurriedly, I had no identification—nor even any money on me.

"OK, lady—where's your I.D.?" said the gum-chewing middle-aged cop testily, oblivious to my bleary-eyed and obviously distressed appearance. I thought it best to turn on my most upper-class British accent as fast as possible. "I'm awfully sorry, officer—but I *cahnt* seem to remember putting it in my reticule when I left my flat."

I realized "reticule" was going a bit far—a Victorian word he probably had never heard of—but "flat" hit the spot, and I knew Americans were slightly in awe of aristocratic up-market British diction. He was no exception. Instead of calling in to his headquarters, as he should have done when finding someone driving over the limit—in which event I would have been computer-checked and they would have found I had a dozen unpaid traffic tickets which *could* necessitate spending the night in jail—he gallantly offered to escort me on his motorcycle back to my "flat" while I retrieved my driver's license from my "reticule."

"Oh, you American policemen are so wonderful," I gushed admiringly, and he, by now mindful of the tears drying on my cheeks and feeling perhaps a bit sorry for a British damsel in distress, left me to my misery.

So I listened to Zsa Zsa at lunch—grimly—more determined than ever to try and break off this disastrous affair with George.

"Dollink, he's vonderful," said Zsa Zsa, tossing her blond and beautifully coiffed curls, her doll-like blue eyes glistening with evangelical fervor at the thought of playing Cupid. I usually avoided blind dates like the plague. Men who were interested in meeting well-known actresses were usually creeps—but I let her have her say while munching my way through as much lunch, and as many glasses of wine, as possible, to dull the pain.

"His name is Rafael Trujillo—you've heard of him, of course?" She looked at me questioningly. I shook my head, mouth full of spinach and bacon salad. Zsa Zsa sighed. Women like Zsa Zsa always seemed to know intimately every head of state, prime minister and tycoon of all the minor countries of the world. Since my

involvement with George and my constant sessions with the
analyst, my enthusiasm for current world events had waned, and
I had not even read *Time* magazine lately. If I had, I would certainly have heard about the Trujillos. Zsa Zsa painstakingly started
to fill me in, and I listened halfheartedly.

"His father, of course, is the President of the Dominican Republic and—" she bent forward conspiratorially—"he has sometimes been known as *El Jefe*, 'the chief,' and 'The Caligula of the
Caribbean.' " Now I remembered reading about him. Although he
had successfully lifted his country from a depressed economic
state, in which it had been when he assumed control and took
over the government in 1930, he had never tolerated any opposi-
tion to his regime and suppressed dissent with arrests, tortures and
executions. He guarded his country with a curtain of fear, terrorizing and exploiting his frightened people.

Everything of value in his country belonged either to him or his
family. It had become a police state, in which his glassy-eyed photograph appeared in every public building. Major buildings and
streets were renamed for him, and he awarded himself numerous
titles of importance—he had come a long way from being one
of eleven children in a poor peasant family. All in all a very
unsavory character indeed, the Idi Amin of his day. A holiday in
the Dominican Republic would be at the bottom of my list of
favorite places to visit.

But dismissing my protestations about the father's injustices
with an airy wave, Zsa Zsa proceeded to fill me in on the son. He
was a polo-playing friend of Zsa Zsa's close friend Porfirio Rubirosa.
He had recently finished an army stint at Fort Leavenworth in
Kansas and now, therefore, had the title of "General" Rafael
Trujillo. "And . . ." Zsa Zsa finished triumphantly, "he's twenty-
nine years old—unmarried, *very* handsome, very rich and dying to
meet you. Vat do you say, dollink?" I considered carefully while
devouring chicken pancakes. Well, why not? Even if his father
was the Great Dictator, it didn't necessarily mean the son had to
be a baddie too.

"Will you come along too?" I asked Zsa Zsa, who was now surveying me like a mother hen looking at her first new laid egg.

"Oh, dollink—I can't—I can't get to Palm Beach right now. I'm doing a show."

"*Palm Beach?*" I gasped. "You didn't say anything about Palm Beach. I mean, this is Beverly Hills—I'm not going four thousand miles for a *blind date.*"

"But, dollink," she wheedled, "his boat is there now. He has to be in Palm Beach for the next ten days on business—he can't get here. Surely, dollink—" she lowered her voice conspiratorially and bent her blond head coyly closer to mine—I could smell Arpège and observe that she wore navy blue mascara on her false lashes— "surely you can leave this awful George for a couple of days." She smiled mysteriously and leaned back to sip some more Chablis, her mission, if not accomplished, at least message delivered.

"No way, Zsa Zsa." I lit a cigarette and shook my head violently. "I'm not going all those miles for a date with a guy I don't even *know*—however cute and rich he may be."

"But dollink, you told me you were going to be in New York next week for the opening of your movie. Palm Beach is next *door* practically. He'll send his plane for you, naturally." She continued her argument through the raspberries and ice cream but I was unenthusiastic about the idea. Besides I had to get back to the apartment. George was coming over at three-thirty, and even though he was always late, nevertheless I was always there. Today I had things to discuss.

I dashed back to Shoreham Drive. It was a beautiful sunny Californian afternoon but I felt chilly. He arrived at four. Handsome and tanned as ever, wearing an immaculate Prince of Wales plaid suit, which on any other man would have looked tacky and on him looked like a cover of *Gentleman's Quarterly.* His socks matched his tie, I noticed, and the new shoes obviously cost plenty. I tried to remember a present, a card, or even a flower he had ever bought me and realized he had never brought me anything but himself. I wondered if that was supposed to suffice.

Our usual afternoon ritual was to chat, kiss, and take it from there. Today I was in the mood only for the first item on the agenda. I needed a drink. To broach this tricky subject was not going to be easy. He accepted the vodka and tonic I handed him and sat opposite me in the armchair, jacket off, leaning back, arms behind head—surveying me with benign satisfaction and a faint smile. I was his property, his little princess in an ivory tower in the hills of Hollywood. Behind him the afternoon sun glinted on his shiny shoes, his gold cuff links and, it gave me a moment of satisfaction to note, his slightly receding hairline. Serves him right, I thought to myself bitterly. I hope it all falls out *soon*. I downed the vodka in one great gulp and came right out with it.

"You told me that you and Cloris sleep in separate rooms, but I don't believe you." I stared at him, hoping against hope he would come up with a good story and that it had all been just a figment of my imagination.

He stared back. He downed his vodka, a look of pain across his face. He lit a cigarette. My God, he never *smoked!* What was going on? OK, George, admit it now. *Admit* you slept with your wife. Come out with all the old clichés: *She* was there, you weren't. I thought about you all the time. I only did it once. She tried, but I couldn't do it. . . . Say *something*, but don't sit there at half past four in the afternoon looking like a death in the family and smoking cigarettes. Admit it—tell me—I'll cry a bit and then we'll make up. These thoughts raced through my head as he continued to stare and smoke.

"Cloris is pregnant," he said flatly. "We only did it once, believe me, Joanie, and she's goddamn pregnant again." I stared at him numbly. Pregnant—it wasn't possible—or was it? She already had three kids, with about two years between each one.

"How . . . I mean why . . . ? When?" I could barely speak. There was a lump in my throat the size of a fist that only vodka would make go away. I silently filled our empty glasses with straight Smirnoff while he filled me in on the details.

One afternoon seven or eight weeks previously when he had been in my apartment, she had suddenly started knocking on the front door and screaming, "George is here—I know he's here—make him come out." We sat fearfully up in bed, he motioning me to shut up as I attempted to go to the door and assure her that George was not in my apartment. After five or ten minutes the neighbors complained and she left. I was in a mild state of shock for I was not aware that anyone other than Cappy Yordan and Marlon knew about our affair. But rumors in Hollywood are like the jungle drums and obviously word had reached her that his Cadillac was parked on Shoreham Drive several times a week. At that time—according to him—they *were*, in fact, occupying separate bedrooms. He slept in the study on a couch because they were going through some sort of tacit separation while he was trying to sort out his very mixed-up emotions and feelings about me. When he returned that evening she threw everything she had at him—tears, hysteria, even suicide threats. To protect me, and prove to her that he was *not* involved with me, he had slept with her—just the once—and this was the result.

"So now you'll be the father of four," I said, my voice sounding as if it came from my boots. I picked up the vodka bottle and drank it all down—about a quarter of a fifth—and then hurled it across the room at him with all the force I could muster. It crashed into the window behind his head and glass flew everywhere. He jumped up, amazed. I took an ashtray and threw it at another pane in the middle of the bay window, then a glass, a pillow—anything I could lay my hands on, while sobbing and screaming at him hysterically, "That's *my* baby she's having—mine—how could you make *another* child with her? How could you, you bastard?" I threw myself about the room, all reason gone. He tried to calm me. He knew I detested physical violence, had never hit anyone in my life, and that this outbreak was the signal that I was going over the top.

I wouldn't let him touch me. My lungs were raw from yelling and screaming. All the pent-up months of patience, hope, of putting up with his lateness, his lies and his deceptions, were unleashed. If I had had a gun I might even have killed him—a true *crime passionel*. I never knew I possessed such feelings of rage. The dam burst but a tiny objective part of me watched the proceedings with great interest. As an actress I would be able to call on this experience for the future. "Well done," said the little voice admiringly. "What a great performance, dear." The grief, rage and passion that overcame me at four o'clock on that sunny afternoon in North Hollywood was never matched in my life—until my daughter Katyana was hit by a car and hovered between life and death in an intensive care unit some twenty years later.

Hours later he left. To his credit he saw me through the tempest and to the shore of oblivion—sleep. As he tiptoed out of the apartment at nine o'clock he left a groggy, helpless wreck lying in bed exhausted, overwrought, filled still with rage and an atavistic desire for revenge.

The next afternoon I called Zsa Zsa. "I'm leaving for New York tomorrow," I said crisply. "Tell your friend Mr. Trujillo to call me at the Plaza."

She had not been too wrong about Trujillo. He was good-looking in a glossy black-haired, olive-skinned Latin way. His manners were impeccable and his admiration for me was apparent. We dined on his palatial 350-foot yacht, the *Angelica*, surrounded by the trappings of wealth that only the very richest can afford. The vast table was set with a hand-embroidered white organdy cloth; the dishes were gold, as was the flatware; the glasses at each place setting were of the most beautiful pale-amber Venetian glass; flowers were everywhere—orchids, lilies and lush tropical plants. There was caviar in profusion, vintage wines and exquisite food. It was a balmy beautiful night in Palm Beach. The moon was full and reflecting on the water which lapped gently at the boat.

Apart from a crew of about eight, not counting the band, there were a few people there—Palm Beach socialites, his equerry and some aides from the Dominican Republic. The talk was frothy— the usual jet-set chat about parties and places and people. Some of them I knew, some of them I didn't. I didn't really care. It was good once again to be in the company of a man who obviously found me thrilling and paid me lavish compliments. Your word is my command seemed to be his attitude. What a change from trying so hard to please George and not succeeding.

We had coffee and cognac on the upper deck where, on the distant shore silhouetted against the navy-blue sky, the palm trees waved lazily in the breeze and the calypso songs brought back memories of locations in the Caribbean. We danced, and I felt lightheaded, lighthearted and more than a little drunk. I had not slept the previous night—thoughts of George's impending fatherhood tormented me. I wanted to go back to the hotel at Palm

Beach and sleep for a week. I was tired and told "Ramfis" so, but he insisted that I stay the night in the luxurious stateroom that had been prepared for me.

So why not? I was young, footloose and fancy free. My love affair and my commitment to George still occupied all my thoughts but it was doomed. Why not stay the night with this attractive strange gentleman who treated me like a piece of rare crystal? I had never before slept with anyone unless totally carried away by passion or love. This time my motivation was mental and physical exhaustion, mixed with gratitude for a consolation missing from my life for months. I had been completely faithful to George for over a year, but he had not to me, so this, finally, would be how our affair would end. On a beautiful boat, on a perfect Florida night, with the son of the President of the Dominican Republic.

Autumn came to New York, and it was a frenzy. Interviews, photo sessions, press luncheons and guest shots on TV. *Stopover Tokyo* opened to mediocre-to-lousy reviews. Most of the movies I was making at Fox seemed to get poor reviews, and I would get comments like: "Joan Collins seems to be an actress with more talent than she is able to show in the purely decorative roles she has been playing."

In the half-dozen years my fledgling career had spanned, I had appeared in fifteen films, in some of which I had starred. I had worked with some fine actors and excellent directors. Basil Dearden, who directed *I Believe in You*, was noted for his down-to-earth realism and for bringing a feeling of actuality to all of his film characters. My role of Norma in *I Believe in You* was, I think, one of my better acting jobs in all my early movies. Although it was my first major role, I had yet to experience the agonizing self-consciousness that the early Hollywood years instilled in me, and because of the scruffy way Dearden wanted me to look, I didn't care about my appearance at all. In *I Believe in You* that wasn't important. I was not yet aware of how an early "leap to fame" can leave you up for grabs by every critic around, professional or amateur.

Because of my youth and inexperience, my early films were judged, and fiercely so, on my meager acting talent which, I admit, was somewhat limited then. But to have one's mistakes lambasted and criticized constantly while trying to learn one's profession under the scrutiny of Hollywood moguls, gossips and critics, could be, and *has* been, the finish of many a fledgling career. Self-consciousness is *death* for a performer, but one of the hardest things to overcome on the screen.

I was lucky enough (or stupid enough) not to let the torrent of adverse criticism affect me too deeply, when many more faint-hearted than I might have contemplated ending it all.

I plodded on, appearing in turkey after turkey, gritting my teeth and learning at least *something* from my every movie, play and TV appearance.

Sometimes it was tough to experiment, to try out new ideas as an actor, to stretch. Sometimes I tried and failed dismally, as in *The Good Die Young*. Lewis Gilbert, a fine and sensitive director, cast me wrongly, I felt, as Richard Basehart's bourgeois sweet and long-suffering wife—the archetypical girl next door role. This was not only wrong for me, as I was only nineteen, considerably younger than Basehart, but I did not have the emotional range or experience to portray the suffering the girl was meant to be feeling.

I was much better in *Our Girl Friday*—young, spoiled, rebellious and playing comedy, for which I felt I had a flair even then.

If I had to advise any young actor or actress about to embark on a career today I would strongly advocate *learning* before plunging into actual performances. Two or three years at a really good drama school is essential, I think. Studying as many great movie actors as possible during this time is a benefit that my generation was not lucky enough to have.

One can now see on TV reruns every day the movie greats of all time: Spencer Tracy, Katharine Hepburn, Barbara Stanwyck, James Cagney, John Garfield, Claudette Colbert, Humphrey Bogart, Bette Davis, Cary Grant, Henry Fonda, Joan Crawford, James Stewart, Carole Lombard . . . the list is endless. And one can learn so much from them. What an opportunity to learn from masters!

I think it is a great pity too that the repertory theater, as I knew it, is no longer with us. For an actor to play dozens of diversified roles in a season is the most wonderful training of all. I cherish the six weeks I spent at Maidstone Repertory Theatre in England during my summer vacation from RADA.

I was lucky enough to be hired at three pounds ten a week—the equivalent of fifteen dollars then—as third assistant stage manager. This was about as low on the totem pole as one could get. The job necessitated being prompter for all the six plays that were staged there, as well as learning at least four of the roles as an understudy. We did the usual repertory fare—*French Without Tears, An Ideal Husband, Private Lives*, and such. I never got to even understudy Amanda, but I have yearned to play her ever since, and one day I *will!*

I regret really that I had so much success so young, and that it all came to me with relative ease. I realize my good fortune in being able to drop out of the "stardom" race for many years, years in which I grasped the opportunity to find out what the hell I was doing actingwise, how and why, and to take stock of myself objectively both as an actress and a woman.

Of course there are so-called "natural" actors, but experience and technique are absolute necessities for sustaining a career, and one can never, ever stop learning. I love the quote by Laurence Olivier in his autobiography about the start of his career. It goes something like: "Most people become actors to express themselves. I began for the simple reason I wanted to show off!" How true in so many cases.

Land of the Pharaohs gave me my first opportunity to portray clichéd Hollywood glamour and out-and-out villainy, with which, on the screen, I was to become strongly associated. *The Bitch, The Vamp, The Sex Goddess, The Femme Fatale*—all of these labels could be used to describe many of the characters I have portrayed in the more than fifty films I have made.

Since it should, I hope, be apparent from this book that I really am none of these (although there is a part of me that *could* be), perhaps one could say that my acting teeth were sharpened on such films as *The Opposite Sex, Rally Round the Flag, Boys, Up in the Cellar, Alfie Darling, The Bawdy Adventures of Tom Jones, The Moneychangers* and, of course, *The Stud* and *The Bitch*. In all of these I played a vamp or a villainess, as I did in many TV shows.

However in the following movies I played more-or-less "nice girl" roles: *The Virgin Queen, The Girl in the Red Velvet Swing, Seawife, Island in the Sun, Stopover Tokyo, The Bravados, Seven Thieves, Esther and the King, The Road to Hong Kong, The Executioner, Quest for Love* and *The Devil Within Her*.

Alexis in "Dynasty" put the stamp firmly on my villainess image, and it's a hard one to shake. Not that, at the moment, that is my desire. In spite of all her villainy and plotting and scheming, I quite like her!

It was party time in New York. By now the New Yorkers had returned to their favorite haunts, "21," Pavillon, El Morocco and the Little Club, back from their summers in St. Tropez, the Hamptons and the Greek islands.

Around my neck I now sported a dazzling diamond necklace from Van Cleef and Arpels, a gift from Trujillo, which had arrived the day after I returned to New York from Palm Beach. It was an exquisitely beautiful choker in the shape of several flowers consisting of about twenty-five carats, and although I had tried to contact Trujillo to return it, his aides informed me he had returned to Santo Domingo and would be most offended if his "token of esteem" was returned. It would be "an insult," they informed me frostily.

When I phoned Cappy Yordan in Beverly Hills, she was horrified at the thought that I should return it, and so was Zsa Zsa. "Dollink, from him, he is so rich it is like sending a basket of flowers," she scoffed. So I kept it. If you've got it, flaunt it, was one of Cappy's philosophies. So I did.

It was the first piece of valuable jewelry I had ever received. Arthur Loew, with the family millions, had given me little gold pins and rings with a few quarter-carat diamonds strewn around, and Nicky Hilton was not noted for his largesse with women. It's a pity, I thought, that the one piece of jewelry of any value was given to me by a man with whom I had a relationship of no value to me. True, he was nice, charming and handsome, but I had no desire to see him again.

My week's whirl of publicity work ended when I was called back to Los Angeles to start another picture. Nicky Hilton, whom I had started seeing again, and Peter Theodoracopolis, another man

138

I had been dating, had almost come to blows over me one night at the Plaza, and it was time to get out of town and get down to work.

George Englund was out of my system now, I thought. But I was wrong.

One red rose and a note, "Forgive Me. G.," was delivered the day after I got home. I didn't need to know who it was from. I tried to pretend that I didn't care as I sped to the studio to fit costumes for *Rally Round the Flag, Boys* but I couldn't deny that I was exceptionally cheery and full of *joie de vivre*. Was it only because of the note?

My message service called me as I sat in consultation with Charles Le Maire, who was designing the clothes for *Rally*.

"Mr. Cunningham's called you three times today," said Teddy, at the answering service, who knew how many times I would casually ask when I checked in, "Has Mr. Cunningham called?" and how disappointed I was if the answer was negative. Mr. Cunningham was George's telephone alias.

My heart skipped a tiny beat. The mind is controllable but not the heart—mine certainly wasn't.

"If he calls again tell him I'm in wardrobe," I said, and went back to discussing the dresses with Charles, trying to concentrate. Ten minutes later George called. "Before you say anything," he said hastily, "I just want to say three things—I love you, I miss you, and how the fuck is Peter, Theodore, whatever the-fuck-his-name-is?" I giggled. I couldn't help it.

"We're just good friends," I laughed, fingering the antique diamond brooch that Peter had given me as a parting gift. Suddenly the men I met had become Santa Claus. George didn't have to beg terribly hard for me to agree to see him. He whetted my appetite by telling me he had portentous news of great benefit to both of us. But I insisted we meet at La Scala. Since I considered our affair over, what was there to hide?

"Cloris lost the baby," he said flatly. "It happened a couple of days after you went to New York. We had a lot of fights—heavy ones." He paused to sip his vodka. I hung on his words.

"We've decided to definitely get a divorce. I've consulted a lawyer and . . ." He took another sip. I leaned forward, not really believing what I was hearing.

". . . And I've moved into the Beverly Comstock, on Wilshire—
'The boulevard of broken dreams' "—he referred to the fact that
there were dozens of hotels along Wilshire in the Westwood area
where newly separated or divorced men went to sort out their lives
while their lawyers fought it out with their wives for custody of
their property, houses, Cadillacs, paintings and children. The wives
usually got it all anyway—unlike my farcical divorce settlement
with Maxwell Reed. That section of Wilshire Boulevard, which
also housed a lot of stewardesses, models and actresses, had become known as a swinging singles paradise.

"So where do I fit into all this?" I asked.

"With me you fit in, of course. I mean I love you. Do you still
love me?" My look should have told him that. "And when it's all
over maybe we can . . ." He took another drink—this seemed
hard for him to get out—but I had to hear it. "D'you fancy being
stepmother to three boys?"

It was too much to take. He had finally decided to commit himself. I was the happiest girl in the world. We ordered a bottle of
Dom Perignon to celebrate—and while we drank it he informed
me that his lawyers had advised him that he must not be seen
publicly with a woman alone—particularly me—since Cloris was
considering naming me as corespondent. In the unenlightened
days of 1958, scandal could still be ruinous to an actor's or an
actress's reputation and career. I had as much to lose as he. We
agreed on complete discretion until his divorce was final.

We started going to obscure restaurants at the beach and in
the Valley. Sometimes we would double date with Marlon Brando
and his pretty and dynamic Puerto Rican girlfriend Rita Moreno—
an actress usually typecast in "spitfire" roles, and a faithful worshipper at Marlon's shrine. She adored him, but he treated her in
a rather cavalier manner, never letting her know where she stood
in their stormy affair, which lasted on and off for eight years and
culminated in her taking a near-fatal overdose of pills. I sympa-
thized with her. Marlon, too, was having marital problems with
his estranged Indian wife, Anna Kashfi. I don't think Marlon ever
went out with a blonde—he loved exotic women. Marlon and
George were preparing to make a film together called *The Ugly*

American. I hoped that George might find a feeling of nepotism in his heart and would cast me in the role of Marlon's wife.

Alas, it was not to be. But I was finally playing a role I really liked and had fun with· witty, outrageous Angela in *Rally Round the Flag, Boys.* Fox had originally wanted Jayne Mansfield to play the sexy young vamp, living in a small town, married to a boring businessman, who tries to seduce Paul Newman away from Joanne Woodward. Joanne and Paul had insisted to director Leo McCarey that Mansfield was far too tarty and obvious for Angela, that the character should have a touch of class and an impish sense of humor, and they persuaded him to cast me. They were good friends and I appreciated their loyalty. Few actors go out of their way to try and get a role for a friend, but the Newmans have always been generous and supportive in their relationships with people they care about. The picture was a happy experience—although again, like most of my movies, neither a critical nor a financial success. Leo McCarey was a famous and beloved director who had made such films as *Going My Way* with Bing Crosby, for which he won an Oscar. But now he was old, seemingly feeble, and had lost the zest and comic flair which had flourished in the thirties. Why did I always seem to work with famed directors who were on their last legs careerwise?

My love life was lyrical now, working with the Newmans was a treat, and finally I was allowed to express my comedic talents, which had been lying dormant since *Skin of Our Teeth.* Critically this turned out to be my most favorable film. I received excellent reviews, expressing surprise an attractive woman should be funny too. I was able to be inventive in ways I had not been allowed before. The laughing scene, where Paul and I get drunk together while I try to teach him how to do the cha-cha, had some hysterically funny moments. We had to laugh all day—take after take—from dawn till dusk. Mascara ran endlessly down my cheeks, and it got so that just the sight of each other would set us off. "Angela—I'd know that face anywhere," groaned Paul between gasps of laughter as he came face to face with my rear end. I was doubled over on the floor, gasping for air, and when he said the line I deflated like a balloon and fell flat on my face. Another cut, and

Paul was swinging literally from the chandelier back and forth while I hung onto a pillar for support, weak from laughing. We became so carried away that we couldn't stop even when we sat on canvas chairs between takes and tried to be coherent. It was catching. The crew were laughing helplessly too. Everyone was having a wonderful time. Pity it didn't work that well on the CinemaScope screen.

In the five and a half years I was contracted to Fox, and in fact for several years before and after my tenure there, their record at the box office was appalling. And artistically it was even worse. The studio that had turned out such hits as *Gentleman's Agreement, Grapes of Wrath, Razor's Edge* and *Letter to Three Wives* now turned out things like *The Girl Can't Help It*, with Jayne Mansfield, and *How to Be Very, Very Popular* with Sheree North. Depressing. Especially for the stockholders. Zanuck was less and less involved in the everyday production. Buddy Adler was head of the studio now, and everything he did turned to dross. At this time the studio was deciding to make an expensive blockbuster—*Cleopatra*, the story of the *femme fatale* of all time. In first position for the role of the fascinating Serpent of the Nile was the contender from Great Britain—the "pouting panther" herself—J. Collins. However, the studio, and Walter Wanger, the producer, would not accept me as I was. Grooming had to take place. I had to learn to walk and talk and move like an Egyptian queen. Specialists in the art of walking and deportment (what have I been doing so wrong all these years, pray?) were called in to turn this sow's ear into a silk purse. My body must be slimmed down. At one hundred and twenty pounds I was too curvy for Cleo, so they told me.

I dieted; I exercised; I sat for hours in the makeup and hairdressing rooms while makeup man Whitney Snyder applied unusual and elaborate designs on my face. "I know she had slanted eyes but this is *ridiculous*." I gazed into a pair of astonished green eyes outlined from nose to temple in black and purple eyeliner; silver sequins outlined the liner, and a glistening blue-black wig cascaded to my shoulders. No less astounding was my costume for the test I was about to make.

A pleated toga of pale violet chiffon stopped at thigh level.

Silver sandals laced to the knee—causing me to worry about early varicose veins. A teeny weeny silver bikini bra from which hung baubles, bangles and bric-a-brac of various hues of purple and silver. A giant collar of amethyst and silver inhibited my vocal cords and made moving my head an effort. Immense silver earrings jangled to and fro and constantly tangled themselves in the wig.

The costume was finished off with arm bracelets from wrist to elbow of sturdy sterling silver, nine or ten large rings all representing snakes, and a billowing cloak of purple velvet and silver lamé. This was attached to the giant collar and was so long that if I misjudged my step I would trip and almost strangle myself. In this sensuous, enticing gear I hobbled to Stage 16 to try and act some of the most appalling dialogue ever written opposite an actor who, though obviously chosen for his looks and virility, had as much acting talent as Minnie Mouse—maybe less.

I tried hard. Walter Wanger and Co. persevered. If the first test wasn't too good, maybe it was because the costuming was wrong. Test again—and we did. Three tests, in three outrageous outfits, I made for the coveted role. How I ached to play her. Shaw's Cleopatra had been my test piece for the RADA entrance exam and I knew it was a role suited to me. Naturally they were considering other actresses too, and naturally eventually the casting couch reared its all too ugly head. Spyros Skouras, an elderly Greek gentleman, was the chairman of the board of directors at Fox. He had much to say about the casting of Cleo and he said it. To me and often. Phone calls, suggestions and skittish forays around his desk. He should know better, I thought, as I skipped out of his clutches. He's old enough to be my grandpa.

But with typical Greek tenacity he continued his entreaties and persuasions. An eye for an eye, a tooth for a tooth—a screw for a part. No thank you very much, Mr. Grandfatherly Greek—I have my hands full at home. I tried to be as graceful about it as I could in the circumstances. Greeks don't take kindly to rejection, but he still persisted in calling me often to tell me what a terrible career mistake I was making by my unreceptiveness toward him.

This did not help my relationship with George, who now spent several nights a week at my apartment, considered me his prop-

erty, and heard the phone conversations. He became enraged at
the ancient Greek's audacity. Stupidly I had told him about the
young Greek, Peter, and endured several hours of tongue lashing.
I had hidden the little diamond anchor he'd given me, and when
Peter came out for a visit I hastily sent him back to jet-set land.
But George's jealousy was boundless. Too broad a smile at the
delivery boy and his dander was up, and off he went again: "Why
did you . . . ?" "How could you . . . ?" "Why can't you . . . ?"
I knew his dialogue inside out and it was making me a nervous
wreck. I started to get occasional attacks of hives, especially after
I ate lobster or shrimp. After several tests my doctor discovered I
was allergic to shellfish and must stop eating it completely. Quite
a blow. I liked it, but my reactions had been getting worse each
time I ate it, and Doctor Sellars had warned me that these allergies
could become dangerous.

At the end of the shooting of *Rally Round the Flag, Boys* I
gave a small dinner party. Although I went to many parties I was
not accustomed to giving them. Most of the people who crowded
into my tiny and modest apartment were, I thought, used to a
more lavish setting for their revels. I fluttered insecurely around
trying to be the perfect hostess to people like Milton Berle, Paul
Newman, Joanne Woodward, Sammy Davis, Stanley and Marion
Donen and about twenty others, and imbibing quite a lot of
wine.

La Scala was doing the catering, and I had chosen the menu
with care. But not quite enough thought had gone into my choice.
After a heaping plate of cioppino I started to feel my cheeks flaming
and large welts appeared on my neck and shoulders. "Gosh, you
look like a suet pudding!" laughed one of my English girlfriends.
I rushed to the bathroom mirror and saw a flushed and swollen
face and startled green eyes set in a sea of broken red capillaries
and puffed-up eyelids. Dr. Sellars had told me to call him at any
hour if this allergy came upon me. The hour had come. I leaped
to the phone in the bedroom. Sammy Davis was on it talking
earnestly with his hand over his ear to shut out the babble of
voices around him. "Kim, baby, you know I care—I don't give a
damn what the papers say, baby . . ." I interrupted him in mid-

Kim. "Sam—I've *got* to use the phone—please." He didn't hear my frenzied plea and continued his soliloquy . . . "Of course not, baby—how can that bastard Harry push you around like that? . . ."

"Sammy, *please!*" He looked up and gasped, "What happened to your face?" I grabbed the phone from him, yelled a breathless "Sorry, Kim!" and dialed Al Sellars. A group of concerned on-lookers had gathered to observe my transformation from dazzling hostess to Dracula. I felt hives swelling like tomatoes all over my face as I breathlessly explained to Sellars my predicament. "Get over here immediately," he said authoritatively.

"I'll drive you," said an anxious Stanley Donen. "Quickly!" I yelped, my desire to escape from my own party and the anxious stares of the guests uppermost in my mind. I grabbed a scarf and we rushed down the stairs, my breathing already starting to feel strange and forced.

Stanley drove fast and erratically through semi-deserted Sunset Boulevard. My face felt as if it was being blown up by a bicycle pump. I shot a feverish glance into the rear-view mirror. "Oh, my God! Stanley, don't look at me!" I threw the scarf over what was the most grotesque sight I had ever seen. My face had become the size of a football, and it was getting bigger by the second, and turning purplish red. My eyes were disappearing into the rapidly swelling surrounding tissue. My lips were bananas, so thick I couldn't talk, and worst of all, I realized that I could not get enough air into my throat to breathe properly. It too was swelling rapidly. I was choking for breath.

"Jesus H. Christ!" Stanley's look of frozen horror and his sudden acceleration to one hundred miles an hour and through all the red lights was proof enough of my plight. I couldn't speak—I could hardly breathe. I lay back with the scarf over my face so no one could glimpse this horror, and realized I was probably dying.

"I'm dying . . ." I gasped.

"You'll make it, kid—you'll make it." Stanley's desperate voice was reassuring, but his face, a study in paralyzed fear, was not. At the same time as I was facing death, the little voice in the back of my head was telling me to keep the scarf over my head so no one would have to see how hideous I had become. "Live fast, die

young and have a good-looking corpse." It was a Bogart line from
Knock on Any Door. I had done the first, was about to do the second, but the last was by now far beyond me.

I hope they cremate me before anyone can see what I look like,
I thought hazily and then fainted, right into the loving arms of
the most beautiful sight I'd ever seen—a nurse. As I was wheeled
through the corridor—yes, the wheelchair had been waiting, too—
Sellars pumped an injection into my arm and I heard through a
haze his Dr. Kildare voice saying ". . . Probably have to give her
a tracheotomy." That's all I need, I thought. A tube through my
throat. That should photograph attractively—if I live to ever appear on the silver screen again.

The prognosis seemed unlikely. My face was like a revolting barrage balloon floating above me, alien from my body, which felt
like ten thousand mosquitoes had just lunched on it. As I was propelled through the hygienic corridors of the Roxbury Medical Center a few passers-by observed this pathetic creature obviously in
final death throes and her entourage. A solicitous nurse pumping
adrenalin into her arm, calm yet concerned doctor taking her
pulse, a frantic-looking tousle-haired film director, and the creature
herself, oblivious to her imminent death, concerned only with
keeping her ghastly visage far from the madding crowd.

Magically, my body responded instantly to the adrenalin injection the nurse had administered in the lobby. By the time we
reached the doctor's office, I could at least breathe a little easier
and the dirigible that used to be my face was deflating slightly.

Death did not claim this young victim just yet. My astrologer
had told me that I would always "be saved at the eleventh hour,"
whether from financial ruin, certain death or bad emotional involvements. I was just happy to get my face back. Stanley Donen
couldn't get over the fact that at death's door my main concern
had been that I should not let anyone see my ugliness. Such is the
vanity and insecurity of a young actress under contract to a studio
whose entire emphasis throughout her working day is placed on
the illusion of retaining perfection of face and body at all times. I
couldn't let myself look awful in front of somebody else, even if I
was at death's door.

· · ·

George came back from his nineteenth trip to the Orient, location scouting, and we rather daringly decided to attend a large industry party together.

In the beautiful private room upstairs at Romanoff's all was glitter, glamour and glib talk. *Le tout* Hollywood was there. Everyone from Buddy Adler to Darryl F. Zanuck had put on his best bib and tucker and—to hell with early calls—decided to party.

I wore the Trujillo necklace. It looked divine with the white strapless silk dress and diamond earrings, which I had bought myself from my *Island in the Sun* expense money while in London. Clever kid, living at home and not having to pay those hotel bills. Much smarter to blow the money at Cartier than the Connaught.

George and I made an attractive couple, and by now several people at the party knew of our relationship. I was so happy to be out with him, to feel as though we belonged together. Soon—he had assured me only yesterday—we would be married, a thought too exciting to contemplate without chills running up and down my spine. It was a delicious evening. To be out with the man I loved, publicly for once, to be able to dance with him, touch him, look into his eyes, talk to him and not have to pretend to be enjoying the company of someone else.

"Is that the necklace Trujillo gave you?" I couldn't believe my ears. One of my girlfriends, the only one other than Zsa Zsa and Cappy who knew of it, had plopped herself down next to us as George and I were having a tête-à-tête on a banquette. She was somewhat the worse for wine.

"N–n–no—it's wardrobe," I stammered, noticing out of the corner of my eye George's nostrils flare suspiciously.

"It looks *just* like the one you described to me," she tattled on, squinting close to get a good look.

"Mmm—yes, well they really are doing good things with costume jewelry these days, aren't they?" Her husband mercifully appeared to whisk her onto the dance floor, and I turned, flushing hotly, face to face with George's angry brown eyes.

"Trujillo?" His questioning and menacing tone sent shivers down my spine of a different kind from those I was experiencing only a few minutes ago.

"Trujillo who, may I ask?" His tone became even more menacing and his hand, which had been gently on my knee, now turned into a vice. There was no possible denial—my flaming cheeks and blazing diamonds were proof enough. I was undone, unfaithful to my unfaithful lover—bad, bad girl. I falteringly, stammeringly, haltingly told him all. He extracted every detail from me, his face a mask of rage which he was trying extremely hard and unsuccessfully to control. My tactless friend had realized her *faux pas* and was grimacing "I'm sorrys" at me across the room. By now the nearest onlookers were riveted to our obvious discussion.

"Slut," he whispered savagely into my ear. "You're worse than a street-corner harlot." His fingers gripped my knee even harder and I winced, tears of pain and humiliation squeezing themselves from under my carefully painted eyelids and making little gray streams down pink cheeks. With an uncontrollable epithet bursting from his lips, he ripped the necklace from around my throat and flung it savagely across the room, to the astonishment of several observant ladies to whom diamonds have always been a girl's best friend. And he was off and away, leaving me to grovel for the broken baubles on hands and knees in front of *tout* Hollywood.

A few girlfriends joined in the hunt for those tiny carats—so precious and so useless—but which certain women could not do without. I was not joining their ranks. The insurance alone on this bauble was preposterous, and George's attitude and my humiliation did not seem enough of a price to pay for the privilege of parading this bit of chemical junk around the "A" party circuit. I knew a lot of the older wives of men in the business—producers, directors and executives—did not approve of me. They felt I was a threat to them because of my so-called "loose" morals. Because, strangely enough, with the paradoxical double standard of the day it was considered "OK" for a girl to sleep around with casting directors, producers, agents, to get on and up the ladder. But going to bed with men because it was enjoyable branded one as cheap and frivolous. So, no doubt, some of those ladies contemplating this sad little scene at Romanoff's restaurant were smugly thinking that I was getting what I deserved. Having an affair with a married man, indeed. Serves her right.

We stayed until two-thirty piecing together the bits of necklace on a table like some glittering jigsaw puzzle. It had shattered into

about a hundred and fifty pieces—but none of the diamonds themselves were lost, and although the necklace was in pieces it was
not irreparable. The waiters joined the treasure hunt and finally
we retrieved it all. "Into the vault with this as soon as it's fixed," I
said grimly. "It's more trouble than it's worth."

George and I made up, of course. It seemed half of our relationship was making up. We both apologized. He for making a nasty
spectacle of me, I for being a faithless sex fiend when his wife was
pregnant. For a few weeks all was sweetness and light until suddenly the papers got the goods on Trujillo.

"Gifts for the Girls" screamed the tabloid headlines. "Diamonds for Kim Novak and Joan Collins," yelled the tabloids.
" 'Say it again and I'll sue,' " said Zsa Zsa. The yellow presses were
running at full speed to print startling and colorful stories of sex,
sin and costly baubles in Hollywood.

It started when Congress, while voting on foreign aid to the
Dominican Republic, was asked by a Congressman if the Republic
really *needed* help. It had been discovered that the young Trujillo,
with a wife and six children, appeared to have lined his pockets
with over six million dollars which could only have come from
American aid, and had proceeded to lavish gifts on various well-
known film actresses. The catalogue was impressive. To Zsa Zsa
Gabor: 1 Empress Chinchilla Coat—value $8,500; 1 Mercedes-
Benz—value $5,500. To Kim Novak (whom he now professed to
love and hoped to marry in spite of the six children): 1 diamond-
and-pearl ring—value $3,500; 1 pair of diamond earrings—value
$1,500; 1 Mercedes-Benz (he obviously liked that car)—$8,500.
And—in spite of some weak "No comment" and halfhearted de-
nials to the press—Collins finally admitted all: 1 diamond necklace—value $10,000.

Zsa Zsa sprang fiercely to Trujillo's defense, and even more
fiercely to her own when the Congressman accused her of being
"the most expensive courtesan since Madame de Pompadour." Zsa
Zsa with her typical Hungarian wit countered: "I was born in the
wrong century—I would have made a bum of Madame de Pompadour." One up to Hungary.

Miss Novak also jumped to his defense. Photos of their hand-
holding had been appearing in the tabloids. "He is a wonderful

gentleman and an honor to his great father who is doing a world of good for his country. He is a real goodwill ambassador." So much for Poland.

The British contingent, after grudgingly admitting the existence of the trinket, categorically refused to discuss the man and his affairs at all. I desperately wanted my name out of the headlines, and revealing nothing was the surest way of achieving that.

But the publicity rekindled George's anger and jealousy. There were more scenes, more tears, more making up. I started getting minor allergic reactions again. "It's nervous tension," said my doctor. "Get out of town for a while until this blows over."

I went to New York to do the Steve Allen television show. Walking down Madison Avenue one fine afternoon I stumbled upon an intriguing shop. "Jolie Gabor Jeweler" it was called.

The boutique was filled to overflowing with authentic-looking jewelry. The jewels were in fact paste—glass and rhinestones, but so cleverly designed that they looked like the most expensive diamonds, emeralds, pearls and rubies. The shop had many photographs of the three Gabor girls and Mama, looking delicious and wearing Jolie's jewelry creations, which she designed herself. Madame Gabor, Senior, was there that afternoon in person. A vision in pale beige crepe and pearls, smelling wonderful and looking like a younger, more glamorous Barbara Cartland. By contrast, in my gray pleated skirt, loafers and black polo-neck sweater I looked like a college girl.

Madame Gabor obviously didn't think someone dressed as I was would do anything more than browse, so when I pointed to a "diamond" necklace in one of the showcases, she showed it to me with a marked lack of enthusiasm.

"For your mother, dear?" she inquired in her Zsa Zsa-like husky Hungarian voice.

"No, for me," I said excitedly examining the necklace. It was incredible. It was practically identical to the one Trujillo had given me. An idea had formulated in my mind.

"How much is this?"

"One hundred and twenty-five dollars," said Madame Gabor, quite surprised to see this student type willing to pay that much for something that would be out of place at Vassar. Without makeup and simply dressed, I could easily pass for seventeen or eighteen.

"I'm a friend of your daughter's," I explained as I scribbled the check and showed her my I.D.

"Ah, of course!" She smiled, no longer surprised. With Zsa Zsa anything was possible, and who knew what possibilities lay behind my baggy clothes and innocent face?

"I wish you much success with it, dollink," she said, giving me the package. "It vil look vunderful on you. With the right outfit, of course," she added hastily.

"Thank you, Madame," I trilled, tripping into the Madison Avenue sunshine. George had a surprise in store for him.

We had a romantic candlelit dinner *à deux* at a cozy bistro on the beach at Malibu. It was a perfect California night—a little chilly, but the moon was a miniature crescent, the sea dark and calm, and the beach pebbles crushed softly beneath our feet as we walked hand in hand along the shore. I had drunk a bottle of Liebfraumilch singlehandedly and was feeling rather giddy. We were celebrating our first anniversary of on-and-off togetherness. Ups and downs seemed to be my destiny and I was adapting to them like a trouper. He wasn't an easy man. Fascinating yes, witty and good-looking certainly, but his tempers, his jealousy and his ambivalent attitude toward his divorce proceedings did not make me feel secure. I *still* never knew where I really stood with him. I was about to play a trump card.

"Darling," I cooed, "I know how upset you have been about the diamond necklace." I put my fingers to his mouth to stop his retort. "No, don't say anything, darling. I realize it was an idiotic thing to do, to accept a gift from someone I had—er—hardly known." Again he started to speak but I stopped him. "So, because I love you so much, I'm going to do something that I hope will stop us from bringing this subject up *ever* again."

I brought out the necklace from my bag. The diamonds glittered in the moonlight and I dangled them in front of his eyes. "George, my darling, look, your love means more to me than all the diamond necklaces in the world—" and with that I hurled Jolie Gabor's $125 masterpiece into the waves, where it sank instantly.

He looked at me in stunned amazement. "Jesus, babe, you just threw ten thousand dollars to the sharks."

"I know," I said softly and serenely. "Oscar time," said my inner voice. "Because I love you so much I don't want anything like this to ever come between us again."

He seemed truly moved by this noble gesture and gathered me into a passionate embrace. I felt it was a devious and underhand ploy—one I was not proud of—but I hoped that this would close the Trujillo chapter forever.

It did. But when, a week later, I found him locked in another passionate embrace in a car on Beverly Drive, with the blond wife of one of TV's handsomest Italian singers, I knew that I was dicing with disaster.

I walked into his office the next day, unannounced, and confronted him. He denied it. He was a brilliant liar (I'd heard him with his wife), and he almost convinced me. But not quite. I called the singer's wife in Palm Springs: "You're playing it too close to home, my dear," I said icily. "Lay off George Englund or I'll tell your husband, I swear I will." She spluttered and cried and finally admitted it was true, and I hung up, disgusted. Was I becoming a hard, bitter bitch? Or were circumstances just ganging up on me to turn me into one?

The phone rang. My agent.

"Can you ride a horse?" he inquired.

"Of course not," I replied warily. "They scare me to death."

"You'll have to learn then," he said. "You've been cast opposite Peck in a Western to shoot in two weeks' time in Mexico. Get your ass down to the Fox ranch in Santa Monica tomorrow morning at nine o'clock. You leave for Mexico in ten days so you'd better learn fast."

"But I'm *terrified* of horses," I bleated piteously. "What happens if I can't learn to ride?"

"You'll go on suspension again, and I know you can't afford that," he said crisply. "Get it together, kid." And he hung up.

I lay back on the bed and gazed at the California "cottage-cheese"-style ceiling, a fixture in most West Hollywood apartments. A Western! Me! The British Bombshell in the saddle—

what a joke. But at least it would get me out of town, and away from him. He had a hold on me like Svengali had on Trilby. I knew it, I hated it and loved it: Was I becoming a total masochist? My analyst assured me I was still looking to conquer Daddy and that the George and Cloris situation represented this, but I felt that there was more in it than that. George's attraction was so strong that I knew it couldn't just be a father fascination. When things were going well with us I felt so completely *right* with him, infinitely more than I had ever felt with anyone else before. It was total "oneness." The kind I never could believe existed.

I believe that loving someone, whether it be a lover, parent or friend, is accepting them for the way they really are and not trying to change or shape them into a behavior image of what *you* want them to be. Loving is being happy that the other person is doing something that is making him happy, even if it means that you cannot always be together. Therefore I let George do whatever he wanted. He was still so full of doubts and guilt about his divorce—fine, I would understand and try and help him, support him, and not make him feel more guilt-ridden by bringing *our* relationship problems into an already difficult situation. He felt a need to see other women occasionally because he'd been trapped in his marriage for so long and had gone straight from that into an affair with me, with never a chance to look around to see where the action was—well, that was a harder pill to swallow, but I understood that too. I tried like hell to understand, because I loved him so much that that was all that mattered. My own pride and self-confidence was on the wane. Being an understanding mistress to a mixed-up and often thoughtless lover was taking its toll. But I was resilient, persistent and tough, and I hung on in. Looking back, he obviously didn't love me enough. But I loved him too much to give him up.

On the occasions that we have bumped into each other throughout the years, he has always been enormously flattering and ruefully reflective about the fact that "if only" I had been more patient and understanding we would have ended up together. I wonder. There is a limit to anyone's patience and understanding.

• • •

153

Brooding endlessly about my romantic problems, my rear end hurting violently from two weeks of riding practice, I flew to a primitive little village on the outskirts of Morelia in Mexico for *The Bravados*. On location again. My God, did I ever seem to spend more than two or three months in one place without whisking off to foreign parts? My astrologer Ben Gary's words about my gypsy life came back again as I looked around the dank and insect-ridden little adobe hut that was to be my home for the next seven weeks.

The Bravados had a good script, a fairly good director, blustering, blunt Henry King, and an excellent cast: Gregory Peck, Henry Silva, Stephen Boyd, Albert Salmi and Lee Van Cleef. However, I was not cast to advantage as an arrogant, tough, hard-riding American ranch owner. I was meant to look as if I'd been born in the saddle and as though I and the horse were bonded to each other. Instead I felt I looked out of place and awkward, and I certainly did.

I had dutifully spent every morning for the past two weeks in comfortable jeans and T-shirt riding, with Henry, Albert and Stephen, stiffly round and round the Fox ranch on a docile nag called Dulcie, who had a temperament like an old shoe, and whose age seemed to put her in the running for the glue factory. Now, dressed in stiff black jodhpurs, narrow boots constricting my feet so that all circulation immediately left my toes, a ruffled white shirt, black gauntlet gloves and a black Stetson slanted sharply over my eyes (over a heavy wig of course), I was shown the horse I would ride in the picture. Imagine a diesel engine attached to a dragon, and that was Pancho. A black stallion, in his prime. Glossy, glistening, beautiful and *dangerous!* I could feel his animal energy palpitating beneath me as four husky handlers forced me protestingly into the saddle.

Pancho, of course, knew I was nervous. Scared shitless was more like it. I leaned over and patted his nose tentatively to let him know I cared. I offered him two large lumps of sugar. He practically took off my hand. I wrenched it back, startled. He was snorting and tossing his great black mane. His hooves were doing a tap dance on the grass. This baby wanted to *go*. He was about to show this crew of strange people lolling about moving arc lamps and cameras who was the boss. I already knew. I leaned over and whispered to the handlers and my riding instructor to stay nearby at all times. Pancho pricked up his ears, half turned his head and neighed jeeringly. He had heard me. I swear that horse *knew* how scared I was.

"Nothing to worry about, honey." My tough, tobacco-chewing teacher, fifty years in the saddle, patted the horse's rump and gave me a reassuring wink. "It's safe as houses if you'll just *relax*—I told you a thousand times. *Relax*, honey, Pancho can feel your tension."

"Please stay near me, *all* of you, until Henry calls 'Action,' " I hissed to the four laconic, weathered old ranch hands, all highly amused by this nervous English lass sitting petrified in the saddle of Mexico's wickedest horse.

As shooting progressed, Pancho and I became even less close. As soon as he sensed me in the vicinity he reared up. His eyes rolled around in his head, and he bared his yellow teeth in a sadistic smile to welcome me to his back. I had begged for a double for the long shots, and finally Henry King, a stickler for realism and a man who couldn't fathom how anyone couldn't *adore* horses, let alone be frightened of them, had grudgingly agreed. However, I think his motives were more for artistic than altruistic reasons. I had put on about ten pounds in two weeks. A mixture of terror and boredom had driven me into the arms of the great pacifier Food! Every night the hotel served pecan pie, my favorite dish. Every night I would persuade the jovial Mexican cook, who loved my appreciation of his food, to give me the left-over pies. I took them to my lonely prefabricated, Holiday Inn-Mexican-style hotel room with the single fifteen-watt light bulb, put on the record player and gorged. To the sentimental ballads of Sinatra, Tony Bennett and Johnny Mathis I devoured slice after slice of pie until, like some early Roman glutton, I fell into an exhausted nightmare sleep, filled with grinningly ghoulish red-eyed fearsome horses, ready to eat me along with their bale of hay. The next morning I'd stuff what remained of the pie in my bag with the script and finish it off as a little midmorning snack. After ten days of this gluttony, the wardrobe woman unsuccessfully tried to zip me into the pants which, tight before, now fitted like a sausage skin. This necessitated her constantly having to reinforce the splitting seams. She asked me if I was pregnant! I wasn't, but looking at my once slim waist, which had gone from twenty-two to twenty-seven inches in less than a fortnight, I could see where she and the rest of the crew might imagine I was three months gone. Round, chubby cheeks hid my once photogenic cheekbones, and my bosoms could rival Mansfield's.

My midnight feasts did not go unnoticed. The director decided to use my riding double as often as possible, hoping that this would relax me and keep me away from pecan pie. They even got a double for Pancho! As though to prove me right about horses being dangerous, and out of pique at having been thwarted of his fun every morning by terrifying me when I mounted him, Pancho, in retaliation, kicked up his heels one day at my riding instructor. He broke the poor man's ankle in three places, and from then on everyone had a healthy respect for this noble, cunning beast.

I gave up pecan pie and started playing cards at night, and developed a sudden newfound equestrian skill in the saddle of my friendlier new horse, Adonis. I started to do most of the riding myself. Gregory Peck and I had a scene where we had been riding together for three days searching for a kidnapped girl. The hairdresser insisted on setting my wig each night till it was pin-curl perfect, and then glumly watched me as I pushed dirt and twigs through it and messed it up as much as I could. I rubbed mud and dirt in my face and scrubbed off as much globby makeup as I could. "That girl's going to ruin her career," said the hairdresser bitterly to the makeup artiste, as she watched her attractive hairstyle being destroyed. I tore bits and strands out to look as though I'd really been riding for three days. I still looked like a Hollywood actress sitting fully made up on a prop horse, with tight jodhpurs and a wig. Realism was an unfashionable word in 1959. Actresses were supposed to be goddesses. Untouchable. Plastic. As pristine as a box of candy. I'm sure that the public's notion of beautiful movie stars who can't act is partly the result of overzealousness on the part of the costumer, hairdresser and makeup department. Everyone looked like a store-window mannequin. I managed in

The Bravados to look fairly unpresentable, but by today's movie standards I was still ridiculously well groomed.

I had not exchanged many words with Gregory Peck until we came to the scene where he and I ride together fast and expertly for days. He was quite shy and did not socialize with the cast, spending his time with Veronique, his attractive French wife. The cast and I were in awe of him. He was a very big star and seemed rather austere, aloof and uninterested in the rest of us.

He was a wonderful-looking man, tall and rangy, with a classically handsome profile and a strongly carved nose. His aloofness, I found out when we rode for so long, was a form of shyness. He was basically not at ease around new people. I found he had a wonderful sense of humor, and, knowing my fear of riding, he was considerate toward me. But on the last day he teased me unmercifully by riding so fast that I was sore for a week. "Come on, Collins!" he yelled as we cantered faster and faster beside a deep canyon that I knew with a sickening lurch meant plunging to certain death if Adonis placed a hoof wrong. "They say you English women can ride," Peck said mock-scornfully, digging his spurs in and making his mount fly even faster. "Let's see you show 'em *all*, Collins—show 'em you're a real horsewoman, will you?" He galloped even faster. The wind almost took off my Stetson and I jammed it down like Greg's until it covered my eyes. It was enormously exhilarating. I felt in command of that three hundred pounds of sinew and muscle beneath me; I wasn't afraid at all, in fact it was a wonderful, free and joyous feeling I had of space, power and purity.

The camera car was hard put to keep up with us. They hadn't expected Greg to gallop so fast, and even less expected that I would be right alongside him, urging my horse to ever greater speed. Even when Henry yelled "Cut," we continued galloping faster and faster into the distance. I was laughing now and so was Greg, as we heard the assistant director plaintively calling us back to our positions. We reined in the horses. I amazed myself with my newfound expertise and galloped back.

"Thank you, Greg," I yelled over my shoulder. Now I was outracing him!

157

"For what?" he called back.

"For curing me of my fear of horses—you really did it. I'm not scared anymore."

"Don't mention it, ma'am." He smiled gallantly.

I am still not an enthusiast about horses but thanks to Gregory Peck I can at least get on one now without becoming a nervous wreck.

The Hollywood pinup factory ground out hundreds of shots like this. Here is my "pouting panther" look, usually achieved because I was bored stiff.

My first Hollywood movie, *The Virgin Queen*. I was not Bette Davis' favorite lady-in-waiting.

Party time in Hollywood with Arthur Loew, Jr. For some reason, Errol Flynn is pretending to be a dog.

With *The Girl in the Red Velvet Swing*, 20th Century–Fox launched me in a blaze of publicity that culminated in this *Life* cover.

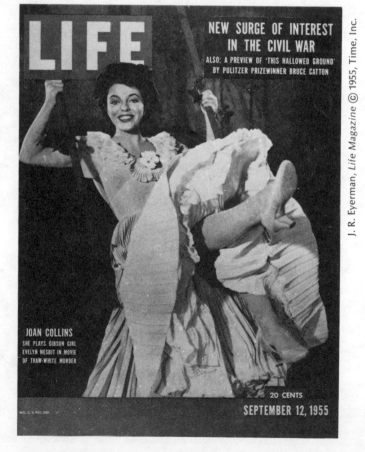

Loaned out to MGM for *The Opposite Sex*, I had my first "grown-up" role. I played an utter bitch, ironically called Crystal.

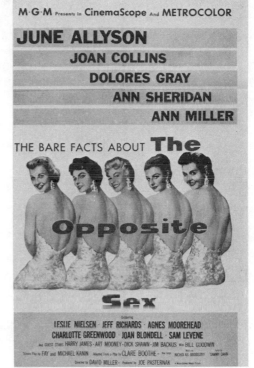

Oh, the agony of sitting in this bubble bath for three days. Particularly when served with divorce papers and demand for alimony while in it.

My sister Jackie came with me to Santa Monica Court when I got my final decree from Maxwell Reed.

Playing a novice nun wrecked on a desert island with Richard Burton in *Seawife*. We weren't allowed to kiss in the movie. Fox allowed this symbolic palm tree as a substitute.

In Barbados with the splendid Harry Belafonte for *Island in the Sun*.

Trying to remain cool for a close-up while three handlers hold the horse for *The Bravados*. I was meant to look as if I'd been born in the saddle, but I didn't succeed.

This is from a "wallpaper role" in *Stopover Tokyo* with Robert Wagner. The picture was so bad we dubbed it "Stop Overacting."

As the sluttish alcoholic wife in Steinbeck's *The Wayward Bus* I got some excellent reviews. Many people were amazed that I could act!

20th Century–Fox

Pictorial Parade

With Marlon Brando at a New York opening. My real romance was cropped from the photo and the gossip columns revealed Brando and me as a "new twosome."

UPI

Nobody did it better than Candy Barr. The strip routine she taught me for *Seven Thieves* was so hot that most of it was censored from the film.

The laughing, dancing drunken scene from *Rally Round the Flag, Boys* was Paul Newman's first, and I believe *last*, attempt at hoofing.

Official engagement photo, 1961. We both look wary.

Playing poker with Vivien Leigh and Warren while visiting him on the set in Rome for *The Roman Spring of Mrs. Stone*. Miss Leigh's flirtatious glances at him were not unnoticed by me.

From the last of the "Road" films, *The Road to Hong Kong*. I was Dorothy Lamour's new replacement. With Bing and Bob, it was business as usual.

Leaving the hospital in New York with Anthony Newley and our gorgeous brand-new son, Sacha.

CHAPTER

Seven

I SAT IN LA SCALA WITH BARBARA
and Mort Viner, feeling despondent. My relationship with George
had been dragging on for over a year. In spite of six or seven
separations, he had eventually always returned to Cloris. He was
separated from her now and had promised me that when he returned from the Orient he would definitely divorce her. I felt
cynical about it. My love had turned to resignation. There were
so many obstacles to overcome; nothing ever seemed to go the
way George said it would.

I had been in trouble with Fox several times in the past year
for turning down scripts that I thought were wrong for me, and I
had gone on suspension. I had spent the early part of 1959 exten-
sively preparing to play Cleopatra, but in spite of several tests I
wasn't holding much hope for it now. I was drowning my sorrows
in Chianti and cannelloni when I became aware of a young man
staring at me from the opposite table.

I returned his gaze, which was becoming rather bold. He raised
his glass and smiled. I looked away. Flirting with attractive
strangers in restaurants can get one into trouble, and I had other
things on my mind. I couldn't resist another look when Barbara
said, "That boy who's looking at you is Shirley MacLaine's brother,
Warren something or other." I looked over and studied him co-
vertly. He was about twenty-one or twenty-two. Blondish slightly
curly hair, worn rather longer than was fashionable, a square-cut
Clark Kent type of jaw with a Kirk Douglas dimple in the chin—

159

rather small greenish eyes, but a cute turned-up nose and a sensual mouth. From where I sat it looked as though he suffered from a problem I had once had—*spots!* He wore a blue Brooks Brothers shirt and a tweed jacket. All in all, he looked rather appealing and vulnerable, and my interest was somewhat piqued.

"Who's the girl he's with?" I asked Mort, who knew everyone. "Henry Fonda's daughter, Jane," he said. "She's out here to make some basketball picture with Tony Perkins. It's her first movie." "Are they an item?" I asked casually, sipping my drink. Mort looked at me, amused. "Interested, are you?" "Oh, Mort, really, can't I even ask about somebody without the world thinking I fancy them?"

I had only to look at a man these days and people would start surmising I was having a flirt. Because of my secret affair I had been dating a lot, and the gossip columns were full of my supposed "latest loves." What they didn't know was that my dates were a cover-up.

"She's quite pretty," I said taking a look at Jane. "A bit full in the face. I wonder how she'll photograph." "They're working on her cheekbones," said Barbara. "She goes to that woman in the Valley, she does wonders with problem areas." I looked at Jane Fonda. She was pretty in a fresh, scrubbed, wholesome way, and she had long, fair, thick hair. She bore a strong resemblance to her father, Henry. She was hanging onto Warren's every word. They made the perfect all-American couple. I turned back to my cannelloni and continued talking about other things. Out of the corner of my eye I saw Warren looking me over occasionally, but I didn't return his glances.

I thought nothing more of Mr. Beatty. I was busy rehearsing every day at Fox with Candy Barr. I was playing a stripper in *Seven Thieves* and I was lucky enough to have Candy, who was about the best stripper in America, as my teacher. For two or three hours every day she taught me how to move and dance, bump and grind, and strip. How to peel off my gloves, dress and stockings in the most provocative and sexy manner. How to turn men on in an overt and truly sensual fashion. She taught me more about sensuality than I had learned in all my years under contract. Candy was a down-to-earth girl with an incredibly gorgeous body and an angelic face. She had recently been sentenced to a long jail term for possession of a tiny amount of marijuana. From her ebullient attitude one would never guess this was hanging over her. She was amusing and gay and we had great fun together choreographing my sensuous stripteases.

Needless to say, Stage 6 at Fox, where we rehearsed, suddenly became the most popular spot on the Fox lot. It was amazing how many agents, writers, producers and crew members used Stage 6 as a shortcut to Stage 5 or Stage 4, or even the commissary. They would linger and watch while Candy put me through my paces. Actually we rather enjoyed getting an honest audience reaction, and the guys were certainly appreciative. But she was a hard taskmaster, so when John Foreman called and asked me to a party at Debbie Power's house, I tried to beg off, exhausted from all the bumping and grinding. Stripping may look easy, but to do it expertly is physically demanding.

John was insistent, so reluctantly I agreed. I didn't feel like getting dressed up. I was getting bored with having to look like a glamour queen every time I went out. The studio frowned on my Bohemian hippie look. I was trying halfheartedly to be chic, but not succeeding very well, because I had recently made Louella Parsons' "10 Worst Dressed Women" list. I think I'll live up to that tonight, I thought—and took from my wardrobe a pair of gray flannel boy's Bermuda shorts, long gray socks, sneakers and a green Brooks Brothers shirt. I scraped my hair into a ponytail and left off the makeup. I liked the look. A cross between Jackie Cooper and Betty Coed.

Debbie Power was the widow of Tyrone Power. Rumors abounded that she was about to marry my ex-boyfriend, Arthur Loew. Her house, in the flats of Beverly Hills, was filled with people when we arrived. The usual mob doing the usual things— drinking, gossiping, talking box-office grosses, whiling away another forgettable evening. I wandered around chatting to a few people and wishing I hadn't come. My outfit caused a few amused remarks. It didn't bother me. I liked being outrageous sometimes, although at other times I felt like being extremely conventional. Gemini coming out again.

"That piano player is really good," I said to John. "Who is he?" John, who was tall, craned his neck above the crowd and said, "I think it's Shirley MacLaine's brother, Warren something-or-other." Aha, there he is again, I thought. Even if he didn't make it as an actor, he was a superb pianist and could definitely make a living in a cocktail lounge if need be. He was doing imitations of various pianistic styles: Erroll Garner, George Shearing, Oscar Peterson. It was clever and I drew closer to watch and listen. He noticed I was there and smiled, but he appeared totally absorbed in his music. John and I left after a couple of hours and Warren was still immersed in his piano playing.

The next day was Sunday, gorgeous and sunny. I drove to the beach for my tan and then came back to go to a cocktail party for songwriter Jimmy McHugh. Gardner McKay was my date. When I checked my answering service, there were six messages to call Warren Beatty at the Chateau Marmont. Surprise! We had not exchanged a word and yet he had managed to get my number. Immediately I hung up, the phone rang, and a soft voice said, "Hi, did you get my messages?" He didn't say who he was, and I admired his assurance that I would know his voice.

"Yes, I did," I said crisply. "You can't be a poor actor. It costs twenty-five cents a call from the Chateau." He chuckled and said, "Do you want to have dinner tonight?" I thought swiftly. The party was from five-thirty to seven-thirty and although Gardner probably thought I would have dinner with him, nevertheless I had not actually said I would. Gardner, a black-haired six-foot-four actor at Fox, was, according to *Life* magazine, the handsomest man in America. We had been going out in a platonic way for a few months. Fox was pleased to have two of its stars "dating" and we went to various industry functions with their approval.

"OK. I have to go somewhere first. I'll meet you in Beverly Hills." I didn't want him coming to the house and bumping into Gardner.

"Eight o'clock at the corner of Rodeo and Santa Monica," he said. "I can hardly wait." Strangely enough, neither could I. This was odd. Somebody I hadn't met—hadn't spoken to—and I was excited at the thought of having dinner with him.

Rushing home after the party—I pleaded exhaustion and an early call to Gardner—I ripped off the black faille cocktail dress and the flowered organdy hat and jumped into a pair of jeans and a shirt. I brushed my hair and took off some of my makeup. Warren was obviously slightly younger than I. I didn't want to look too done up.

He was waiting at Rodeo and Santa Monica in a rented Chevy. I locked my rented yellow Ford and joined him.

"Hi," we said simultaneously and looked at each other. "Do you like Mexican?" he said, after we had each taken a good look. "Mexican what?" I asked, coming down to earth. He was better looking than I remembered. True, he had a few spots—probably left over from his adolescence, which couldn't have been too far behind him—but his eyes, although small, were clear greenish-blue, and I noticed that his hands were beautiful.

"Food, of course," he said as we moved into the Santa Monica traffic. "I thought we'd go to the Casa Escobar—they make terrific Margaritas."

"Sounds good," I said gaily.

Over dinner and Margaritas we couldn't stop talking—or looking. He was in Hollywood hopefully to start his movie career. He had done stock, a lot of TV, and had made a few tests—the usual things young actors do—and was hoping to get the lead in William Inge's new play A Loss of Roses. He was an Aries and was, curiously, born on March 30—the same date as Sydney Chaplin. I gravitated toward Aries men. Having recently become interested in astrology, I realized that my sign of Gemini had certain compatible signs. These were Aries, Libra, Gemini and Aquarius.

We talked and laughed until past midnight. He dropped me at my car and said he would follow me home to see that I arrived safely.

My Shoreham Drive apartment was about half a mile from his hotel. As I drove through the deserted Beverly Hills streets, I wondered if I should ask him up for a nightcap. I realized what this meant. I was not an innocent virgin. Asking him up for a drink could be construed as an invitation to other things. I was still in love, albeit unhappily, with George. If I asked Warren up, I was taking one giant step.

I liked Warren. I liked his mind. I liked his humor, his conversation—and his physical packaging.

My mind was buzzing with indecisive ifs and buts, pros and cons. As I drove into the underground garage he decided for me. "I'm coming up," he announced, pulling his car in behind mine, "for coffee"—and the die was cast.

We became inseparable. Apart from physical attraction, we seemed to have everything in common. We would stay up all night talking, laughing, discussing, and I would stagger wearily to the studio in the morning to work on *Seven Thieves*. He would call me eighteen times a day. We couldn't bear to be apart. Every second we could be together we were. He hung around the set for hours. We drove to the beach and gazed at the ocean and each other; we went to piano bars to listen to music. Sometimes he played. He played magnificently—after acting, the piano was his main passion. We played poker with my friends, who were all surprised by this sudden romance. "Don't you think he's a touch young for you?" said Cappy one afternoon, after Warren and I had been entwined on a beach chair all day. "He looks about seventeen—and how can you stand those *spots*?"

"Oh, Cappy, for goodness' sake, he's not that young. He's twenty-two and I'm only a couple of years older. Don't you see he's the best thing that's happened to me? I've got to get George out of my system and Warren is really helping me to do that."

"But, darling," she said, "he's penniless, he's an unsuccessful, unknown actor, and he's probably using you to get ahead." Dear Cappy! She usually called the shots right—but I ignored her remarks this time, although her advice had usually been on the nose.

"For once in my life, someone is trying to make me happy. Someone is caring about how *I* feel, someone is taking an interest in my mind, in my work, and helping me over my insecurities. It doesn't matter that he's poor and not successful. He's a terrific actor and he's going to make it. You can bet on it." Cappy looked dubious. "Have you told George?" she asked. We were primping in her lavish dressing room.

"Oh, Cappy. I don't know how to tell him," I groaned. "He's in Hong Kong with Marlon. Every time he's phoned, I've been out."

"You must send him a cable," she said firmly. "It's only fair to him. You've been seeing no one else but this Warren for three weeks now. You know George will find out as soon as he gets here. Send it now."

I sat down and reluctantly composed a "Dear John" cable. Although Warren and I were in the midst of a flaming love affair, it was still very hard for me to break off with my married lover after nearly a year and a half of being together. He had treated me callously, I knew—but I also empathized with his marriage problems and the three kids. I understood his problems only too well—that was *my* problem!

"Can't see you any more," I wrote, "In love with someone else—very sorry—love JC." "How's that?" I said, showing it to Cappy.

"Awful," she said, "but better than nothing. Send it."

George returned from the Orient two days later and immediately called. He was charming and persuasive. He couldn't believe I had fallen for someone else. Not after all we had meant to each other. He would definitely and absolutely get the divorce immediately and then we would be together forever. I had heard this line so many times, but he was my weakness and he knew how to manipulate me. He persuaded me to meet him for a drink the following afternoon at the Cock and Bull, an English-style pub on the Strip.

"At least you owe it to me to say goodbye properly," he said, "and not just a damn 'Dear John' telegram."

I told Warren I was meeting George.

"How long will it take?" he asked petulantly.

"Oh, just forty-five minutes or an hour," I said airily. "Just to end it civilly, like friends—we owe it to each other."

"You'll probably realize it's him you love and not me," he said moodily, doodling on a piece of paper and fiddling with the phone. He *loved* the telephone. He made twenty to thirty calls a day, often to the same people three or four times.

"I won't," I said, putting my arms around him. "I know I won't. You don't have a thing to worry about."

I left him doodling on his pad, the phone, like some extra part of his body, hanging from his ear, and went to meet George. He was tanned from his trip and beautifully turned out in a beige suit, pale green shirt and a dark green tie. He looked great. I felt sick. I was about to kiss off a year and a half of my life. I was about to get rid of Daddy! I was about to say goodbye to fifteen months of misery, unhappiness, jealousy and hysteria, but also to closeness, intellectual stimulation and, at times, more joy than I'd ever had before.

He ordered Pimm's for us and got down to business. He already knew all about Warren. "He's just a kid," he said. "How can you, a sophisticated woman, be interested in a *kid?*" I started to protest that Warren was twenty-two, but he went on, "Listen, Joanie, I know how tough it's been for you this past year. I know I've been a shit and I understand this little fling of yours had to come. I understand it and I forgive it, and I'll forget it ever happened if you just end it now and come back to me. . . ."

He went on in this vein, ordering more Pimm's and talking in his clever and fascinating way. I began to waver. Maybe he was right. George was a man—a grownup—Warren was a boy. George knew about life, and although Warren was clever and bright and razor-sharp, he was still inexperienced, naive and gauche. My good intentions started to falter. I was so weak. So stupid. After all the lies and promises George had made to me, I was starting to believe him again.

I looked at my watch. Eight o'clock. We had been there for three hours. "I've got to go." I got up hurriedly and he threw a ten-dollar bill on the table and followed me to the parking lot. He grabbed my shoulders as I stood trying to open my car door. "I'm going to give you a week to decide," he said, conceding heavily. "You're a smart girl, you're *not* going to throw your life away on an out-of-work actor who's probably only using you." He bent down and kissed me. A fervent kiss. It felt good. Too good.

"Goodbye," I said faintly as I stumbled into the driver's seat, trembling violently. Oh, God—could I love two men?

"I'll call you tomorrow—I know it's not easy, babe, but don't forget what we had and what we *can* have when I get the divorce."

I pulled away into the Sunset Strip traffic in a turmoil. Warren was not in the apartment. He arrived five minutes later. Furious. "I saw you," he said, ripping off his glasses and jacket, throwing them on the sofa. "I saw you necking in the parking lot." He tried to look menacing and walked toward me. He tripped over a stool—without his glasses he was practically blind.

"We weren't," I said helplessly, and more than a little drunk. "He kissed me goodbye, that's all."

"Oh, sure," he sneered. He had been driving around and around the Cock and Bull for two hours, steaming with jealousy. We fought all night. Yelling, crying, recriminations and declarations of a passion neither of us was really positive about. We ran the gamut of emotions as only actor and actress can. My indecisiveness drove him mad, but it drove *me* mad, too. I wanted to do the right thing for me, but I was so unsure. Did I really love Warren? Enough to end it with George?

The next day I had an early call on *Seven Thieves* to shoot a scene in the Monte Carlo Casino with Rod Steiger. I was a wreck. I had hardly slept and my eyes were swollen from crying. The makeup man, used to the overly developed emotions of actresses, did his magic tricks and I was poured into a tight black satin evening dress, hair swept into a chignon and diamonds in my ears. I looked nearly new, but I couldn't play the scene. I kept blowing my lines—something I *never* did. Henry Hathaway, the director, became furious with me. The angrier he became, the more I blew my lines, until finally I broke down completely and left the set in tears. Rod came to console me. He was a kind and considerate actor—hard to reach on a personal level but wonderful to work with. Very giving.

Warren came for lunch in the commissary and we again hashed over our problems. I told him I was going to see my analyst at five-thirty and that I would try to sort things out.

On the familiar brown couch I tried to be analytical about my problem. I owed nothing to nobody. I should not go to George just because of my "investment" of time, but only if he could make me truly happy—which most of the time he had not managed to do. If Warren made me happy I should be with him. An hour backward, forward, inside out—get rid of my father—for that's what the married man represented. But to chuck out that

167

year and a half when attainment was so close? Or was it? George had lied to me so often—maybe this was another lie. Finally I made a decision. I left Dr. Greenleigh's office and walked, elated, down Bedford Drive to my car. A tap on the shoulder. It was George. Full of confidence and vigor from the hour of uninterrupted soul searching, I told him, "I love you. A lot. I probably always will. You're the brightest, cleverest man I know, but you haven't made me happy. I want and *need* happiness now. I want to be with Warren—he loves me, and we're good for each other now. Please don't try to stop me." He pleaded and remonstrated, but I wouldn't listen. "I hope we can always be friends," I said, meaning it, and walked away.

That night Warren and I celebrated our commitment to each other with his sister, Shirley MacLaine, at La Scala. We had been together nearly a month and everything was blissful.

He left the following week for New York to start rehearsals for Inge's *A Loss of Roses*, with Carol Haney and Betty Field. It was a wonderful break for him. One for which he had been waiting for months. Inge's plays were always critical and commercial successes and Warren's part—that of a tormented young man with a slight Oedipus complex who falls in love with a much older woman—was meaty enough to guarantee he would be noticed and hopefully discovered for films. For, unlike me, Warren's first love and preference was for movies rather than theater.

Inge's plays included *Bus Stop, Come Back Little Sheba, Picnic* and *Dark at the Top of the Stairs*, all major dramatic works which had earned him accolades as one of America's most important playwrights. Warren was nervous and excited about the assignment and he plunged into rehearsals with enthusiasm and optimism. I stayed in Hollywood to finish *Seven Thieves* and then planned to join him. We talked on the phone constantly. I watched him in a TV show called "The Affairs of Dobie Gillis"— he was quite good. He had talent and looks and blinding ambition. I felt he was bound to succeed.

In November, *Seven Thieves* was finished and I caught the midnight plane to Washington, where *A Loss of Roses* had just opened to less than rave reviews. I was tired. Apart from shooting, the strip sequences for *Seven Thieves* were arduous. I had also been cramming in photographic and wardrobe tests for the next film I was supposed to start—D.H. Lawrence's *Sons and Lovers*.

We stayed at the Willard Hotel in Washington. I met his parents, who lived in nearby Arlington. They were kind, humorous people whom I liked instantly. I could see from whom Warren and Shirley had inherited their intelligence and good manners.

As Warren was busy rehearsing all day and performing at night, I had time to myself—something I relished. I took long walks and read, went to the Smithsonian, and thought about our relationship and what I wanted from it. I didn't know—I was happy just taking each day as it came. Warren and I seemed to be good for each other. We didn't want marriage. I didn't want babies. I just wanted to live and enjoy my life.

When the final script of *Sons and Lovers* arrived, Warren decided I shouldn't do it. Not only did he think the story was unappealing, but he did not want me to go to England and leave *him!* Had the film been a comedy, I would probably have done it anyway. I had been nagging Fox to let me do more comedy roles, but apart from *Rally Round the Flag, Boys,* the funny parts went to other actresses. So I rebelled, realizing this would mean a suspension of salary. Once again! The previous year I had refused two roles, one in *The Last Wagon* and the other in *Madison Avenue.* Both turned out to be flops, but for the duration of the shooting of these films I not only did not get paid but could not accept another job. Since I was by now earning $2,500 a week, forty weeks a year, this financial sacrifice was not easy, but I was becoming discontented with not having any decisive say in my career. Now Warren—the bossy Aries side of him coming out—was making career decisions for me.

I was a "utility infielder." If Fox couldn't get Susan Hayward or Gene Tierney for the role, they'd use me. I was usually cast at the last minute in decorative and unrewarding roles. My agent would call and tell me to get over to wardrobe right away. Once there, old Lana Turner or Maureen O'Hara costumes were refitted and refurbished to fit me and off I would go, to Tokyo,

Mexico or wherever the wind blew me, my secondhand finery following. I was not stretching myself at all as an actress and Warren understood this more than anyone.

Jerry Wald, the producer of *Sons and Lovers*, had promised various script changes that would have made my role in *Sons and Lovers* more palatable and interesting. When I read the final script these changes had not been made. Warren encouraged me to walk out of the film. His motives were not exactly selfless. He needed me with him—he was getting lots of publicity over our relationship and it was a tricky time of his life. With me in England he would feel forlorn and lonely. "Don't go, Butterfly," he begged. "Don't leave your Bee." I moved back to New York with him, into the Blackstone Hotel, and *A Loss of Roses* opened. It was not Inge's greatest work. The critics were unkind, but Warren's personal reviews were good and everyone thought he was excellent as the sensitive boy. Interest was stirring for him in Hollywood. The play ran for only three weeks but after it closed we stayed on in New York seeing friends and plays, going to the Harwyn Club—an up-marked Manhattan boite where they let us eat free because of the publicity they got from our going there— arguing and making up, neither of us earning a bean, broke, but loving life and each other a lot.

We moved back to California at the beginning of 1961. We rented a small studio apartment at the Chateau Marmont and started looking for work. Financially I was in good shape again. My suspension from *Sons and Lovers* had ended and I was back on salary and preparing to test for another Western epic called *Big River, Big Man.*

Warren coached me for this test. He was an excellent director and a patient teacher, with an intense and intellectual approach to exploring the depths and details of a characterization.

The endlessly sunny winter and spring California days passed quickly. We spent a lot of time at the Aware Inn, eating health-burgers and drinking carrot juice. Warren was a health freak and was now trying to persuade me to stop both drinking and smoking. After we ate we would walk to Turner's drugstore and flick through a pyramid of movie magazines looking for pictures of us together. The movie magazines loved the "new twosome."

Warren was heavily involved in trying to get the lead in Elia Kazan's *Splendor in the Grass*, again written by his friend William Inge. This necessitated his making three hundred and fifty phone calls a day—two hundred and fifty to his agent, twenty-five to Bill Inge—who was doing all he could to get Kazan to test Warren—twenty-five to me, wherever I was (although when I was working or doing an interview, he was never far away), and the rest to his by now numerous friends and business acquaintances. He was never happier than when he was on the phone, and he didn't need a phone book to remember the important numbers he constantly called. Ten years later, meeting him at a party he said, "CR—— do you remember what that was?" I didn't but he told me it was the telephone number of the apartment on Shoreham Drive where I lived when we met.

Telephoning, however, was secondary to his main passion, which was making love—and he was also able to accept phone calls at the same time. I had heard that men were at their sexual peak between the ages of seventeen and twenty-three. If Warren was anything to go by, this was true. I had never known anyone like him before. It was exciting for the first few months, but after a while I found myself feeling like an object.

One Sunday morning, exhausted, I left him sleeping soundly—another thing he did well—and staggered upstairs to visit an actress girlfriend from New York. She had been happily married for several years to a handsome superstar and idol of millions. "I don't think I can last much longer," I said, lighting a much needed cigarette—frowned upon by Warren. "He never *stops*—it must be all those vitamins he takes."

She smiled warmly, dispensing coffee and sisterly advice. "Just like my husband," she said.

"After all the years you've been together!" I said incredulously.

"Oh, yes. In fact it gets better."

"Better—oh, God. Please." I leaned back and took a drag on the cigarette. "In a few years, I'll be worn out."

"Take my advice, Joan," said my friend. "Don't reject him. If you do, he may find it necessary to go with other women."

"Perish the thought," I said jealously. But her warning lingered in the back of my mind and we continued with his favorite occupation whenever it suited him. Of course, the inevitable happened.

"I think I'm pregnant," I said coming into the kitchen one day, where he was preparing one of his health concoctions in the blender. He stopped slicing bananas and pouring wheat germ, took off his glasses and stared at me. Without his glasses he was quite myopic, and I wondered why he didn't want to see me. "Pregnant?" he said in his puzzled little-boy voice. "How did that happen?"

"The butler did it," I said sarcastically, "or maybe it's an immaculate conception."

"This is terrible," he said, putting his glasses back on and looking at me as if for the first time. "Terrible!" He threw down seven or eight vitamin E tablets.

"I know," I said in a small voice. "I'm sorry." Not only did I feel awful about it, but I remembered what happened to my girlfriend at RADA who had gone to a butcher of an abortionist in a London back street and almost died. She would never be able to have children. I did not want that to happen to me. Although I wasn't prepared for motherhood, nevertheless I felt that one day, if my maternal instincts rose, I wanted to have my options open.

We sat on the faded red sofa in the living room, I with a stiff vodka, he with his health drink, and discussed what to do. Abortion was a dirty word in the early 1960s. In fact, so was sex. Even living together as Warren and I did was considered risqué. Abortions of a kind were of course available. I had recently gone to Tijuana, the tacky Mexican border town, accompanying a girlfriend and her married lover. I had listened, horrified, to her screams of agony as a Mexican "doctor" performed the operation *without* an anesthetic.

I shuddered at the memory, downing my vodka. We could get married, of course. But I was not in favor of "shotgun" weddings. The few times we had discussed marriage we had both decided that we were too immature to make it work. Besides which, he was practically penniless, exceedingly ambitious, and to get tied down in marriage at the age of twenty-two was totally impractical.

So marriage was out. And having a baby was *definitely* out. So there was only one solution.

He called a friend in New York. We had heard that the abortion could be done in clinical circumstances there without risk to health. I would not consider a Tijuana-type deal. The friend arranged it. Warren had to go to New York to start preparing for *Splendor in the Grass* and I followed a few days later.

Early that morning I woke up trembling with my oldest and most frightening nightmare. It was as terrifying as ever. I was walking alone up a very dark and winding staircase. The stairs creaked and the wind howled outside. In the distance I heard dogs barking and an owl hooting, and then silence—only my footsteps, which went faster and faster up the crumbling stone stairs. Rats and mice scurried ahead of me, their tiny, furry bodies brushing my bare legs. Suddenly I heard breathing. "It" was behind me. "It" was getting closer. I ran faster and faster up the endless stairs, hearing the breathing getting closer all the time. And then I came to the top of the stairs to a door that said "Doctor." I rapped furiously. The footsteps were gaining behind me. Slowly the door opened. A grinning old man stood there, his white apron covered with blood, a bloody knife in his hand. He came toward me to take me by the hand. Behind me I heard the moans of a woman. I stepped back. A hand grabbed my arm and swung me backward. "I've got you at last, little girl," screamed Maxwell Reed dementedly, his face a mask of cruelty, his eyes those of a madman. "Now you'll really get cut up and carved up, and no one will ever look at you again!" He raised the bloody knife in his hand to bring it slashing to my face. I screamed.

"What is it, what's the matter?" said Warren, groggy with sleep, as I sat up sobbing, the vivid dream still gripping me.

"I can't go through with it," I sobbed. "I can't, I can't. Please don't make me go there, Warren, I'm scared—I'll have the baby—we'll get it adopted—but I can't go there." He comforted me as I sobbed hysterically. It was true. It is an ironic fact of life that the metabolic and hormonal changes that women go through when pregnant bring them closer each day to a protective feeling toward life inside them. I had been feeling—perish the thought—broody for a couple of weeks now, almost accepting what was happening to me, and now that it was going to be taken from me, I wanted to keep it.

"Butterfly, we *can't*, we can't do it," he said helplessly, trying to comfort me. "Having a baby now will wreck both of our careers—you know it will."

He was right and I knew it. Ingrid Bergman, a far bigger star than I, had almost wrecked hers by having an out-of-wedlock child by Rossellini. It was a very serious and far-reaching step. There had been rumors of various actresses throughout the years who had disappeared for several months, and a few months after their reappearance had "adopted" a tiny baby, but it was all extremely hush-hush. With the eyes of the gossip columnists on us, nagging in print for us to "tie the knot," it would have been an impossibility. So I dried my tears, putting his ambition and my career first, and mooched about the hotel room until dusk, when it was time to drive to New Jersey.

I wore thick black stockings, a sweater and a full plaid skirt. "Don't wear slacks," I had been told by a sterile, sibilant voice over the telephone when I received my instructions. My eyes, which were swollen and red from crying, were covered by my biggest black sunglasses, and a head scarf covered my untidy hair. I did not wish to be recognized by anyone.

I chain-smoked as Warren drove a rented station wagon to Newark. We spoke little. He glanced at me with concern several times. I wished I could keep the baby. Practically, though, I knew it was impossible. But the fact that he would not even *consider* that possibility hurt me terribly. He was a man. He took none of the responsibility for me becoming pregnant. That was the woman's department. But pre-Pill, however careful one was, accidents happened, and *she* was the one to face the emotional upheaval that pregnancy causes—and then the unbearably ambivalent feelings it generates.

I tried to convince myself that we were doing the right thing as we entered the Holland Tunnel and Warren started consulting a piece of paper on which were written the directions. I had just turned twenty-six. I had a thriving career, which, if not exactly to my liking as far as the roles I was playing were concerned, was still

174

lucrative and rewarding in many ways. A baby would change all that. I would have to stop working. Fox would suspend me. I might lose my figure. I might be a lousy mother. He and I were not suited to each other in the long run. Was our love just a physical thing? I didn't seem to be able to be with *any* man for a long period of time. We were both selfish, careless, argumentative, combative and just plain immature. It was stupid to think otherwise. Thus I convinced myself—while my mind shrieked "No!"

I dried my eyes and blew my nose as the car drew to a halt in front of an ominous-looking maroon high-rise apartment building.

"We're—um—here," said my gallant lover, nervously wiping his glasses on the sleeve of his tweed jacket. I noticed his face was covered with perspiration. He was probably more scared than I was. We looked at each other and I swallowed hard. "If anything goes wrong . . ." I started to say, but he interrupted me, almost screaming, "Nothing's going to go wrong—*nothing*. He's the best around. Don't even *think* about *that*, Butterfly."

He was close to tears himself. My maternal instinct went into comforting him, and hand in hand we walked to the green-paint-peeling elevator.

I awoke to hear someone pounding on the door.

"Are you still there?" yelled a coarse voice. I looked at my watch. It was one o'clock in the afternoon. I pulled the covers back over my head and tried to sleep again. The voice kept on yelling.

"Open up in there. I'se gotta clean the room."

"Oh, go to hell," I yelled back. "I don't want it cleaned. Leave me alone."

The voice sniffed, "If that's what you all want, you just go ahead and sleep all day, see if ah care." It shuffled down the corridor and left me in peace.

I tried to go back to sleep. Warren had gone to rehearsal and I didn't want to think about what had happened last night. It was too vivid and too painful. We must get out of this fleabag hotel and find an apartment, I thought, as I drifted back to sleep again.

The next day I felt much better and full of energy again. I pushed the horrifying abortion out of my head. Done. Over. Forgotten. That was yesterday—no point in brooding about it, and—oh, good—I didn't feel maternal any more. Not even to Warren. I called a house agent and went apartment hunting in New York. It was a beautiful, clear, crisp day. A rare day in New York. Newborn—I felt newborn myself, as though a great weight had been lifted and I could get back to living again.

As I rummaged through the drawers to find sweater and stockings, I noticed my jewelry case under the sweater. I opened it up and looked at the diamond necklace. It was scrunched up with some junk jewelry, some Greek worry beads—could've used those a couple of nights ago—and gold chains. I put on the gold chains and slid the leather box back under the pile of sweaters. That necklace. What trouble it had caused me. Much more trouble than it was worth. I toyed with the idea of putting it in the hotel safe, then forgot about it as the phone rang and the switchboard announced that the real estate agent was downstairs.

Two nights later, dressing to go to El Morocco, I looked for the necklace. Gone. Probably stolen by the maid, angry because she couldn't make up the room. "I think real jewelry is a drag," I announced bravely to Warren, as I heaped on some imitation pearls and waited for the police to arrive. "I really don't care if I ever have expensive jewelry again."

We moved to a tiny apartment on Fifth Avenue. It was furnished in blue-and-white chintz, English antiques, and had bad plumbing. Warren started filming *Splendor in the Grass* with Natalie Wood.

I had known Natalie Wood since I first arrived in Hollywood in the mid-fifties. She was already a star. Although only sixteen, she was starring opposite Jimmy Dean in *Rebel Without a Cause* and was big at the box office. Throughout the fifties and sixties we consecutively or successively dated some of the same men, and we eventually became good friends when our dating whirl stopped. We sent each other flowers and telegrams at the births of our respective children and exchanged long letters when she was in California and I in London. We "did" Rodeo Drive and the boutiques of Beverly Hills after long lunches at the Bistro or the Polo Lounge, and we spent hours on the phone with each other. She always dressed and behaved like the ultimate star. Spending money with abandon on clothes, furs and jewelry, she was never to be seen in the same outfit twice. Although Natalie was popular both with the young social set in Hollywood and the older group, she was incredibly insecure as a person and about her physical attributes. She always wore high-heeled shoes to maximize her height, and she always wore a thick gold bracelet to cover a slightly protruding bone in her wrist, which was hardly noticeable.

At a dinner party one night, Natalie inadvertently performed one of the most extraordinarily vain gestures I have ever seen. Upon sitting down at the elegant table, she picked up one of the gleaming, polished Georgian knives and, holding it close to her face, examined her lipstick and teeth as though gazing into a compact! Mesmerized by this display of narcissism, I determined to use it as a piece of theatrical business one day. My chance came a few years later while appearing in an Orson Welles television production, *The Dinner Party*, and I was commended by the director for an excellent piece of business!

Natalie and I had a slight falling out in the summer of 1969 in St. Tropez. We were both in between husbands and were staying at a tiny hotel on the beach. We had dined with the usual large group of suntanned Riviera playboys and models at L'Escale, and then drifted on to the open-air discotheque Byblos. There were some cute guys in the group, none of whom were averse to pretty actresses. Natalie and I agreed that we would neither of us go home without the other in tow.

"Promise me you won't go yet," she called, as she was whisked onto the dance floor to dance to the romantic ballad "Monia," sung by Peter Holm. Shortly thereafter I, too, hit the dance floor with a would-be beau to the trendy beat of the Beatles chanting "I'm a Loser," and we discoed for an hour. Coming back to our table I found that Natalie had left. No goodbye, no "Sorry Joan, just couldn't resist Jean Pierre or Francois or whomever. I'll see you tomorrow." Not even a message. I was angry, and I had been saddled with a bunch of people I had little in common with. Earlier in the evening we had had drinks with Roger Vadim and his wife, Jane Fonda, but they were not into the disco life since she was pregnant.

I left a note under Natalie's door telling her I felt abandoned and that she had broken a promise. Instead of an apology, she didn't speak to me for three years! It was only the intervention of a mutual friend, Asa Maynor, that eventually got us back together, via a series of lunches. We renewed our friendship, and nothing was ever mentioned of the incident that had caused the rift. Natalie hated confrontations and always felt she was right in her opinions. Those who cared about her did it her way, otherwise they were *out* of her group.

While Warren was filming *Splendor in the Grass*, I went to Berlitz every day and took Italian lessons preparatory to leaving the following month for Italy to film *Esther and the King*. I was unhappy about leaving and so was he, but I was not about to let him interfere with my career again. Not only did I need money, but *Sons and Lovers* had turned out to be a good picture, infinitely better than most of the stuff I had done at Fox. Mary Ure, who had played my role, was nominated for an Oscar the following year. I deeply regretted having turned it down thanks to Warren's insistence. His career was now well and truly off the ground, while mine was stagnating in a stew of forgettable films. I was now getting toward not only the end of my seven-year tenure at Fox, but I had also passed my first quarter century—an age that young actresses had learned to dread ever since the studios had decreed back in the dark ages of moviemaking that twenty-seven was the end of beauty, freshness and youth. New faces were on the horizon. Younger than mine. Fresher. My career was in the doldrums and I knew it. Nine mediocre films in five years are no guarantee of eternal longevity at the box office. As these realizations began to crystalize, I tried even harder, through the efforts of my lawyer, to get out of the remaining eighteen months of my contract. I wanted to be free to accept some of the interesting independent films that were being made in the early sixties. But no, it was not to be. . . .

I had now been on suspension so many times that Fox thought I was crazed. In five years, five suspensions. Is this a record? I wondered as I sat on the set of New York Filmway's studios and watched Elia Kazan direct Warren and Natalie in a scene.

He was a sympathetic, sensitive, brilliant director. Lauded, and rightly so, for a multitude of great movies: *Streetcar Named Desire, Viva Zapata, On the Waterfront, East of Eden* and many more. He had discovered Marlon Brando and James Dean. Would Warren be next? I wondered as I saw "Gadge," his arms around his two young stars, patiently talking, explaining, extracting from them every nuance of thought, meaning and expression for the scene. Warren was very lucky to have Kazan as his first director. Maybe he really would become a big star.

I thought back to what my astrologer, Ben Gary, had said recently, when he had done my chart in conjunction with Warren's. Ben was a psychic astrologer and his predictions had always been uncannily accurate. "You know Warren's birthday is March thirtieth, the same as Sydney Chaplin's," said Ben triumphantly. "He's got all the usual Aries traits," continued Ben. "The ram, of course." I nodded agreement on that. "The ram is the first sign in the zodiac—it represents birth. 'I want' is the Aries credo; they usually get what they want."

"Hmmm, Maxwell Reed was an Aries too," I remembered. "And so was Hitler."

Ben fixed me with his beady eyes and I shut up. "He is stubborn and aggressive, but he is unyielding in his ambition and because of his tremendous drive and energy will have an early and immense success." I listened carefully as Ben continued. "However, after a short period of success, he will go into a dry period for a couple of years, make several career mistakes, but finally will become a major star again—probably in the late sixties. He's very sexual, you know—" he looked at me questioningly. I looked demure. "Most Aries are, of course. Ruled by their cock. How delightful for you, my dear."

"Sometimes," I said cryptically. "What else? Go on, Ben—what about us?" He consulted the hieroglyphics on his chart, peering through his nearsighted eyes and taking a long draught of beer. "You have an affinity for Aries men, you know, my dear—you'll probably marry at least one more of them. But it won't be him!"

"It won't?" I said disappointedly. "Why not?"

"He will not marry for a long time," said my soothsayer. "Probably not until he's forty-five or older. I do see many, many women, though."

179

"Terrific," I said gloomily. "Are they around him now?"

"No, dear, now he only needs you—later he will need . . ." He pored again over the chart and paused, making little notations with red pencil on the indecipherable squiggles on the paper. "He will need a constant inflation of his ego—one woman will not suffice to satisfy him sexually."

"So where does that leave me?" I asked, trying to look over his shoulder at the squiggles.

"Ah, my dear—you have only just begun to live your life."

This is encouraging, I thought. I seem to have lived so much already.

"You have only just begun your career, which will last for a very, very long time and you will reap the rewards when you are in your forties."

"Forties!" I gasped. "That's ancient, Ben!"

"You are a late bloomer, dear," he admonished. "You are going to surprise a lot of people when you are much older. There will be other men in your future. You will be married again within two years to a . . ." He squinted at his squiggles again, ". . . a writer—no, a producer or director, also an actor. A very multi-faceted man—he does many things."

I giggled and looked over at Cappy sitting on the couch. I believed in astrology, but I couldn't take it completely seriously. However, it was fascinating to hear one's future, even if one took it with a pinch of salt. "This marriage will last six or seven years," continued Ben. "From it will come two or three children—two of them probably twins, or very close in age. Shortly thereafter you'll marry again . . ." He stared at the paper thoughtfully. "It's hard to see that far. I think he is a businessman—maybe an executive in some company."

"Rich?" I said hopefully.

"My dear, you never fall for rich men," said Ben, fixing me with a steely glare. "Your heart rules your head. You will always make enough money to take care of yourself. You will continue working for a very long time—your career will have many ups and downs but you were born under a lucky star. You are truly a survivor."

Ben's prophecies for himself came ominously true several years later. He had always foreseen that he would die when he was thirty-two. On his thirty-second birthday he shut himself in his house with a close friend to take care of his needs. He was ultra-careful. He did not touch anything electrical or mechanical, not even a telephone or a fridge. He insulated himself from anything that could cause him physical harm. A year later he was dead. From malnutrition. His diet of beer, pretzels and potato chips had finally caught up with him.

As of this writing *all* of his prophecies for me have come true.

"I feel like having some chopped liver," said Warren, looking up from studying his script. It was three o'clock on Saturday afternoon. We had only recently finished lunch.

"It's in the refrigerator," he said, going back to his script. "I got it yesterday at Reuben's." I opened the fridge and got the white plastic carton. "Did you find it?" he yelled from the living room. "Yes," I shouted. "What do you think of it?" I opened it slightly. "Umm—smells delicious," I said

"Does it fit?" he called.

"Fit? Fit where, on a bagel?"

The man was obviously working too hard. "Well, try it on," he said anxiously, appearing in the doorway of the kitchen. "Oh—" he looked sheepishly at my surprised face. "Oh, you haven't found it yet." I followed his eyes to the carton of chopped liver and looked at it more carefully. Stuck in the middle of it was a gold ring encrusted with diamonds *and* pearls. "Oh, darling—it's beautiful," I cried, extracting it from the liver and wiping it off so I could see it in its full glory. "Absolutely beautiful—what's it for?"

"It's your engagement ring, dummy," he said, grinning like a Cheshire cat. "I figured, since you're going away soon and we'll be separated we should um, well, um, you know . . ." He shuffled embarrassedly. Took the glasses off. Put them on again. Grabbed a couple of Vitamin C tablets and crunched them. "Get—well, engaged. What do you think?" He looked anxious.

"I think it's a great idea—just terrific," I squealed happily. "Are you sure you really want to—I mean you're not just doing this to make me feel secure, are you?"

"No, Butterfly, I'm not—you know I don't do anything unless I want to . . . and . . . um . . . well . . . um . . . I guess I

want to. We . . . er, could get married at the end of the year."
He took his glasses off again and we burst out laughing.

The fact that Warren may have bought me the ring out of a
strong guilt feeling because of the abortion crossed my mind. I
put it on the third finger of my left hand and left it there for a
long, long time. I wore it all the way through *Esther and the King*
since it fitted in with the Biblical costumes.

That night we celebrated our engagement by dining at Danny's
Hideaway and then going to hear Bobby Short at the Carlyle. I
flashed my left hand casually wherever we went, and within a week
the columnists were pleased to announce that we had officially
become engaged at last.

I was dismal about going to Rome. Although it was my favorite
city in the world, I was desolate at leaving Warren, and so was he.
He was jealous at the thought of me being around other men.
Especially Italian men. I tried to convince him not to worry, that
I would be fidelity personified—but Aries men are exceedingly pos-
sessive, jealous and stubborn, and he would not be convinced.

At Fiumicino airport I was greeted by Raoul Walsh, the roister-
ing one-eyed director, bearing pink roses, also by my Italian agent,
two Italian actors from the film, two producers from the film, a
bunch of staring tourists and twenty paparazzi.

I was surprised at the number of paparazzi, those Italian photographers who make their living from photographing celebrities
outside restaurants, at airports, shopping along the Via Veneto
and, oh, major coup, coming out of a lover's apartment after a
"romantic interlude." Some do have ethics and respect for people's privacy; others are scavengers feeding on tidbits of celebrities'
love lives. One of their favorite tricks is to incite an actor to such
extreme rage that he will attempt to either smash the photographer or the camera. These photos—the more irate the actor the
better—are usually worth several hundred lire, and will garner a
two-page spread in *Tempo, Gente* or *Oggi*.

I was quite popular in Italy, and the number of photographers
proved that they still liked me although I hadn't set foot in that
country since *Land of the Pharaohs*, five years previously.

Instead of staying in a hotel, where I might get lonely and

tempted to accept dinner invitations, Warren had insisted that I stay with Marion Donen in her apartment. Immediately after I arrived, he started bombarding me with telegrams and letters protesting love, fidelity and commitment forever. When we talked on the phone, he sounded so forlorn and depressed that I decided that I would surprise him and fly to New York the following weekend. Twelve days after leaving New York I was back again. I had not yet started shooting the movie and he was over the moon to see me. Not many fiancées fly more than eight thousand miles for three days. He should be *deeply* thrilled. We spent the weekend, what was left of it, in our apartment. Monday and Tuesday I watched him filming again and Tuesday night I was back on Alitalia to the Eternal City. Exhausted but happy.

We had decided to marry in January. I wanted my dress designed in London. I called my English dressmakers, told them to start making up some designs, and started filming *Esther and the King*.

It was an awful film. It was full of pseudo Biblical banal Hollywood dialogue and, with the exception of Richard Egan, Denis O'Dea and myself, an all-Italian cast who spoke their dialogue in Italian, to which we replied in English! There were also a Spanish and a French actor who spoke their lines in Spanish and French respectively. It was a veritable League of Nations.

It really was terrible stuff. Warren had advised me not to do it. He suggested that I behave so badly when I was in Rome that they would fire me, but atrocious as the film was, my professionalism got the better of me and I tried to do the best I could with the part of the simpering heroine.

Warren's first letter contained some jocular rules and regulations on "How to make a Biblical film." They included:

1. It is always best to try to show as much emotion in all scenes as possible. It is generally best if the actor cries in each scene, taking special pains not to be out of control or realistic to the extent that members of the crew or other actors will be made to feel embarrassed. All gestures and facial expressions should be worked out in front of a large mirror. These should not be deviated from. Remember that the audience is not involved until the actor cries. Be very careful not to let the mascara run.

2. In doing Biblical pictures it is best to try to imagine how Jesus Christ would have said the necessary lines and done the prescribed movements and then to emulate his work.

3. Never change the words in a movie script. These have been written by great creative forces.

4. Do not challenge the director, or especially the producer. These are dedicated men.

5. Do not tire yourself out with thinking about the script between takes or at night away from the set. This destroys spontaneity.

I was still trying to renegotiate my contract with Fox to have some freedom to accept outside offers. But for some reason they wouldn't let me go, although they were dropping other contract players like hot potatoes.

Every night I was in bed reading, or had early dinner with Marion or my agent. I was bored and miserable, hating the movie and missing Warren. I constantly wore, besides the flashy engagement ring, a tiny gold butterfly that he had given me, from my favorite jeweler, Buccellati.

I visited London one weekend and started choosing wedding dress fabrics. Warren's phone calls and letters became more intense and desperate every day: "Can't wait to see you in dress" was the gist of most of them, and "Missing you more than I can bear."

Eventually I could stand it no more. After a pleading consultation with the production manager, he allowed me to fly to New York again for the weekend. Three and a half weeks after I left for Italy, an exhausted wreck deplaned at Idlewild airport on Saturday night and left again on Monday night.

In those forty-eight hours Warren and I did nothing but fight. He was convinced I was having an affair. Nothing I did or said could persuade him otherwise. The fact that I had flown those more than eight thousand miles twice in five weeks just to see him should have been proof enough to him that I loved him. Apparently it wasn't. His insecurities got the better of him, and I became the butt of them. Could it be, I wondered on the plane back to Rome, that *he* was the one who had been unfaithful?

And with his co-star Natalie Wood? They had certainly seemed more than close when I observed them at work. My suspicions were now aroused.

Sullen and angry, I returned to the awful film. I mouthed pious and pontificating language while I seethed with rage inside. How dare he treat me as if I were his piece of private property with "For Warren's personal use only" stamped in large letters all over the packaging? I had spent three thousand dollars on air fares alone, never mind the massive phone bills.

He yelled at me for something I hadn't done—maybe I *should* do it. He probably was. With Natalie Wood yet. "Ruled by the cock," Ben had said. Oh, God!

I started returning the flirtatious glances and remarks of a young Italian actor on the movie, Gabriele Tinti.

I always had a penchant for Italian men. I like their appreciation, often verbalized, of women, I like their attitude toward life. I even like the way they dress! This year everyone, including the young actor, wore black shirts open to the waist, a plethora of gold amulets and charms around the neck (to ward off evil, to make them more virile, or just to glisten on a tanned chest) and white cotton or linen pants. Quite a devastating look when teamed with black curly hair, sparkling white teeth in a brown and unbelievably handsome face and amazing slanted green eyes. As I thought of pimply, bespectacled, white-faced Warren, seriously emoting his way through his first movie role and getting angry at *me* all the time, Gabriele was a welcome change.

We launched into what the Italians call a "flirt." My mother and brother, Bill, were by now staying with me, so I was chaperoned at all times, which suited me fine. This was to be a "flirt" and nothing more, since my deep-down monogamous instincts and loyalty to Warren won out over the Italian's passion. But oh, what sitting and hand-holding in a corner of the studio and being told one was *bellissima,* and *meravigliosa, simpatica, più bella del mondo* could do for one's slightly fractured ego. Not to mention the boost in the arm it gave my Italian vocabulary.

Although I wouldn't go out with Gabriele officially, since I was *fidanzata* to Warren, I spent half an hour a night on the phone listening to his protestations of *amore.* Somehow, in Italian the words had far more meaning, although I could not take them seriously. Italian men love to use flowery phrases to their women— just as Englishmen court a woman between going to soccer matches and boozing it up with their mates at the pub. It's all part of the international mating call of men. One must read between the lines (or lack of them) to understand what the man is really *saying*. But when all was said and done I was in love with Warren. This "flirt" was my usual immature way of getting some sort of revenge for the pain he caused me.

Warren's suspicions solidified when he tried to phone for an hour one evening, with the line constantly busy. His suspicions would only be assuaged by another visit from me, which I dutifully and foolishly made. This accomplished nothing more than to alienate the producer and director of *Esther*, get myself splashed all over the New York and English tabloids, including the front page of the *Daily News* as a runaway, renegade actress, and generally achieve nothing more than a temporary truce in our battles. Warren never visited me in Rome. He sent me a telegram on the first anniversary of our meeting: "My life began one year ago." Letters and phone calls and cables continued, but the quality of the relationship started deteriorating.

The phone in the rented house of Sunset Plaza Drive rang, waking me out of a deep sleep. I picked it up, noticing it was barely nine o'clock. Our friends knew better than to call before ten.

"Joanie, it's me," said the anxious voice of my agent. "Can you be packed and ready to leave for London by the end of the day?"

"Oh, no, not again!" I sat up and searched fruitlessly for my eyedrops. "I've only been home a couple of weeks, whatever is all the rush for?"

"It's Elizabeth. They think she's dying. They want you to replace her in *Cleopatra*," he said tersely.

Dying! Liz Taylor—God, I *don't* believe it—this is a ghastly joke. My eyes snapped open. I nudged Warren awake.

"It's not a joke, sweetheart," the agent went on. "I wish it was. She's so ill they don't think she's going to make it. All the sets are finished at Pinewood. The cast and crew are already on payroll. It's costing them thousands of dollars a day while she's in the clinic. If she dies they've got to start shooting with a new Cleopatra within three days. Fox are way over budget already. They can't afford to screw around any more."

I listened horrified. I couldn't believe the heartlessness of the Fox moguls. All that mattered to them was money—and power, of course. This was all dollars and cents. What did they care if Elizabeth Taylor was dying of pneumonia? All that mattered was that the show must go on. Get someone, anyone, to take her place. Alter her costumes, put her wigs and makeup on the replacement—lights, camera, action—instant Cleopatra—just like Nescafé. It was awful. It was Hollywood. Except that it was happening in London and Elizabeth was fighting for her life in the London clinic across the street from Harley House where I had spent so much of my life.

I looked at Warren, who had awakened and was trying to listen to what was going on. "I can't—I couldn't do it—I know Elizabeth . . . I would feel too *ghoulish* stepping into her shoes like this." It was true—my whole body had turned to goose bumps during this conversation. However desperately I had wanted the part in *Cleopatra* last year, the thought of finally playing it because the favored choice had died was appalling.

"Sweethcart—don't get so emotional," said my agent, trying to calm me down. "Let's hope she doesn't die—on the other hand, think of your *career!* This is Fox's biggest movie of the year—it's going to cost over six million. It'll make you a Big Star. Besides which, if you don't do it, you'll go on suspension again," he said flatly. "I'll call you in a couple of hours after the next medical report." He hung up and I stared at the receiver numbly.

"What do you think?" said Warren, getting up and jumping into his jeans.

"It's horrible," I said lying back with my arms folded behind my neck and staring at the ceiling, "really horrible."

"It's show biz, baby," said he, pulling a crumpled blue Brooks Brothers shirt out of the eternally half-unpacked suitcase lying open on the floor. "As in there's no biz like it." He looked at me seriously, his unspectacled eyes squinting slightly. "I think it's horrible too!"

"God, I hope she doesn't die," I said.

"She won't," he said confidently, going out to the kitchen to squeeze fresh orange juice and take the fifteen mysterious vitamins he fortified himself with. "She's got nine lives, that woman. Don't worry about it, Butterfly. All you have to worry about is making breakfast." He disappeared into the kitchen.

I refused to pack as much as a powder puff until I heard any official news. On the other hand, my agent had told me not to leave the house and to be instantly available. I prowled around unhappily, chain-smoking, biting my nails and fervently wishing for Elizabeth's recovery. We talked on the phone to friends who had the "inside" track on her condition. All the radio and TV news reports seemed to differ. Some said she had pneumonia, others, a chest infection. Some said three doctors were in attendance, some said there were nine doctors, including the Queen's personal physician.

I imagined myself in Elizabeth's place. Hovering between life and death in a sterile hospital room, tubes in my throat and in my arms—what must she be thinking? Did she live her life fully enough? Or did she feel cheated of many more decades? Did she know she was possibly dying? Or was she doped up?

The last time I had seen her she was married to the English actor Michael Wilding, and Arthur Loew and I had dinner with them at LaRue in Hollywood. She was extraordinarily beautiful: deep blue eyes, hundreds of black eyelashes, and a heart-shaped face. She was down to earth. We chattered and gossiped animatedly all evening, practically ignoring Michael and Arthur. She was dying? It seemed unbelievable.

At six o'clock my agent phoned, gave me permission to go out to dinner but to leave a message on the service where I could be reached. Warren and I munched on a nut, celery and carrot salad at the Aware Inn and gloomily discussed the situation. The next morning my agent called bright and early.

"Good morning, sweetheart," he said cheerily. "You're off the hook. Liz is going to make it."

I heaved a deep sigh of relief. "Good," I breathed. "She does have nine lives after all."

Warren went to London to make *The Roman Spring of Mrs. Stone* opposite Vivien Leigh. I went too, but for a twofold purpose. My mother had been operated on for a malignancy and I wanted to be close to her. My sister Jackie got married amidst great pomp and ceremony. I had tried to dissuade her from this marriage as she was very young, and my own mistake was still fresh in my memory. But she did it anyway.

Warren and I were not getting along. The idea of marriage no longer seemed appealing to either of us. The beige chiffon wedding dress lay carefully packed in tissue paper in my closet in Hollywood, and I moved once more into Harley House in the bedroom recently vacated by Jackie.

We were spending less time together. He had recently done his two or three weeks reserve duty at George Air Force Base in Victorville. While at the base, he had bombarded me with telegrams and phone calls in L.A. expressing his misery, loneliness and undying love. So why did he fight with me and harass me all the time when we were together?

Many of his messages stressed how much he was longing to see me in the wedding dress, so, being unable to resist him when he was enchantingly persuasive, I jumped on a plane and went to spend the weekend near him at the Apple Valley Inn, a sweet, rundown hotel in Victorville close to George Air Force Base.

Being in the service definitely did not agree with Warren. He was upset, nervous, depressed and argumentative. Furious that he had to take precious time from his burgeoning career to dedicate to his country. After the initial elation of our first glorious meeting, our relationship once again deteriorated into petty fights and arguments, culminating with me getting on a plane and away from Victorville and back to L.A. as fast as possible.

We seemed to argue about anything and everything. Since Maxwell Reed, and maybe even *because* of him, I have never been the type of woman who is subservient to a man. I believed in total equality in all things and would not tolerate the idea that women were inferior to men. Consequently I was overaggressive sometimes when it wasn't necessary. Warren, being insecure and aggressive and determined to always get his own way no matter what, and I made a volatile combination. I would not give in to his often very childish demands, and he wanted his own way all the time. I had finally been released from my Fox contract after six years of slavery, and was eager to accept some of the tempting offers I was receiving, but as soon as he read the scripts he would contemptuously throw them aside.

"It's crap, sweetheart, junk—you can't do it."

"But darling, it's seventy-five thousand dollars," I demurred—and the row would start. True, he was a perfectionist, but he had been spoiled by his first film's being of high artistic caliber, and now he wouldn't settle for anything less—and he thought I shouldn't either. Unfortunately, 90 percent of the films made are *not* of high artistic caliber. I had made eighteen movies. Of those eighteen, maybe only two or three had some artistic merit. But acting is a business as well as an art. Sitting around waiting for the phone to ring and my agent to come up with the plum role of the decade was not likely to happen in the foreseeable future. Bakers bake, writers write and actors act. I wanted to work. To practice my craft until the day when, and if, a wonderful and fulfilling role would come along. Meanwhile Warren threw the scripts I was offered into the wastepaper basket.

I went to see a producer about a part I really wanted. He sat behind his giant mahogany desk, his five feet five inches elevated by an extremely high-legged chair, and surveyed me through a haze of cigar smoke.

"You've been around awhile now, dear," he said. "How old are you?"

"I'm twenty-six," I said.

"Twenty-six . . . hmmmmm . . . y'know, that's not young in this business any more, dear."

I was speechless. Not young in the business any more! What cheek! This elderly asshole—fifty if he's a day, telling *me* that twenty-six is not young any more. That epitomized the attitude that pervaded Hollywood at that time.

Discovered at sixteen—Hollywood star at twenty—washed up at twenty-six, I thought despondently. No wonder Daddy wanted me to become a secretary. I surveyed my face in my compact mirror as the elevator glided me smoothly away from this repulsive man. Not over the hill quite yet: I had my own hair and teeth and no wrinkles. What a stupid jerk, I thought, angrily shutting the

190

compact and striding out onto Sunset Boulevard. Trying to make me feel insecure, and angry because he tried to seduce me once in New York and I had rejected him.

"Men. They only want one thing," said a tiny voice in the back of my mind. "They use you. They abuse you. They're all a bunch of bastards."

I sat in Warren's canvas chair on a dark and dank stage at Elstree Studios outside London and watched Warren, dressed and made up like a young Italian gigolo, make love to Vivien Leigh. Vivien was a beautiful woman in her late forties. As the aging Mrs. Stone, an American lady looking for love and companionship in Rome, she was cast perfectly. The great beauty of her early films was no longer much in evidence. Her life, never very happy, was compounded by ill health and drinking, and she looked tired and older than her years. "Beauty is a gift. You should not destroy it," someone said to me once at a party, as I downed a vodka and tonic. Looking at Vivien, and how her lifestyle had taken its toll on her looks, I hastily ground out my cigarette and vowed to take better care of myself. She did not take kindly to me, Miss Leigh, but she certainly did to Warren. He, never one to miss an opportunity, was his most beguiling and adorable self around her.

"Why do you spend so much money on clothes?" she asked me sharply at lunch in the studio restaurant one day. "It's an *absolute* waste of good money. Why, I've never seen you in the same outfit twice." She looked at me accusingly. "And what is that you are wearing today? It looks like a man's suit."

"It is," said I, digging into my steak-and-kidney pie. "It was made for me." Men's suits for women were unusual in the early 1960s. London had not yet become the trend-setting fashion capital of the world, and ladies wore skirts in England.

"You should spend your money on jewelry, my dear," said Vivien, elegantly lifting a glass of wine with her be-ringed and brace-leted hand and scrutinizing me disapprovingly. "Jewelry is such a *good* investment. Why, with good jewelry—some pearls and rings, or an attractive brooch—you could wear a little black dress every day and look marvelous."

A little black dress every day. How boring, I thought, looking at

Warren devouring his fish and chips, and apparently oblivious to this catty exchange. He looked devastatingly handsome. There was little trace of the spotty boy I had first seen sixteen months ago.

His hair had been darkened for the part of the Italian gigolo. He had a deep tan, which, although it was out of a bottle, looked as if it came straight from Portofino. He wore a beautifully cut beige silk suit from Brioni, a cream crepe de chine shirt from Battaglia, and a brown-and-beige Saint Laurent tie. No wonder half the females in the restaurant were tripping over themselves to get a glimpse of him. The Warren Beatty sex-symbol image was beginning to emerge. Women adored him. He was loving every minute of it.

"What do you think, Warren darling?" asked Vivien, lightly resting her aristocratic hand on his arm and fluttering her beautiful pale blue eyes.

"Um, I think she looks cute," said Warren, giving me a sly wink. "No use trying to get Joanie to change her way of dressing. She does what she wants. You look like—umm—a little man," he said fondly. I raised my eyes heavenward and observed Vivien's eyelashes batting in his direction. I was not above having a touch of the green-eyed monster myself, so I gave him a swift kick under the table and he quickly went back to his fish and chips. Vivien gave me a sharp look. She was a perceptive lady and *she* knew that I knew that she fancied Warren. Whether this May–December flirtation was ever consummated I do not know. Warren was getting plenty of opportunities to be unfaithful if he chose to do so. Women were going gaga at the sight of this vision and he was pleased and flattered by their attentions.

I was worried about my mother. After the operation to remove the malignancy, she seemed in good health and spirits, but the surgery had been debilitating and upsetting to her. With Jackie married and out of the house, I again became the resident daughter, which made her extremely happy.

She worried about me. Would I ever settle down like Jackie and find a man to make me happy? She adored Warren—most women did: he charmed them all—but she was aware of our bickering and realized he was not really the kind of man who could make a woman happy forever. I knew marriage with Warren was not the answer, but I still loved him. Since I found it hard to make major decisions in my life, I continued to let the relationship drift along.

Warren had rented Peter Glenville's house in a charming square near Harrod's for the duration of filming. He was up at dawn every morning, so I preferred to luxuriate in my old familiar bed in Harley House every morning and have Mummy bring me tea, toast, marmalade and mother-and-daughter chat.

Warren and I took a trip to Paris one weekend to visit Joanne Woodward and Paul Newman, who were filming there. We took long walks along the Seine, browsed through the bookstalls and the endless art galleries, and whiled away happy hours in the cafés. I toyed with the idea of buying some paintings. After six years in Hollywood, making a healthy salary, I had almost no possessions except clothes, hundreds of books, a stereo and thousands of records. Not a chair, a teapot or a lampshade had I ever purchased. I had been encouraged by my business manager always to rent furnished apartments and to lease a car while my money was "invested" for me. I had nothing, which meant I was free to go where the wind blew me. And the wind was still blowing in Warren's direction. I knew little about art, but looking at some of Vasarely's abstract lithographs, I found the idea of spending a ton of money on these funny squares and triangles rather formidable.

The Newmans took us one evening to the Carousel, a gay night club in Montmartre. It specialized in beautiful young men and boys dressed in women's clothing who sang, danced and mimed on the tiny stage. The club was packed, mostly with tourists, but also with a sprinkling of the *haut monde* and a large group of homosexuals. All eyes focused on our table as Newman, of the fabled blue eyes, and Beatty, not so famous but with a definite aura about him, sat and sipped Poire William, a particularly potent liqueur made from pears.

The "girls" who performed were gorgeous. Divine creatures, each with her hairstyle, makeup and clothes patterned after a particular movie star. There was Marilyn Monroe—Ava Gardner—Audrey Hepburn—each one a vision, and each one more breathtaking than the last. Joanne and I began to feel rather ordinary next to all this glamour. The "girls" performed especially for our table. "Diamonds Are a Girl's Best Friend," huskily sang a vision in red lame and feathers as "she" slithered her boa invitingly over Warren's shoulder blades. "*Je t'aime, je t'aime,*" intoned a masculine but soft voice, looking into the eyes of Paul, "her" makeup so fastidiously applied that it must have taken hours.

Paul and Warren grinned sheepishly at all this attention, while Joanne and I giggled. The songs were performed for our two men, the suggestive glances and gestures directed toward them.

"We should take lessons in sex appeal from this bunch," I said to Joanne. During the finale a dozen pairs of false bosoms and false eyelashes shook and batted triumphantly from the stage as they performed their final number with bobbing ostrich feathers, beehive hairdos, and slit skirts, cleverly covering their strategic areas.

The "proprietress" came up to us after the show. "The ladies would like to 'ave you visit zem backstage—oui?" she breathed. An ancient crone in a three-foot-high red wig and black sequins who on close inspection proved to have a heavy five o'clock shadow under her pancake makeup.

"Oh, c'mon, let's," I giggled, the Poire having loosened my inhibitions.

"Um—er—do ya think we should?" said Warren, nervously glancing at the crone, whose vast false bust was resting on the shoulder of his best blue suit, while she gazed smolderingly into his eyes.

"Yes, yes. I want to see them up close. Come *on*—don't be square."

The two men reluctantly trailed behind us while Joanne and I followed "Madame" backstage to the dressing room. We walked in. Squeals and shrieks of joy from the assembled gentlemen—or ladies. It was hard to tell. Some had on full makeup but had taken off their hairpieces to reveal short-cropped hair. Some were in elaborate underwear with lace and frills and garter belts that would not have been out of place in *Playboy*. One or two had removed their lower garments, revealing that they definitely were not female.

The smell of perfume and powder was intense, as was another, subtler scent that would become more familiar as the decade progressed. They passed a joint to me but I refused. I was trying to drink it all in: the drying stockings; the photos of Jean-Paul Belmondo and Marlon Brando taped to the mirrors; the high-pitched girlish chattering. But these were men, some more gorgeous than many women I knew.

Strangely it was not Paul and Warren whom they oohed and aahed excitedly over. It was Joanne and me!

"Your 'air—eet ees so beautiful," crooned the Monroe look-alike to Joanne. " 'Ow you get that colaire—ees natural, *non?*" "*Mais oui—naturellement c'est naturel*," indignantly said "Jayne Mansfield," running her fingers through Joanne's bob, as Joanne tried to suppress a smile.

"Ooh—*regardez—regardez les* lashes," said a "Sophia Loren" pointing at my eyelashes. Three or four of them descended on me, avidly discussing my lashes.

"On *le bottom*—oh, *c'est très, très originale*," said "Sophia," her eyes staring into mine. " 'Ow you do eet?"

I explained how I sometimes stuck fake eyelashes on my bottom lids—a fashion trend in London. They listened enthralled.

Our dresses, jewelry and hair were examined and fingered. The two men stood forgotten in the corner of the cramped dressing room watching amusedly while Joanne and I were plied with questions about our looks. Eventually we escaped, laughing hysterically, into the Place Pigalle, and strolled over to a nearby bar. The evening was unforgettable for giving me the worst hangover I have ever experienced in my life. On waking, my head felt like a balloon. A sledgehammer was inside it pounding so hard I thought it would explode.

"It's the Poire!" said Warren who, although not a drinker, had done his share that night. "It's ninety proof."

"Oh, God," I gasped, catching a glimpse of my dissipated white face in the mirror. "If the 'girls' could only see me now!"

"Somehow I think that tonight in Montmartre there will be two new stars," said Warren. "Joanne Woodward and Joan Collins starring at the Carousel—authentic down to the last bottom eyelash."

. . .

After Warren finished filming *The Roman Spring of Mrs. Stone* we returned to Los Angeles and my house on Sunset Plaza Drive— and the smog and the rows. We argued so much and over such mundane and petty things that the last few months of our relationship are a hazy blur. My mother came to visit with fifteen-year-old Bill, who tended to hero-worship Warren.

"Why did you let them come?" Warren hissed at me loud enough for Mummy, who was sunbathing in the garden, to overhear. "We never have any privacy now—ever." He rummaged through his usual messy suitcase, which was lying on the floor with his shirts and jeans falling out of it, and glared at me accusingly.

I glared back. "She's my *mother*," I said flatly. "I pay most of the rent on this house, and I have every right to have her visit, so stop being such a rat."

My eyes filled with tears. I didn't let him know how much he hurt me by his antagonism toward Mummy. I tried to never let him know he hurt me now. I felt terrible about her recent illness. I wanted to try and be the perfect daughter to her and make her happy as I hadn't done since I was a child. My sister was pregnant now, and Mummy was thrilled, hinting strongly that it was time I took a turn in that direction.

It was obvious I had to be the one to end it with Warren. He seemed content to let it drift sloppily along. What happened to the glorious romantic fun we used to have? Why did all of my relationships with men turn sour? Was it my fault? Was I too strong? Or was I too weak? Or was it—and this I knew deep down to be the truth—that I really *wanted* only the neurotic ones, the men unable truly to love, truly to support and truly to give. Only by gaining the love of one of these impossible men could I prove to myself that I was a worthy person.

Finally I accepted an offer from Norman Panama and Mel Frank to go to London to play opposite Bob Hope and Bing Crosby in *The Road to Hong Kong*.

"It's crap," said Warren, throwing the script to the floor. "Crap! Why do you need to do it?"

I looked at him. "Two reasons," I said simply. "For the money— and to get away from you."

We stared at each other for a long time. It was the end, and we knew it. We held each other tightly. Nearly two years of loving and fighting had passed. He had become a man and almost a star, and I had marked time.

It was time to move on.

CHAPTER

Eight

THE SIXTIES WERE YOUTH. THEY
were freedom and "flower power." They were "doing your own
thing"; "letting it all hang out," and throwing convention to the
winds. Nowhere epitomized the Swinging Sixties more than London. It was the place to be, and that's where I was. The decade
was young, there was excitement in the air, a feeling of vibrancy
and great expectations in people's attitudes. Optimism, originality
and enthusiasm were the *modus operandi* of the day. Everyone
seemed young, enthusiastic and fresh.

The "Mersey Beat" was starting to drift down from Liverpool,
where four mopheaded youths in their early twenties were getting
started and a new kind of music was beginning to be heard. They
called themselves "The Beatles." Discotheques were sprouting all
over England. The youth culture happened with a vengeance.
Mary Quant had burst upon the scene with the miniskirt. Girls,
and women too, were showing more and more legs. Although there
was a war in Vietnam, it was a great time—a wonderful time to be
young.

I sat in the White Elephant, one of the most fashionable of
London's new restaurants, and observed the scene at lunch. Half
of Hollywood seemed to be there making deals, setting up pictures
or just sitting there. Many American movie people had decided to
leave smog-ridden, heavily taxed Los Angeles and move to tranquil, civilized nonfoggy (thanks to the Clean Air Act in the mid-1950s) London. The restaurant was abuzz with conversation and

198

activity. Crystal sconces glittered; the Italian waiters moved swiftly from table to table. "Cubby" Broccoli, the American producer, stopped by my table to chat. He told me he was producing a film based on Ian Fleming's James Bond spy stories, and they were off to the Caribbean soon. I wished him luck and watched as he said hello to two young men seated at a nearby table.

"That's Tony Newley," said my girlfriend. "You know, the fellow who's just had a big success with that new show *Stop the World—I Want to Get Off.*"

Ah, yes. I remembered reading the reviews when it had opened a few weeks previously. The critics had been harsh, but very intrigued by this practically one-man show in which Newley, in white clown-type makeup and baggy pants, played an amalgam of Everyman. He also directed it and wrote the book, music and lyrics with Leslie Bricusse, who, my friend informed me, was the man lunching with him.

Newley looked familiar. I stared, trying to remember where I had seen that face before. Then it came to me. He was Artful Dodger in David Lean's film of *Oliver Twist*. He was about fourteen then, but still had the same cheeky Cockney face, darting intelligent eyes and strong Romanesque nose. He was now in his late twenties, I thought, satanic and intense looking, with thick, dark brown hair and beautifully expressive hands that he used constantly in the conversation. He met my glance and a flicker of recognition crossed his face. I looked away. I was heavily off men right now. Besides, glances in restaurants had caused me trouble before.

I thought no more about him until Robert Wagner, who was also making a movie in London, called and said he had tickets for *Stop the World* and invited me to go. R.J. and I had been friends since the disastrous *Stopover Tokyo*, and since his separation from Natalie Wood we had gone out together several times in London.

The newspapers and gossip magazines jumped on this hot "new twosome" immediately. Numerous articles appeared to the effect that we were "consoling" each other while Natalie and Warren were now dating openly. These reports were fairly irksome. Enough that Warren and I had ended our relationship with honesty and objectivity, trying to remain friends, but to have the eager eyes of the yellow press announcing avidly that Natalie and Warren had been carrying on a passionate affair while she was still married to R.J. and Warren was engaged to me was aggravating, although I knew there might have been some truth to it.

However, Warren, ever quick to make hay while the sun shone, had not found it disadvantageous to his burgeoning career to be dating Natalie, a major star, and since he was fond of seeing himself in photographs with well-known actresses, it served him well. As one wit remarked, "I knew Warren before he only bedded household names." While their relationship developed, R.J.'s and mine did not. Although he was very attractive, I was still neurotic enough to be truly interested only in complex, difficult men—and R.J. was gentle and sweet and too nice for me. We were—hello cliché!—"just good friends." The tabloid-reading public, however, found it hard to believe that an attractive man and woman could merely be friends. Consequently there was plenty of gossip and speculation about our friendship.

I was completely enthralled by *Stop the World—I Want to Get Off.* It was one of the most brilliant, creative and excitingly original shows I had ever seen, made all the more so by the magical presence of Tony Newley. His was a *tour de force*, bravura performance, and although many of the critics belittled it, his talent was the maypole from which the ribbons and form of the musical flowed.

The premise of the show was simple. It was the story of "Littlechap," a sort of Everyman of the world, alternately bumptious and vulnerable, belligerent and sensitive, aging from brash youth to elder statesman, and in between running a veritable gamut of emotional highs and lows, punctuated by show-stopping songs that culminated in the classic "What Kind of Fool Am I?"

At the end of the show I was drained but exhilarated. I hadn't witnessed anything in the theater that had moved me so much for ages. Not only the show, which I had been informed was autobiographical in flavor, but by Newley himself.

"Let's go backstage and say hello," I suggested to R.J., as the cast took their final bows to tumultuous applause. He, as impressed with the show as I was, agreed, and we made our way through the labyrinthine musty back corridors of the Queen's

Theatre to Newley's dressing room. A gruff, heavyset man greeted us suspiciously, asked our names and told us rather uncharmingly to wait, as the "young master" was removing his makeup.

R.J. and I raised our eyebrows at each other at this rather grand epithet, used previously, I recall, only by Noel Coward himself. We waited. And waited. And waited. After twenty minutes of staring at the seedy, cracked and waterlogged walls of this far from elegant anteroom, and without being offered so much as a glass of water, my Gemini impatience got the better of me and we decided to leave.

"We're going," I called to a shabby green velvet curtain that separated the waiting room from the star's dressing area.

"Oh—hang on a minute, love. Just putting on me drawers," called a voice in a beguiling Cockney accent. The curtain drew back with a flourish and there stood Littlechap in the flesh. Little he was—at least not very tall. Thin as a rail, white as a sheet, blue of eye and black of hair and rather sexy. He was toweling traces of white pancake from behind his ears, and his intelligent, deepset eyes were still encircled by the heavy black eyeliner he wore in the show.

"How d'ja do. How d'ja do, sorry to keep you waiting. This muck takes forever to scrub off." We shook hands and R.J. and I gushed how much we *loved* the show, and how wonderful he was. He seemed genuinely pleased to hear this and listened with deep interest to our comments.

The heavyset man hovered disapprovingly in the background, fiddling about with stuff on the dressing table, making it obvious we were not at all welcome.

"Well we better take off and get something to eat," said R.J., intercepting a basilisk stare from the vigilante at the dressing table.

"Why don't we have a bite together?" said Tony. "Unless you two have other plans?"

"No, no, come on—come with us," said I, my interest in "young master" Newley slightly piqued.

"Shall we go to the Trat?" said Tony, putting an old green tweed jacket on top of his baggy gray flannels and black polo neck. "I usually have a table there."

"Sounds good," said R.J., and after Tony bade his surly retainer a brusque "Ta-ta, Ter," we crossed Shaftesbury Avenue to the stylish new Italian bistro, the Trattoria Terrazza. We were greeted effusively by Mario and Franco, who led us down the tiny winding staircase to a marble-floored, white-stucco-painted room hung with Chianti bottles and humming with conversation. In fact, the acoustics at the Trat were such that conversation had to be conducted three pitches above normal level.

This, added to the proximity of the tiny tables to each other, the excitable Italian waiters—who occasionally burst into either song or rage (a trolley laden with desserts was constantly getting in the way of one of the waiters, who would angrily ram it against the patrons' tables)—and the appetizing smells made the evening quite stimulating.

"What will you have, pretty lady?" said Mr. Newley, frowning at the wine list. "Pretty lady"!—an effusive compliment for an Englishman, I thought.

"Verdicchio, please," I said—and we plunged into animated conversation.

We had many friends in common, and the talk flowed easily, punctuated by Tony's sudden bursts of staccato laughter. He had a keen Cockney humor, which I appreciated. I was able to slip easily into the vernacular of London slang or Beverly Hills small talk, having spent all my adult life between these two opposite poles. Two hours and several bottles of Verdicchio later we bade each other fond farewells outside the restaurant and wended our respective ways home. It had been a stimulating evening. Tony was bright, amusing and attractive, intelligent and likable.

Joyce Blair came to lunch at Shepperton a few days later and I was surprised to hear, "Whatever did you do to Tony? He fancies you like mad."

I sprawled on the couch in my portable dressing room and peeled an apple.

"What did he say, then?"

"Oh, you know. The usual. How fantastic you look and what a great body. All that sort of thing."

"Oh, did he say anything about my mind?"

202

Joyce giggled. "I think old Tone's a bit of a male chauvinist. He didn't mention your mind. He thought you were funny, though."

"Oh, goody," I said sarcastically, taking a bite from the apple. "That must mean then he *does* think I've got a mind."

"I'll tell you something about Tone," said Joyce, leaning forward confidentially. "He's a super person—really super—I mean we were at Aida Foster's together so we've known each other since we were kids and I've always adored him, but do you know—" she lowered her voice and leaned forward even more—"do you know that he's *never* been in love?"

I stopped in mid-munch. "Never?" I said incredulously. "What is he—gay?"

"No, no. He loves ladies. No, he's just never been able to fall in love with anyone. Can you imagine, darling, twenty-nine and never been in love. Awful isn't it?"

"*Very* interesting," I said, studying my apple core. "Is that where the song comes from at the end? You know, the fool song?"

"Yes, yes," she said excitedly. "Those lyrics are *exactly* the story of his life. What kind of fool am I, who never fell in love, it seems that I'm the only one that I have been thinking of."

"Oh, please, save us from *that*," I said, throwing the apple core in the wastebasket. A man who has *never* been in love. How sad— but how challenging. I looked at Joyce and she looked back mischievously.

"Oh, no, dear. I'm *not* interested in making him change his ways," I said hastily.

"Well, a little lunch wouldn't hurt," she said lightly. "He called me yesterday, drove me *mad* for your number. I finally agreed that I might be able to persuade you to have lunch with him—and me too, of course," she added quickly, seeing my dubious look. "Oh, come on darling. Whatever can happen at *lunch*?"

"You'd be surprised," I said, finding myself, against my will, intrigued by this ambiguous Newley character. I stood up to get ready for the scene. We looked at each other and I smiled at Joyce.

Never been in love, eh? Well, we'll see about that.

• • •

I found myself thinking about Anthony Newley during the next twenty-four hours. I was, for nearly the first time in my life, absolutely free of all emotional entanglements. I had no roots; no home; no husband, lover or parents to answer to; no children to look after; no studio contractual obligations. I could do what I liked, when I liked. It was bliss. If I wanted to fly to Paris or Rome for the weekend, all I had to do was pack a bag and jump on a plane. This feeling of total freedom and disencumbrance was so heady and refreshing after my disciplined childhood, disastrous marriage, studio contracts with Rank and Fox, who had controlled my every career move, and then, total involvements sequentially with Sydney, Arthur, George and Warren, that I almost didn't know how to handle it.

I was like a bird that had just learned to fly. The world was mine and I intended to keep it that way for a while.

Occasionally I would get a flicker of envy as I would see some cherubic infant being fondled by its loving mother. Feeling "broody" came upon me now and then, but I pushed these strange maternal feelings away without stopping to analyze and dissect them. I had felt a sense of loss since the abortion. Sometimes when I saw a tiny baby I would automatically calculate what age mine would have been had I had it. But, as with all my deep and subliminal feelings, I would not allow myself to dwell on them. Life was gay. Life was fun. Life was for doing and seeing and going places. There was no time for ruminative self-pity or unhappiness. I wanted to live to the hilt. In doing so, however, I lost touch with a certain basic reality. Never stopping to analyze my constant mistakes, I blindly rushed in where angels feared to tread . . . and Tony Newley was no exception.

Any woman with any horse sense does not fall in love with a man who openly proclaims to the world in song and verse that he is unable to love. She might like him. She might admire his talent and personality—but if she is smart she will not get involved in a relationship with "doomed" written all over it.

Poles apart—we were worlds apart. He was a Libra, quiet, intellectual, home-based, deeply involved in his work and himself. His capacity for *joie de vivre* was not great. He was uncomfortable and out of place except with close, old friends, and in familiar sur-

204

roundings. He hated to travel—disliked new things. He was nothing like my father, yet the feelings he generated in me, as in all the men to whom I became deeply attached, were exactly those of that little Joan of so long ago, trying to make Daddy love her. I was everything that he shouldn't want in a woman: Gemini—mercurial, moody, exuberant, inexhaustible, extroverted, highly energized and quick-tempered—thinking only of today, dismissing yesterday and letting tomorrow take care of itself.

But despite our different lifestyles and personalities, we became involved. It did not, of course, happen to us simultaneously. First I became infatuated and then persuaded him to feel the same way. Three weeks after our first meeting we became lovers. Not long after that he *professed* to love me.

So, now that I had won his hard-earned "love," what did I intend to do? Was I going to play the little woman role and cook liver and bacon every lunchtime for him at Leslie and Evie Bricusse's flat in Stanmore? Was I going to sit night after night applauding wildly in the stalls as he performed, reveling in the adulation of his enthusiastic audiences? I didn't really know. I was playing it one day at a time.

My mother was dying. I knew she was dying—so did Daddy and Jackie. Only sixteen-year-old Bill was protected from the truth, although with the wisdom of adolescence he no doubt suspected. The final illness came upon her so swiftly that it took us all by surprise.

After a brief period of hospitalization she came back to Harley House to spend her last days with the family. I had to be there. I could not face the fact that she was dying. I refused to believe it. Even now I cannot really believe she is gone. Her photographs are with me all the time: her always smiling, happy face, with the fair curly hair, sparkling blue eyes and high cheekbones, which last I inherited from her, as well as her tremendous *joie de vivre*.

Unfortunately my mother was the product of a strict Victorian authoritarian upbringing. She was nervous about her intellectual capabilities and consequently had a tendency to sometimes play the "dumb blonde" role. She so adored my father that she even gave up all her own friends when they first married and his friends became hers. He was sometimes critical of her and seemed to never let her be her own person and enjoy herself. He, being a male chauvinist before we even knew the meaning of the phrase, ruled the roost totally. His word was law, and woe betide any of us who disobeyed it.

"I pay the bills around here," he would roar if anyone even dared remonstrate or argue with him. "If you're so clever, you make the money to support us all. Then I'll listen to you."

He would shout at Mummy often. It is from him that I inherited *my* impatience and tendency to fly off the handle at petty irritations. But it didn't matter how much he yelled at her—she *adored* him! I could never understand how she could be so warm and loving to someone who sometimes treated her so badly, even though during my early adult life I obviously did the same with my men. Her mentality was such that she believed in the superiority of the male, but at the same time acknowledged men as "the enemy."

She was filled with a host of misconceptions and superstitions that she drummed into me at an early age. I painstakingly exorcised them on the analyst's couch years later. A lot of these adages I deliberately set out to disprove as soon as I became aware of the male sex. *But,* there is a lingering residue of her teachings bouncing around in the subconscious somewhere that agrees with a lot of her philosophies: "Men are no good." "They only want *one thing* from a woman." "He'll have *no respect* for you if you let him *have his way* with you." "Nice girls don't let men *touch them* unless they are married." And so on, and so on . . .

She was not alone in her viewpoints. Millions of women in the 1930s, 1940s and 1950s felt the same way and brought up their little girls to feel the same guilts and unclean feelings about their sexuality. Hopefully, today my generation of women have been able to learn from the sexual revolution of the sixties, and from their own ashamed and furtive early years, how *not* to indoctrinate *their* children.

Be that as it may, I loved my mother, and it was unbearable to know that she was leaving us. Her forte, of course, was motherhood. The kind of mothering that keeps you home from school if you wake up with so much as a sneeze; that sees that you get three good nourishing meals a day, plus at least ten hours sleep; that makes sure all the doors and windows are locked and that there is a light on in the hallway when you go to sleep, in case you get frightened during the night. And who, after nagging you to pick up your dirty clothes, will sigh heavily and pick them up for you. We were taken care of very well. Even during the years of rationing during the war we always had meat, eggs, sugar, and sometimes even candy.

Mummy had her reward from Jackie: a beautiful little baby girl, Tracy, a few months old and the apple of her eye. "If only Joan would get married and settle down," she would say wistfully to Jackie, as they played each afternoon with Tracy in the photograph-laden living room of Harley House. The room was now an absolute shrine to the Collins sisters. Literally hundreds of pictures of us hung on the walls, clustered on the mantelpiece, sideboard and TV. She certainly was proud of her children, and I felt guilty that I had not been able to be closer to her in the past few years.

I refused to leave England and go back to the States while Mummy was so sick. We had taken her to many different doctors and specialists, but the prognosis was always pessimistic. We were told she had only a few months to live, and I was determined to be with her as much as I could.

The Road to Hong Kong was finished. It had been fun. I liked Bob Hope immensely. He was the consummate comedian: confident, aggressive, always completely in command and never at a loss for a joke or a quip. He was consistently charming, warm, and down to earth. He was also a Gemini.

Bing Crosby, on the other hand, was a different breed: offhand, grumpy and vague. He appeared to me always as an old man acting very young, or a young man who looked old. His face was like a piece of crumpled tissue paper and I never felt his eyes when he looked at me. They looked *through* me. He did not endear himself to the crew, and he had the revolting habit of spitting on the set or wherever he happened to be. We spent days shooting

207

on a stage that had sawdust on the floor, and he would clear his throat and aim a great wad of pipe spit on the piles of sawdust scattered around, to the chagrin of the tiny Cockney in charge of sweeping the set.

"Blimey if I 'as to clean up any more of that old geezer's spittle, I'm goin' to ram it dahn 'is bleedin' throat, I swear I will," he muttered furiously, as he collected the debris in his spade and deposited it in a bucket. Crosby puffed away on his pipe, oblivious to all the activity going on around him. We were standing in the middle of the set getting the final light checks for our love scene, and Bing had spat at least three times that morning.

"How'd you like to have to kiss him?" I whispered to the little Cockney as he angrily brushed at the sawdust around my feet. "Ooohh, you poor little darlin'. I'd rather kiss Hitler," said he, and sniffing disgustedly he walked away.

I arranged my face into the correct loving expression to gaze into Crosby's bland blue eyes and smell his rancid breath and wondered again how people could think an actress's life was just a bowl of cherries.

Tony—Tony Newley—I was obsessed by his outrageous talent, by his brilliant performances. He astounded me with his virtuosity. I and many other people, including himself, thought he was a genius. But genuises are complicated. And being infatuated with one wasn't a bowl of cherries, either, for although professing love for me, *he* was also interested in a young blonde, in the cast of *Stop the World*. This had been gathering momentum ever since rehearsals had first commenced in April, and various difficulties of consummation only increased Tony's interest.

Blissfully involved in the first passionate throes of an exciting romance with an exciting man, working hard on *Hong Kong*, and devoting what time I had left to spending it with my ailing mother, I had blinkers on as far as another girl in his life was concerned. It wasn't really until six years later, when he wrote, produced, directed and starred in an autobiographical film called *Can Hieronymus Merkin Ever Forget Mercy Humppe and Find True Happiness?* that the full extent of his infatuation with the girl was crystallized for me.

But these were the days and months of what to me has always been the best time of a relationship. The beginning. I was well aware of the familiar pattern and how things started to wear off. I knew I expected too much from men. I expected them to be perfect. I couldn't seem to cope with human frailties and idiosyncrasies. Certainly I was not perfect myself. So was it asking too much to demand faultlessness from others? But now I was giving Tony the benefit of the doubt and making myself well aware of all his failings and foibles before I committed myself. I had decided he would make a fine father for the children I felt I was now ready to have. All I had to do was convince *him*.

I threw myself into the role of "camp follower" with a vengeance. I turned down all movie offers to the despair of my agents who, after working hard to get me out of Fox, now could not cash in on the money I could be making. I devoted myself to being the perfect wife. I cooked. I cleaned. I shopped. Culinary arts I did not know I possessed suddenly blossomed in me. Sausages and Mash, Toad-in-the-Hole, Shepherd's Pie, Irish Stew, Bread-and-Butter Pudding, Rhubarb and Custard—I became an expert in these simple English dishes, and a regular customer at the supermarket on Marylebone Road.

I had competition for his attention though. His mother, Grace, his manager, Terry, and various others all vied with me and each other to be close to him.

His mother worshipped the ground he walked on. She was a sweet birdlike little woman who had given birth to him illegitimately and had been made to pay the price for this (then) outrageous transgression. She had brought him up practically singlehandedly, and she lavished all of her love, attention and adoration on him. He took this as his due. Although she had married, finally, during the war, nevertheless each day she appeared regularly at his cozy, shabby little flat off Earl's Court Road to make his breakfast. She then stayed for the rest of the day doing the housework and just being in his orbit.

I first met her one wintry Monday morning when the door to Tony's bedroom opened at nine o'clock and a perky little face, not unlike his, but crowned with a mass of gray curls, said "Good

209

morning, son, what would you like for your breakfast today? I've got some lovely kippers, or I'll do you some bacon and eggs and fried bread. Or would you rather have some nice porridge, seeing as how it's such a nasty cold day?"

She did not acknowledge that there was another person in the bed with him, and after he had placed his order for porridge, she scampered away without so much as a glance in my direction.

"Do you think I could have a cup of tea?" I asked meekly of the "young master," who seemed not at all surprised by this unusual confrontation—or lack of it.

"Oh—Flower, of course. Mum—Mum," he called, and the little lady scuttled back in again, gray curls bobbing, and wiping her hands on her apron.

"Yes, son," she said nervously, glancing at me.

"Mum. This is Joanie, and she'd like a cup of tea."

"If it's not too much trouble," I said hastily, trying to look innocent and beguiling.

"No—no. Not at all. How do you like it—er—Joanie?"

"Oh. Two lumps please." I smiled sweetly, hoping she would think what a delightful daughter-in-law I would make. "I'll come and help you make the porridge if you like."

"No—no. That's all right. Not to bother, dear. I'll do it." And she quickly disappeared again, no doubt thinking what loose morals the girls of today's generation had. Later Grace and I became friends and, in fact, some of the feelings that I had for my own mother were transferred to her. But at the beginning she was wary of any woman that Tony became involved with.

I instantly became great friends with Tony's best friend and collaborator, Leslie Bricusse, and his beautiful wife, Evie. It was rare to have a four-sided friendship in which any combination of the individuals got along like a house on fire, but the four of us did. At Leslie's and my urging, one cold December weekend we forced Tony on a plane to Paris and away from his ever-present entourage, to sample some of the delights of another environment. He needed a lot of persuasion. It was hard for him to leave the comfort and security of his snug flat in London for "foreign parts," even for two days, and Gallic cooking did not agree with his sensitive stomach. But I was determined to make him get away from his hermitlike existence and get used to some of the better things in life.

One of the songs in the show epitomized the renaissance that Tony was experiencing with his newfound success and acclaim. It was called "I Wanna Be Rich."

> *"I wanna be rich*
> *And live in L.A.,*
> *Go crazy at nighttime*
> *And sleep in the day,*
> *An Italian car*
> *As long as the street,*
> *And the local broads will arrive in hordes,*
> *It'll knock 'em off their feet.*
> *I wanna be famous*
> *And be in the news,*
> *And date a T.V. star*
> *Whenever I choose,*
> *Give me half a chance to lead a dance*
> *And make my pitch*
> *And I'll be dirty rotten filthy stinking* RICH." ©

I fitted well into the "go out with a T.V. star" line. Tony was starting to acclimatize himself to a more sybaritic life as he became more successful.

Leslie and Tony's idol was the Scandinavian filmmaker Ingmar Bergman. So admiring were they of his work that they adopted part of his name and incorporated it into their own names. They still refer to each other by these nicknames to this day Newley became Newberg, and Bricusse became Brickman. Our sons, who today are great friends, also now call each other Newberg and Brickman.

The four of us had wonderful times and a great kinship. I relied heavily on the camaraderie of this four-sided relationship to help me through the dark days of my mother's failing health and death. Her death, early one May morning in 1962, was almost a relief, as she had been in great pain. She must have known what was happening although we all desperately tried to keep her from knowing the truth.

A few days before she died I sat at her bedside gossiping and telling her jokes, hoping to make her forget her pain. Suddenly she took my hand and looked me in the eye and with great lucidity asked, "What are you going to do with your life? It's time you settled down. You're not going to be young and beautiful forever, you know."

My mother rarely confronted me with this kind of probing question. She had let me live my own life for a long time now. I was taken aback at this, for her, frank approach.

"Well, Tony and I will probably get married—when he gets his divorce," I said, crossing my fingers and sounding confident.

"Ah—I'm glad, darling. He seems good for you. He's stopped you from gadding about." She closed her eyes and breathed deeply and I thought she had gone to sleep. I gently withdrew my hand from hers, but as I did she opened her eyes and looked at me with such love in her face that I could hardly keep from crying.

"You'd be a marvelous mother, darling," she whispered. "I hope you have a baby one day. I hope you have one soon." She closed her eyes again and I gazed at her, the tears streaming down my face. I mentally kicked myself for the fact that there was no way now that she could ever hold a child of mine in her arms. It was too late. I knew it was only a matter of days. My tears fell on her hand and she opened her eyes and smiled at me.

"You're so easily led," she whispered. "And you're so strong too. It makes it difficult for you, difficult." Her voice trailed off and she closed her eyes and murmured as she drifted off to sleep, "I hope you have a child soon. Have it soon, darling. . . ." She loosened her hand in mine and slept. Her hand was so thin and vulnerable, the blue veins standing up like tiny rivers on the frail white skin. My mother. The only person really in my life who had ever cared about me. She was going. And I could do nothing to save her. I went to my room and sobbed for two hours. I then made a resolution. If I did nothing else, I was going to try to do something to please her and make her happy. Although I did not believe in an afterlife, in some way I knew that if and when I had a child she would know about it and be happy.

I cried all my tears for Mummy that evening. When Daddy came into my room at six-thirty the next morning and said, "She's

212

gone," I had already faced the loss and the tears had been shed. But the resolution remained. I had an ambition and a goal now. For her. And I was going to make it happen—come what may.

I rented yet another house in Los Angeles. Tony and the Bricusses came to visit for two weeks. Cordell Mews was nestled in the Hollywood Hills behind the fabled Doheny Estates. It was a tiny house, eclectically furnished in chinoiserie and Melrose Avenue pseudo-English antiques. The master bedroom featured a giant bed with an ornately scalloped gold-painted headboard. Tony took one look at this Hollywoodian masterpiece and fell on it gasping for breath. "Ha, ha!" we all shrieked. "What a sense of humor the young master does have." Unfortunately he was not being humorous—a flu bug had attacked him even as he had surveyed the palaces of the affluent during the drive to the house, and he was seized with simultaneous headache, stomachache, throat ache and muscle ache.

"Oh, God, Flower—I'm so sorry," he moaned, as Evie and I scurried about bringing him aspirin and hot lemon and honey—his staple drink, which usually warded off attacks on his ever delicate throat.

"Never mind, darling." I bustled, doing my Florence Nightingale impression. "It's just jet lag. You'll be up and about tomorrow."

"Please God," he groaned pitifully, and sank back onto the carefully arranged pillows we had surrounded him with to protect his head from the wooden monstrosity looming behind him.

"I think I'll have a little kip," he said, putting large wads of pink waxy substance in his ears and placing a black eye mask over his feverish eyes. He wore pajamas—the only man I had ever met, other than my father, who did so—and arranged a decrepit old camel-colored scarf around his neck. He pulled the covers up to his nose and fell instantly asleep. He was, enviably, always able to fall asleep any time, anywhere. I looked at him snoring and tiptoed out to join Leslie and Evie in the living room. What a start to a romantic, whirlwind holiday.

I had planned dinner on the patio, where we could look at the twinkling lights of Los Angeles spread out like a sequined shawl and listen to the newest Sinatra and Mathis records on the excellent stereo system. I had prepared my favorite dish, *Pomme Paysanne*, which I had been introduced to by Laurence Harvey. Actually "Peasant Potato" was the pseudonym for a large baked potato filled with fresh sevruga caviar, butter and sour cream. Even with caviar at fifty dollars an ounce, I had not stinted myself or my guests. I managed to eat several ounces and two potatoes trying to get over my disappointment at Tony's indisposition.

One could not be downhearted for too long, however, around Leslie and Evie. They were young, fun and in love. Evie, with her flawless olive skin, huge dark eyes, lustrous black hair and hourglass figure, was one of the warmest, kindest and funniest girls I knew. She still is. And Leslie, with his Cambridge-fair, typically English looks, owllike glasses and biting humor, was stimulating and witty enough to make me forget Tony wheezing away in the huge "Hollywood" bed. They are two of my closest friends to this day.

Leslie was a great planner. That evening, after several bottles of white wine, we plotted and planned our two-week vacation every minute from dawn to dusk. It was organized with soldierlike precision. Leslie was a grabber of life, and each new day was an adventure to be discovered and savored and enjoyed to the utmost. So he and I had a lot in common. We both had new Polaroid cameras, which we used constantly. Because of the Bricusses, I saw Los Angeles and California through new eyes, discovering places and things about the city that I had not seemed to be aware of before. Life became a constant photo call. Not the boring, uncomfortable sessions in the sterile portrait gallery at the studios but spur-of-the-moment funny photos snapped wherever and whenever.

"Quick, get the Polaroid. Tony's drowning," someone would squeal and off we'd go. Snap—tear—count to ten—pull—*voilà!*

"Oh, it's good of you, Evie"—"Oh, no, I look *awful*—but you look *great!*"

The coffee table was heaped with dozens of pictures. Mugging it up outside Dino's on the Strip, Tony wielding a large comb and trying to look like Kookie "Lend me your comb" Byrnes. There we were at Disneyland, surrounded by Mickey Mouse and Donald

Duck, and falling down with laughter. There were Evie and I in the bathroom, in the process of teasing our hair to immense bee-hives fourteen or sixteen inches high, wearing bras and tights, caught openmouthed with surprise. There was Tony by the swimming pool in Palm Springs wearing football boots, drooping black socks and long gray shorts, lifting with mock effort a huge pair of dumbbells.

There we were, the four of us, clustered around Sammy Davis, Jr., in his dressing room in Vegas, our faces full of admiration, for there was a mutual exchange of hero worship between Tony and Sammy. Sammy often "did" Tony in his act, and was Newley's and Bricusse's first and biggest booster in the States. He, not Tony, had the first big hit with "What Kind of Fool Am I?" Quite a few Newley-Bricusse songs were getting air play now in the States, especially on KLAC. We would often hear the strident Cockney tones boom forth with "Yes, We Have No Bananas," and "Pop Goes the Weasel," but he was still a virtual unknown as far as most of America was concerned.

Leslie had the incredible knack of combining extremely hard, prolific work with a large measure of holidays, vacations and pleasure trips. He could make a simple outing to the zoo a gala event. He was able to turn the most mundane situation into a great adventure. It is a priceless gift, and he has managed through the years to continue doing it, juggling his and Evie's and their son Adam's lives and balancing them with their several homes all over the world, and their dozens of friends. Wherever "Brickman" goes there is always instant action.

All too soon the brief vacation drew to a close. Time for them to return to London and for Tony to start *Stop the World* again for a few months until they would bring the show to New York for the fall season under the auspices of the "King of the Broadway Producers," David Merrick. During his summer break Tony was also going to star in a very demanding role in a movie called *The Small World of Sammy Lee*, while also working with Leslie on two future projects for musicals—*Noah* and *Mr. Fat and Mr. Thin*. On top of that he was appearing in three or four TV specials, his own TV show—called "The Johnny Darling Show"—and cutting at least two or three records. I realized that for the next few months the boy was going to be very, very busy indeed. How I was going to fit into his crammed schedule was a puzzlement. I allied my fortunes with those of the Bricusses. We planned at least three trips during the spring and summer. I had made my own mind up as far as Tony was concerned. I had decided to marry him, and I had made it clear to him that this was what I wanted from our relationship. Having already been married and still only separated from Ann Lynn, he was ambivalent and dreaded another marriage, but he was also terrified of losing me. His feelings vacillated back and forth like a yo-yo. One day totally enamored, he could not consider life without me. The next, careless indifference. Adamant that he would be a disaster as a husband and that we were from two different worlds . . . "What can a rich, young, beautiful film star see in a married Cockney, half-Jewish git?" he would ask me ruefully, sitting behind his shabby, top-heavy dressing table backstage at the Queen's Theatre, in his ancient moth-eaten navy blue dressing gown from Marks and Spencer, a brown hairnet scraping his heavy wavy hair off his white forehead, while he scrubbed the cold cream around and around until his black-and-white makeup turned into gray mud.

"I'm half Jewish too, Newberg, don't you forget it. A half-Jewish princess from Bayswater via Sunset Boulevard. I think we make a great combination." I put my head close to his and we studied ourselves in the fly-specked mirror. "If our children have my looks and your brains there'll be no stopping them. It will be an *unbeatable* combination!" He smiled faintly.

"Ah, Flower, you always look on the bright side, don't you?"

"You bet," I said optimistically. "But wouldn't it be awful if the children had your looks and my brains!"

Tony had started divorce proceedings against Ann Lynn, from whom he had been separated for three years. The English courts were notoriously long-winded as far as divorces were concerned, unlike the States, where divorce is as easy to get as a cold. I knew it would be a long and difficult time but I felt confident we were going to win.

While Tony was rehearsing in New York for *Stop the World*,

the Bricusses and I spent a week in Jamaica. It had been five or six years since *Seawife*. I revisited the beaches and lagoons with nostalgic interest. Leslie and Evie thought the idea of Tony and me married was super. Even when we sat one evening listening to the ominous tones of the radio announcing that President Kennedy was going to stand firm and not allow Russian bases on Cuba (we were holidaying right in the middle of the Cuban missile crisis!) I was still preoccupied with Tony. We realized that Jamaica was rather too close to Cuba for comfort and that even getting *out* of Jamaica and back to the States might be a trifle dangerous. We flew back to New York.

Tony met us at the airport, thrilled to see me, but at the Philadelphia opening he was cool. First-night nerves, the Bricusses assured me. He's scared; everything is on the line now. But things weren't the same between us. He confessed he was having a fling with the young blonde from *Stop the World*. He realized that she was in every way wrong—but what could he do? The flesh is weak. I knew that. We decided to separate. Heavy-hearted, I flew back to Los Angeles carrying a French poodle named Ladybird that Tony had given me. Now she seemed destined to be my life's companion. I had promised the Bricusses and Tony that whatever personal problems we had, I would definitely attend the first night of *Stop the World* in New York. A week later I flew back and stayed at the Drake Hotel. I was fulfilling my duties as a friend, but I couldn't fight Tony any more. If he preferred another girl to me, that was the end as far as I was concerned. I had offers of movies in Hollywood and Italy and I must get on with my life. Now I could reap the rewards for the years I had spent doing Fox's potboilers.

After the opening of *Stop the World* we went back to Tony's suite at the Navarro and waited for the reviews. They were not good. The critics, although admiring Tony's immense talent and the Bricusse-Newley score, which was magnificent, did not like the show. They felt it was self-indulgent and pretentious. Paul and Joanne Newman had come in from Connecticut, and with Michael Lipton—Tony's best friend—the Bricusses and a few other close mates, we sat reading the scathing reviews by Bosley Crowther and Walter Kerr and felt the kiss of death on the show.

The Newley relationship was over. This was it. Finished. Done with. Goodbye baby and amen. Another year down the tube. We all said tearful goodbyes to each other in the early hours. Leslie and Tony were convinced that Merrick, on the strength of the appalling reviews, would take the show off and that they would go back to London and start writing another one. I was going to accept one of the movie roles. Preferably one that would be ten thousand miles away from Tony. Gloom was rampant.

The next morning, however, an amazing thing happened. There were lines around the block outside the theater. Hundreds of people waiting to buy tickets for *Stop the World*. This time the word of mouth of the public proved stronger than the critics' scathing words. The show became an instant hit.

I was thrilled for Tony, and Leslie and Evie, who were also staying at the Drake Hotel. I had a celebration drink with the Bricusses in the bar a couple of nights later, while Leslie excitedly told me about the great audiences and standing ovations they had been having. "He still loves you, Joanie," said Evie sympathetically. "He really *needs* you. He's miserable without you."

"That's too bad," I said calmly, watching my date for the evening come in. "He's got another girlfriend now and I'm not a groveler, Evie, you know that."

"We certainly *all* know *that*, Jace," said Brickman as the young man came over to our table and sat down and had a drink with us.

I introduced them to Terence Stamp, who was extremely handsome. He had just had a critical success in William Wyler's film *The Collector*, with Samantha Eggar, and having just played the title role in *Billy Budd* for Peter Ustinov, was in New York doing publicity and movie promotion.

"See you later," I said after twenty minutes as Terry and I got up and left for our dinner. Evie shot me a knowing and penetrating look. "He's gorgeous," she whispered to me. "Tony will be *livid* when he hears." He had no right to be livid even if I was subconsciously going out with this very attractive man to make him jealous.

Terry was a Cockney boy, full of whimsical Cockney assurance. His success had not gone to his head and he found all the fuss and hullabaloo "a bit embarrassing." He and Michael Caine had shared a flat when they were penniless actors a few years previously. Now Michael's career was taking off, too. It was the time of the English actor. Albert Finney, Alan Bates, Peter Cook and Dudley Moore, Peter Sellers and now Terence Stamp and Tony Newley were taking America by storm. England was where the action was, and suddenly anything and anyone British had enormous appeal.

Terry was also staying at the Drake Hotel, which certainly made life less complicated. Tony called me three times later that night. I didn't return his calls. I was trying to get over him, and I wasn't going to jump through his hoop whenever he decided to set it up. After a dozen or so phone calls during the next two days in which he begged me to meet him to "talk about things," we met on neutral ground. A bench in Central Park. It was a cold, blustery November day. The trees in the park were stark and bare of leaves. A few brave people walked around with dogs and bundled-up children. We sat huddled on a hard bench. The collar of his navy blue raincoat was turned up, and he wore his usual woolly scarf to protect his valuable vocal cords. He came to the point quickly. He wanted me back. Under any circumstances. Whatever I wanted was fine by him. Anything.

What did I want? Looking at his sad, pale face with the permanently ingrained pained expression I felt compassion and love for him. "I don't think you *really* love me, Tony," I said carefully. "I think you're fascinated with me, infatuated, call it what you will, but I don't truly think it's love, do you?"

"I don't know, Flower, I don't know what the bloody word *means*, for Christ's sake." He got up and strode up and down the path, the wind whipping his thick dark hair, his face a mask of agonized concentration. "I've been miserable the last couple of days. *Miserable*. You've been running around New York with Terry Stamp—oh, yes, all of my friends told me about it." He smiled bitterly. "I think, I really feel, I can't live without you now, Flower." He sat down next to me and put his arms around my shoulders. I was shivering. Whether from the cold or the emotion I didn't know.

"What about the young blonde?" I said evenly. "A month ago it was she whom you couldn't give up. How do you feel about *her* now?"

"I can't deny it, Flower—I can't deny I find her very attractive, but . . ." He paused, groping for words, his dark blue eyes searching my face as though hoping to find the answer there. ". . . I'll really try and truly love you—if you try and help me to. Can you help me, Flower?" I didn't know the answer to that one. I didn't know where altruism ended and ego began. But I knew what *I* wanted and needed out of life now. I wanted to marry and have a child. If it wasn't Tony, it would be someone else eventually. I was in love with Tony but I'd been in love before. Love was like measles. You could get it again.

I told him that if he truly wanted to be with me, then we would have to marry. "Otherwise I'm leaving for Rome next week to do a movie," I said flatly. "You can't keep turning me on and off like a tap." I had been an actress for over ten years now. I wanted to be a wife and mother. I wanted to have children, settle down. Give up this life of furnished apartments and hotel rooms, locations and airports, living out of suitcases. Stop the World—I Want to Get *On*. I want roots. I want to belong. I want to buy my own furniture, get my books and records out of storage, make a nest.

I told him all this and he understood. And he agreed. A week later we moved into a huge unfurnished penthouse apartment on Sixty-third Street. He started immediate divorce proceedings and we haunted Bloomingdale's and furniture stores on Third Avenue for furniture for our nest.

Six weeks later I was pregnant.

The good years had begun.

CHAPTER

Nine

TARA CYNARA NEWLEY WAS BORN
at Mount Sinai Hospital in New York on October 12, 1963. She
was without a doubt the most beautiful creature I had ever set
eyes on from her perfectly shaped pink head, with just the tiniest
blond fuzz on it, to her enormous blue eyes, rosebud lips and
perfect little body. She was so infinitely precious and wonderful
that I sat and stared at her in wonderment for hours. She was
mine. Ours. Our baby daughter. Tony had wanted a daughter. I
didn't mind as long as it was a healthy baby, but I was overjoyed
to see his reaction to this gorgeous elf.

I had her by natural childbirth, having done all the right things
while I was pregnant: vitamins, rest, tons of milk and eggs and
fresh vegetables; natural childbirth classes; special breathing exer-
cises so that she wouldn't have to have any medication or anesthetic while she was experiencing the trauma of birth.

Joanne Woodward had told me I *must* nurse her myself. Although I loved the symbolism of the whole thing, Mother Earth
incarnate, I wasn't too sure whether I could really handle it.
Having gained thirty-two pounds, I was eager to shed them and
get back into my clothes again. Nursing entails drinking two or
three quarts of milk or beer a day to keep everything on tap, so
to speak. The nurse on my floor was surprised at what I was doing.
"We haven't had a mother do that for years—except in the wards,
of course," she added hastily. The wards were where the poor
Puerto Rican and black women from Harlem were delivered.

I was on the third floor, where the private rooms were. They were occupied by lovely young creatures having their first, second or maximum third child, who would never consider defiling their svelte figures by anything as barbaric as breastfeeding. I was trying hard to do it successfully.

It was 1963 and a whole movement was afoot to popularize not only natural childbirth but the natural way of feeding the child too. I gritted my teeth. I was quite a curiosity on the third floor as nurses and interns would pop in to see how the movie star was coping with her young. It was a source of much amusement to them and to some of my friends.

"Joanie, I just can't watch this—it's too disgusting," said horrified Sue Mengers, an agent friend noted for her outspokenness.

When Tara was three days old the hospital sent us home. None of this languishing about in bed eating grapes and being waited on hand and foot applied any more to modern-day obstetrics. Drop the kid and go home was the new method. As Chinese peasant women in the rice paddies did.

I called Joanne. The baby was screaming her head off. I was in agony. I had bosoms the size of watermelons and the consistency of granite, and a four-day-old infant starving to death. "I cannot do it, Joanne!" I cried. "This is for mammals and peasants, it's not happening. Tara is *dying* of malnutrition."

"Don't worry," said the calm and assuring tones of my friend. "It's always like this, the fourth day is the worst. Perseverance—I know it hurts but believe me it will be worth it in the end—you'll see."

She persuaded me for forty-five minutes, while I rocked the squalling, and by now terrifying, babe in my arms, the slightest move her little head made against my chest causing me to wince in agony.

"Give it twelve more hours," pleaded Joanne. "I promise you it will get better—I've done it myself with Nell and Melissa. Don't give up on it, my dear—it's worth it." I had a sleepless night. But suddenly the next morning I was the perfect advertisement for Madonna and Child, propped up in bed behind my flowered pillow, hair flowing, along with everything else. Pleased as punch and twice as frisky. What a great feeling of achievement. It infinitely surpassed anything I had ever done on the screen.

Tara bloomed. When she was six weeks old she had her first checkup with the pediatrician. "What have you been feeding this baby? She's enormous," said the doctor in surprise, bending over the bonny gurgling princess, already aware of what was going on around her.

I noticed as we drove home in a cab through the crowded New York streets that many people were behaving strangely. Cars had pulled over to the sidewalk. People were standing about in clusters looking depressed and unhappy. I leaned over to the driver. "What's happening? Is there something going on somewhere?"

"Beats me, lady," he drawled in the charming way New York cab drivers have.

As soon as I opened the apartment door I heard our cleaning lady weeping loudly. It sounded like a wake. Tony strode out of the study and beckoned me in. He looked somber and on the brink of tears. The television was on full blast and an ashen-faced announcer was reading a news report.

"Jack Kennedy's been shot, they think he's dying," said Tony.

"Oh, no—oh, God—it's not possible." I sank onto the sofa, the little pink bundle cooing placidly in my arms. We listened and watched in stunned horror for the rest of the day. It wasn't possible that J.F.K., this extraordinary man—a symbol to the world over that America was trying hard to create integration and to erase poverty and unemployment, who was endeavoring to make the nation truly a democracy, who really cared about people—had been assassinated. Friends came over. None of us could do anything other than watch the box, still unable to believe what had happened.

"Shit," said Tony, angrily switching off. "Let's get out of here, Flower—I want to go back to England."

He wrote a song about that terrible day on November 22, 1963. We were both tremendous admirers of the Kennedy family, especially of the President. Tony's homesickness for England probably had a lot to do with his decision to leave the States. He had never felt as though he really belonged in America. Though he was idolized each night by throngs in the audience and the hordes of fans who waited backstage for a glimpse of him, he still felt more his own man in England. He wanted to live in a little hut on the coast of Cornwall, and he would often talk nostalgically of his hut. It had no water or electricity, was in the remotest part of the coast overlooking the fierce coastline, and was made of tin! Probably left over from World War I.

I, more pragmatic about amenities, did not indulge in his enthusiasm for the little hut. But the assassination brought home to him all the things he disliked about New York. He wanted out.

The show was to close soon after Christmas. We were going home again. Who says you can't?

We arrived in Paris on a frosty February day in 1964. We had to wait until the tax year ended on April 6 to enter England. We decided to stay in Paris for a couple of months, where Tony could relax and start writing his new show. It was sad getting rid of our apartment in New York. It had been my very first proper home. The first place for which I had actually bought wallpaper and carpets, had chosen, albeit not terribly tastefully, lamps, sofas and tables, and tentatively started my hand at interior decoration, which was to become a minor passion in my life and, in view of the future moves, a necessity.

What to do with all of this stuff? Records, books, photographs, scrapbooks, junk and mementoes. "Sell it or ship it," said Tony, leaving *me* with the problem of how to do that. I had called my agent in Los Angeles and told him I was going to England "indefinitely" and that I wouldn't be available for work. He hadn't been pleased when, six months earlier, he had excitedly phoned to say that he had a firm offer for me to play Jean Harlow in the movie of Harold Robbins' sexy book *The Carpetbaggers*.

"It's a wonderful part, honey, a terrific role—and the money is great. They really want you."

"Would they really want me if they knew I was six months' pregnant?"

"Joanie . . . What?" My agent was understandably annoyed. Actresses who got pregnant were a nuisance.

"All the time and effort we spent getting you out of Fox—you can't blow that, sweetheart. Not now—it's finally paying off for you."

"It's too late," I said, surveying my bump. "I would look awful in white bias-cut satin."

"You're crazy," he said grimly, "Crazy. You're too young to give up your career. You've worked too hard to pay your dues—it could be really happening for you now, sweetheart. Don't you *care* about working any more?"

"Yes, I *do* care," I answered truthfully. "But my personal life, Tony, Tara and our happiness have to come first. Right now my life is with Tony, and wherever he goes Tara and I go too."

I thought about this as I wheeled Tara in her chic French pram down the boulevards of Paris each morning. After a breakfast of hot croissants and coffee, Tony would settle down to write for three or four hours, and Tara and I would take our morning constitutional. I felt very much the young bourgeois housewife as I sat in the Bois de Boulogne with the other mothers and babies feeding the pigeons and watching the older children on the swings.

Sometimes we would parade down the Champs Élysées and Tara and I would look at the giant movie posters outside the cinemas. *Road to Hong Kong* had just opened, and there was a painting of me fifteen feet high outside one of the theaters. Bouffant hair, glistening red lips and eyes painted an unimaginable shade of grassy green. How far away that life seemed to be already. Pushing the baby carriage in a camel coat, sensible shoes and headscarf, with hardly any makeup, I was unrecognizable as that movie queen up on the billboards. I was, however, for the first time in years, extremely contented.

Tara brought me infinite joy. I had eschewed the idea of a nanny—I wanted to look after my four-month-old infant myself. Although we lived in a suite at the Hotel Grand Point, nevertheless I still had to make and mix her formula myself. I'd stopped nursing her at three months. I washed her clothes by hand, played with her, bathed her and did all the other dozens of things a tiny baby needs. I didn't want anybody else to do this for her. She was my baby and I was going to do right by her.

One night Tony woke me up with a sharp nudge. "What's all

that commotion?" I said sleepily. "Sounds like a drunken orgy next door."

"Sounds like they're breaking all the glasses and windows in the place," he said, jumping out of bed in his blue and white striped pajamas. "I'll see what's happening." He opened the door of our bedroom, which led to the hall, and recoiled coughing violently. The hall was filled with smoke. He banged the door shut and turned to me, trying to keep the panic off his face. "I think there's a fire," he said quietly.

"Oh, God . . . Tara." My knees turned to water. I leaped from the bed and rushed across the living room which separated her bedroom from ours. It was almost impossible to breathe in her room. Thick black acrid smoke everywhere. I could barely see. "My baby!" I screamed, fearing the worst. She was lying in her cot, gazing with surprised blue eyes at this interesting substance floating around her room. Another minute and she could have suffocated. I grabbed her and fled back to our bedroom.

Tony was talking to the concierge on the phone. "There's a fire . . . um . . . *oui, un feu* . . . er . . . Oh, Christ . . . *un grand feu ici*—help us, *s'il vous plaît.*" His calmness hid the panic he was trying to cover. His atrocious French was not an asset. I heard the concierge yelling excitedly.

I looked outside. It was not a reassuring sight. We were seven floors up. In the street stood a lonely fire truck surrounded by five incompetent firemen lackadaisically trying to connect the hose pipe to a nearby water pump. A knot of mildly interested Frenchmen, obviously on their way home from the local bordello, as it was four in the morning, stood idly by smoking Gauloises and offering advice. Some of them chuckled occasionally. Several people were hanging out of the windows above and below us and screaming frantically. Flames were shooting up from the top of the building, and smoke spiraled from the top floor—the ninth. We were on number seven. The people on the eighth were understandably hysterical. Of the people on the ninth, there seemed no evidence. Dead? Or escaped? A middle-aged German, naked except for a string vest and green socks, was on the balcony immediately above us, jumping up and down and yelling incoherently. I couldn't help a hysterical giggle at the fact that he was so unaware of his nudity—he seemed even more bizarrely naked because of his vest and socks.

I realized I myself was only wearing a see-through short night-gown and nothing underneath. I grabbed a pair of jeans, a sweater and slippers and thrust Tara into Tony's hands. "I must get her bottles." I dashed into the living room, where smoke was seeping in below the door, and snatched three bottles of formula from the fridge. I took my mink from the closet and my jewelry box from the desk. Although frightened to death, I still felt we would be saved at the eleventh hour. Finally finding all this happiness and then getting fried to death in a second-class hotel in Paris could not be my destiny. Or could it? Tony thrust the baby into my arms again and jumped onto the balcony like Errol Flynn. "Where are you going?" I screamed. Was my bridegroom about to commit suicide, or was he going to scramble to safety alone—leaving me holding the baby? I stood shaking helplessly on the tiny balcony watching him maneuver round the side of the hotel to where the smoke seemed less dense. I was suddenly very alone and very frightened. "Help! Help! Please help us!" I screamed.

A small crowd had now gathered in the Champs Élysées to watch with laconic interest sixty people die horribly. They ignored me. The firemen were still fiddling about with the nozzle of their equipment, and my opinion of the French plummeted. What disorganization. They couldn't even get the bloody water connected. We could all go up in flames and they would still be messing about. "Au secours! Au secours!" I yelled, hoping that French would do more good than English. Maybe the reason they were so indifferent to our plight was because they knew the hotel was full of German tourists. A *petite* revenge for their occupation. Maybe if they saw a poor young Frenchwoman clutching her tiny babe, a future president of the Republic *peut-être*, they might get their act together and put out this *fucking* fire.

The smoke was getting denser. Sparks were falling on us. A woman on the ninth floor let out a horrifying scream. No wonder—her hair was on fire! It was too, too horrible. A nightmare from which surely I must finally awake. After what seemed a year, Tony scrambled back along the balconies, disheveled, his face blackened from soot and his hands cut and bleeding.

"The fire's in the elevator shaft," he breathed shakily, gasping for air. He was not much of an athlete. "It's on the top floor and burning downwards—we've *got* to get out of here, Flower!"

"I know, but how?" I wailed. Tara started to cry. The three of us held on tight together. Horror stories of mutilated bodies found in burned-out buildings filled my mind. I could hear screams, and breaking glass—cries and groans from the floors above us. I saw the headlines on the *Evening Standard* placards in London. "Famous Stars and Baby Die in Paris Hotel Fire!" That would sell a few papers. Everyone would want to know who the stars were and how horribly they died. Circulation would soar.

We stood there trapped. If *we* were too young to die, what about Tara? Four months old—what a tragedy. I tried to imagine my whole life passing through my mind. Wasn't that what supposedly happened when people knew they were doomed? I couldn't think of anything except that my baby's life hadn't even begun yet.

And then—the door to the bedroom burst open and two burly firemen appeared in masks and heavy asbestos gloves. It was the most glorious sight I had ever seen. They yelled at us in French.

One of them grabbed Tara and gestured us to follow him as he crawled on all fours down the corridor. They dampened towels from a bucket of water, and made us cover our heads with them. The floor was burning hot, and acrid smoke filled my lungs even with the wet towels. The ceiling was an ominous red, and bits of plaster and ash fell on us like confetti. The noise was horrifying. In a dream I crawled behind the huge garlic-smelling fireman, who was clutching my most precious possession, Tara. We reached the stairs which were next to the lift. "*Allez! Allez-vous!*" said the fireman, pushing us to the stairs. I looked up the lift shaft and saw the whole top in flames. I had never "allezed" anywhere as fast as we whisked down those seven flights.

Saved at the eleventh hour. Ben Gary was right again.

I never again have stayed in any hotel room without checking thoroughly to see that the fire escape was within immediate access. Once burned, twice shy—you better believe it!

. . .

We left immediately for Switzerland. It was unthinkable to stay in the suite. Everything was blackened by smoke, there was no hot water or electricity. The management begged us to be patient—normal service would be resumed shortly; but the event was so awful that we wanted out.

St. Moritz in early March was just coming to the end of the season. It was the most exclusive, elegant and glamorous ski resort of the international set. The Palace Hotel was where the *haut monde* congregated. My best friend Cappy was now married to Andrea Badrutt, the owner of the Palace Hotel. Cappy had become the doyen and social arbiter of the St. Moritz social calendar. She knew everyone and everyone knew her. Niarchos, Onassis, Agnelli, Thyssen, Von Opel, Gunther Sachs, Charles Clore. The cream of the jet set was partaking of the pleasures of the Palace— probably the least of which was skiing. Intrigue, romance, big business, deception, seduction—all took place, and had for dozens of years, beneath the portals of this magnificent hotel. Set in the middle of the quaint village of St. Moritz, where the simple villagers rubbed shoulders with international playboys and princes, the atmosphere was at once deliciously decadent and jolly healthy.

Into this hothouse atmosphere, redolent of sex, sin and sport, arrived one deranged-looking British actress—grubby and unkempt from twenty-four hours on the train, one Cockney genius, already with a sore throat and incipient flu, who absolutely loathed anything to do with high society, and one adorable female baby— good as gold and who never cried, probably because she hardly ever left her mother's side.

I took Tara everywhere. To lunch at the Palace Grill, where Madame Dewi Sukarno, elegance personified in the simplest of underplayed après-ski clothes, would lunch with Madame Badrutt, a vision in sable ski hat and velvet trousers, Baroness Thyssen (the former model Fiona Campbell-Walter), lustrous red tumbling curls and beautifully cut shirts and jodhpurs—and me. I had not come prepared for the joys of skiing and had to make do with some itchy polo-necked sweaters, tight jeans and a John Lennon black leather cap. Not at all what the *haut monde* would consider *haute couture*. My clothes were liberally sprinkled with baby food and crumbs, since, parked on my lap or nearby on her portable chair, little Tara would sit and gurgle happily away. The ladies and the staff did not exactly approve. The atmosphere was far too refined to have children around, let alone babies, who were usually seen by their parents only between four and five in the afternoon for nursery tea.

"Joanie—you can't go on like this," said Cappy. "You can't go walking about St. Moritz with that baby slung on your back like some African peasant woman. Get a nanny, for goodness' sake, dear."

"I don't *need* a nanny," I said defensively, spooning up a trickle of cereal oozing from Tara's mouth and realizing that it was time to change her diaper again. "What's the *point*, Cappy, in having a child if you don't take care of it yourself?" Tara burped happily in agreement, and beat a little tattoo with her messy spoon on my grubby sweater.

"Look at you!" said Cappy. "Look at your hands—you've *ruined* them by washing her clothes, and whatever else it is you wash." She had glanced distastefully at the beautifully decorated marble bathroom now festooned with drying diapers and tiny garments of all descriptions. "The role of hausfrau does not become you," she said sternly. "Neither does this role of camp follower to your husband. You must settle down, darling. Buy a house, get some roots, and you should get back to *work*."

"I know we need roots," I said ruefully. "But we can't go back to England until April because of Tony's tax situation, and honestly, Cappy, I *enjoy* looking after the baby—I really do. And as for work—who needs all that waiting around on sets all day? I've done it since I was sixteen. It's fantastic to be free." I picked Tara up and threw her expertly over my shoulder to burp her, then placed her on the bed to change her.

"I find this delightful domesticity a little hard to take," said Cappy, glancing in the mirror at her patrician features and elegant body, fetchingly clad in gray fox hat and coordinated pale gray ski clothes. "I don't exactly consider you free, dear. At least I hope you can get a baby sitter tonight so you can come to my party at the Corviglia Club."

"Darling, I promise you I will not arrive at your party embar-

rassing you with egg yolk down my dress and dishwasher hands."
I was able to make the transformation from harassed housewife
during the day to soignée sophisticate at night with little effort.
Geminis thrive on changing roles. It was much more fun to be
the perfect mother all day and a vision of glamour by night. But I
could never come close to Cappy in the glamour department. She
was truly always a vision of beauty, coordination and sophisticated
elegance. Years later I based my visual interpretation of Alexis
Carrington Colby in *Dynasty* on Caprice Caprone Yordan Badrutt.
She was one of the most elegant and stylish beauties who ever
lived. And infinitely nicer than Alexis!

John Crosby of the *Herald Tribune* wrote an article about me in
St. Moritz called "A Most Peculiar Mother."

> *St. Moritz*—There's a very peculiar mother here named Mrs.
> Anthony Newley, otherwise known as Joan Collins, a movie star
> of some renown, who takes care of her own baby!
>
> In this citadel of the rich, this is a throwback to primitive be-
> havior patterns almost unknown in these parts since they intro-
> duced the Roman alphabet.
>
> Other mothers in St. Moritz, who are barely on a first-name
> basis with their babies, stare at Miss Collins in considerable
> awe: "Washes her own bottles" they whisper to each other.
> "You know, the things they feed the baby with."
>
> "All the women here think I'm mad," said Miss Collins. "If
> they have one child, they have one nurse, two children, two
> nurses. Three children, three nurses" . . . Joan Collins's pe-
> culiar behavior started in Paris when she assumed executive con-
> trol over Tara Cynara, washing bottles, changing nappies and
> all the other unnatural practices for mothers.

On April 7, 1964, Tony and I, and all the other British performers, writers, sportsmen and others who had gone nonresident
for a year, returned to London. We rented Keith Michell's house
in Hampstead and Tony and Leslie Bricusse plunged feverishly
into writing a new show, *The Roar of the Greasepaint, The Smell
of the Crowd*. Evie had just given birth to a little boy, Adam, my
godson, and the six of us were now playing "Happy Families" together. Except I hardly ever saw my husband. He was enslaved by
his work. He scribbled away morning, noon and night, with little
time for much else. Although I now hired a housekeeper, I was

231

still preoccupied with the baby and my newfound domesticity. I spent days looking for houses in the country, but near enough to London, and finally found a wonderful house at Elstree, full of character and charm, an old Edwardian mansion with three stories, stables, grounds—just right for the large family we planned on having. I was expecting another baby, and although I thought it was rather too hot on the heels of Tara, nevertheless I was completely happy and busy as a little bee.

Friars' Mead, the house was called, and it needed a monstrous amount of renovation and decoration to make it habitable. It had cost the astronomical sum, in those 1964 preinflation days, of twenty thousand pounds. Tony thought this was far too expensive, but I had convinced him it was worth it as we now planned on living in England forever. The days were full. Playing with Tara, who was becoming more adorable all the time, consultations with architects and Robin Guild, our interior designer, and shopping, for wallpapers, fabrics and furniture for this new home. Goodbye Gucci suitcases—hello roots. At *last!*

Tony moaned about the cost of everything. His humble background had not accustomed him to the fact that things cost money, but he was learning to like the better things in life, not all of which are free, unfortunately, and I was an expert teacher. My own bank balance, however, was diminishing rapidly. Always used to making money, I was equally used to spending it. Tony was not financially secure, certainly not in the league of being able to fully support a wife who was used to buying her clothes at St. Laurent and Thea Porter.

When an offer materialized for me to go to Rome and star opposite Vittorio Gassman in an Italian comedy, Tony persuaded me to do it. I had just lost the baby I was expecting and was feeling rather blue. Tony was on the road in Manchester and Birmingham, on out-of-town tryouts for *The Roar of the Greasepaint, the Smell of the Crowd.* Leslie, Evie, Tara, Adam and I were of course all there, too.

Tara was one year old when I left for Portofino, Lugano and Rome to make *La Conguintura.* It was the first separation since our marriage. I was very unhappy about it. Although fairly pleased with the idea of getting back to work again, and realizing that to live the life I had been accustomed to for the past several years I needed money, nevertheless I had a foreboding that even with Tony's protestations of "Yes, Flower, do it—you know it'll be good for you. You know you love to work," he did not really mean it. Deep down I think he wanted a wife who would stay at home, cook and take care of the family's needs.

La Conguintura turned out to be one of the most successful movies I made. At least in Italy. It was number eight at the Italian box office the following year. Unfortunately, it was never shown in England or America. A pity, because I was doing my favorite thing, comedy. Tara had a wonderful time on location. She even appeared in a scene in her pram when Gassman trips over her in a mad dash around the hotel in Lugano. Tony, Evie and Leslie all came to Portofino after the London opening of *Greasepaint*. Their faces told the sad story.

Disaster had struck. The critics had given the show every nasty epithet in the book. A lot of love, care, time and talent had gone into it. Tony was upset, not only because of *Greasepaint*. He had discovered that his tax structure was such that it was impossible for him to live permanently in England without paying 90 percent of his income to the government. To top it all, David Merrick, having come to Manchester to see the show, had made an offer they could not refuse. Tony was to play Mr. Thin in *Greasepaint* on Broadway.

Joan, the camp follower immediately did all the right things. Sold the beautiful house at Elstree—we had not even moved in yet. My dream house at last. I begged Tony not to sell it—I would pay the twenty thousand pounds to keep it, but he was adamant, and so was his tax adviser. Neither of us could own property in the U.K. Even though I had been a resident of America for seven years, it could seriously disrupt him taxwise if we kept it.

Out came the twenty Gucci cases, and once more, amidst poignant farewells to our friends and family, we flew to New York. I was pregnant again and liked getting on planes less and less. I was deeply upset by this latest move. This time we moved into a furnished apartment on 72nd Street. With Tony's mother, Grace, now as nanny-cum-housekeeper, I once again found myself living in someone else's house surrounded by someone else's possessions, plus several families of giant cockroaches. At thirty I still owned *nothing* except clothes, books and records. Would I ever have roots?

Alexander Anthony Newley was born on September 8, 1965. In the same hospital and in the same room as his sister Tara. It was unbelievably thrilling that I now had a boy too. He was exactly what we wanted. We were now a complete family unit. Indestructible. I was totally involved with my all-consuming role of wife and mother.

Things were going well for us. *The Roar of the Greasepaint*, starring Tony and with Cyril Ritchard playing the other part, had opened to mixed reviews, but praise for Tony's performance was high. He had developed a big following and was a major draw on Broadway now. Our living arrangements, however, were less than satisfactory. That summer we had rented a house on Long Island where I lazed around happily playing with Tara, swimming, sunbathing and barbecuing for the cast on weekends. Tony would leave for the theater around four, and I would have the rest of the day and evening to read, write, think and generally be a placid, bovine lump. My friends were amazed at my transformation. From an energetic, volatile, vigorous creature, who was only happy doing things, going and being where the action was, I had turned into Mother Earth, happy to laze away the days. The high spot of my week was a visit to the local supermarket, wheeling baby Tara in the basket.

A week before Sacha was born, we moved into Paul and Joanne Newman's apartment on Seventy-second Street and Fifth Avenue. It was a beautiful, airy, tastefully furnished apartment, filled with early American furniture and English antiques—a tribute to Joanne's good taste. I had visited her in the hospital a couple of months previously. Her third baby, Claire, was born three months before Sacha. Now my fear of flying had become an obsession.

We were in Toronto, Canada, on tour with the show. I preferred to take the overnight train to New York and back rather than spend two hours in a plane. We had had a bad experience on a short jaunt from Boston to Cleveland in a blinding snowstorm. As the jet, its wheels already descended, was coming in for landing, two hundred yards from the runway it suddenly zoomed back into the air again. My stomach gave a sickening lurch. The cabin crew went green. I asked one of them what happened. She replied shakily, "Probably something on the runway."

"Probably something on the runway!" What, pray, I wondered, could that something be? Another plane? A stewardess taking an afternoon stroll? A stray dog? It was too horrible to contemplate that one hundred tons of metal carrying sixty or seventy human beings could be wiped out by "something on the runway." When the plane finally landed, I decided never to fly again unless there was absolutely no other alternative. Now with Sacha's arrival and Tony playing to full houses each night, I hoped that there would be no plane trips in the immediate future.

If having one baby and taking care of it alone was novel and fun, suddenly two little babies, one a few days old and one twenty-two months old, both in diapers, became much too hard to handle. I hired a German nanny—Renata. She arrived with excellent references a few days before the new baby was expected.

The hospital, as before, briskly sent me home when Sacha was only three days old. They obviously believed that the more kids you had the less time you deserved for lying about. With terse instructions to "get into bed and take it easy for at least a week" I entered purgatory. As soon as twenty-two-month-old Tara, the pampered and adorable apple of her parents' eyes, got a glimpse of brand-new, excitingly different and magnificently masculine Sacha she smiled, stroked him and begged to be allowed to play with him.

But as soon as he was settled comfortably on my lap in bed, propped up against the Porthault sheets, she flew into a raging fury. She wanted to be where he was. When I held him, she wanted to be held, when I changed him, she wanted to be changed. Her potty training of the past six months went to pot. I couldn't let Sacha sleep in a crib in our room as I had done with Tara, because *she* wanted to be allowed to sleep there too! So he slept downstairs with her and Renata. My German treasure obviously was stone

235

deaf, for the babies could cry and scream all night and she would not be roused. Staggering downstairs at ten or eleven at night, Tony at the theater, Renata dead to the world, I could carry baby Sacha and drag little Tara by the hand up to my bedroom and try to placate them both. Tara got a cookie, Sacha got Mummy, if he was lucky. I was so exhausted he sometimes had to settle for a bottle. At 3 or 4 A.M. the same thing, and again at nine or ten in the morning. The only time Renata was conscious, it seemed, was between eleven in the morning and nine at night. The poor girl needed her sleep—but so did I, and all this traipsing up and down the stairs was a strain. After a week, I woke up one morning feeling like death. The doctor, on examining me, came right to the point.

"You're lucky," he said. "A few years ago this disease carried them off like flies, in the wards."

"What disease?" I said weakly. I had never felt worse.

"Puerperal fever—or childbed fever as it's called now," he said briskly, injecting me with some wonder drug. "Yes, it's a terrible thing, my dear—*was* a terrible thing, I should say, only ten percent survived. We don't see much of it nowadays—only—" he looked at me suspiciously—"with those mothers who *do too much*. Have you been doing too much, young woman?" I nodded weakly. "Keep the children away from her. It can be dangerous to the baby," he told Tony. "We need to get a nurse for her and a new nanny for the children, no doubt." He had caught a glimpse of frail, white-faced Renata, hovering on the landing, clutching a whimpering Tara by the hand. And Sacha's demanding yells for lunch were issuing from the downstairs bedroom.

The new nanny turned out to be a capable treasure, and I was able to relax more. We became friends with a girl who had become the toast of New York in *Funny Girl*, Barbra Streisand, and her husband, Elliott Gould. Elliott was an actor who was finding it hard to get work. His wife's astonishingly sudden and well-deserved success had not rubbed off on him. He was in the unenviable position of being "Mr. Streisand" to the hordes of fans who clustered around the stage door each night and inundated Barbra with their idolatry. She did not take too kindly to giving autographs. She would sweep disdainfully through the crowds to the waiting limousine and rarely deign to scribble her signature.

We had seen her only a year and a half earlier at the Blue Angel, where she was starting out. The magnificence of her vocal talent and originality as a performer took New York by storm instantly. She became a "must see" for anyone and everyone. Barbra and Tony developed a mutual-admiration society. They were similar in temperament—high-strung, hard-working, dedicated to perfecting their craft. We often dined together, talking, laughing and joking late into the night. She had an eloquent Romanesque nose, bouffant hair and porcelain skin, and with her way of dressing, sometimes quaint and kinky, sometimes in the highest of *haute couture* clothes, she was an imposing and unusual-looking woman, in addition to having that exceptional, extraordinary talent. She was about to make her first movie, *Funny Girl*. She questioned me at length about makeup techniques and matters pertaining to motion pictures. Barbra was like Marlon Brando with her thirst for knowledge. Her mind was a sponge—it soaked up everything. She had an intense desire to learn and improve herself in every way.

I found these qualities admirable and enviable. My mind was more like a sieve—the more that went in, the more went instantly out with the vegetable water. Although I was an avid reader and went often to the theater, concerts and movies I still, due to my mercurial tendencies, was hard pushed to remember anything I had read, seen or listened to for more than a couple of weeks afterwards. I could learn an entire script in an hour—memorize it by heart—and a month later I couldn't remember a line.

Negotiations had begun for Tony to appear in a major musical for my old alma mater, 20th Century–Fox. It was to be a lavish, mammoth spectacle for which Leslie Bricusse was writing the book and lyrics. *Dr. Doolittle* was adapted from the children's book by Hugh Lofting. Rex Harrison would play Doolittle. Tony was excited about being in such an important production. He was interested in becoming a film star now. He vowed that *Greasepaint* would be the last time he would appear on the stage.

We took the train to California. It took three days. Tony wrote and I stared at the scenery and played with the kids. Tara loved dashing through the carriages and stopping at all the stations to buy souvenirs. At two and a half she was a tiny, beautiful little girl. Bright and funny.

In L.A. Tony was perfectly content to reside in the rented house that Leslie Bricusse had found for us. I wasn't. I insisted we *must* have our own home. We could not continue to dash all over the globe, with two children, seventy-four suitcases, a nanny, a mother-in-law and crates of books, records and junk. Not to mention all of our stuff still in storage.

We started house-hunting in Beverly Hills. Tony was working on another project. Tara started nursery school and Sacha was well taken care of by Rosie, our new nanny. I suddenly started feeling rather useless. I began thinking about acting again. My career—which with the exception of the Italian film had been sublimated for over three years—started to have new meaning for me. Maybe this was because I was living in Hollywood again, where everyone eats, sleeps and breathes motion pictures. Television was a major industry force now, instead of the poor relation to the movies it had been during my Fox days. The William Morris Agency contacted me. Would I be interested in doing some guest shots on TV in various dramatic shows? Why not indeed? I looked as good as, if not better than, when I had arrived in Hollywood a decade previously. Certainly I was a better and more experienced actress. If I was going to continue acting at all I had better start now by stretching myself and accepting some of these roles—even if I considered them somewhat unrewarding.

It's so easy not to work, to let things slide and "think about that tomorrow." One day tomorrow arrives, and it's too late, baby. Much too late. Industry people have memories as short as matchsticks. I had made a series of mediocre films a few years ago and then evaporated to virtual retirement as far as they were concerned. It wasn't going to be particularly easy to get back into anything like the position I had had before. A whole new generation of actresses was on the scene—Candice Bergen, Julie Christie, Faye Dunaway, Raquel Welch, Samantha Eggar, Barbra Streisand.

These were the stars of the mid-to-late sixties. As far as the American public was concerned I was practically unknown.

"Who's that pretty girl?"

"Oh, that's Anthony Newley's wife—didn't she used to be an actress?"

"Oh, yeah—Joan something-or-other. Whatever happened to her?" Such is life in the tropics of Hollywood.

Luckily, stardom had never been something I strove for. It was acting I enjoyed. The creation, portrayal and characterization of another person. I loved wandering on the back lots in the studios, awed by incredible and beautifully detailed sets that still remained standing after decades.

Tony and I lunched at the Fox commissary. I was amazed at what had happened to the giant back lot I knew. It had been sold for an astronomical fee—no doubt to pay back to the stockholders some of Fox's debts, a few of which surely must have arisen from the turkeys I had appeared in. I felt the urge to work become stronger. I knew my energy and enthusiasm should be channeled into some sort of creative direction. If not acting, then interior designing or writing. Much as I adored my children, I realized that I was not the sort of woman to whom home, hearth and family was the be-all and end-all of feminine existence. Tony, while not discouraging me, was totally absorbed in writing his new show. It was preferable to him to have me occupied and out of the way so that he could concentrate on his work. Tara and Sacha had Rosie Riggs, their fresh-faced English nanny, to look after them and I realized that the day-to-day grind of cooking, washing up and changing diapers was no longer as enthralling as it had been.

Oh, fickle Gemini! Only another of the same sign can truly understand the vagaries of the Mercury-ruled mind: the compulsion to do too much; to take on too many projects; to be able to do six things at once and still have time for one more; the way the mind flitters like a butterfly from one subject to another, from one project to another, never alighting long enough to put down roots.

We are the "butterfly" sign of the zodiac. Youthful in spirit, and often in body, we are open to the new, the unusual, the unexpected. Routine is the kiss of death for the Mercury-ruled sign.

Much as I hated to admit it, I still needed the stimulation, joy and excitement that I received from acting.

The signs had been in the air for some time that things were not going well with the marriage. As a way of coping with many things that upset me, I did my Scarlett O'Hara act and thought about it "tomorrow." It certainly was an excellent device for me to avoid dealing with the realities of misery and disappointment and unhappiness. By putting off the moment when I had to analyze and evaluate a particular situation, I successfully managed to never have to think about it at all. Even the most traumatic experience of my life—the death of my mother—I did not completely realize and mourn for until several years later.

It was, and is, of course, a great way of getting through life as happily as possible, and for an actress whose lot is often heartbreak, rejection and frustration, it's a way of keeping sane. But marital problems must be sorted out. Festering sores should be discussed, however painful. Tony's offhand attitude, not wanting to rock the boat and to keep things on an even keel, my "keep it under for another day" attitude, guaranteed that important issues in our marriage were deeply buried.

We did talk. We discussed, sorted out, even argued in a mild way, but Tony hated it. We never dug deep enough to explore our most intimate psyches, secrets and emotional problems. In the end this lack of communication began corroding our marriage.

One night, crossing the street in the pouring rain with my sister Jackie, we almost got hit by a bus. Tony had darted ahead of us. When, later, I told him off, he sulked. Making no waves became the *modus operandi* of our marriage.

Whenever I asserted myself he called me bossy, masculine and ball-breaking. He could not seem to understand that my feelings and ideas had value. Each time we disagreed, the gulf between us widened.

Finally we bought a house in California. Once more the lure of the palm trees and the sweet smell of success beckoned us to tinsel town. I finally attempted to put down those longed-for roots and make a permanent home for us and our two children.

Tara was now three, and I desperately wanted her to have some stability in her life. Born in New York, she had spent more than half her short life in hotel rooms all over America on the never-ending *Greasepaint* tour. Rented houses and apartments everywhere from London to Paris, Rome, Portofino, Lugano, Liverpool, St. Moritz had been her life. Her passport looked like that of an international playgirl. I was determined she should have what most other little girls of her age had. Her own room in which she could play with her toys, secure in the knowledge that this was her *home*. The security that she would stay there, hopefully, for a long, long time. Sacha, at eighteen months, was still too young to feel the effects of the constant changing of scenery, but I knew that he, the most gorgeous hunk of blond curly-haired baby boy, needed his security too.

Hollywood in the late sixties had not changed much from the time I had first arrived. The same lavish and star-studded parties were still being given by the ever diminishing ranks of the movie moguls. Darryl F. Zanuck was gone. Fox was desperately trying to get itself back on its feet after horrendous losses over the past several years. Spyros Skouras, the wily old Greek, was dead; so was Lew Shreiber, my mentor and father confessor during my contract days. Harry Cohn, feared head of Columbia Studios, who ruled the lives of Rita Hayworth and Kim Novak with a rod of iron, was long gone. His place had been taken by a group of corporate executives to whom the word "creative" was anathema.

Bob Evans, under contract to Fox at the same time as I, had taken over the reins at Paramount Studios. He proved to be infinitely better at running a studio than he had ever been as an actor.

Jack Warner was still the boss at Warner Brothers, which was in the process of changing its name to The Burbank Studios. So many independent productions—both TV and motion picture—used the Burbank lot that they changed the name to a more nonspecific one, so as not to invite petty jealousies from other independent studios.

Universal, home of the tacky sand and sin pictures, was now the biggest force in television production. Strongly controlled by the redoubtable Lew Wasserman, former president of MCA and

241

a shrewd and clever businessman to boot, Universal Inc. had amalgamated with the octopus-like MCA agency, which at one time seemed to represent 90 percent of the top theatrical talent in America.

The contract star system had virtually finished, the only exception being likely prospects for TV series at salaries of around two hundred dollars a week. The big superstars were commanding gigantic amounts of money for their movies. Paul Newman, Steve McQueen, Barbra Streisand, Clint Eastwood, Charles Bronson were superstars on a level not seen previously, and their agents now had unprecedented power at the studios. And what do you know? Even Warren Beatty was having a phenomenal success with *Bonnie and Clyde* which he had starred in and produced. He was well on his way to his first million. After Warren's initial impact with *Splendor in the Grass,* he had made a series of indifferent films. Now he was on the crest of superstardom, as well as becoming the most famous stud in the Western Hemisphere. The shyly myopic, pimply-faced, skinny boy who had caused much mirth among my acquaintances when our romance had first started was now a handsome, mysterious, charismatic, sexy movie star, and a brilliant producer too. He had become irresistible to throngs of females. No woman, it was rumored, could resist those greenish-blue, shortsighted eyes. His charm and success with females of all ages had become legendary, and his prowess between the sheets was the subject of much Hollywood tittle-tattle. Although he had always had a "live-in lady" in his life, he apparently was able to cram in an endless amount of extracurricular activity and was on his way to becoming the successor to Errol Flynn as a ladies' man and lover par excellence.

"I must be the only woman in L.A. and New York that Warren hasn't tried to *shtup,*" said my agent, Sue Mengers, laughingly. It seemed to be true, although Warren was clever enough never to admit his conquests.

So much of what my astrologer, Ben Gary, had predicted was coming true. Warren's fast rise to fame, fade-out for a few years and then superstardom. My marriage to "actor or writer or director" Newley—he was all of those. And two children: Tara petite, Sacha husky, almost the same size, and who, since I often dressed them alike, were often mistaken for twins. The gypsylike existence Ben had predicted for me had also come true. I didn't want to think about his last prediction, however—that my marriage would last for only seven years. We were barely making it through the fourth.

CHAPTER

Ten

THE DAISY WAS A BEVERLY HILLS discotheque that overnight became a mecca for everyone in town. Perhaps they were trying to compete with the Swinging Sixties scene in London. As miniskirts rode thigh-high and men's hair began to hang over the collar, dancing frenzy gripped Hollywood the likes of which had not been seen since Joan Crawford Charleston'd her way to fame in the 1920s movie *Our Dancing Daughters*.

Every night the Daisy was jammed with the beautiful people, the trying to be beautiful people, and the not so beautiful people in Hollywood. Stars, starlets, agents, writers, producers and producers' wives all crammed onto the dance floor to "Let it all hang out" (and it often did) or to sit and observe. A sort of madness gripped everyone. Outrageous clothes and extroverted behavior had become the norm. No dinner party was complete without a trip to the Daisy afterward. Everyone was doing the Monkey, the Funky Chicken. It was sheer madness—but lots of fun.

Even Tony would occasionally accompany me there, although he was now busy rehearsing for his role in *Dr. Doolittle* and also writing a new script tentatively based (yet again!) on the story of his life. On the evenings at home he would immediately return to his study after dinner to work on his script. We had virtually no communication; he was wrapped up in his work, and although he told me he loved me, I was dubious.

I was not happy. The beautiful house in Beverly Hills, complete with pool and all mod cons, and the two gorgeous children, the light of my life, couldn't make up for the emptiness I felt. When I managed to extract conversation from Tony about our marital problems he would become irritated and talk about the immense problem he *himself* had in loving and giving fully. Yes, he loved me in his own way—but who was I to him? An attractive stranger who shared his bed, mothered his children, and sat once a fortnight at the head of his dinner table.

When we gave dinner parties I was never sure he would attend. We had a sit-down dinner for fourteen in honor of Peter Sellers, which I had spent a week organizing. Tony pleaded a stomachache and stayed in the bedroom, leaving thirteen for dinner, and me getting fiercely drunk in front of a monosyllabic Sellers.

Tony didn't like dinners or parties anyway, even though they were part of the Hollywood social scene. Often I would go to them with a platonic friend or a married couple or a glamorous gay. I loved dancing, especially at the Daisy.

A young man asked me to dance. He looked vaguely familiar: brawny, blond, tall, a face like a handsome boxer. He looked as though he might get his nose broken one day, or maybe some of those perfect white teeth. He was obviously an actor, although tight blue jeans and a shirt open to well-muscled chest didn't necessarily mean in Hollywood that he was. Physical perfection was the achievement of all in Beautiful Beverly Hills—agents, writers, producers. The gyms were full of them flexing well-tanned biceps and heaving their way through fifty sit-ups a day. The hair stylists couldn't keep up with the demand for the romantically tousled long-haired look, copied from swinging London.

Ryan O'Neal had it going for him in the looks department and he wasn't lacking in charm and humor. Or the sex-appeal department. He was the first man I'd found attractive for a long time. So we kept on dancing for an energetic hour or so. Mick Jagger was singing "I can't get no satisfaction." It sounded like the title song for my marriage.

The fact that I was married didn't seem to faze Ryan. He wanted my telephone number, which I wouldn't give him. Tony would just love that. But Tony must have subconsciously realized that letting me go out alone two or three nights a week to the Daisy was asking for eventual trouble. A nun I had never been—only in the movies.

Ryan was funny and endearing. He had an open, boyish personality and a droll self-mocking attitude toward himself. He was part Irish—with a name like O'Neal what else?—married and divorced and had, like me, two children, Tatum and Griffin, the same age and sex as Tara and Sacha. But attractive as he was, my marriage vows still meant a lot to me. I was not about to open up this can of beans, however inviting the label.

The next afternoon, idly flipping channels to find cartoons for the kiddies, I came across him again, being boyish and sincere with Mia Farrow in the soap opera "Peyton Place." I watched with interest. He definitely had star quality. It flashed across the screen, along with sizzling sex appeal, even with the banal plots and dialogue of "Peyton Place." I switched the channel to the cartoons the children were clamoring for. He was forbidden fruit.

I hankered to play the main female role in *Dr. Doolittle*—that of the haughty British belle who falls for the Cockney-Irish charms of Newley. Although this was a Fox film produced by our friend Arthur Jacobs, they didn't think I was right and the part went to Samantha Eggar.

My Hollywood movie career appeared to be fading fast. Although I received scripts from England, Italy and Spain, I could not land a decent film role in the States. I had been away too long and was no longer a new face. Thank you, Warren. Thank you, Tony. She gave it all up for love. What kind of fool was *I*? Television offers, however, came aplenty. I had my pick of the top shows and I accepted most of them. Now I could be a wife, a mother and an actress all at once. A neat little package deal. I was trying to please Tony but I really wasn't pleasing myself because guesting on episodic TV shows was not tremendously fulfilling either.

The truth was I enjoyed working—why did I feel pangs of guilt when I admitted it? Why wasn't I just content, like most of the young Beverly Hills matrons I knew, to be a faithful wife (albeit ignored) and a dutiful mother? Content to run the house with my trusty Portuguese couple, to lie by the pool and ruin my skin and then go to the facialist and the dermatologist to repair it, go to the analyst, the hairdresser, the manicurist, the gynecologist, the numerologist, the group-therapy session, the tennis lessons, the tap-dancing classes, the kaffee klatches, the hen-party lunches, the backgammon games, the beach and the gym? Young Beverly Hills matrons had a *slew* of things to do with their day. Why was I so discontented?

Apart from the above there was always shopping—a major occupation for a California lady of leisure. God forbid one didn't pop into Saks or Magnin's at least once a week to blow thirty or forty dollars on some new lipsticks and skin lotions, meander upstairs to Lingerie and buy a few cute robes at eighty or ninety dollars apiece, and top it off with a bauble or two from the cut-price jewelers on Beverly Drive. A solid-gold "his 'n hers" key for "their" house, a solid-gold ankh for good luck, very popular that year, everyone was wearing them, or the latest rip-off from Tiffany's— whatever it was. Money was spent like water. Certainly the average net nut of the moderately wealthy was close to a quarter of a million dollars a year. This went through their wives' sieves as fast as it came in. The men dropped dead of heart attacks and stress younger and younger, while their widows pushed, pulled, tucked, trimmed and taped (no one over sixty-five ever looked a day over forty), collected the insurance money and paid it out over and over again to Saks, Magnin's and the Rodeo Drive boutiques.

I could never understand why everyone had such huge closets overflowing with finery never worn. The usual invitation was "Come to dinner casual or informal." If a brave hostess had the temerity to suggest, "Come to dinner—black tie," there were moans and groans of anguished protest. It was a paradox. Why did they buy all these clothes if they never wore them? Everyone looked more or less the same. The teens, the twenties and the actresses wore jeans and T-shirts, the thirties and forties wore linen pants and silk shirts, the over forties *haute couture* or polyester and dacron permapress pants suits with coordinated accessories.

I surveyed my large closet, full of the latest fashions from London. I didn't need a thing. I had everything to wear. I didn't want to learn to play tennis, backgammon or tap dancing. I didn't intend to ruin my skin at the beach or the pool, didn't need the analyst and the gynecologist and didn't believe in numerology or group-therapy sessions. Girls' lunches I liked, but once or twice a week was enough. I wanted to work—I needed the roar of the greasepaint—the lights, the cameras, the action! It was in my blood.

So I worked. "The Man from Uncle" with my ex-classmate from RADA, David McCallum; and "Batman" and "The Bing Crosby Special," and "Mission Impossible" with stalwart Martin Landau and impeccably groomed Barbara Bain. And "Star Trek." "City on the Edge of Forever" became one of the most popular episodes. As Edith Cleaver, a young mission worker for down-and-out men in New York in the Depression, I try to prove to the world that Hitler was a nice guy. Bill Shatner as Captain Kirk falls in love with Edith, and Dr. Spock—he of the ears—allows her to get run over by a truck lest her teachings lead the world to total destruction.

In the evenings I came home and frolicked with the children, who were totally endearing. Tony and I gazed somberly at each other across our Wedgwood dinner service.

One night I got out all the letters we had written to each other and reread them. My letters were full of love, compassion and understanding. "Please try and understand me," I cried out in red ink on Beverly Hills Hotel notepaper. "The only thing I want is for us to be together—to communicate with each other—I understand your problems—I want to help you—I love you."

Try as I might, the contact and the communication weren't there. Had they ever truly been?

I gazed at my perfectly made up face in the dressing-table mirror. Porcelain skin, helped along by Revlon and Clinique; arresting green eyes, all the better for double sets of eyelashes from the Eyelure company; and a weak chin. I narrowed my eyes and surveyed my chin. Yes, it was definitely the chin of a coward and a weakling; a person unable to make decisions, solve problems or keep the love of her husband. I slammed the makeup drawer shut and stalked into Tony's study. He was curled up on the sofa, wearing his usual black sweater and gray flannels, a plaid blanket covering him up to the chin.

"We're late," I said sternly, as he looked wearily up from the script of *Dr. Doolittle* he was studying. "We're late for Arthur's party." Since Arthur was Arthur P. Jacobs, the producer of *Dr. Doolittle*, I expected him to attend this one.

"Sorry, Flower," he said, a smile attempting to flit across his face and failing. "I'm beat. Why don't you call Brickman and Eve and go with them?" He sighed and turned back to his script. The troubles of the world seemed to sit on his shoulders recently. I couldn't understand why. He was starring in an important film and had many good offers lined up.

"OK," I said flatly, not showing any of the emotion that he detested. "Arthur won't be pleased, you know. After all, you are one of his stars. Rex and Samantha and Dick Fleischer will be there. Are you sure you're too tired?"

"I'm exhausted, luv." He rubbed his eyes and yawned as though to emphasize his fatigue. His face did look white and strained.

"Go on, Flower, have a good time. I'll see you in the morning." He gave another sigh—I knew he wanted to be alone. We brushed cheeks. He went back to his script and I went to make my by now inevitable phone call to the Bricusses to pick me up.

After Arthur's party, it was disco time. I hadn't been to the Daisy for several weeks, but even the usual excitement that the place generated couldn't get me out of my depressed lethargy. I gloomily sipped a Brandy Alexander and surveyed the frenetic scene. Legs, legs, legs—a veritable forest of them, kicking and stomping and pirouetting to the latest Beatles and Stones and Supremes discs. With every song that was played I seemed to be able to find some special meaning in its title—"Can't Buy Me Loove," sang McCartney and Lennon, their young voices cascading in a crescendo, and "She Loves You"; and I cynically yeah yeah'd myself into my third Brandy Alexander.

She loves *you* all right, I thought cynically, although it's evaporating rapidly these days. As if to answer my thoughts, Tony's voice crooned over the sound system the words to his most famous

song, and the one which made me realize now what he was all
about:

> *What kind of fool am I*
> *Who never fell in love*
> *It seems that I'm the only one*
>   *that I have been thinking of,*
> *What kind of man is this?*
> *An empty shell*
> *A lonely cell in which an empty*
>   *heart must dwell.*
> *What kinds of lips are these*
> *That lied with every kiss*
> *That whispered empty words of love*
> *That left me alone like this*
> *Why can't I fall in love?*
> *Like any other man?*
> *And maybe then I'll know*
> *What kind of fool I am?* ©

My eyes misted. The words applied to Tony totally. I had
known it, though. He had warned me he was incapable of love,
but I had thought my love could change that. What kind of fool
was I?

"Like to dance?" Ryan stood there looking arrogant and nervous
at the same time. I got up.

"Sure."

"Haven't seen you around lately."

We gyrated in front of each other amidst the flashing lights and
the flashing legs.

"I've been working a lot," I explained, becoming caught up in
the music and the dancing. It started to blow the blues away.
Jagger was suggestively intoning "Under My Thumb." He was
good. Ryan looked *very* good. He had enormous energy. Although
he had to be on the set of "Peyton Place" at seven in the morning
he wasn't concerned about his beauty sleep.

He was an Aries. They were compatible with Gemini because

of their vitality and spark. Sydney—Max—Warren. Aries men were my weak spot.

We danced on until closing time. The ridiculously early California licensing laws dictated that all drinks must be off the table by one forty-five. He insisted on driving me home but I was nervous in his car. God forbid Tony looked out the window and saw his dutiful wife arriving home at two in the morning with a good-looking actor.

"Give me your number," he urged as we approached the drive way. "We can have lunch or tea. English ladies always have tea, don't they?" His blue eyes twinkled. He was definitely adorable. But trouble. Trouble I did not need.

I took *his* number and promised to call him sometime.

"Promise!" He leaned over the steering wheel to kiss me, which I avoided by stumbling hastily out of the car.

"I promise, I promise," I whispered, hoping that my Portuguese couple hadn't seen us.

"I'll be waiting then," he called. His sports car made a 100 degree turn, and with a screech of brakes he zoomed off down the hill.

I didn't call. I couldn't. I wasn't a teenager calling a boy for an innocent date. He knew what it meant if I called him. I knew too. I was Sadie, Sadie, married lady now, and even if it wasn't a wonderful marriage and my husband slaved over a hot script all day, I still wanted my marriage to work.

Tony went to New York for a few days and I went to work at Universal, guesting on "Run for Your Life," with Ben Gazzara. It was the usual cops-and-robbers shoot-'em-up TV trash, and I played the usual glamorous villainess. The spy with a heart of brass.

Tara came to visit one day. She watched a scene in which Gazzara tells me off angrily for not being a good enough spy. Suddenly her baby voice piped up indignantly, "Don't you talk to my Mummy like that, you naughty rude man!" Ben and the crew broke up—Tara was showing her mettle at an early age.

Ryan showed up and insisted on buying me lunch at a Chinese restaurant on Ventura Boulevard. For forty-five minutes he was

251

captivating, witty and triumphant that we were lunching at last. He was enormously appealing in a roguish way. Not to be taken seriously, but he had all the sparkle that was lacking in Tony's personality. He positively glittered with exuberance and enthusiasm.

"What about dinner?" he said as we drove through the gates of Lew Wasserman's big black glass film factory.

"Never," I said faintly and unconvincingly.

"What are you doing tomorrow?" He never gave up. I liked that. His butterfly net was always out.

"Tomorrow's my birthday. Tony's coming back from New York. We'll probably celebrate with a hot dog in front of the TV set," I said firmly, surprised by the bitterness in my voice.

"I'll call and wish you Happy Birthday then." I jumped out and went back to Ben Gazzara and Co. feeling lighthearted.

Tony did not make it back in time for my birthday. The meetings in New York were taking longer than expected. He sent a huge bunch of flowers and a regretful phone call.

"Happy Birthday, English lady—where's your husband taking you tonight?" said the husky familiar voice, the sound of which always brought a smile to my face. I certainly didn't want the crew of "Run for Your Life" to notice that.

"He's not," I said simply. "He's stuck in the Big Apple, with only his record producer for company."

"Oh, you poor kid," he clucked sympathetically. "Well, er, we wouldn't want you to be alone on your birthday, would we?"

"No, we wouldn't." There was a pregnant pause. I suddenly decided what I wanted for my birthday present. A girl should get what she deserves on her birthday. And she did.

A few weeks later my sister Jackie married for the second time— Oscar Lerman, an American businessman. Her first husband had died in tragic circumstances and I really hoped that now she would find the happiness she truly deserved. Certainly it had eluded me most of my life. Oh, yes, there had been passion and infatuation and what, for months or sometimes years, I had thought was love. As I stood behind Jackie and Oscar at the simple wedding ceremony at our house I realized definitively that nobody had ever really loved the real me. They had professed their love, but when the chips were down, none of it meant a damn thing. But *I* had chosen these men, and I'd usually picked Mr. Wrong.

I knew why, now—that was the irony of it. I *had* to pick the toughest ones—those who couldn't, wouldn't, or didn't know *how* to commit. *Why* did I constantly make the same mistake? To get Daddy, obviously. Because he had always been undemonstrative. I never felt he loved or cared about me enough. If I could get a difficult man to fall in love with me, *then* I could say to my seven-year-old self, "Wow! I'm a worthwhile person at last. Daddy loves me, and I've *got* him!"

If I had guts I'd end my marriage. Tony's love for me was not based on reality. He professed love when I was being a good little, sweet little, home-loving obedient Joanie—Flower. But if I showed any of the other sides, the strong side, the ambitious side, the assertive side, the argumentative side, he couldn't *stand* me—and he admitted it. It was the same with the other men I'd loved. Total adoration when I was behaving myself and no understanding at all when I wasn't what they expected me to be.

I knew I had my faults. But show me a faultless person and I'll show you a dull one.

I decided to go back into analysis and try to sort myself out again.

Tony left for England and *Dr. Doolittle* locations. I stayed on in Beverly Hills for a few weeks. I was enjoying being with Ryan. He had a tiny apartment on Doheny Drive and the afternoons flew by.

Several people suspected our relationship by now. Although we had been discreet, we had often been in each other's company. We even went to dinner with the newlywed Lermans. I realized I was playing a dangerous game when I read the blind item in a gossip column one morning:

Mr. X, talented British-born performer, seems unaware that his sexy actress wife Mrs. X is doing more than just polishing her

253

dance steps with handsome Mr. Z, up and coming star of one
of America's favorite soap operas. . . .

Oh, God—if the columnist knew about it, that meant it was almost in public domain. I didn't relish at all Tony's becoming the
town cuckold, with all the sniggering innuendos.

I packed my bags, and flew to join him in London with my
children and the nanny. My little fling was over. I had to now
work out whether there was any hope or life left in our marriage
before the rot really set in—for the sake of our precious children.

Rumblings had obviously reached Tony about Ryan. He had,
in fact, brought Tatum and Griffin up to our house to swim several times with Tara and Sacha. He did tricks with them in the
pool. People weren't blind. We'd been seen together often enough.
Tony wasn't stupid. Suddenly he obviously realized my dissatisfac-
tion and the possibility of losing me. He was aware I was attractive
to men, more now than in my Rank and Fox days, because I had
gained an aura of sophistication. He made a genuine effort to
become the loving husband he had been at the beginning of our
marriage, and we sailed happily through the next year on more-or-
less calm water.

The following year, along with Paul Newman, Sammy Davis,
Peter Lawford, Ronnie Buck and two or three other businessmen,
Tony and I went into the discotheque business. The Factory became an overnight sensation. It was on the top floor of an old
abandoned factory on Robertson Drive, in Hollywood, and decorated in a melange of Art Deco, Art Nouveau, English antiques,
stained-glass windows and flashing disco lights. With a live band
augmenting the recorded sounds, it was flashy, fun and fabulous.
Opening night, the club was jammed with major stars and celebrities. The huge dance floor was packed with dozens of the most
famous people in Hollywood. Word gets around fast and even
at three hundred and fifty dollars a membership, everyone wanted
to join. Night after night the most illustrious and glamorous people—some of whom had never even set foot in a disco before—sat
and stared at the incredible goings-on. Marlon Brando came. So
did Barbra Streisand, Steve McQueen, Loretta Young, Liza Min-

nelli, Dean Martin, Peter Sellers, Bobby Kennedy, Vanessa Red-grave, everyone who meant anything at that time—a Who's Who couldn't do it justice. Tony and I spent practically every night there. He even got to like dancing.

We couldn't believe how quickly the success of the Factory happened. But just as quickly as it started, it faded. Too much too soon. Goodbye Sweet Factory. In a little less than a year its vogue had passed, just like many a Hollywood career—and Tony and I were back in London again.

Tony was achieving his life's desire to write, direct and star in an erotic musical-comedy-fantasy, based on his life story. It was succinctly called *Can Hieronymus Merkin Ever Forget Mercy Humppe and Find True Happiness?* This was an avant-garde satirical Fellini-esque movie about a successful actor-director (Newley-Merkin) who, at the age of thirty-eight sits, miserable and bitter, on the beach outside his Beverly Hills mansion screening a montage of film clips from his life, while showing them to his two tiny children and his old Cockney mother. His main fantasy in the film revolves around a deliciously nubile blonde, Mercy Humppe, for whom he has been searching all his life. He considers her his suppressed desire and the penultimate sexual object. She is a slave to his whims. He is desperately torn between his love for her and for the beautiful, headstrong raven-haired Polyester Poontang (guess who?) who becomes the mother of his two children and puts up with his philandering with every Jane, June and Jenny who crosses his path, or, as they were more poetically named in the film, Filigree Fondle, Trampolina Wham Bang, and Maidenhair Fern!

Incredibly, I decided I had to play the part of Ms. Poontang. Who other than I could play it better? Since our two children—now four and two and a half—had been cast at the insistence of Tony as his children in the film, Thumbelina and Thaxted, I would have to be in London and Malta in any case for four or five months, being a stage mama. Universal thought it a great idea and I got the part, for which I was paid the princely sum of two thousand pounds!

Tony wrote a song for Polyester to sing to Hieronymus. It was a cute song. He even dedicated it to me, since it was based completely on our relationship. Before I sing the song there is a symbolic scene where the two meet for the first time. Polyester looks at the mask (Newley-Merkin's alter ego) and says:

POLYESTER (*sympathetic as she looks at* THE MASK)
Typical Libra. You bruise so easily!
HIERONYMUS (*leering to himself*)
Typical Gemini . . . you gonna get it.
(*They stare at each other in a kind of mutual fascination.*)
POLYESTER
You realize, of course, we have absolutely nothing in common . . . *And* POLYESTER *sings,*

How did you get into my horoscope
You funny irascible lovable dope.
Isn't it clear from the stars that you haven't
    a hope with me?
Anyone else would have known in advance,
Libra and Gemini haven't a chance.
Anyone else would have seen at a glance it
    could never be—
Chalk and Cheese—we're as different as Chalk and Cheese.
Were there ever two people more out of step before
More unalike if you please
Souls apart, we are opposite, poles apart.
When I think about me and you saying, how do you do?
Maybe it wasn't so smart.
Me, I'm bright, got a groovy scene.
I like to be where it's at!
You're up-tight as a tambourine
What kind of music is that?
Chalk and Cheese—who would ever blend things
    like these?
On the other hand people say love is here to stay
Hurray for the birds and the bees!
I'm a fool maybe—but I don't mind chalk with
    my cheese.

256

I performed this little ditty clad in a clinging white Grecian gown, while Tony (talk about upstaging) wore nothing except a giant toy key sticking out of the bottom of his spine! He was playing his alter ego, and an actor stood next to him, his face covered by a pink mask on which no features were shown, and dressed in Tony's clothes. A motley selection of hankies and camera tape covered Tony's full frontal which, although never actually revealed to the camera in this scene, one could catch glimpses of later in the sensuous graphic underwater love scenes with the virginal Miss Humppe. This part was played by flaxen-haired *Playboy* centerfold Connie Kreski, after a search rivaling that of the quest for Scarlett O'Hara.

Tony and Connie became extremely close on this movie. Since she was a novice to films, he obviously had to coach her a lot, and they spent many an hour together on and off the set rehearsing their scenes.

She, however, was not the only pebble on the beaches of Malta. Women featured heavily in Hieronymus Merkin's life, and there were dozens and dozens of girls to be interviewed, talked to, rehearsed, prepared and built up for the many roles in the film.

I had a sick, horrible feeling when I first read the script of *H.M.* Tony seemed to have spelled out the death of our marriage with this totally revealing picture of his life.

Hieronymus has a sidekick producer and mentor—Good Time Eddie Filth (Milton Berle), who encourages him in his philanderings. Newley-Merkin has a scene where he sits on top of the mountain having the following dialogue with God:

> There has never been a woman who commanded a moment of my regard after I'd made love to her. I realize I have no respect for women—I really believe I hate them, and take my revenge in sex. The ritual murder, forever stabbing and reopening the divine wound.

After this speech, Good Time Eddie, dressed as Satan, officiates at a ceremony in which dozens of robed candle-holding monks

257

surround an altar bed on which lies a naked woman. Hieronymus is ceremoniously derobed and mounts both the altar and the girl to ritual moans.

The finale of the movie finds Hieronymus at dawn, still on the beach, surrounded by his paraphernalia—skips, wardrobe hampers, sky-high cans of film and scrapbooks, mementos of his career, and his whirring projector. The two kids are asleep on Grandma's knee. Hieronymus sings a plaintive ballad summing up his misery and disillusionment with life. It was called "I'm All I Need":

> I'm all I need, if I got me—I
>   got rainbows
> If I got me—just you see how the rain
>   goes away
> 'Cos I've got somebody who cares
> Someone who likes my company
> While I've got me—I've got a sky full
>   of bluebirds
> When did you see someone as lucky as me?

He continues in this vein. As the song finishes, a squad car approaches on the beach and disgorges two Los Angeles cops and a distraught Polyester-Joan, who has been calling throughout the movie for her husband.

She rushes toward him, gathering Thaxted-Sacha in her arms and Thumbelina-Tara by her tiny hands, and a torrent of words pour out. "Darling, are you *crazy?* . . . Have you been here all night? . . . I've been calling . . . didn't you hear me calling? I didn't know what to think. I called the police. Your agent called the police. I called the hospital. You do this sort of thing, you do it all the time. You don't think and you don't care. Well I've had enough. I'm taking the children—yes I am—I'm taking them back to Europe and this time I mean it. This time *I really do mean it*— I really do."

Exit Polyester-Joan, sobbing hysterically, with Thaxted-Sacha and Thumbelina-Tara, leaving Hieronymus-Newley unmoved and slightly puzzled.

The playing of this scene affected me so violently that during and after each take a positive torrent of real tears burst forth—all the anguish I had been concealing for six years. It was true. Our marriage was badly cracked, and when I finally saw the film in a private screening room in London a few months later I knew there was no hope for us ever to live as husband and wife again.

CHAPTER

Eleven

"THIS IS RON KASS."

My heart said, "Oh, nice!" It had done so before, of course, so I was used to it. The man sitting on the couch in my living room in London was an extremely attractive American. He was tall, with fair hair worn, happily, somewhat shorter than in the current vogue for shoulder-length locks, amazing green eyes in a deeply tanned face, sensual mouth and a warm, open and endearing smile. He was sartorially perfect in a beige suit and black sweater— dressed, I guessed correctly, by the tailor Doug Hayward. Doug had been a close friend of Tony's and mine ever since Evie Bricusse and I used to go with our respective husbands to his tailor shop, then in shabby Shepherd's Bush. Now he was the top tailor of the Swinging Sixties London set. He had a chic shop in Mount Street, near Park Street, where Tony and I were temporarily living while he cut and edited *Hieronymus Merkin*. And hello, hello! a mere two blocks away from elegant South Street, where Ron resided. We were all within a stone's throw of each other, were we of a mind to throw stones, which indeed I was not after meeting the attractive Mr. Kass.

We had dinner at the Club dell' Aretusa, the fashionable Italian restaurant-disco on King's Road, where rock stars rubbed shoulders with MPs, and debutantes, models, managers, photographers and actresses hung out. It was wall-to-wall "in" and lots of fun. Anybody who was anybody was usually there each night.

Evie Bricusse was Doug's "date" for the evening, I was with

260

Tony, and Ron was alone. He was recently separated from his wife of several years. She and their three sons were living in Lugano while he was in London, managing director and president of Apple Records, the Beatles' recording company.

It was a fairly sparkling evening at Aretusa. Michael Caine was there with Bianca Jagger. So was Jean Shrimpton, London's top model, with Cockney photographer David Bailey, the hottest photographer in England. The Swinging Sixties were regretfully drawing to a close, but many of the people who had made them swing were at Aretusa that night. Bailey dropped by the table. He wanted to arrange to take a picture of Tony and me for his book to commemorate the dizzy decade. Seven years after publication, nearly all the couples Bailey pictured in *Goodbye Baby and Amen* were divorced or separated, some by tragic circumstances—Susan Hampshire and her French husband, Dudley Moore and Suzy Kendall, and Roman Polanski and gorgeous, ill-fated Sharon Tate among them.

Tony was not unaware of the interested looks I was trying not to exchange with Ron, but shortly after dinner he excused himself and telling me to "have a good time, Flower," went home to work.

Doug, Evie, Ron and I sat sipping Sambuca in the discotheque. I was attracted to Ron, not only for his warmth and easy personality but also for the energy and enthusiasm that emanated from him. He was an Aries. Not only that, his birth *date*, March 30, was exactly the same day as Sydney Chaplin's and Warren Beatty's! Surely the chances of that were two million to one.

We started to see each other. Just for lunch or tea at first. I was treading extremely warily. Aside from the physical attraction, I felt that Ron was a man who could be a friend. I could talk with him about any subject under the sun. We exchanged ideas, explored each other's minds. He was mature, although only thirty-three, and had an enormous zest for life. Here at last was a man who was a match for my physical energy and stamina. Seemingly indefatigable, he ran the Beatles' company, jumped regularly on a jet to New York, Rome or Geneva at least twice a week and was able to stay up until three or four feeling no jet lag even after a sixteen-hour day.

He was a doer and an organizer, as well as a very dominant male. He was also the first man I had become involved with who

261

was not either an actor, a producer or a playboy. He was substance. He was, in fact, a supervisor, businessman and executive with a Bachelor of Science degree in business (as a graduate of UCLA business school), an Associate of Arts degree in music, and had a keen and intelligent mind. He always knew what he wanted and he usually got it. And what he wanted was me.

But married butterflies who have difficulty in making decisions are not so easily caught, and our relationship had stormy waters to ride. He was the first man I had ever met who thought of me first and himself second. This was an exceptionally novel experience for me. Ron literally swept me off my feet. Try as I did to stem the tide, I found myself becoming more and more attracted to him, not only in an emotional and supportive way but in the need we discovered in each other as human beings and friends. I grew to lean on him and depend on his advice more and more.

Because Tony was still completely enmeshed in his work I was able to see Ron often. Since Tony never asked where I went, I had considerable freedom. Tara and Sacha were now both at school, and my supply of American TV shows was not in evidence, so Ron and I managed to spend much time discovering each other. And the more I discovered, the more I liked. We did not launch into a flaming affair immediately. Perhaps now I was finally realizing that here was the man I had been searching for all my life. I wanted to be very careful. I didn't want to injure our blossoming friendship and love by jumping instantly into bed. So we lunched at the Connaught, had tea at Claridge's, met for drinks at Trader Vic's and bided our time.

I went to Trieste to make an "intellectual" film. At least, my Italian agent had assured me it was an intellectual film. "Not much money, cara, but aah—the prestige!" The director was a dedicated Communist, the crew numbered a mere seventeen; my salary was minimal, and I was not allowed to smile once in the film, since the director considered smiling a cheap and shallow Hollywood device.

"Do you see smiles in a Bergman film?" he roared. "Or an Antonioni film? Maybe you have only one smile in my film, when you are very, very sad."

I played a desolate young widow who becomes involved in a

love affair with a seventeen-year-old boy. For this I had to do my first nude scene, which made me very nervous. It was nearly 1970. Nudity on the screen was suddenly fashionable, all the rage, yes, sir. No more ruby in the navel, flower in the too-plunging neckline. Goodbye, chaste kiss and fade-out to the sound of sensual violins. Hello, take off your bra and jump into the sack or the sofa or the back of a truck—wherever it would be the most "artistic" to shoot the scene. Our director finally decided, after mulling it over for days, that our love scene would perhaps play better in bed. Thus, one freezing winter afternoon in Trieste, a town on the border between Italy and Yugoslavia and one of the most dismal and depressing cities I had ever stayed in, I took off my all for "art."

Mathieu Carrière, the twenty-year-old actor playing the boy, was not quite as nervous as I, perhaps because he was allowed to keep his shorts on. I wore a vast assortment of tights, socks and leg warmers to keep out the freezing air (Michael Caine told me he wore Wellington boots for his love scenes in bed in *Alfie*). I still had to be bare above the waist, however. The director had assured me repeatedly that this was an "art" film. He was not interested in showing anything as vulgarly commercial as a nipple, but he just needed the two bodies in the throes of sexual passion anyway—so throb we must. I decided to cleverly camouflage the basic bits of my anatomy with camera tape. Camera tape, unlike ordinary sticky tape, is very strong. It is used to attach weights to cameras, and has a thousand and one other uses in the studio. Italian camera tape is bright blue. In my dressing room I carefully attached a neat X of camera tape in the middle of each breast. Great ad for Blue Cross, I thought, surveying my surrealistic image in the mirror.

Mathieu arrived with a bottle of brandy, thoughtfully sent by the director to "warm us up"—whether for the love scene or to keep out the bitter cold we knew not. Half a bottle of brandy later I found myself drunk and panicky, tucked in between the sheets with young Monsieur Carrière who was, if anything, even drunker and more panicked than I. Peering hopefully at us behind the hand-held camera was moustachio'd *Il Regista* himself, sizzling with artistic fervor. The Italian crew lounged nonchalantly about, pretending indifference to the simulated coupling they were about to see. I kept on my robe, while the director tried to get the perfect angle for this piece of celluloid passion. Mathieu appeared to have fallen asleep—it was comfortable in the bed and a tiny snore escaped from his beatifically smiling countenance. I nudged him awake. We clutched each other stolidly. Two great hunks of flesh, neither of us about to do anything remotely sensual until the magic word "*Azione!*" was screamed. It is always screamed by Italian film directors. The director feels that this electric word will galvanize his cast into dynamic performances.

"*Va bene—va bene. Allora,* Joan." He turned to me. "Take off the roba."

"Shit," I muttered. The moment of truth had come. What the hell was I doing here, thousands of miles from my loved ones, making a lousy uncommercial Italian art film which no one would probably see anyway? Lying in bed with a young lad barely past puberty, with blue camera tape covering my chest. Oh, the degradation! I bravely ripped off the robe and threw myself onto Mathieu's scrawny chest to cover my by now embarrassing blue crosses.

"OK. O.K. *Azione!*" screamed the director excitedly. The whirring cameras could not keep up with the sound of his yelled instruction "*Kees*—beeg beeg kees." I pressed myself even more fervently to Mathieu and we locked lips and simulated lust. "More *sexy!*" roared Romano. "You *woman,* he *boy*—ees veree veree beeg *thrill* for you." God, this was like making silent movies. Sound was not a big issue in Italian pictures; everything was dubbed later. Our director was going a bit far, even so. His vocal efforts were causing me to giggle. I tried to prevent it by biting my lip, and found Mathieu's there instead.

Squirm, squirm—wriggle, wriggle—pant, pant—we wrestled around on the bed. I felt as passionate as a cat on a cold tin roof. To top it off, my suppressed giggles caused me to get hiccups. I was determined to keep my back to the camera all the time but the staccato heaving of my shoulders every three seconds made the director furiously yell "*Cut!*" We disengaged lips—a thin line of saliva connected us—I disconnected it, giggled and hiccuped. Mathieu was dissolved in hysterical drunken laughter. We disengaged arms. I tried to back off from his chest and found I couldn't. The edge of one of my blue crosses had attached itself to Mathieu's chest. We were Siamese twins. Like courting couples who are found locked in the throes of sexual embrace and who, unable to separate, have to be taken to the hospital while they put them under a cold shower and administer nonstimulating drugs to cool their ardor. Mathieu, aware of what had happened, became even more hysterical with laughter and, hiccuping wildly, so did I. The crew were puzzled until they saw what had happened, and guffaws abounded. But the director remained aloof and cold. He hated people to smile, let alone laugh. The wardrobe lady eventually separated us and I put on my robe and staggered, still hiccuping, to my dressing room to recuperate.

"We will shoot the rest of the scene tomorrow," said the director coldly, "when you 'ave both sobered up." He stalked off briskly, moustache bristling.

After downing a double espresso I proceeded to try and remove the tape. It was stuck solid as a rock. It would not budge. Alarmed at the thought of permanently blue breasts I rushed back to the hotel and, after soaking in a hot bath for an hour, attempted to pull off the offending tape. The agony was such that after it was finally removed, and my bosoms were raw from the pulling, I vowed, to hell with false modesty—in the future if I had to do any nude scenes they would be au naturel.

Tony and I by now had an unspoken "arrangement." He went his way and I went mine. I was in a tremendous dilemma. I wanted to be with Ron, I felt he was the man I had been searching for—he combined the qualities of leadership, dominance and intelligence with love, warmth, communication and compassion. I still loved Tony, but in a completely different way. I felt sadness for him and for his inability to give himself totally to anything except his work. And he was also the father of my children. This was my biggest problem. I dreaded having to break up the children's secure and happy home. To take away their roots, which I had fought hard to get for them. Every time I made the decision to separate from Tony, I changed my mind again because of the pain and hurt it would bring my children, who were the most important entities in my life. How could I ruin their innocent lives?

265

It would be selfish and rotten of me. At the same time, I realized that living in a house without real love was probably much worse for them. I agonized for months, completely torn, completely unable to decide one way or another. I hated myself for being so weak, for not being able to take the decisive initiative and end the marriage. Meanwhile I juggled my quadruple lives and tried to put on a happy face.

I had always had a hankering to be a singer. At one time I took singing lessons in Hollywood before auditioning for a Broadway musical. Luckily I didn't get it since it closed after three performances. My voice was quite good but weak (rather like my character). I had crooned a passable duet with Bing Crosby in *Road to Hong Kong,* called "Let's Not Be Sensible," by my Oscar-winning friend Sammy Cahn, and I had also sung the notorious "Chalk and Cheese" opposite my naked husband in *Hieronymus.* Now Tony's record company in London had approached him about producing and writing an album on which I would perform. The irony of this close working relationship commencing at about the same time our marriage was going down the drain did not escape us.

We were in the process of an amicable "trial separation" although still residing in the same house "for the sake of the children." I had told him about Ron, and I knew about Connie Kreski and various others. We were going to attempt to get through this exceedingly difficult period as normally as possible. It was naive of us to think it could be so.

The album was to be called tentatively *And She Sings Too!* and would feature on the sleeve a photo of me looking beguilingly sexy. My voice was sort of breathy and girlish. Streisand definitely did not have to worry. Tony wrote a song which he gave me. I sang it for the album. It was a hard-driving rock song, better performed by someone with the vocal strength of Petula Clark. It was called "Why Do You Try and Change Me?" and it said it *all* about our marriage.

> *You tell me you love me*
> *But if you love me Baby*
> *Why do you try and change me?*

I don't want to change you baby
You know you have faults as well
I accept them 'cos I really love you.
You can lead a horse to water
But you'll never ever alter me.
I'm free—I'm me . . .
Life is a Mardi Gras and I refuse to miss the party.
I want to dance the night away—
You want to keep me home a perfect little household pet.
But I don't want to be your mother
Take me as a friend and lover
That's the only way I want us to be.
Strange, when I think at first
You seemed to be so mad about me
Why should you suddenly complain?
If you go on and on insisting that I do things your way
You are going to drive me from you
After everything we've gone through
Tell me what you want
I wish that you'd say.
Didn't I change my name for you?
Didn't I play the game for you?
Didn't I make it wild for you?
Didn't I make a child for you?
Take me the way I am or leave me alone
Didn't I stay at home for you?
Didn't I give up Rome for you?
What do I have to do to show you I care? ©

I awoke at six o'clock with a distinct feeling of foreboding. I was having a dream of such reality that I forced myself to awake from it. Could it be true? I had to find out immediately and the only way to do that was to make a phone call to Brazil. To Rio de Janeiro, where Ron had gone for the annual song festival. He had wanted me to go with him and I had been sorely torn. For weeks I anguished about the ramifications a trip to Rio would bring. I wanted to go. Traveling—experiencing new places, sounds, vibrations, meeting new people—was one of my greatest pleasures, and Rio had always been one of the places I wanted to visit. To go with Ron would be an extra bonus. But although Tony was aware of my relationship with Ron, it simply wasn't cricket to openly attend a highly publicized music festival, at which the press of the world would be, with my lover. I was quite popular in Latin America. If we went to the festival together it was tantamount to taking an ad in *Variety*.

But reason prevailed. I needed time—time to think about my children, and what divorcing their father could do to them. I couldn't decide. I knew what I wanted: I wanted Ron. But I was still trying to have my cake and eat it too, a practical impossibility.

I drove later that morning to Ron's rented house on Coldwater Canyon to phone him in Rio. When his voice came through, faint and surprised, yet happy to hear from me, I didn't beat about the bush. The dream was too vivid in my mind.

"Who's this dark-haired twenty-six-year-old socialite you've been going out with?" I said sharply. Diplomacy and tact were never my strong points.

"Whaat?" His voice from a distance of more than six thousand miles sounded fuzzily amazed. "How do you know about her? Who told you?"

It was true then. My dream was a reality. "I just know, that's all," I battled on bravely. "How long has it been going on?"

"My God, Joan." He was the only man who had ever called me by my proper name. A good sign—maybe he saw the real me, and not some plaything or imaginary goddess. I had always been Honey, Sweetheart, Babe, Joanie-bird, Butterfly, Flower, or Jaycee before Ron.

"It hasn't really been 'going on.' I met this girl—she's a lovely girl—" I gritted my teeth. "But we haven't got really involved or anything—yet."

Yet! Yet! Oh, I was such a fool, an absolute fool. I had let this extremely handsome man of thirty-four go off to Rio telling him that, after over a year of knowing each other, I "had to have more time to think things over" and expecting him to stay faithful to me. He was only human. And he was a man.

I realized that I was close to losing the one man who had really understood me and with whom I had true communication.

We talked for an hour. An hour in which I finally resolved my horribly ambivalent feelings and faced up to what losing Ron meant. I knew now what I wanted, needed, and what he wanted too. We had to be together. It was the only way.

If anyone imagines that divorce for an actor or actress is easy, let them think again. This parting was infinitely more horrible than my divorce from Maxwell Reed had been. I really did still care about Tony. My conscience was deeply affected by what I was doing to my two innocent children. But the sparks of love between Tony and me were not enough to rekindle our marriage. We liked and respected each other, but living together any more was out of the question. The split was amicable. Painful, hurtful, but amicable. I wasn't the right woman for him and he knew it. We had been staying together for the children's sake for far too long. Even they, at the tender ages of six and a half and four and a half, were aware of it.

The beautiful house on Summit Drive went on the market. I took no alimony—only a property settlement derived mostly from the sale of the house—which was soon bought by Sammy Davis, Jr. We agreed on a sum for the children's support. They were my responsibility now, and since I had let my career take a secondary position for seven years, the prospects of my earning enough money again to support them were dim, to say the least.

Ron already had a wife and three kids in Lugano to whom he had to pay alimony and child support. I could hardly ask him to support my two children as well.

My marriage to Tony had lasted seven years, just as uncannily true as Ben Gary had predicted.

I assured Tony that he could see the children whenever he wished. The last thing I ever wanted was to have them hurt or used as a pawn in the marital upheavals, as I had seen so many selfish spouses do.

I returned yet again, bags, baggage, furniture and children, to my beloved London.

Ron was now president of MGM records and Robins Feist and Miller Music Publishing Company. He had plush offices in New

York and spent much time commuting between continents. I refused, for the children's sake, to move into Ron's Mayfair townhouse with him, and instead took a cramped and overpriced furnished flat around the corner. I plunged into getting the children settled in new schools, trying to set up my career once again in a different country and generally sorting out all our lives. I was in love with Ron, although we fought a lot. We both always said what was on our minds. It was instant combustibility. But at least it was honest. I felt that at last I had found true, dedicated and supportive love in Ron. However, I did not wish to traumatize the children even more by a new "Daddy" suddenly appearing on the scene. My main concern was to take care of their needs and adjust them as well as I could to their new and strange life. London life is very different from sunny Beverly Hills, where most families have a swimming pool in their backyard.

It was the spring of 1970. Ron bought me a new minicar. I raced around London hunting again for a suitable house. Ron wanted us to marry, but I was convinced that, as Oscar Wilde said, "One should always be in love—that is why one should never marry." Two attempts at marriage had made me realize I wasn't very good at it. And it was too soon.

Luckily I was able to start working in films immediately. I made several in quick succession. In the early part of the 1970s I made *Three in the Cellar* in New Mexico, before I left for England. It was a comedy—a rather abortive one. I played Larry (J.R.) Hagman's wife. J.R. and Alexis in the same movie! I had known Larry since I was at RADA. He was Mary Martin's son, then appearing on stage in *South Pacific* with her. (He was in the chorus.) We dated a couple of times casually, little dreaming that some thirty years later we would be the reigning villains on TV. He was very different from his J.R. image—quiet, shy and self-effacing. I made *Quest for Love* and *Revenge* for Rank at Pinewood Studios, my old stamping grounds. Over fifteen years had passed since the "coffee bar Jezebel" had crossed those hallowed portals to portray wayward teenagers and sexy delinquents. Now I played leading ladies, sometimes if I was lucky with a touch of humor or evil thrown in. None of these films were by any means either box-office bonanzas or works of art, but an actor acts and a baker bakes and I needed the bread.

Then came a quick series of horror films which were euphemistically referred to as "psychological melodramas": *Fear in the Night, Tales from the Crypt, Dark Places* and *Tales that Witness Madness.* I became known by the British press as Queen of the Horror Films—a title I didn't particularly relish. But I was resilient. A survivor. I considered myself lucky to be working so much after such a long period away from the British screen, particularly since I was well into my thirties. The critics were sometimes kind. "Miss Collins—an actress always better than her material," said the *Evening Standard*—and "Joan Collins is an actress who only improves . . . and brings beauty, luminosity, and compelling charm to the screen." How nice!

I had always thought that if my acting career collapsed I might become a casting director. I could see the potential in some unknown actor or actress and say "There's a future star." It first happened at MGM while making *The Opposite Sex.* A young guy, about my age, who worked in the mail room and sometimes delivered my fan letters, used to whistle at me as I sailed by in my tight-waisted Helen Rose creations to the commissary for lunch. One day I stopped to chat. He was cute—boyish, with black curly hair, wide blue eyes, a sense of humor and a certain offbeat sex appeal. He must have had a lot of confidence in himself for he asked me for a date, which I refused. He told me he was an actor, and his name was Jack Nicholson.

In 1972 Ron and I finally found the perfect London house we had been searching for. It was, from the outside, a rather ordinary looking semidetached 1930s house, not unlike forty or fifty others on the same avenue, but it was exactly what we wanted. A warm family home into which Ron, Tara, Sacha and I happily moved, and with the added excitement of a new addition expected to our already large family. Ron's three husky young sons—David, Robert and Jonathan—visited us each summer and at Christmas time at our house in Marbella. When baby Katyana arrived we had a his, hers and theirs brood.

271

Ron and I sat with friends Paul Wasserman—Ron's best friend—Peter Kameron, and Burt and Maxine Kamerman in Mr. Chow's ten days before the baby was due. We doodled possible names on the paper tablecloth. Ron desperately wanted a girl—after three boys, who wouldn't? Pete was sure it would be a girl. Pete was one of Ron's closest friends. He had given up most of his material possessions and had spent several years traveling the world and searching for the truth. A true guru!

He had just returned from a trip to India and meeting with that extraordinary Indian, Saha Baba, a holy man held in the highest esteem. Pete had a small phial of gray dust, and he dabbed some of it on my forehead and cheekbones. It was a substance that Saha Baba had created himself—out of thin air, literally—and it had, so I was told, powerful properties. Pete was a great believer in getting your "karma" right.

After he applied the ashes he told me that the baby would be a blessed child, possessed of immense personal magnetism, intelligence, beauty and luck. "You'll have her tomorrow," he said gravely, convinced it was a girl.

"Nonsense—it's not due for at least ten days," laughed Ron. We wrote down some names—mostly Russian, from his ancestry, for his original family name was Kaschinoff—Tatiana, Katya, Katyana. I wanted something completely original but with a Russian flavor. Four hours later, after consuming an immense Chinese meal, and Ron consuming a powerful sleeping pill, I went into labor. Unable to rouse Ron from a deep sleep I poured three cups of strong coffee down his throat before he could get himself together enough to drive me to the nursing home!

I was having this child, again by natural childbirth, helped along by Ron's encouragement, and a fierce Scrabble game which lasted almost until the birth.

When James Schneider, my obstetrician, said excitedly, "It's a girl!" I argued with him. "You're just saying that to make Ron happy," I said. "He always gets what he wants and you don't want to disappoint him." Ron was at the birth, beside himself with joy. Katyana Kennedy Kass brought us even closer together.

I was extremely concerned about the effect a new baby would

have on Tara and Sacha. It hadn't been easy for them adjusting to a new country, new friends, new house, new school, new stepfather. I remembered how horrible I had felt attending all those different schools and having to make new friends when I was a child. But they adored Katy and seemed to adjust to their new situation.

Katy was born on June 20, 1972. Being a Gemini too, she and I probably understand each other better than anyone else in the world.

I was now in what without a doubt was the happiest time of my life. If one can measure the highs and lows of one's life, the years between 1970 and 1975 were almost perfect. I loved my husband. I adored my children. I was happy living in England with my family and working on some things I really enjoyed.

Buzz Kulik, who had directed me a few years earlier in a ghastly potboiler, *Warning Shot*, with David Janssen, asked me to play Lorraine Sheldon in *The Man Who Came to Dinner*.

This was a prestigious NBC Hallmark Hall of Fame two-hour special and, although shot in England, it was to be shown in America for Thanksgiving.

Lorraine was a wonderful part based on the character of Gertrude Lawrence. Flamboyant and eccentric, it was the sort of part I had been wanting to sink my teeth into. Finally a decent role. I hoped it was not going to be a flash in the pan, after which I'd drift back into my usual wallpaper parts or horror films.

Buzz gathered an excellent cast. Lee Remick was to play Maggie, Sheridan Whiteside's loyal secretary, immortalized in the screen version by Bette Davis. Marty Feldman played the mad Groucho Marx character, Don Knotts the catatonically shy doctor, Peter Haskell the journalist, and last but definitely not least, Orson Welles himself as Sheridan Whiteside. *The* man who came to dinner.

He comes to the house of a respectable middle-aged Connecticut couple, breaks his leg, and stays, creating havoc, turmoil, and humor. It is a marvelous comedy. Sheridan Whiteside is one of the best (and longest) comedy roles ever written for an actor. He dominates every scene, is bitingly witty, ruthless, scheming and hilarious. Hallmark felt they had a major coup in getting this giant of the entertainment world to grace them with his august presence. He was treated like an emperor.

We rehearsed for three weeks, during which time Mr. Welles consumed vast quantities of burgundy-colored liquid from teacups and read every one of his lines from massive cue cards three feet by three feet which were held in place by two wide-eyed nervous students from RADA.

I felt like a wide-eyed nervous girl from RADA myself in the intimidating presence of Welles. He was immense, literally and figuratively, and frightening. His reputation for not letting anyone get the better of him preceded him. I practically curtsied and would have pulled my forelock reverently if I had one, such was the awe he instilled in us. After all, he was the boy wonder of the movies who, at the age of twenty-five, had made *Citizen Kane*, one of the greatest movies of all time. Awesome Orson I called him. I was playing a poised, sophisticated actress, whom nothing fazed, but I had to steel my nerves while working with his mightiness.

He was rehearsing a long speech to me one afternoon. I was standing on my mark when he suddenly ended the speech with, "And I can't read the rest of the lines because *Miss Collins* is standing in front of the damn cue cards!"

"But I'm on my mark, Orson," I muttered feebly, catching a sympathetic grimace from Lee Remick. It didn't matter that he was in the wrong. I had blocked his view of his lines so I must stand in another position where his Highness could view them without obstruction. I meekly did what I was told. Welles looked triumphant. His secretary brought him another cup of "tea"— which he insisted was Coca Cola but which we all knew was red wine. Not even vintage.

Peter Haskell, however, was not intimidated by Welles one bit. He bounded in the following day performing an airy speech about its being a beautiful Christmas day tra la and the snow was on the trees and frost on the ground etc. Welles boomed out in a sarcastic stentorian tone, "You read that just like a goddamn faggot."

"What did you say?" said Peter, menacingly quiet and advancing toward Welles with measured stride.

"I said you read it like—a—er—faggot. But, dear boy, I was only joking, I assure you—ha ha ha! Dear boy, I *know* you aren't a faggot—I'm sorry." His huge laugh boomed and reverberated through the drafty rehearsal hall. Some of the crew laughed with him sycophantically. Peter, slightly placated, continued the scene. Orson seemed to admire him after that and they became quite chummy. Welles obviously enjoyed people brave enough to stand up to him. He relished putting the fear of God into lesser mortals, however.

Don Knotts was not so lucky. Lee Remick and I sat in the transmission room watching a dress rehearsal on the monitor while Don had his best and funniest scene cut to ribbons by Welles. Welles insisted on restaging so that all of Don's best lines were shot on the back of his head. He insisted on cutting anything that he felt detracted from his own performance.

During the three-day studio taping, which extended to five and a half days, while another TV company stamped their feet in frenzy outside our studio door, Orson Welles read *every single line* of his part from the cue cards. Buzz Kulik tried to remonstrate with him. During the staging of each scene Welles insisted on being center stage facing the camera (and his cards). Kulik suggested that perhaps some of the other actors should get a close-up occasionally. Welles boomed angrily, "*I* am the star. This is *not* an ensemble piece. This play is about Sheridan Whiteside. The rest of the troupe are just supporting players!"

Buzz gave up and Welles did it his way. Needless to say, it was one of the unfunniest productions of *The Man Who Came to Dinner* ever. And the ratings for NBC were exceedingly poor.

I received a fine compliment from Kitty Carlisle, the widow of the co-author, Moss Hart. She came to visit during the filming and told me that I was the best Lorraine Sheldon she had ever seen— and she had seen every actress play it since the 1940s.

Although my quest had been for a father figure, not a mother figure, I was sorely conscious of the lack of a mother in my life, especially with three beautiful children to whom having a granny

275

would have meant so much. The family unit was important to me. I missed my mother. What a pity it took me so long to realize it. I found I thought about her more and more, especially as Tara grew older. I could identify so vividly with my own childhood feelings.

My feelings for my father were not as vehement now. I realized his weaknesses and failings, but I cared about him and felt compassion for him.

He had married again and had another daughter, Natasha, when he was sixty-five. His wife was also an agent and artists' manager. Irene was about the same age as I, which was interesting. I wondered if she had ever searched for a father figure too?

But my mother's image still haunted me and I dreamed about her more often. Jackie had become enormously close to Mummy in the years before her death, and I regretted that I had not been able to do so because of leaving for America while still too young to appreciate her. A boy needs a father some of his life, but a girl needs a mother all of her life. Or is it the other way around? In any case I prefer my own version.

Ron was co-producing with David Putnam *The Optimists*, starring Peter Sellers. Putnam went on to become one of the most successful producers in Britain, his success culminating in the Oscar-winning *Chariots of Fire*. Sellers was going through the turmoil of another divorce, and was feeling rather put upon and lonely. He had adopted Ron and me as his new best friends of the month. I had known Peter since 1963 when he, Tony, Leslie Bricusse and I had made a comedy album called "Fool Britannia," which was based on the sexual excesses of certain members of Parliament and aristocrats in Britain at the time. Now Peter was down in the dumps. He had recently started a short-lived romance with Liza Minnelli. Short-lived it was indeed, for a scant ten days was about how long it took before the gilt wore off the gingerbread. Now the romance was teetering on its last legs and Peter needed someone to pour his heart out to, and we were the recipients of his confidences. At 11 A.M. one Sunday the phone rang.

"Hello," said I, busily fixing bacon and eggs for the family in our sunny kitchen.

"Joanie?" said a wary voice. "It's me—Pete. What's happening? Are you and Ron up to anything today?" "No, we're staying in. Do you want to come over, Pete?" I asked, spooning scrambled eggs onto eighteen-months-old Katy's plate. "We're here all day."

"All right—yes—I'd love to." Then, dropping his voice dramatically, "Fleet Street's on to Liza and me. They've been doorstepping us all night. It's been hell. I've got to get out. I'll leave by the back entrance of the Dorchester. See you in an hour."

Shortly afterward he arrived. In deep disguise. This disguise consisted of an SS officer's uniform, complete with leather jacket liberally festooned with swastikas and an SS armband, a steel helmet covering his whole head. He drove a black Mercedes-Benz with tinted windows, obviously bulletproof. Sheldon Avenue was a predominantly Jewish neighborhood. On a sunny Sunday afternoon most of the residents took a little constitutional to nearby Highgate park with their dogs or children. The sight of a sleek black Mercedes containing a Nazi SS officer authentic down to the last swastika must have been quite a shock to them.

When the doorbell rang and I saw this apparition standing there I convulsed. "Let me in, quick. I was followed by half of Fleet Street, but I think I lost them," hissed Sellers, black leather quivering.

In the garden he regaled us for two hours with hilarious stories of his ill-fated romance with Liza Minnelli. When it was time to leave I suggested it might be better to hide the steel helmet and swastika-studded jacket. He wouldn't hear of it. With typical Sellers humor he zoomed into Sheldon Avenue, and then with right arm extended stiffly out of the window of the Mercedes proceeded down Sheldon Avenue, declaiming loudly "Heil Hitler! Heil Hitler! Sieg Heil!" in his most guttural German to the disgust of the residents and Ron's and my helpless laughter.

I finally fulfilled one of my major ambitions. To play in a Noel Coward comedy. Ron had obtained the rights to several Coward plays, among them *Fallen Angels*. We had tried, unsuccessfully, to obtain *Private Lives*. I still longed to play Amanda. *Fallen Angels* had been originally produced in New York in 1927 with the young Tallulah Bankhead and Edna Best in the leading roles. Two women, best friends all their lives and now happily, if boringly, married to dullards, had shared a passionate romance in the past with an attractive Frenchman. It was a *tour de force* for two actresses, and Tallulah and Edna made enormous successes on Broadway. Since then the play had been constantly revived, but always with older actresses in the roles which should have been played by women in their late twenties or thirties. Perhaps managements thought that only mature actresses could play these roles, as they were extremely funny, outrageous and rather camp. Hermione Gingold and Hermione Baddeley had played them, among others.

We made a deal with Sir John Woolf, the head of Anglia TV, and started pre-production. For the first time I started to become instrumental in the production side. Ron was producing, and with my casting director's hat on I suggested that Susannah York would be perfect to play Julia, and Sacha Distel, the French heartthrob, to play Maurice. This role, probably because it was small, has usually been played by some lackadaisical nonentity, but it was, I thought, extremely important to the plot that if Susannah (Julia) and me (Jane) spent three quarters of the play extolling the virtues of this wonderful Frenchman with whom we were both still secretly in love, by the time the audience sees him he should be sensational.

The adaptation for television worked well. Susannah and I had good chemistry together and Sacha Distel looked suitably stunning as the devastating Frenchman. It was screened in England over the Christmas holiday and received good reviews and ratings.

"*Soak the rich!*" screamed Chancellor of the Exchequer Denis Healey in the headlines of the British papers. "Tax them till they bleed. Squeeze them dry!"

It was too ominous for us. Ron, American born and living in Europe for over ten years, could not stay. He was now president of Warner Brothers Records in the U.K.

There was nothing for it but to escape from Healey's claws. I had worked hard all my life. The possessions I had accumulated—

a house, furniture, a Mercedes, jewelry, some paintings and my collection of Art Deco objects and 1920s figures—would, it seemed, be subject to an immense wealth tax each year. The newspapers editorialized that England would lose much of its creative talent by this governmental blunder, but Mr. Healey was adamant. He wanted his last pound of flesh.

With astonishing alacrity, dozens of writers, directors, producers, sportsmen and actors left England. Many Americans, U.K. residents for years, were forced to leave also.

Nevertheless I fought tooth and nail not to leave. I was desolate. Destroyed. I couldn't *bear* the thought of packing up everything once more. Taking my children from the schools and friends to whom they had become so attached, and hitting the long and winding road to Hollywood, California—again.

I adored the house on Sheldon Avenue: I had been sublimely happy at last. Why did Ron, who knew that I had been striving to put down roots for so long, insist that we uproot ourselves yet *again* for California?

I wept for days as the impending inevitability of our departure approached. It was 1975 and I was shooting a horror movie called *The Devil Within Her*, a sort of *Exorcist*-inspired thriller, which was later moderately successful in America.

I was gaining a toehold in the fading British film industry again. The day that Ron brought the final papers to me to be signed for the sale of Sheldon Avenue at lunch in the studios I rushed to my dressing room and wept for so long that the director was unable to shoot on me for several hours. All my deepest instincts, which I usually chose to ignore, screamed at me that this move to L.A. was a *major* mistake. But inexorably we had to leave. Off we went, transporting a houseful of furniture, children, the car and the clothes. I felt like a snail who carries its life on its back.

Ben Gary's prediction for me in 1961, seventeen years earlier, was accurate again: "You will *always* be a gypsy. You will strive to have roots, but you will constantly be on the move and have to keep on putting down new roots." It was in the stars. Could Ben, I wonder, see from his grave how accurate he had been about my entire life?

"You are amazingly resilient," he had said to me. "You will always adapt, and you will always adjust to what life has in store for you. You must always work. It is essential that you be involved and creative. Nothing will ever defeat you or depress you for long. You will always have the capacity to make money and you will eventually achieve happiness because you are basically a happy person and one of life's survivors."

CHAPTER

Twelve

I WASN'T HAPPY LIVING IN HOLLY-wood again however—my third permanent move there in twenty years. We bought a vast modern house with a tennis court, marble floors and a mirrored bar on Chalette Drive in Trousdale, and I started decorating. I also started the thankless task of trying to get a job. To say there was little demand for my services was putting it mildly. Joan who? Oh, yes, she's been around awhile. Must be a bit long in the tooth by now. Well, let's take a look at her. Maybe we can use her in *something*. After all, she *was* a star. . . .

Although I had endured the normal amount of career rejection in the years between 1975 and 1977, I nevertheless managed to scrape by workwise, guest-starring on TV shows like "Baretta," "Mission Impossible," "Future Cop," "Switch," "Policewoman," "Space 1999" and even "Batman," where I donned silver lamé and played the role of "The Siren" whose piercing falsetto scales could stop her enemies and even Batman himself in their tracks.

It wasn't exactly rewarding creatively, but it helped to pay the bills. Ron's career was not doing so well. He had left his good job as president of Warner Brothers Records in London and was now the head of a new film company called Sagittarius.

Sagittarius was the brainchild of Edgar Bronfman, the heir to the Seagram whiskey millions. He had taken over as chairman of the board of MGM briefly in the early seventies. He had acquired a taste for show business and had been actively involved in a few film productions in England.

Edgar was a good-looking man in his mid-forties. He had been married for over twenty years, had five children, a taste for pretty women, and his own brand of whiskey. We all became jolly buddies, double-dating with Samantha Eggar, Sue Lloyd or whoever was his lady of the moment, jetting in the Seagram private Gulf Stream jet to San Francisco, New York or Acapulco, where Edgar had a villa.

He was also a Gemini. With all his *joie de vivre*, wicked humor and almost childlike enthusiasm for certain short-lived projects, he had his dark side too. Although incredibly wealthy, he could be amazingly stingy. He seemed paranoid that women might be interested in him only for his money and not himself—a prevalent attitude among many wealthy attractive men.

But this was by the by. Ron adored, practically worshipped, Edgar. Edgar became godfather to our daughter Katy, who was born on his birthday. I liked Edgar and enjoyed his company, but there was still something about him that I instinctively couldn't trust.

I started the Hollywood rounds again. I renewed old acquaintances, friendships and contacts. I knew practically everyone in Hollywood, having arrived as a green young starlet twenty years earlier.

I plunged into the decoration and renovation of Chalette Drive with enthusiasm and a limited budget, organized Tara, Sacha and Katy in new schools, made the odd TV appearance and went back to the little wife role.

Ron was working hard at his job with Sagittarius and taking trips with Edgar whenever Edgar wanted him to.

When Edgar's eldest son, Sam, Jr., was kidnapped, it was Ron who flew to New York and stayed by Edgar's side waiting for the phone to ring and for the kidnappers to tell Edgar where to deliver the ransom money. They were as close as two men can be, both as friends and business associates.

When Edgar asked Ron and me to give his second son, Edgar, Jr., his twenty-first-birthday party at our house, Ron agreed. I pointed out to Ron that Edgar knew very few people in Hollywood and that we were being used; however Ron insisted on a big Hollywood "bash" with as many socially acceptable producers, agents, stars as I could conjure up. The planning of this elaborate party went on for weeks.

I was helped by my friend Judy Bryer. I had known Judy since she came to work for Tony Newley in 1968. He was then preparing *Hieronymus Merkin*, and although she was working for him as his secretary, she and I quickly became friends. This friendship has become stronger through the years, and she is now my secretary, closest friend and confidante, as well as being my stand-in on "Dynasty." A regular Jill of all trades. Naturally, she's a Gemini.

I cherish the relationships I have had with my women friends. It has always been tremendously important to me to have at least two or three close female friends with whom I can share so many things. Men may come and go in one's life, but girlfriends last forever, and I consider myself very lucky to have several who are in my corner when the going gets tough—which is when the tough get going.

Sadly my lovely friend Cappy Badrutt succumbed to cancer early in 1981. It was a tragedy and a deep blow to me.

I was in charge of the organization and every detail of the Bronfman party from the guest list to the table placement, the flowers and decorations, to the choice of music the band would play. It was fun but I was concerned about the cost. Ron said Edgar had budgeted the party to cost five thousand dollars, which I knew was too low, and I told him that it would inevitably be closer to eight or ten thousand. Ron assured me that Edgar would foot the bill, but I wasn't thrilled about laying out large down payments to the tent people and the caterers out of my personal bank account. We certainly couldn't afford to give a party of this magnitude.

It was a warm May night and the guest list was sparkling: David Janssen and his wife, Dani, Audrey and Billy Wilder, Dionne Warwick, director Dick Donner, soon to do *Superman*, Janet and Freddie de Cordova, Tina Sinatra, Susan George, George Segal, and many others. It was certainly a terrific party, which went on past 2 A.M.—in Hollywood a major coup.

The next afternoon I was basking in my laurels as the hostess with the mostest. The phone had been ringing all day with congratulations, and thank-you flowers were arriving from the more well-mannered guests. It was six o'clock and time to help nanny Susan DeLong get the children fed and watered and ready for bed. Ron walked with a heavy tread into our green-and-white bedroom, slightly overdecorated with bowers of palm-tree wallpaper. "Edgar's fired me," he announced wearily, his face ashen.

I could not believe it. After weeks of preparation for Edgar's son's twenty-first birthday party, after years of friendship and business partnership, after shlepping our family across the Atlantic again, his boss had *fired* him. Just like that. It was unthinkable. But it was true.

Giving a new meaning to the word "cowardly," Edgar had sent Ron a "Dear John" letter. It was probably written while we were in the middle of the final preparations for the social event of the season. Ron at least deserved a confrontation face to face—man to man. But it was not to be. Edgar had paid Ron off to the end of the month, closed up the Sagittarius film offices on Sunset Boulevard and was incommunicado to both of us for over four years.

Katy regularly received a little gift and card on her birthday and at Christmas; since Edgar's birthday was the same as hers, and since she was his godchild, it seemed the least he could do. My instincts not to move to L.A. had been right all along. Now here we were stuck with a house with a giant mortgage, three children who had recently adjusted to new schools, and neither of us working.

I was bitterly resentful of Edgar Bronfman. I had never in my life been bitter and resentful toward anybody, but now the major breadwinner of the Kass family was out of work, thanks to him.

I don't think Ron ever fully recovered from the traumatic disappointment, pain and shock that Edgar caused him. Certainly this became a turning point in our up until now happy marriage.

"My marriage is a fiasco!" I said dramatically to Stuart Emory, conductor of the workshop for the exploration of human potential called "Actualizations." It was the time of "finding yourself" and I had gone to the Biltmore Hotel with Tina Sinatra, who was also considering leaving her husband, to try and find some answers.

We had been there fourteen hours a day for two days. Sitting on hard chairs, starving, dying for a cigarette, and watching eighty other confused and unhappy people get up onto the podium to reveal the misery and failure in their lives. It was an interesting experience. Listening to the pain that came from the hearts of so many lost souls, Tina and I considered ourselves lucky that really our only major problems were the men in our lives.

Eighty pairs of sympathetic eyes and ears watched and listened while I poured out my saga of woe. I *was* unhappy. Ron had changed. Subtly, but he was no longer the man I married. He was not working creatively, and money was a big problem. Living in L.A. was difficult. Because of our financial situation we had had to sell the house on Chalette Drive and move to another glass palace on Carolyn Way. With the profits we made on the sale we were thus, according to Ron, the controllers and doyens of our money matters—able to live in a style which we were used to. I was making around $2,500 a show, occasionally guesting on episodic TV, and for the odd ten or fifteen thousand, scooting off to Spain or Italy to star in some celluloid nonsense that I sincerely hoped would never see the light of day in either the U.S. or the U.K.

This was peanuts in terms of what I had been making. I had now been an actress for a quarter of a century but still had little to show for it in terms of savings. I knew I could have lived more simply and been happier had we only been able to move back to England and turn the clock back eighteen months. Before Edgar Bronfman entered our lives. But that was impossible.

Stuart Emory, all Australian charm and intelligence, smiled at me benevolently after I had finished my piece. "Don't you realize that your husband is surrounded by the barracudas and piranhas of the business?" he said pityingly. "Don't give up, Joan, he needs you. It's been a tough time for him. Stand by him, give him support—you'll both win in the end."

He waffled on. I listened, baffled and confused. The bottom line was that he was telling *me* to be patient, that Ron would come out of his Bronfman-induced decline, and that I must be more supportive and help him over his depression. What about *my* depression? Who was helping me over that? I was physically intact, if not even better than when I was younger. I was trying to live a normal family life in an environment I no longer had a taste for. My children were at school and growing up. Ron wasn't working. We had enormous financial drains upon us, not helped by his ex-wife, Anita, who had got her claws into a bunch of money from the sale of our house and was not about to let it go. She had three growing boys to support, Ron's sons, and although he had been paying her alimony and child support she wanted more. We had lawyers coming out of the woodwork, and creditors, too. It was sinister.

I had always read with fascinated horror the stories of famous actresses who ended up living in poverty or working as waitresses to support themselves. Lonely, unloved, unlucky. Had they given up? Believed the credo that after thirty-five it was all downhill from then on? I only knew that I was now going to have to fight like hell to try and resurrect my career and my personal life, not only for myself, but for Ron and my three children.

Two weeks later Tina Sinatra separated from her husband, and I made a major and far-reaching decision: to find a suitable commercial film property for myself and put the expertise I had gathered throughout the years into getting it financed and produced.

My sister, Jackie, had written a book called *The Stud*. It had become a best-seller in England and Europe. I persuaded her to let me have the film rights. I wanted to try to set it up as an independent film. I considered myself the right casting for the rich elegant socialite Fontaine, who sets up her "stud," Tony Blake, as the "greeter" in London's hottest disco, Hobo, and uses him for her own pleasure, sexual and otherwise. It was a modern, steamy, sexy premise, and one which I felt in my bones could be the commercial vehicle to put some juice in my career, which was going nowhere. *Saturday Night Fever* had just gone through the roof with its disco background and its sexuality. *The Stud* had the possibility to do, if not the same outstanding grosses, at least reasonably well.

Meanwhile I continued, albeit reluctantly, to "guest shot." The "Starsky and Hutch" gig had been the final blow.

"Want to do a 'Starsky and Hutch' in Hawaii for eight days?" It was my agent's voice on the phone, as I maneuvered the four-foot extension cord around the kitchen, and attended to the poached eggs on the point of overpoaching, the toast about to turn black and three children clamoring for breakfast.

"Starsky and Hutch" was one of the "top ten" TV shows of the previous season. Its two stars, David Soul and Paul Michael Glaser, were the current hunks of the moment. Thirteen-year-old Tara let out a whoop of joy when I told her I might do it.

"But I haven't read the script yet, Tara," I protested, shoveling hard, soggy eggs onto blackened toast.

"Oh, Mummy, you must do it, you *must*. Maybe I'll get to meet David Soul! Oh, wow!"

"That's not the reason I would do the show—so *you* could meet David Soul," I said firmly. "I'll let you know if I'm going to do it when I've read the script, darling." This of course was a white lie—I would have to do it because we needed the money.

The script turned out to be a rather chauvinistic, slightly amusing story to be shot in Hawaii. Thick with voodoo, witch doctors and gorgeous gals, it was typical TV fodder.

I sighed—but a buck was a buck was a buck—and I was still trying hard to get *The Stud* financed.

So, in the summer of 1976 I went to Hawaii to film the two-hour episode. Paul Michael Glaser was sitting on the lawn of the location paradise we were shooting in. Palm trees waved and lush tropical plants shimmered in the hazy morning heat. He was absorbed in his script, and, although wearing an outrageously unflattering outfit of baggy Bermuda shorts, cheap printed Hawaiian shirt, red ankle socks and tennis shoes and an Andy Capp cap, he managed to look charismatic. He had a slight look about him of Charlie Chaplin and Tony Newley.

In Hawaii at the hotel Hawaii Surf sat Peter Borsari, a photographer. He was gloomily bemoaning the fact that he had been sent by the *National Enquirer* to do a story on Glaser and Soul, but they had refused.

"They are so into the vork," moaned Peter gloomily, in his Hungarian accent. "Vork, vork, vork, that's all they care about . . . no pictures, no interviews, nothing. They'd do it for the glossies—*People* or *Cosmopolitan* they'd do—but not the *Enquirer*."

I commiserated, little realizing that within five years I would be in Glaser and Soul's position vis-à-vis the tabloids and the more prestigious media. Right now, though, to get my photo in the *National Enquirer* would have been a major event.

That night at a cocktail party for the cast and crew at the hotel, I felt mature and overdressed. "We're too old to be part of this group," I joked to Samantha Eggar, who'd been cast as Charlotte, "No one's over twenty-three." David Soul joined us: tall, blond and tanned, he wore glasses and chain-smoked Marlboros. He shook his head at the army of girls parading up and down and being ogled by the crew.

"After all the effort and care Paul and I have put in trying to make this show a success, now we're doing a tits-and-ass piece," he murmured sadly.

On the first day of shooting we drove through spectacular scenery. The location was probably the most beautiful I've ever seen: an estate of over a hundred acres of lush tropical jungle garden with foliage and trees that looked as if they'd existed for two thousand years, and probably had.

The crew were setting up a scene in which Starsky and Hutch, as trespassers, were attacked by several fierce Alsatian dogs. I recalled that Paul and I had met briefly at Pinewood Studios four or five years ago when he was making *Fiddler on the Roof* and I was guesting in "The Persuaders."

"Yes! You were sitting with Roger Moore and Topol brought me over and introduced me to you, right?" I remembered that at the time I thought he had magnetic eyes.

In a coral strapless silk dress with a tropical flower behind one ear, I was handed a gun by the prop man. I asked Paul to show me how to hold it. I've often had to work with guns and I hate them—I always have the feeling a real bullet might have been left in.

I am always nervous on the first day of anything. It seems ridiculous, but I'm comforted by the thought that Laurence Olivier often feels like throwing up before a performance. Since he is also a Gemini, I feel it's a good omen.

Miss Patti, Playmate of the Month, was ensconced in a chair with "Guest Star" emblazoned on it. Hairdressers and makeup men hover. She is queening it—why not? Someone seems to have ordered the star treatment for this lady. She asks me how old I am—a question I feel should never be asked of anyone over twenty-one. I ask her to guess. She surmises thirty-five. "Around there," I reply airily. "How old are you?"

"Twenty-five," says she.

"Oh, you look younger."

"Good," she says.

A lot of the girls and crew keep telling me condescendingly how good I look, as though anyone over thirty-five is a candidate for the mortician's parlor.

Both Samantha and I asked for canvas chairs but there were none. Once Bunnies appeared, however, chairs sprouted like broccoli.

My dressing room, a two-by-three-foot space, was occupied by Debbie, who rather huffily said that there was no room for her and so the wardrobe girl put her in with me. Her clothes and makeup were strewn all over my clothes and makeup.

The wardrobe girl apologized. It's a SAG rule that leading actors do not share dressing rooms with bit players, and she promised she would move Debbie.

I felt depressed and unable to get over this feeling of really hitting bottom careerwise.

The perils of "Starsky and Hutch" were relived off the set, too. Arriving at muddy, swampy, cold and rainy location to shoot runaway scenes in the car with the boys and the actor playing my father, everyone was uptight because of the weather.

In the car, Paul drove with my on-screen father in front, David, me and a wheelchair squashed in the back. We drove fast through gates that are supposed to burst open on impact. Three Jeeps filled with yelling stunt men pursue us hotly.

Take 2: Paul skids and we almost turn over as we plummet into a ditch. The crew rush up to see if we're OK. Charlie Picerne, the stunt coordinator, screamed angrily at Paul. "What the fuck do you think you're doing, for Christ's sake?" He was furious; Paul was furious.

Another scene: I'm in the car and the gun I'm holding inadvertently goes off when Paul swerves to avoid a truck. I horrifiedly point it at David's gut, then realizing what I've done, throw it out of the window. A print, but . . . "what's wrong?" asks David, seeing a look of alarm cross my face.

"I think a boob came out when I threw the gun!" I said.

"As long as we didn't see any nipple," says Paul. We ask. The camera is rigged to the car so no one is sure. We think it's OK. Nipples are a no-no on network TV.

Oh, the perils of TV stardom: At the base camp, as David sits reading his script, a lady tourist comes up and asks him wheedlingly if she can take a photograph. A crowd has gathered instantly, as we're on a main road. He politely says no. She insists. "It's for my daughter. Please." He tells her if he poses for her he'll have to pose for everyone else, and he's studying. She is pushy. He yells at her. She laughs and takes his photo anyway, while he's yelling. "Oh, my daughter will love it, she'll just love it," she cackles. David sighs. I don't envy him.

The perils of stunt men: Down on the pier, I climb into a camera boat with the crew, Samantha, Paul and David. All of us are festooned with cameras as this is going to indeed be a stunt worthy of a feature film.

Anticipation and excitement are in the air as the two camera boats position themselves. This stunt can only be filmed once.

After an hour of suspenseful waiting the director cries "Action." The black Cadillac comes speeding down the coast highway at what I consider an excessive speed of forty-five miles per hour. It drives up fast onto a specially constructed small ramp. I hear a laconic grip remark, "It'll never hold up," and over into the murky green water, head first, fall four doubles dressed as Starsky, Hutch, me and my father. There is a gasp from all on board. The car is supposed to land flat on the water and sink. It has been specially weighted for such an effect, but with stunts anything can happen.

But soon four little heads appear. Everyone bursts into spontaneous applause and cheers as they realize the stunt was successful.

Candy, my double, told me to be careful of "our" dress. Hers had come off completely in the water, leaving her topless. I told the wardrobe girl.

Her attitude was nonchalant. "Nothing we can do. You worry about such silly things," she sniffed. Ah, the caring attitude of TV people. It wasn't important that the dress I had put on had shrunk from cleaning and was now four inches above my knees. "It'll never show," she said, bored to tears by it all. Brought up as I was in an era when every detail of an actress's wardrobe was of immense importance, I found it appalling that the matter of a skirt length's being five inches out of whack was inconsequential to her. God, I hated TV. I vowed this would be my last episodic guest shot.

I prepared for the "wet" scene. We were in the middle of the ocean, shooting the scene following the car stunt, our characters having just been rescued from the ocean depths.

For three hours we sat in the boat, soaking wet. I had cleverly left my makeup ashore. It was baking hot. We filmed my final close-ups with me teary and bleary-eyed, sunbaked, makeup-less, my dress falling precariously every time I moved.

My shoulders were in an agony of sunburn. I requested some towels but they never arrived. Sunburned and soaking wet, we finally raced back to shore, arriving at the wharf to find the whole crew gone, and not a towel in sight. Stoically dripping, I walked barefoot the five hundred yards to my trailer, a bedraggled wreck. My enemy, the wardrobe girl, handed me a small towel. Silently I thanked her. It was time to move on in life.

Ron was now involved with Peter and Burt Kameron in a production company called Triple K; they had all invested money in it but Ron was not bringing home the bacon. Although Tony Newley was paying me $1,250 a month for Tara and Sacha, that was not enough to support them. We considered selling the house on Carolyn Way and moving to the Valley. This would mean the kids changing schools *again*.

I had, by lying vehemently about my age by ten years, fought for, and got, the part of the glamorous call girl, Avril, in NBC's big miniseries "The Moneychangers" with Kirk Douglas and Christopher Plummer. For this I had been paid the magnificent sum of five thousand dollars. I was considered lucky to have got it. True, true—I was. Hollywood was not noted for its benevolence toward actresses over thirty unless they were into character roles. See the over-thirty-fives dressed too cute and young at restaurants and parties, desperately trying to turn back the clock.

Looking objectively at the rushes of "The Moneychangers,"

and also in my mirror, always situated in the harshest northern light possible, I saw a woman who could pass for twenty-eight but was in fact past forty.

After the "Starsky and Hutch" gig, when Samantha Eggar suggested I should apply for unemployment benefits I was shocked. "I've seen Rudy Vallee there," said Judy Bryer. "Many actors go. You're entitled to it, after all. You've paid all your taxes and contributions." Thus persuaded, but dubious, I reluctantly set out one sunny afternoon in 1976 in my gold Mercedes to the Department of Unemployment on Santa Monica Boulevard. Judy had suggested I go there rather than the office in Hollywood, so that I wouldn't be recognized.

I wasn't keen to go at all. I had been a working actress for over twenty years now and it seemed somewhat an anticlimax, to say the least, to be on the dole. Not how I had foreseen my life at all. No way. I hadn't really wanted to be dripping with diamonds, sables and Ferraris; on the other hand, I loathed the state of constantly hovering on the brink of serious financial problems.

I had just been the hostess at the opening of a new English boutique on Sunset Boulevard. My Mercedes overflowed with flowers. I was wearing an expensive chiffon dress, a matching turban and a few gold and diamond trinkets. I tore off the turban and stuffed the jewels in my purse after I hit Sunset Boulevard to the fond farewells of my friends and the paparazzi. Putting an old trench coat over the four-hundred-dollar chiffon, a creased scarf on my head and a pair of *extremely* dark shades over my eyes, I pulled the Mercedes into the unemployment office parking lot, next to a battered '64 Chevy.

I stood in a slow-moving line for forty-five minutes trying to look as nondescript as possible. In Charles Jourdan shoes and with two inches of expensive flowered chiffon peeping out from beneath the raincoat, I realized I looked slightly out of place, to say the least. Most of the people standing around were Hispanic or black, and they seemed as if they definitely could use the money. No one looked like an actress just popping down to the dole so she could afford to pay the maid. I began to feel guilty.

"Name?" asked the bored, gum-chewing clerk when I finally reached her desk. "Er, Kass—Joan—er, Kass," I whispered nervously, hoping that the two Puerto Rican gentlemen eying me from behind and discussing my merits in Spanish, of which I knew a smattering, couldn't hear me.

"Maiden name?"

"Collins," I croaked conspiratorially. Rivulets of sweat ran down my back. It was 93 degrees—hardly the weather for Aquascutum raincoats.

"Joan Collins?" shrieked the desk clerk with suspicious delight. "Didn't you used to be her?"

"Yes" I mumbled, silently cursing Samantha, who had sent me on this little trip with airy assurances of how easy it would be. "I still am her," I muttered ungrammatically, aware of the slight buzz of excitement emanating from the queue behind me.

"I just saw you on 'Policewoman' last week," yelled the clerk with unbounded glee. "What are you doing down *here?* Aren't you working?"

"Hey, Debbie," she called excitedly to her co-worker. "Hey, Debbie, look, it's Joan Collins!"

"Joan who?" said Debbie, peering at me. I pulled up my collar to hide my face, now crimson with embarrassment.

"No, I'm not working at the moment," I replied with as much dignity as I could muster, aware of the entire roomful of people now riveted to the little scenario unfolding before them. It was probably pretty dull standing in line down at the Santa Monica unemployment office every week.

"Er, things are a bit slow now—I'm resting," I explained, using the actor's timeless euphemism. Twenty pairs of eyes and ears clocked the action. A few more embarrassing questions were fired at me. Had I been trying to get a job? Yes—my agent had started refusing my calls, pretending he wasn't in. I knew the ploy. I used to do it with my father when he had a performer he wanted to avoid. "Tell so-and-so I'm out," he'd hiss as I answered the telephone and dutifully lisped, "No, Daddy's out and I don't know where he is," to some anxious singer or clown desperate for work.

Other questions. Had I tried getting another job other than

293

acting in the six weeks I'd been out of work? Well, no. Waiting on tables was not my style, and I couldn't type worth a damn. Eventually I escaped. Humiliated and clutching not the $120 I had expected, but a chit that entitled me to that amount two weeks later when the Department of Unemployment had checked me out with Social Security—thoroughly.

"Can I have your autograph, please?" asked a small black boy as I opened my steaming car, now filled with the scent of a hundred flowers dying for a drink. I signed and fled.

Wending my way through the Santa Monica traffic toward the charming but at this moment heavily mortgaged home in Beverly Hills, I made a vow. I would never get myself in this situation again. I *must* work. If I couldn't cut it as an actor, then I would write or do interior decoration. I couldn't abide the humiliation of receiving a handout. I had started modeling at sixteen so I wouldn't ever have to ask my father for money; I had certainly never asked for any from my husbands. I had to succeed now by myself. I couldn't accept that this was to be the way my career would end.

To hell with my agent. He didn't give a damn whether I worked or not. A hundred other actresses were in his stable. It was all up to *me*. No one was going to extend their efforts on my behalf. *I* had to be the mistress of my destiny. If I didn't want to be broke, I had to pull my finger out and start thinking of a suitable project for myself. A viable and commercial project that would ensure my future as well as my children's. And *The Stud* was the catalyst.

If I thought I had been rejected as an actress, it was nothing to the rejection I received as a producer trying to get financing for *The Stud*. Producers I had known all my life turned me down flat. Lew Grade, Nat Cohen, Plitt Theatre Chain, Sam Arkoff . . . the list went on, but I persevered.

I convinced Jackie to write her first script from the book. It was good. It was hot and it was right for today's market. I knew, I just *knew* in my bones that if I could get it made, it would not only reactivate my career but could be a commercial success as well.

I was shlepping *The Stud* all over on both coasts, but I still needed a job. I got one. More than I bargained for, to say the least. *Empire of the Ants*, an H. G. Wells classic (so they said), to be shot in Florida.

This was physically the most difficult picture I had ever done. The Florida swamps in November are dirty, dark and dank—infested with crocodiles, rats and other creepy crawlies too unspeakable to think about. But we needed money, so off I trotted, along with Robert Lansing, Jacqueline Scott, Robert Pine, John David Carson, Albert Salmi, and nine or ten six-foot plastic ants, the brainchildren of Mr. Bert I. Gordon, our director.

The story of a group of people trapped on a remote Florida island infested by giant man-eating ants who stalk their hapless victims one by one and then devour them was not going to win any of us Oscars. In fact it seemed more of a certainty that this film would guarantee none of us would ever get a job again—such was the quality of the story, script and direction. As it eventually turned out, most of us went on to rather better things: Bob Lansing to star opposite Elizabeth Taylor in *The Little Foxes*, Robert Pine to play a continuing role in "Chips." But in November of 1976 we considered ourselves lucky to be working at all.

After a week of slogging through the swamps, sometimes knee-high in slimy water and freezing weather, we were all thoroughly fed up. The only way we could go to the loo was if one of the principal ladies (i.e., Jackie or me) insisted on it. A motorboat would whisk us from the swamps to the mainland, wait, then whisk us back to where we were shooting again.

We became so irritated by this that with much coercing from the cast—who persuaded me that *I* make the demand since I was the so-called "star" of this epic—we insisted on having a portable loo on the huge open camera barge that was our headquarters while shooting. Several days later it arrived. And there it sat in all its glory on the barge . . . no doors, no privacy. It caused much hilarity, and after a bit more yelling and screaming by Jackie and me a makeshift curtain was encircled around it—but we still preferred the speedboat ride back to the mainland to using it.

One windy morning, the wind almost hurricane-like in its intensity, I left the motel at 6 A.M. to go to the location. The door of the unit station wagon was held open for me by one of the many teamsters we had on the crew, but he let it go as soon as I entered the car. The wind slammed the door shut onto my face with hurricane ferocity. Blood gushed from my eye and I screamed for help, but no one could hear. My teamster friend had disappeared, it was pitch-dark and the wind was blowing at seventy miles per hour.

Eventually I wrestled open the door and staggered into the lobby of the motel where some of the cast and crew were assembled. Someone screamed.

I was a sight straight from one of the more gruesome horror movies I'd had the pleasure of starring in. Blood was pouring from a gash in my eyebrow. It had already become a bump the size of an egg. How I wasn't killed or brain-damaged by the force of the door was a miracle. I was left with an unsightly black-and-blue eye that took the makeup department half an hour to conceal. And they were unable to shoot on me other than in extreme long shots for four days.

I was not thrilled to be told one day that since our stunt doubles hadn't arrived from L.A., we were to do the canoe-capsizing stunt ourselves. I was horrified, in fact.

"We're putting stunt people out of work," I expostulated to the director, ever mindful of Gene Kelly's warning some years before.

Bert Gordon poo-poohed my fears, intimating I was a bad sport, difficult and uncooperative. Since the rest of the cast seemed resigned to their fate, I had no choice but to go along with it or be called a first-class prima donna bitch and therefore lessen my chances of ever doing another horror flick for A.I.P. again.

I took off my knee-high boots and threw them to the wardrobe girl, safe on the security of the big barge. One or two crocodiles still lurked at the edge of the swamp in spite of the prop men's having fired blanks from their rifles to frighten them away, and the crew's using them as target practice by aiming their midmorning bagels at the sinister greenish-black hulks.

"Action!" yelled Bert. Two frogmen crouched under the raft, pushed it over, completely capsizing it, and four petrified actors fell into the swamp. The water was absolutely disgusting, foul green slime. It probably hadn't moved in two thousand years and it was thick and warmish. I tried to keep my head above the loathsome liquid while acting convincingly terrified. I swam as fast as possible to the sanctuary of the camera barge. Under the water my legs and feet became entangled in the submerged giant roots of a swamp plant. I thought of swamp snakes and kicked with all my might, trying to untangle my legs from this moving mass of God knows what. I crawled onto the barge like a beached whale, blood oozing from at least a dozen cuts on my legs and from the gash over my eye. I'd swallowed some of the putrid water and felt definitely ill.

The makeup people immediately poured bottles and bottles of pure distilled water over us, and produced eyedrops, eardrops, nosedrops and throat spray, which they insisted we use immediately. The motor launch arrived promptly to rush us to a nearby hotel; we were told to shower *immediately* we got there. The women were given douche kits by the nurse and instructed to use them. "That water is a major health hazard," said the nurse, busily trying to patch up my legs as the launch carried us, wet and shaking, to safety. "You could get serious infections from it. I told them not to let you all go in. They wouldn't listen."

Within two days the cuts on my legs started festering. Some looked so bad I joked I was getting gangrene, but it wasn't fun. We still had three weeks of shooting left, like it or not.

Each day the wounds on my legs were dressed and bandaged. On top of the bandages were tied brown plastic garbage bags, attached with camera tape, which was wrapped round and round my legs until they looked mummified; and over these, the tan leather boots. I looked and felt a wreck, convinced I was scarred for life, and was never so delighted and relieved as when the last day of shooting arrived and it was finally my turn to be asphyxiated by the giant queen ant. Six cast members had already gone to the big anthill in the sky; only four of us were left.

We had miserably spent both Thanksgiving and Christmas in this hellhole, and were desperate to get out and back to L.A. for New Year's Eve.

We were shooting in a sugar refinery in a tiny town in Florida.

297

The smell of the cane being melted was so strong and sickening that everyone wore masks the entire time we weren't actually shooting.

By now I had been turned into a zombie "ant robot" by some forgettable plot twist and was standing in line at the kiosk where the queen ant was to blow her magic breath on me so I would become even more of a zombie and do her ant bidding. As I stood face to face with this ludicrous creature, Robert Lansing burst in with guns blazing and a flare. The ant expired and fell on top of me, exuding lethal ant gas. How would Alexis have coped? I have sometimes asked myself.

The sight of this grotesque papier-mâché insect face and flaying tentacle legs—which were actually attached to moving sticks held by prop men—was so hilarious that every time I had to expire with the giant ant on top of me I burst into gales of giggles, which quickly subsided when Mr. Gordon said if I didn't stop we wouldn't get out of Florida until January 2. Perish the thought!

And that, I am happy to say, was my last horror picture. At least in terms of ants.

Wherever I went, there went the script of *The Stud*, becoming more dogeared and worn every day.

It was at the Cannes festival in May of 1977, where I had gone at the request of A.I.P. to promote *Empire of the Ants*—and finding little that was noteworthy to say about it—that I finally struck oil.

I was seated at Hilda and Sam Arkoff's annual luncheon at the Carlton Hotel next to a man who Hilda told me was a distributor of B flicks in England, interested in getting into full-time production. A likely prospect, thought I.

I tentatively offered my by now slick opening ploy. "Would you be interested in making a commercial movie from my sister Jackie's best-selling novel *The Stud* with a disco theme and erotic love scenes, etc., etc. . . ." I droned on enthusiastically. I knew these words by rote now.

"As a matter of fact, I would. That's just the kind of movie we're interested in producing," said burly George Walker, ex-boxer and now head of Brent-Walker.

"Have you got a script?"

"Just happen to have it at my hotel, the Majestic, next door." I smiled as sweetly as I could. "Would you like to read it?"

"Yes," said Mr. Walker. "Can you come to dinner at the villa tomorrow night and we can discuss it then?"

"I think I'm free," I murmured, barely containing my enthusiasm.

Within a week the project was set. Brent-Walker loved it. No fools they. They wanted to start shooting within two or three months. Ron and Oscar Lerman, Jackie's husband, would co-produce. I would star, with the proviso I do some tasteful nudity. Yes, I could do that. I'd done it in Italy already. This was no longer the dark ages. Look at Diane Keaton in *Looking for Mr. Goodbar*, Jane Fonda in *Barbarella*, Glenda Jackson in *Women in Love* and dozens more. Actresses of far greater stature than I had stripped to the buff for films. It was even becoming rather boring. Certainly no big deal as far as affecting their careers was concerned.

I thought the sex and eroticism would sell the movie. So did Ron. So did Brent-Walker. A vast publicity campaign masterminded by Ron started in England. "Over forty and she takes her clothes off!" screamed Fleet Street in fascinated frenzy. I decided I wouldn't let it bother me, although it seemed the press picked on me constantly. We had supposedly finished with racism and sexism. Now I thought it was time to end ageism.

I knew how I looked (objective I always was). What was this barrier about being over forty? Did over forty have to mean over the hill? Not in my book it didn't. And not in the book of the man in the street in England either. *The Stud* became a giant success in England—the biggest British moneymaker other than the Bond films for years.

I became a household name, face and body in Britain yet again, although I was still virtually unknown in the States, my early films forgotten, thank goodness.

Since my aspirations to become a "star" had always been minimal, this wasn't of too much concern. What was of concern to me was that my personal life was falling apart again.

Although Ron and I were residents of the States and had again traded in our glass-and-chrome modern Italian house on Carolyn Way for a mock Tudor mansion in Beverly Hills, I had been forced to spend a lot of time in England, shooting and promoting *The Stud*. Katy, at five, was at a stage in her schooling that presented no problem in switching to a British school. However, Tara and Sacha at fourteen and eleven were at a more difficult stage of their education. I did not want them to leave their California schools and change to English ones just because this was where my bread, careerwise, was suddenly being buttered. Tony and I discussed this amicably. We decided that Tara and Sacha should stay with him and his new wife and child while I was working in England.

The children decided that life at the Newleys' was more settled than life at the Kasses' and opted for living permanently with Tony. This caused me much heartache. I adored my children, even if I was not the "typical mum." I believed in the quality of my time with them and not the quantity. I could have said "Forget it" to my new career, but unfortunately I was becoming the breadwinner in our family, and apart from the fact that I was enjoying my work, it was now an absolute financial necessity that I continue it.

And so I did. Back to California for a highly forgettable movie called *Zero to 60* with Darren McGavin—off to South Africa and an even more forgettable one with Richard Harris called *Game for Vultures*, with a script so full of complications that none of us understood it at all. Since "Fallen Angels" had been quite a hit on Anglia TV, Sir John Woolf, the head of the company, asked me to appear in one of the anthology series they were currently making. Called "Roald Dahl's Tales of the Unexpected," they were dramatized half-hour versions of some of Dahl's cleverest short stories. Dahl was an expert storyteller, his tales always ending with a macabre or ironic twist of fate. I was asked to star in "Neck," the story of a glamorous, ruthless aristocrat married to a bumbling fool whom she cuckolds with various handsome young men who come to their grand country manor for weekend visits. The only person who has the slightest control over her is the butler Jelkes, played by Sir John Gielgud.

I was delighted at this casting. I had been an admirer of John

Gielgud's since my student days at RADA, when three of the most promising students had been selected to visit Sir John and Pamela Brown at the Queen's Theatre where they were appearing in Jean Anouilh's *The Lady's Not for Burning*. After a few days of shooting on "Neck" I reminded Sir John about this meeting— I had been one of the students chosen—but, understandably, he did not recall what had been a red-letter day in my student life.

Sir John, as the cast deferentially referred to him, was exceedingly charming and witty, with exquisite manners and the ability to recall in minute detail the most interesting anecdotes about every actor and actress he had ever worked with. Since this was 1978 and he had started his career in the 1920s, he had fifty years of memories with which to regale us. "Neck" was directed by Christopher Miles, brother of Sarah, and also starred Michael Aldridge, Peter Bowles and a young actor called Paul Herzberg, who so admired Gielgud that he kept a small notebook into which he inscribed Sir John's every bon mot.

Although we were shooting at Greystone Manor, a stately home in the midst of the Norfolk countryside, we were staying at the rather tacky English seaside resort of Great Yarmouth in a small beachfront hotel.

My first meeting with Sir John took place one windy fall morning in the unit car outside the hotel, just across the road from the amusement pier. Cockney mums and dads in beach gear with assorted children and dogs and buckets and spades and picnic baskets struggled down to the beach, oblivious to the great actor who sat in solitary splendor smoking cigarettes in the front seat of the car.

"Good morning," I mumbled shyly, falling into the back seat, a morning wreck as usual in faded jeans and T-shirt.

"Good morning, my dear," he twinkled, turning his head around and extending a well-manicured hand. He was dressed impeccably in that elegant but slightly faded style that becomes actors of the old school. Gray flannel trousers, highly polished shoes—years old, but obviously of the best quality—a tattersall shirt, tie, pullover and a good tweed jacket. Elegant. So unlike most of the actors with whom I've worked, who usually look like slobs in the A.M. Never at my best at the crack of dawn, I tried to keep up my end of the conversation during the twenty-minute ride to Greystone Manor. He, unfazed by my mumbles and ineffectual chat, told several amusing anecdotes, culminating in a Noel Coward-ish "Very flat, Norfolk," when I remarked at the prettiness of the surrounding countryside. I enjoyed his company, and our off-set chats which, as long as they were not too early in the morning, were extremely stimulating.

One day a reporter was interviewing me—it was a beautiful, mild autumn day and we were seated in canvas chairs in the garden of the manor. The journalist asked the usual boringly predictable questions, finishing off with his *pièce de résistance*, "So how old are you *really*, Miss Collins? We never seem to read the same age twice for you in the papers."

At this point, Gielgud, who had been reading *The Times*, peered at the journalist frostily over his spectacles and in biting tones informed him, "Never ever ask any lady over twenty-five, particularly an actress, how old she is, young man."

"Why not, *sir?*" asked the hack sarcastically.

"In my day," said Sir John reprovingly, "it was considered unutterably bad manners to even *discuss* a lady's age, let alone ask *her* about it. How do you think the great actresses of the past could have played Juliet, Ophelia or indeed any of the heroines or leading roles had the public known that they were over thirty, forty—sometimes even fifty? Illusion, young man, illusion. The public should never know too much about an actor or an actress."

The reporter slunk away, chastened, and I thanked Sir John for his support. Considering the negative attitudes associated with age, I always believed that an actress should have the right of privacy on that subject. If an actress looks twenty-five but is in fact thirty-five, there is no reason why she should *have* to play the latter age on screen. Unfortunately, with the press and public mania for knowing ages, this becomes almost impossible nowadays.

Gielgud also gave me some insight into an actor's ability to project other areas of himself. I had given him a copy of a script I was interested in doing, asking him to read the part of a retired Italian gardener living in a home for old men. He returned the script to me, regretfully declining the part on the grounds that it was too much of a stretch for him to be believable in the part.

"But you're such a marvelous actor, you can play any part," I exclaimed.

"Not true, my dear. Look at my hands. They are not the hands of an ex-gardener." I looked at them. They were definitely up-market hands. "Ralph Richardson could play this part very well," he said. "He could look like a gardener."

"I could play a *gentleman* fallen on hard times, of course—but you must remember that usually an actor is the victim of his or her own physicality, and one must take this into account when choosing the roles one does or does not accept."

I nodded. He continued, "You, for example, could never play an unattractive woman, because you bring to every role your physical presence and it would be difficult for you to play against that, unless you used a great amount of makeup and costumes to disguise the fact."

It was not until four years later that I finally had the chance to get away from my usual physical image when I played the wicked old witch in Showtime's "Faerie Tale Theatre" production "Hansel and Gretel."

And then came *The Bitch*. Whenever I'm asked if I've ever had any regrets in my life—which I don't—the one that might possibly come to mind is why, oh why, did they give it that damn-awful exploitive title, which stuck to me like flypaper through the popular English press for years.

I begged Brent-Walker not to use the title. Cajoled and pleaded to no avail. *The Stud* had skyrocketed—*The Bitch* should do even better. They were wrong.

Made in 1978, a year after *The Stud*, *The Bitch* was a washed-out carbon copy. In their eagerness to reap more financial goodies at the box office, Brent-Walker went into production with an unsatisfactory and, in fact, unfinished script, an unknown Italian leading man whose voice was so weak that he had to be entirely dubbed, and a mediocre director. My wardrobe wasn't even finished.

Ron and Oscar were again the producers. I pleaded with Ron not to start the film before some more work had been done on the script, which it needed desperately—but even he couldn't prevail on Brent-Walker to either change the title or alter the script. They controlled the purse strings and the creative product. And George Walker had been known to yell "Fuck creativity—that doesn't sell tickets. Tits and ass do!"

Ron was certainly an expert persuader. We had many screaming fights about what I considered unnecessary nude scenes for *The Stud* and *The Bitch*. Film nudity was OK by me in certain instances, but not when it was so deviously gratuitous. But he couldn't sway big beefy George.

There had originally been a clause in my contract for *The Stud* to shoot a sequel if Brent-Walker wanted to, but I was extremely unhappy about it. I knew I had exploited myself in *The Stud*, but I had always felt that with a couple of exceptions the film had been done with a certain amount of taste and was certainly entertaining. It captured a part of the late seventies disco scene in London as well as saying a goodly piece about women and their sexuality. One of the reasons *The Stud* was both highly successful and highly controversial was that Fontaine thought like a man, and she used men in the way men had been using women for years. But *The Bitch* was gross exploitation. It did me no good at all, and in fact my name became the butt of many a TV comedian's jokes.

I sat next to Kirk Douglas on the Brent-Walker yacht in Cannes. It was May 1979, festival time again. A light aircraft was trailing a banner all over the Côte d'Azur: "JOAN COLLINS *Is* THE BITCH," it proclaimed, puffs of little white smoke trailing it.

"You made it, kid. That means you're a star," said Kirk, whom I had known since I arrived in Hollywood.

"Oh, Kirk, I think it should say 'Joan Collins *as* The Bitch,' " I protested. "I hate the stigma of 'Bitch.' It's really degrading. After all, how would you like to see 'Kirk Douglas *Is* the Murderer,' for example?"

He thought about this and agreed that perhaps I did have a point. A point, yes—clout with Brent-Walker, no. And they still owed us all money from *The Stud*.

To the outside world I had everything. A handsome loving husband, three beautiful children, career success and money. But there was trouble in my paradise.

I had suspected for some time that Ron had been taking some kind of drugs. His moods changed drastically. Sometimes he wouldn't eat dinner or stop fidgeting during mealtimes. He often stayed up until dawn and then slept all through the day.

I was aghast. A close friend's husband had wrecked his life and almost hers through his abuse of drugs. I had a healthy fear of them. In fact, I loathed and detested any kind of drug taking, and I found people who depended upon them weak and stupid.

I had instilled in my children from an early age the horror that drugs can bring to people's lives. There is no question that they wreck. They ruin. They destroy.

I had vaguely sniffed some white powder at a party in St. Tropez in the sixties, had become high as a kite, and had a post-nasal drip for three weeks. That was the first and last time I would ever try *that*.

I'd also puffed once or twice on the odd joint passed around at parties, but I thought the whole business was infantile. I preferred to be in control of myself. The crazy blurred feeling of fake pleasure and happiness that a drug high gives was not my scene.

I had been upset about Tara and Sacha living with Tony. I missed them terribly. I had expressed my feelings to Ron, who had been sympathetic and understanding. Sometimes I wept for hours. I was embarrassed at the British press's attitude toward me because of my nudity in *The Stud*. It hurt. I didn't understand their mixture of sarcastic bitchiness and grudging admiration.

What about *my* pressure and stress? I wasn't about to let anyone other than my closest friends know what hell I was living through.

I was now a reasonably hot property in Great Britain, so when I was approached by the prestigious Chichester Festival Arts Theatre to do a summer season there I was flattered and delighted. The theater had been in abeyance in my life for too long, and although it had always been my desire to be back on stage again, nevertheless it was difficult to be accepted, particularly since my media image was so controversial now.

The play was *The Last of Mrs. Cheyney*, a frothy 1920s light comedy by Frederick Lonsdale, originally a *tour de force* for Gladys Cooper. Simon Williams, an excellent light-comedy actor, was to play Lord Dilling, the romantic lead, and a distinguished cast gathered one dank February day in 1980 in the grimy rehearsal rooms in Shepherds Bush for the first read-through. I was filled with trepidation. These were all respected West End actors with years of stage experience behind them. I was a "film star." God forbid they believed I was a bitch, too. Oh, that epithet—how it stuck. "Film star" usually meant you couldn't act, either.

I hadn't performed on the stage since I was nineteen. It was a terrifying challenge, but one I was determined to conquer.

Several of my movie actor friends were astonished that I was taking this potentially dangerous career step. I was asking for trouble from the critics—no doubt waiting gleefully, pens poised, filled with vitriol for my performance whether it be good, bad or indifferent. "The Bitch" performing at Chichester. Some had started sniggering already.

Roger Moore couldn't understand why I would put myself in such a vulnerable position now that my movie career in England was bubbling again. But I realized that my days as a "movie star" were numbered. I wanted acceptance now as an actress. This is what I had started out by wanting. Now, thanks to the dubious distinctions of *The Stud* and *The Bitch*, I was going to be able to fulfill my ambition and, hopefully, stay on the stage forever.

That early summer of 1980 was one of the happiest for ages. Tara and Sacha had returned to live with us. Katy was doing fabulously at school. Ron was working on various development deals for me, with himself producing. I was working at the beautiful Chichester Festival Theatre, which was challenging and exciting at the same time. *The Last of Mrs. Cheyney* was sold out for practically every performance. We were the Festival's biggest hit since John Gielgud had played there nineteen years previously.

Grudgingly it was admitted by most critics that I could act a bit. I was playing a reasonably nice woman—not a bitch, not a vamp, not a sexpot. Some found it odd I could play a role like that believably.

Because of the huge success of *Mrs. Cheyney* at Chichester, Triumph Productions decided to mount a West End production, which they wanted more lavish and more beautifully dressed than the Chichester production. The fabled ninety-year-old designer, Erté (Romain de Tirtoff) agreed to do my costumes. After a lifetime fascination with his work, I was thrilled; but he insisted we had to go to Paris to meet with him and discuss the designs.

On August 1, 1980, Ron, Tara and I went to Paris. That afternoon the unthinkable happened.

At two o'clock in the morning on August 2, 1980, in a lushly appointed suite in the Hotel Lancaster, the telephone rang. I was asleep, and so was Tara in the connecting room. Ron had gone to a movie and had just returned. I sleepily heard him answer the phone, heard him say, "An accident—Katy? How bad?"

I struggled out of sleep and he looked at me with a stunned expression on his face.

"It's Katy—she's been hit by a car. She's . . . critical . . . a head injury."

"No!" I heard myself scream. "No, no, no!" I wanted to go back to sleep and wake up again. This was a nightmare. It *must* be a nightmare. "Not my baby, not Katy!" I started to scream and thrash about. All my reason went. I became like an animal. I had no control—just unbearable agony and the frustration of being away from our beloved little girl at this dreadful time.

Tara came rushing in, terrified at the sight of her mother out of control. She tried to comfort me. I felt physically sick, and was. All the time I begged them to wake me up from this nightmare. Ron called all the airlines to try and get us out of Paris. I opened the fridge and found some miniature bottles of brandy and scotch. I drank two or three and calmed down. We had to be practical and keep our heads. We *had* to get out of Paris. We had to push specific thoughts of what had happened to Katy out of our minds and concentrate on finding a way of getting to her. Fast.

We called the hospital and spoke to a doctor. He didn't sound optimistic. He put Katy's headmistress on the phone. When the hospital or police hadn't been able to find any of our immediate

307

family (Jackie was in Los Angeles; my brother and my father out to dinner), they called John Gold, a close friend whose children also went to Katy's school, and he had called the headmistress. She had rushed over and had been with Katy ever since, holding her hand and giving support.

She was comforting. Over the long-distance wires her soothing voice allayed our fears temporarily. She talked as if Katy was in safe hands and would be fine.

We called the British and American Embassies in Paris desperately trying to find a way to get out. They could do nothing. Neither could the concierge. Neither could British Airways or Air France. We were stuck in Paris for at least another seven hours until our 9 A.M. flight to London.

In those hours anything could happen to Katy. It was unbearable.

Icy calm descended on us. We called several friends with private planes. They were all away. Of course. It was August 2. Everyone was on vacation. I called my father in London.

"I don't suppose Roger Whittaker could come and get us in his plane?" I begged helplessly, knowing that Roger had a pilot's license.

Daddy was dubious. It was Saturday night—Sunday morning, and if Roger had had even one drink he couldn't pilot the plane. Daddy said he would try to reach him anyway.

Half an hour crept by. I lay on the sofa numb with shock and apprehension. Tara put ice on my neck and face and tried to comfort me. Ron paced up and down trying to be strong, but he was biting his nails to the quick.

At three-thirty a wonderfully calm voice phoned.

"Joan, it's Roger. Be at Le Bourget at five-thirty—I'm coming to get you!"

In the next two hours every kind of emotion raced through our minds. Elation that we were finally getting out of Paris, despair and frustration that we were not with our daughter at this critical time.

Guilt. How could we have gone off to Paris and left her—even with people we trusted?

Fury. *How* did it happen? and *why?* What carelessness allowed it? Whose fault was it?

Grief. Our baby lying in hospital in what condition we couldn't imagine. And finally the dreadful, ghastly, nagging fear that we would be too late. That she would be dead by the time we arrived at the hospital.

For two hours we paced the suite. We all comforted each other, but I was in by far the worst shape. I felt ill with shock. I kept giving myself ridiculous things to do—as when you are a child you jump across the pavement and mustn't tread on any cracks because if you don't, something good will happen. So I felt that if I threw up—was sick—Katy would live. It sounds ridiculous but some voice in my head, the old ingrained actor's voice of superstition, kept telling me to do this.

As we raced through the darkened streets of Paris in a limousine conjured up by the hotel concierge, the same voice kept telling me again, "If you make the green traffic light before it turns red, she'll live. . . ."

"No, no." I squeezed my eyes shut. I didn't want to have contests with this superstitious inner voice. I held on to Ron, who was like a rock. Very strong, very calm. Inside, though, I could see he was in agony. Katy was his only daughter. He worshipped her.

We arrived at Le Bourget airport at 5 A.M. It was still dark. The ground staff knew nothing about Roger's arrival. Tara and I paced round and round the tiny airport lounge. I chain-smoked and wept. I was in pretty awful shape. I wore a ridiculously inappropriate dress I'd bought in Paris the day before. Red-and-white candy-striped, like a tent, white sandals and a sun visor. It was what I had put out to travel in. It seemed so wrong it didn't matter.

We searched the sky for hours, it seemed. No plane. The sky started to lighten. Dawn was coming. Was our baby still alive?

We called the hospital for the umpteenth time. My brother Bill was there with Robin Guild, another friend. They assured us Katy was holding her own, but I knew they were trying to make us feel better. The more snippets of information that were revealed, the worse it seemed.

Brain injury. The meaning was not clear, but the connotation was horrendous.

Coma. Was it just a long sleep or was it, as I had heard, the closest thing to death?

I closed my mind. I did not know what to expect. I refused to think what could happen.

Tara and I paced around the tarmac for what seemed an eternity, gazing at the ever lightening sky. She was brave, my sixteen-year-old Tara. It must have been hell for her. She had the clarity of adolescence.

"Don't worry, Mummy," she kept reassuring me. "Katy's a big strong kid—nothing's going to get her. You must believe that, Mummy, you *must.*"

She gave me support as we continued the endless wait.

Ron and I looked into each other's eyes and all we saw was stark terror. We could not speak much. We held each other. We cried. Occasionally I would rush to the loo to be sick again. I have been sick only about three times in my life. It was odd. I smoked a thousand cigarettes and prayed desperately.

Roger Whittaker's plane finally landed. By this time Ron's nails were bitten to the knuckle, and I felt close to a complete nervous breakdown. I fell on to Roger's chest and burst into tears. He shook me like a Dutch uncle and told me to shape up, to think positively. He almost shouted at me and strangely it calmed me down.

We hardly spoke during the hour-and-a-half journey in the tiny bumpy plane back to London Airport. Ron and I clutched each other's hands. He was trying so hard not to give in to his terror. He was trying to be strong for me. For Katy. If there was still a Katy.

We drank coffee from a thermos flask Roger had brought. I tried to blot out my thoughts and started to pray to God. To a God I had never really acknowledged existed. Not that I believed he didn't—I was agnostic. Now I prayed for my daughter's life with all my might.

At London Airport they hastened us through Customs. Bill and Robin were waiting. Tara and I went with Bill, and Robin insisted on taking Ron in his car.

We sped through the deserted summer Sunday streets. Bill prepared me for the fact that they had cut off all Katy's hair. He kept assuring me she was going to be all right. I felt he was keeping the real truth from me by telling me this detail. We passed a graveyard. Thousands and thousands of gray and white stones. I shuddered and turned away. Tara was very quiet and I tried to comfort her. We held each other's hands tightly. She was eight years older than Katy but Katy adored her big sister and Tara loved her too.

We ran through the hospital to the intensive care unit. I don't know what I thought I was going to see, but I didn't believe what I saw. My baby was lying in a brightly lit room naked to the waist. Her long blond hair was gone. It was hacked off to the skull. She was white. Bluish-white. She was tiny. Instead of a husky eight-year-old, she looked like an infant. She had tubes in her nose, in her wrists, from under her bedsheet. She had a ventilator life-support system down her throat to keep her breathing. She was still as stone, her eyes closed, her breathing a rasp. Her left fist was clenched and bent above her head. I took her right hand in mine and squeezed it.

"Katy, darling, Mummy's here. I'm here, darling. If you can hear me, squeeze my hand. Please, Katy, squeeze my hand." From the atavistic depths of her being, from the part of her brain that was working, she squeezed my hand. I knew she had heard. I knew she would survive.

To be what, though? We did not know the answer. Ron came in a few minutes later. He too spent some time at Katy's bedside, and while he was with her I saw Dr. Lionel Balfour-Lynn, Katy's pediatrician, who had been present at her birth.

"What are her chances?" I asked.

Tears filled his eyes. "Of survival, sixty. Forty against."

I burst into sobs of disbelief. Ron came out of the intensive care unit and took me to the back door. We held each other tightly and sobbed together. We made a vow to each other. Katy *could not* die. She *would not* die. We would do everything possible to make her live. We would not accept what the doctor's prognosis was, however pessimistic. We would pour into her our love, our faith, our prayers, our strength, our optimism, our utter positivity. All this we talked about in sobbing whispers at the back door of the ICU, surrounded by shelves full of shrouds.

Five minutes later we went in to see our daughter again. I had dried my tears and Ron had dried his. She would not see us cry again. From now on what Katy would receive from us was total positive input and the firm belief that she was going to live and that she was going to recover.

Here is what Ron had to say about those early dreadful days.

"Joan was petrified and asked me to deal with the situation the woman surgeon, Dr. Hunt, was briefing us on at the request of Mr. Illingworth. Joan had talked nearly nonstop to Katy's comatose frail figure for the first 72 hours. I felt Katy knew that it was her mother's voice, a penetrating one that kept her alive during that initial 72-hour critical period. It was right to spare Joan from these things she is queasy about, even in simple situations, so she certainly could not be expected to cope with all these details.

"Dr. Hunt described in detail the surgery that would be necessary when Katy was detached from the ventilator—the machine that breathes for the patient in a life-support situation. It was a common operation—a tracheotomy, which makes a hole in the throat to assist breathing until Katy's injured brain would send the correct signals for breathing.

"Mr. Illingworth told us the operation would not be necessary as he thought Katy would breathe on her own. Dr. Hunt vigorously opposed his opinion—but Mr. Illingworth prevailed. It was therefore decided, much to my relief, and with my having to sign a document, that I, Ron Kass, was taking full responsibility in case anything went wrong. (I had a strong instinctive trust in Robin Illingworth. I know better than anyone that a cool and modest demeanor hid his incredible competence and geniuslike knowledge of the brain.)

"The decision to operate or not was going to be made at the exact time the support system was detached. If Katy could not breathe, I was to stand behind Dr. Hunt to give my on-the-spot permission for the tracheotomy to be performed.

"Mr. Illingworth was standing far enough away to not interfere, but close enough to counsel me whether or not to say, Yes, operate, or No, she is breathing.

"A team of five, headed by Dr. Hunt, had assembled its equipment, normally found only in an operating theater. But Katy could not be moved—it was too dangerous; hence the surgical team set-up in the intensive care unit.

"The tension was high.

"They slowly removed the ventilator tube while Dr. Hunt was having her final scrubdown and having her surgical gloves put on.

"As the tube finally was clear of Katy, a deep wheezing sound, like a truckdriver growling, came from Katy's throat. Then it changed to a kind of heaving. I was alarmed, as it seemed so forced and unnatural. I glanced at Robin for counsel and he had a slight smile of obvious relief on his face—just as the heaving sound lurched out to a recognizable breathing sound.

"Dr. Hunt looked slightly cross, as she is never wrong. However, Robin is never wrong either. She didn't say a word, just directed her team to gather their tools and make a hasty retreat. Gifted people like Dr. Hunt often have sizable egos. I sometimes think of how strange her lack of relief and happiness was, but Robin's expression transcended all as Katy's brain instructed her respiratory system to breathe. This was a big breakthrough, the first being her surviving the first seventy-two hours."

For six weeks Ron and I lived in a trailer parked in the grounds of the hospital. I spent every waking minute at Katy's bedside. Numb with shock, I threw myself with utter desperation into not only her survival—that had been assured after the first agonizing seventy-two hours and the removal of the ventilator—but her return to normality and out of coma as soon as possible.

Ron and I simply breathed and lived and willed life back into her. If ever I believed in *will* and faith and hope and prayer, I used every ounce of it on that child.

The doctors' grim prognosis as the weeks progressed and the continuing of her comatose state did not deter us. She was going to survive. More—she would get back to normal again.

313

"She may be a vegetable for life," they whispered to me. "She may never walk, let alone talk again. You'll have to put her in a home."

How many times we heard it, from doctors, nurses, interns, even friends. It fell on ears of disbelief. We *would* get her back with our strength and God's help.

Each night, while I fell into exhausted sleep for four or five hours, Ron paced the corridor outside the children's ward. Keeping his vigil, watching over Katy while she slept endlessly on.

After a few weeks, we started to piece together the tragic events of how it had happened.

Katy was staying with her best friend, Georgina, and her mother, in a well-to-do residential area in Ascot, home of the famous British racetrack. Jane had assured me she would take care of Katy like "my own," while we were in Paris.

An eighteen-year-old boy, absurdly named Collins, was traveling down the country lane, driving his father home from a medical checkup. The Collins boy aspired to be a male nurse, to specialize in neurology. His father was coming home from a physical for a heart murmur.

The nanny who had been watching the two girls had been distracted and the girls mock-chased a twelve-year-old boy who had been teasing them. Holding hands, they stepped only a few feet onto the lane, which did not look like a public street. A broken gate at the bottom of the garden led into it.

Katy was hit by the on-side fender and bumper by the Collins car and thrown against the concrete curb. The right side of her head took the secondary blow.

A woman picked up a blanket and ran out to help with the appalling scene she saw from her window. Two British bobbies, Police Constable Pollard and P.C. Burredge, were on the scene within minutes, calling into their hand-talkies for an ambulance immediately.

Georgina was screaming blue murder while Katy lay very still with a blank expression in her *open* eyes.

The first ambulance attendant, R. Morris, an ambulance-driver veteran of World War II, recognized Katy's symptoms of brain injury immediately. A second ambulance came a minute later to attend to Georgina while Katy was raced to the local Ascot hospital.

There they sheared off Katy's beautiful long blond hair and prepared for a brain probe requiring holes to be bored through her cranium.

Feeling her case hopeless, the duty doctor telephoned the Central Middlesex Hospital in Acton, a suburb of London. God was on our side; the call was received by Dr. Hussein, a Ceylonese studying under the auspices of the most eminent brain surgeon in Europe—Mr. Robin Illingworth.

Dr. Hussein sized up the problem over the phone and decided Katy could not be treated properly in the rural hospital, which lacked such sophisticated equipment as the EMI brain scan computer device. He was told she probably would not survive the trip, as Ascot to Acton is a two-hour drive, especially with the Saturday night traffic.

In the great British tradition, a call was made to the Thames Valley Police Authority. They immediately dispatched two police escort cars while Katy was being cared for by Nurse Elizabeth Reed, a specialist nurse in a special ambulance equipped with the necessary life-support system.

Nurse Reed later wrote to us how terrible she felt at the time, as Katy's chances were nil, according to her vast experience. This dreaded prognosis was to follow Katy for weeks. Everyone fell in love with this comatose little girl; however they didn't expect her to survive.

The ambulance trip, normally 120 minutes, was made in 35 minutes, thanks to the police outriders, who pulled all the stops out.

She was rushed into the brain scan room, where the first of several revolutionary devices were tested.

It was around midnight when Mr. (surgeons are called Mr. in Britain instead of Dr.—this is a sign of respect) Robin Illingworth came in from his much-needed weekend. No one knew that this eight-year-old's mother was a household name in England. All this urgency and care is what the British are all about. One can criticize them for many things but if ever I'm in another desperate situation I want a British soldier beside me. They excel in *crisis*.

When Katy was wheeled into the ICU of the Central Middle-sex Hospital, the night cleaning lady, Mae, burst into tears. She told me later, "I saw this beautiful little creature come in. I've been working the intensive care unit for many years. I usually can tell when they come in whether they're going to live or die. I *knew* that heaven wanted this little beauty. I knew she couldn't survive through the night, and I've never been wrong yet. I cried then. I cried for her soul and the pity and waste of it all."

Mae told me this as she was cleaning the caravan one afternoon while I was taking my afternoon break.

"I'm so happy I was wrong," beamed that friendly black lady. "For the first time I was wrong."

"Never give up, Mae," I said. "We will never give up on our Katy, I promise you."

Bit by gradual bit, oh, such tiny moments, but so infinitely precious and full of meaning, she started coming back to us, responding to the continual stimuli we gave her. She was a miracle.

On the eighth day she opened her eyes. They were blank, unseeing but it was a marvellous sign. Her weight had dropped drastically. When her physiotherapists worked with her she looked like a little skeleton from a concentration camp with her cropped hair and skinny arms and legs. She moaned like an animal after a few weeks. Another positive sign, meaning her vocal cords could work.

After six weeks the hospital said they could do no more for her. She was, as far as they were concerned, recovered, and they sent her home. That would be the best therapy now. Home. South Street. Her cat, Sam. Her bedroom with the red heart wallpaper and the dozens of stuffed toy animals, books and pictures of horses.

When Ron carried that little stick figure up to her bedroom, her eyes widened and seemed to stare with an inner joy. She knew she was home, but she still didn't speak.

Over the following months Katy's miraculous progress continued. She had to have a day and night nurse constantly. Within a week she took her first faltering steps. It was almost like having a new baby again. I went to Selfridge's department store and bought all manner of mobiles, rattles and toys to stimulate her.

Every day I would point to objects and ask Katy what they were. Silence. No sound from that sweet babyish mouth. But her eyes looked, observed, *knew*. They were the eyes of an eight-year-old, even if she still seemed like an infant.

"What's this, Katy?" I pointed to a horseshoe in her room. She had loved to ride, but it was now over two months since the accident.

A whisper. Had I heard it right? A croak. "Horseshoe." It was barely audible but it was a word—the right word. She was going to be *all right!*

The next week a sentence: "I want a drink." A few days later a smile. More days passed—a little laugh.

No tears yet. It would be six months before she would be able to cry. But her improvement continued. Slowly, oh, so slowly, but surely.

Ron and I were exhausted mentally and physically. To get through the nightmarish time, I had taken to drinking heavily. White wine, whiskey. And chain-smoking. Anything to numb the pain. What Ron was taking to get through his days I didn't want to know.

Life had to go on. Bills had to be paid. Massive bills. Therapists, physical educationalists, doctors, nurses, special beds, wheelchairs . . . the list seemed endless.

While Katy was still in the hospital, we had already decided to continue with the West End production of *Mrs. Cheyney*. Rehearsals began at the Cambridge Theatre the day she said her first word. At the press conference I was ecstatic and babbling on endlessly about how wondrous Katy was. Doing *Mrs. Cheyney* was not anywhere near as important as our darling's recovery.

The photos of me in the newspapers the next morning were pretty depressing. I looked a haggard wreck. I stopped drinking immediately and went on a diet. The years of self-discipline still worked. I was still a professional actress and I had a duty to myself as well as to my daughter. And a duty to the production.

On opening night, Katy came backstage. She had written a little note, her first since the accident. "Dear Mummy and Daddy, I love you so much."

The writing was shaky, but she had written it by herself. The effort of will and strength it took this little eight-year-old girl who had had a part of her brain so severely injured was incredible. I was so much more proud of her than of any of the many curtain calls we took that night.

In November, to celebrate how far she had come, we had a photograph taken for our Christmas card. Katy wore a green velvet dress with a white lace collar. She sat next to a giant Christmas tree with a big smile on her face, clutching her favorite stuffed animal, Lambikins. The message inside was simple:

"Our dreams came true this Christmas—we hope yours do too."

The Last of Mrs. Cheyney was not a massive success in the West End. In the fall of 1980, London theater was experiencing its biggest recession in years. All over town theaters were dark. The public didn't seem desperately anxious to see a frothy period piece of 1920s Lonsdale fluff. Where were the legions of loyal supporters who had flocked to Chichester? Goodbye, name in neon lights on the marquee—hello, episodic TV again. Oh, no!

Ron and I had rashly invested in the production with Triumph. I knew things were heading for skid row when I asked the stage manager for a bit more cash than he usually handed me on Friday night. It was a month before Christmas. Instead of the one hundred pounds advance I took in cash, I wanted extra to buy gifts.

He coughed nervously and looked highly embarrassed. "I, er— I'm afraid I can't let you have *any* money, Joan," he stammered.

"Why, David?" I asked warily. I was sitting in my dressing room, prettily decorated with green and white palm trees specially for me, courtesy the management. It was minutes to curtain time.

"Because, er—because Duncan Weldon and Louis Michaels have a clause in your contract that says if the production starts losing money, your salary is to go toward the deficit."

Happy family, with Tara and Sacha in Beverly Hills. I was content to play the little wife role and I adored my children.

Party time in London. Top, left to right: Alice Cooper, Ryan O'Neal, Madame Sukarno, Tessa Kennedy, Princess Fyrial, Louise and Roger Moore, Fiona Lewis. Bottom: Tatum O'Neal, Ron, me, and Marisa Berenson.

Sunday Mirror

His, Hers and Ours. With my 1972 marriage to Ron Kass I inherited three more kids. From left to right: Robert Kass, Jonathan Kass, Ron, me with sweet six-week-old Katyana Kennedy Kass, my Sacha and Tara, and David Kass.

My least favorite and most grueling film role, *Empire of the Ants*, on location in the Florida swamps. My legs are covered with infected wounds and I am terrorized by giant plastic ants.

Eric Benson

Edward H. Sanderson

On location in Hawaii for "Starsky and Hutch" with Paul Michael Glaser and David Soul. The rigors of this TV episode made me decide to quit doing TV forever!

NBC's remake of *The Man Who Came to Dinner*, with Orson Welles as Sheridan Whiteside and me as Lorraine Sheldon. Mr. Welles read *every single line* of his part from cue cards.

With Robert Mitchum in a remake of *The Big Sleep*, which was not as successful as the original.

With Roger Moore in "The Persuaders," one of my many guest TV roles.

Back on the boards in London in *The Last of Mrs. Cheyney* with Simon Williams. I was putting on a brave face while Katy was recovering from her near-fatal accident.

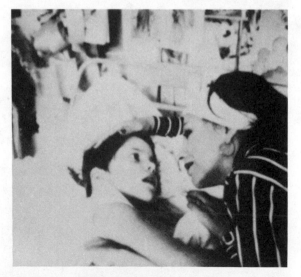

September 13, 1980: "Today's the day—we're going home, my darling."

"Give your boyfriend Joan Collins for Christmas," screamed advertisements for the best-selling video cassette of *The Bitch*. I don't think chauffeur's caps and garter belts worn with fur coats will ever make a major fashion statement!

A thrilling moment for Katy and me—meeting Her Majesty, the Queen, and Prince Philip after I had hosted a charity concert at the Royal Albert Hall in London, 1982.

First day on "Dynasty," August 1981. Alexis gets a grilling from the prosecutor. Although I looked cool, it was 90 degrees in the shade.

John Forsythe and his "Dynasty" women: Linda Evans—*Krystle*; Pamela Bellwood—*Claudia*; Heather Locklear—*Sammy Jo*; Pamela Sue Martin—*Falon*; JC—*Alexis*. In spite of what you see on the screen, we all get along . . . most of the time!

Alexis trying to get the best of *Krystle*. The public loved our fight scenes together.

Winning the 1983 Golden Globe for Best Actress in a TV Drama Series.

My own dazzling Dynasty: Katy, Tara and Sacha.

Peter Holm

February 1984: Show-
ing off with 90 of the
nearly 500 magazine
covers on which I've
appeared.

Playboy

Eddie Sanderson

Which is the real Joan? The Witch in TV's
"Hansel and Gretel" or the witch on the
Christmas 1983 cover of *Playboy*?

I was appalled. "My *entire* salary?"

He nodded. "I could lend you a tenner to buy your round in the pub." I nodded no thanks. He smiled wanly and left. I appreciated his embarrassment. It certainly wasn't his problem. It certainly was mine.

I called my agent, confused. I was the star and Ron was one of the producers, and we were losing money, so was I to be the sacrifice? I was gripped by rage.

We were closing in January in any case. The play had done quite well but it was a wildly expensive production to run and Triumph said it was losing money. Yet our houses looked practically full every night.

In the intermission my friend Barry Langford came to see me. Barry had been doing secretarial work for me and running my fan club for several years. He had come to work at the Cambridge for the run of *Mrs. Cheyney*. I asked him if our houses were really so bad and he said it didn't appear so to him. Barry began doing a head count each night so I could check with the box-office receipts each Saturday.

I smoked furiously. Was there something fishy going on?

For the next five weeks I performed every night on the stage of the Cambridge Theatre for free.

I had been begging Ron to go to L.A. and sell the house we had not lived in for over a year. Our finances, as usual, were shaky.

Six children to support between us. To add insult to injury, *The Stud* and *The Bitch* had come out on video and were hugely successful. From this we were seeing no money either.

The December video magazines featured a picture of me in black stockings, black merry widow, fur coat and chauffeur's cap with the caption "Give your dad or your boyfriend Joan Collins for Christmas!" Exploited again. Would it ever end?

Ron and I went to Equity, the actors' union, to protest and see if they could do anything about obtaining some of the money we were owed. They couldn't. We asked for an audit from Brent-Walker. They hedged. Something fishy here, too, definitely.

Although he had been amazingly supportive through Katy's injury and recovery, Ron didn't seem to me to be functioning well

319

now. Bills and mail lay unopened on his desk. Phone calls went unreturned. Creditors came to the door. It was worrying me tremendously. As soon as *Mrs. Cheyney* closed, I flew to L.A. by myself to try to sell the house. Something had to be done.

In L.A. I realized with a heavy heart the truth about my marriage. The creditors were banging on the door in Beverly Hills too. It was awful—horrible—demeaning. I wasn't a businesswoman—I was an actress and a mother. Financial matters were too difficult for me to understand, let alone control. However, self-pity was never my forte. Action was. I called Ron and told him I wanted a divorce. To have another marital failure was anathema to me, but he had changed too much. I felt he was a different person from the man I had met and married nearly eleven years before.

The next day a close friend, a devout Catholic woman who had helped us enormously by her faith during Katy's hospitalization, phoned me from London. She begged me not to divorce or even separate from Ron.

"God gave Katy back to you but He could take her away from you if you divorce or leave Ron," she urged.

My blood ran cold. Superstitious to an extreme, I had prayed to any God who existed for my daughter's life and recovery. It was only six months since her accident. She still had much more progress to make even though she was now back at school.

My friend spoke for an hour convincingly—so convincingly that I agreed not to leave Ron. I still loved the man I had married. But where was *he?* I told Ron he had to get his act together. Work, put a deal together, take care of our finances.

I did a "Fantasy Island" for Aaron Spelling, in which I finally got to play Cleopatra. This time episodic TV didn't seem so bad. A few people asked me if I would be interested in a series. No, *no, no.* Thank you. It was back to England for me. Back to the boards—that's where I belonged now.

We sold the Beverly Hills house. We moved back to London. The children started different schools—yet again.

I did a play called *Murder in Mind* at Guildford. The night of the dress rehearsal I fell down a flight of stairs backstage that was in darkness and broke my elbow. At the hospital the doctor told me my arm would have to be set in plaster.

"You can't! I open tomorrow night. I *have no understudy!* I can't do that to Duncan."

Triumph Productions had again backed the production, but this time without benefit of Ron's and my investments or lavish costumes and sets.

"I have a responsibility to them," I told the doctor. To no avail.

Plaster-casted from forearm to elbow, I opened in *Murder in Mind,* a thriller a la *Dial M for Murder* in which I was terrorized in my house by three people masquerading as my family. I was severely unglamourized for this and had to wield an immense shotgun with aplomb and authority. I always hated guns.

Opening night I stumbled backward on the step of the stage while trying to threaten my tormentors with the gun and running backwards to open the front door—using only one arm, of course. Not an easy feat.

The audience seemed sympathetic toward me. I had refused to take painkillers, I was in agony, and the discomfort of the plaster, as well as first-night nerves, didn't help.

Everyone, including my insurance man, thought I was mad to go on performing a very physical role with my arm in a cast, but I knew the play would have to close without me, and never having missed a day of work in my career, I had an ingrained "show must go on" syndrome.

In the light of future events it was ironic.

In July we went for a holiday to Marbella, Spain. It was almost a year since Katy's accident. She still had a way to go before she'd be totally the girl she'd been before, but her improvement was fantastic. She was thriving with the sunshine and the swimming.

The phone rang. Tom Korman calling—my agent in L.A. "Joanie, have you ever heard of a TV show called 'Dynasty'?" he said.

"No, never—what's 'Dynasty'?" I queried indifferently. This was

321

my first holiday for two years and I was enjoying basking in the Mediterranean sunshine.

"Well, it's a series—sort of a soap opera, a bit like 'Dallas.' It's been on for thirteen weeks so far. Could become very successful although it's about number forty-five in the ratings right now. They want you for it."

"Oh, no way," I said vehemently. I wasn't inclined to go traipsing back to the USA again. Especially for some obscure TV series I'd never heard of.

"Joanie, you've *gotta* do it. Aaron loves you, so do the Shapiros and the Pollacks. They want you badly. It starts shooting at Fox next week. Can you do it?"

I was silent.

"Hello, hello?" Tom was getting anxious. "Can you hear me? It's called '*Dynasty*,' Joanie . . . D–Y–N–A–S–T–Y. Dynasty. It could be a very hot show. It's a great role. Her name's Alexis. She's a bitch but witty and clever and she has some great dialogue. It could make you a very big star again. Think about it."

"OK, I'll think about it, Tom."

So I did.

The 20th Century–Fox lot again. It had been twenty-seven years since I first set foot on it. The Hawaiian villages, the Western streets, the medieval castles had long gone. In their places were giant steel-and-glass cement buildings, offices, apartments and hotels. Wide boulevards with fountains emulating ancient Roman piazzas. Masses of people scurrying to work. Theaters. Shopping complexes. Big business. High finance. Rich living.

We rented one of the most securely patrolled apartments in Century City. We took it for six months as I didn't foresee the series running much longer than that. I had watched the first thirteen episodes on video and had not been terrifically impressed. The actors were good and so were some of the plots, but I thought it was somewhat dull. In any case, I wasn't a lover of soap operas, particularly ones with a lot of action in the oilfields. But a buck was a buck was a buck, so I was back at Fox again. Older and wiser, but not wise enough.

It hadn't been easy sorting out our lives in order to do "Dynasty." There were so many pros and so many cons in going back to L.A. to appear in an "iffy" series, even if Alexis was a smashing, juicy part which I had been told every actress in Hollywood wanted to sink her teeth into.

I knew I wasn't the producer's first choice. Very few actors and actresses are ever the first choice for any role, be it movies or TV. Sophia Loren and Raquel Welch had been strong contenders. But Aaron Spelling, clever and dynamic Aaron, whom I had known since I was shooting *The Opposite Sex* when he was a hungry actor, and whose every TV show now turned to gold, wanted *me*. And what Aaron wanted he usually got.

A thousand phone calls had gone back and forth in the ten days before I left Marbella. English agents, American agents, lawyers, Katy's school, her therapists, her doctors, my doctors. Agents calling, yelling, coaxing. There were many complications. It was like a "Dynasty" plot already.

Triumph Productions, my old friends Duncan Weldon and Louis Michaels, were expecting me to do a ten-week tour of *Murder in Mind* in the provinces. Since rehearsals were not going to commence for seven weeks and it was just a provincial tour without *any* guarantee of a West End run, I wanted out. Freedom to do "Dynasty."

They had refused to let me go. Ancient Louis Michaels came to see me in Marbella, his wrinkled flesh hanging, and wearing tropical sports gear. He told me the way it was. "The only way we will *not* see you appear in our theaters is if we have your *death certificate* in our hands, Joanie dear—I've got that in writing in a telegram." He waved a piece of paper at me and collapsed into a chair wheezing and coughing.

I stared at Ron and Viviane Ventura. We were in the sunlit, lush living room in Marbella. These people wanted my *death certificate?* What was this—the British mafia? After what I had done for *them?* Going on stage at Guildford with a broken arm? Appearing for five weeks for no money at the Cambridge Theatre?

There were two dozen actresses who could play Mary in *Murder in Mind*. How could they be so unfair to me—whom they professed to like and admire? The part of Alexis in "Dynasty" would obviously mean a major boost to my career, which could eventually benefit them. Surely Triumph realized my theatrical ventures had been less than triumphs?

I offered to do two plays for them for the same money I'd have received for *Murder in Mind* as soon as "Dynasty" finished. At this point I didn't think it would run for more than a season. Forty-fifth in the ratings was pretty damn low even if it was an Aaron Spelling production—and even if he *had* done "Charlie's Angels," "Starsky and Hutch," "The Love Boat" and many other prime time hits.

Triumph threatened my union, Equity. If I walked, they insisted Equity must ban me from working in the States and ever again in England. Equity was concerned. They talked to the Screen Actors Guild. SAG was concerned. Threats were bandied about with abandon. Lawyers discussed suits and countersuits. She *must* do the tour of this play. No—she must fly to L.A. immediately and do "Dynasty." Oh, how I regretted my altruism in performing with a broken arm. If I hadn't, the play would have closed then and there. Finis.

"There will be other parts, my dear Joan," wheezed the ancient Louis. "Other roles in other TV series for you. This is not your last chance, dear."

"It's a big chance, Louis. *Big*. I *know* it. I *feel* it. Even if the gig goes for only one season, with Alexis I think I can make enough impact to be able to do better things. I'll have more box-office appeal. I'll do other plays for you, Louis—I promise."

He shook his grizzled head in despair. "No my dear. No. We *need* you in Brighton, Manchester and Leeds."

Ron went to London to placate Equity, which was placating SAG, which was talking to Tom Korman, who was telling Aaron Spelling that all was well and Alexis-Joan was on her way, picture hat in hand—well, almost. At the family summit meeting we had decided that I definitely should do "Dynasty," in spite of all the difficulties and problems Triumph was creating. At the core of our thoughts were the feelings of the three children.

Sacha was at boarding school in England. No problem there with me going away. He could fly out on his holidays. He was fifteen, a big boy now. Tara, seventeen going on eighteen, was at college in Paris. Time to leave the nest. I had left my nest at her age. She had no objections.

Katy. Ah, Katy. Our baby. The child whose wellbeing meant more to me than all the money and success in the world. All her teachers and therapists and doctors agreed that to be in the sunshine of California for six months or a year would be far more beneficial to her recovery than another cold winter in London. I watched her frolicking in the pool with Viviane Ventura's kids. Tanned, laughing, still a little shaky—but it's only a *year*. Just one year, for God's sake. She's nine years old. My little miracle. Ron's and mine. But mostly her own. Her will and determination got her to where she was today. She was the one who deserved the most consideration.

"Take her," said Robin Illingworth, who had saved her life.

"You'll never work as an actress again," screamed Louis Michaels.

"Take her," said her teacher at school.

"You'll ruin your career," threatened Duncan Weldon.

"Take her," said her speech therapist.

"Take her, and you—you need it," said Cecil Epel, our family doctor.

"Sue her," said Triumph.

"Fuck it," said I, and off we went.

I was extremely nervous on my first day of shooting on "Dynasty." It was mid-August 1981, 90 degrees in the shade, and I was doing the now famous courtroom scene in which Alexis Carrington, oil tycoon Blake Carrington's mysterious ex-wife, walks into the courtroom as the surprise witness to testify against Blake in his murder trial.

The cliffhanger of the previous season had concerned a mystery woman in a large white hat and sunglasses, heavily veiled and wearing a black-and-white suit, striding into the courtroom to the utter consternation, amazement and dismay of the Carrington family and other principals. Today we were shooting a twelve-page interrogation scene between me and the prosecuting attorney. I had most of the dialogue.

I was surrounded by strange new faces of the crew and cast—some friendly, some noncommittal. I had to prove myself. To them I was some British broad come over to take America by storm. Oh, yeah—sure—let's see what she can do. I was being judged. It was par for the course.

Most of the actors were friendly and kind. They had, of course, all known each other, having worked for thirteen weeks the first season. The sole person I knew was Linda Evans, who played Krystle, Blake's long-suffering new wife. I had known Linda since she was married to Stan Herman a few years previously, when Ron and I went to parties at their beach house and hung out with the same group.

Linda had come into my trailer while I was doing my makeup that morning. "We've all done this courtroom bit," she said cheerily. "Last season each and every one of us had to go and sit in that witness chair and testify. We were all terrified!" She laughed.

"Yes, but you all knew each other well," I groaned. "I'm really nervous, Linda. It's hard to play this cool, calm, calculating bitch with butterflies jumping around in my stomach and sweat running down my back." The heat was really intense, and the hot black-and-white wool suit didn't help.

"You'll be great. I'm so happy you're doing this part. We all are. Just remember, we were all in the same place and we are all rooting for you."

I sat staring at myself in the mirror of the trailer. At 20th Century–Fox in the eighties there were no more dressing rooms with built-in bars, sunken tubs and color TVs. Not that I'd ever had one like that at Fox, but I had seen Lana Turner's and Bob Wagner's, which had been palatial.

Au contraire. Neatly lined up outside Stage 8 on the Fox lot were nine identical motor homes. When the cast were on call, we lived in these, like little battery hens, being brought to the stage to do our scenes and then tucked back into our trailers again.

My face stared back at me. I looked scared. I *was* scared. This

Alexis I was about to embark upon playing was a clever, ambitious schemer who lied and manipulated people, caring little for anyone or anything except money and power. I hadn't played a part as wicked as this since Princess Nellifer in *Land of the Pharaohs*. I knew there was a lot at stake. This could—if I played my cards and my performance right—turn out to be a major career break. Or it could be just another gig.

I had no choice of the costume I was to wear. The unknown actress who had played Alexis in the last episode had worn these clothes. I must wear them now. Large wide-brimmed white hat with black ribbon and black veiling. Quite becoming. Serene yet sexy black-and-white suit, hot but chic. Dark glasses. Under the veil, I thought they looked tacky. Again I had no choice.

The second assistant, Alice Blanchard, knocked on the door. "They're ready for rehearsal, Joan." I girded my loins and my veil and walked with trembling legs onto Stage 8. It never changes. Throughout the years, backstage life on a set is always the same. Grips, electricians and cameramen working, moving lamps and props, barking orders, gossiping, swapping jokes, drinking coffee, eating doughnuts. Bejeaned and sneakered. This lot looked jovial and hardworking. They looked like they knew their business—and they did.

Bobby della Santini, the first assistant director, whom I'd met the first day I'd arrived—and who later told me I had a look of horror when he told me the gig was going to shoot for eight months—introduced me to Gabrielle Beaumont, a fellow Brit who was directing this episode. She calmed my nerves, and she told me she was glad I had convinced the producers to let me play Alexis as an Englishwoman, as there had been some talk of me playing her with an American accent. I had thought seriously about this, but realized there were no other Englishwomen on TV and perhaps the American public was ripe for a new voice. I was also very well aware that "foreigners" had never done well on American TV. With the exception of Eva Gabor in "Green Acres," no non-American had sent the Nielsen ratings spinning.

"Middle America" was a term I was to hear often during the next few months. "Middle America will not *understand* you," despaired one of the executives at ABC.

"Yes they will," I argued. "I have very good diction." I was beginning to understand finally—after nearly thirty years—that you have to stand up for your rights in this business. I really felt I now knew much better than most people what was good and right for me.

I sat in the witness stand in the courtroom and gazed nervously at my new TV family. John Forsythe gave me an engaging wink. He was a darling—a true gentleman in the English sense of the word. Gallant, courteous and fun. He had been charming to me, and he was an excellent actor.

John turned out to be one of the most charming and delightful men I have ever worked with. He has been married for forty years to the delightful Julie and they have two grandchildren, and he is without doubt one of the most attractive men I have ever met. Not only physically. His warmth and wit are overwhelming. He truly is the patriarch and the strength of the "Dynasty" cast.

We were chatting on the set the day after I had just been to a friend's fiftieth birthday party. He had been terribly depressed at reaching this milestone.

"That's right," said John. "It's a hell of a birthday. I remember I was in New York doing a play for Gore Vidal when I had mine. I was very depressed and Gore asked me what was wrong. When I told him I had just hit fifty and was now officially middle-aged he looked at me and laughed. 'Oh, no, John, you're wrong. You're not middle-aged *at all*. After all, how many people do you know who are a hundred?'"

Behind John sat "our" children, Steven and Falon. Al Corley was very tall, very blond, very macho; Pamela Sue Martin, tall, slender and pretty, with a zest for life and fervor for new experiences, quests, causes. She refused to wear fur coats on the show, or much jewelry.

And John James—JJ as everyone called him—the resident hunk. Extremely good-looking, but sweet and nice and eager to learn. He played Jeff Colby, Falon's husband.

JJ and Pamela Bellwood, who played the fragile, neurotic Claudia (not that day in court), became my closest friends of the

328

"Dynasty" cast. Katy came to adore Pamela Bellwood, and at parties at my house the two of them would sit together for hours engrossed in conversation.

And last but not least, Lee Bergere—Joseph, the sinister major-domo, with whom I was to have many a fracas before he decided to leave the series after the third season because he didn't have enough to do. Too true. For an actor to play just a butler is anathema. Lee had a clause in his contract stating that he didn't have to do anything menial in his role. When one day I innocently suggested that he carry in a tray instead of the day player's doing it he was outraged. I was learning a whole new set of TV rules.

"Your name?" said Brian Denehhey, surveying the crowded courtroom with an eagle eye.

"Alexis Morrell Carrington," I said with a mixture of defiance and pride.

"Your residence?"

"I've been living in Acapulco for the past several years."

"You were the first wife of the defendant, Blake Carrington. You are the mother of his children, is that correct?"

"Yes, it is."

"Was it an amicable divorce?"

"No," I replied. "It was what you might call an *enforced* divorce."

"Would you please explain that to the court and jury?"

I took off my dark sunglasses and raised my veil slowly for maximum effect. The courtroom gasped. The ABC and "Dynasty" executives gasped at the rushes the next day. The scene was dynamic, and so was I. So they told me.

Never one to believe my own publicity, I merely smiled when my father sent me the front page of the English *Daily Mirror* with the headline "Sophisticated lady Joan is set to beat J.R." emblazoned across the front page picture of me complete with hat and veil and enigmatic smile.

The word had got out, as it usually does in Hollywood, that I was "hot." I had "impact." "Magnetism." Lots of superior adjectives were bandied about. It was said in ancient Rome—and it applies to Hollywood: "Three can keep a secret only if two are dead." There are few secrets in Hollywood, and within days I was getting heavy media interest.

I got the feeling I might be becoming a star again when John Springer, an old friend, and press agent to the stars, called me from New York in November 1981 and asked me to participate in "Night of 100 Stars" at Radio City Music Hall.

"We've got Grace Kelly, Bette Davis, Al Pacino, Paul Newman, Lillian Gish, Brooke Shields and dozens more," John told me eagerly. "We want you and Farley Granger to come on stage as 'Lovers of the Silver Screen' while we show a clip from *Girl in the Red Velvet Swing*."

A buzz of excitement about the show started about three weeks before it was to open. We heard that Grace Kelly was flying in from Monaco, Roger Moore from Gstaad, that Elizabeth Taylor would definitely be there . . . and Gene Kelly, Jane Fonda, Gregory Peck. It could be the event of the year.

I told Nolan Miller, who designed the wardrobe for "Dynasty," "I have absolutely nothing to wear darling!" Everything had been seen dozens of times either on the show or in magazine layouts and TV interviews. Nolan wanted to create a "knock 'em in the aisles" gown. "I mean, if you're going to be with all the movie stars in the world you might as well look the best!" he said jokingly.

He had designed a gold lamé dress slit to the navel for a party scene in "Dynasty." He decided it could be fun to create a similar silver lamé gown. After all, although the fabric was $125 a yard, there were only two yards of material in the dress. And it was superb.

Carefully boxed, tissued and packed to within an inch of its life, the dress, Judy Bryer and I boarded the "Red-Eye" to New York.

The fact that I had arrived back from a quick trip to England only fifty hours earlier, had arisen at 5 A.M. to pack and then shot for twelve hours had not put me in a mood of effervescent jollity. However, we soon started to feel better the moment we got to the airport. Heavyweight stars started boarding: Larry Hagman—J.R. himself—wearing a plaid Western-style jacket, large white Stetson and pink-tinted glasses. Was this a disguise, or did he want the whole world to know J.R. flew TWA? We soon realized it must have been the former when he whipped out a large polka-dot scarf, covered his face and slept for the entire trip.

William Shatner sat in front of us and we reminisced about the "Star Trek" episode I'd worked on twelve years before. Linda Gray arrived breathlessly, straight from the set of "Dallas."

New York was having one of her rare magical days of perfect crisp winter weather when we arrived. A gaggle of early-bird fans and paparazzi with strong flashbulbs and even stronger constitutions was at the airport to meet us. I kept on my dark glasses in spite of impassioned pleas to remove them. I realized now why they called this flight the "Red-Eye."

"Larry Hagman's behind me," I said, winking, and like a covey of starlings they whooped with glee and went off in search of bigger prey.

At the luxurious Helmsley Palace Hotel we were greeted by the sight of some two or three hundred fans surrounding the entrances. The whole of Fifty-first Street had been blocked off, and each darkened limousine was being eagerly scanned for famous faces.

Dozens of burly security men stood by to escort us to the safety of the elevator. The suite overflowed with flowers, champagne, fruit and invitations. The phone rang constantly. Luisa Moore and I discussed where to meet later. After considering Sardi's, Elaine's, a party at Studio 54, where Morgan Fairchild would be crowned "Miss Valentine 1982" and various others, we opted to meet at Regine's at ten-thirty.

That night at Regine's, a veritable hanging garden of red and white balloons, paper chains and assorted heart-shaped novelties hit us about the head as we stumbled through flashing paparazzis' bulbs to the top table. I sat next to Roger Moore, which caused the paparazzi to snap eagerly away, particularly when Regine herself, resplendent in black-and-red taffeta, joined us. When Veronique and Gregory Peck arrived, more photographers hounded them.

331

When Stefanie Powers arrived and sat next to me, more still appeared from out of the woodwork. After an hour of this we began to get slightly miffed. TV camera crews had now arrived and were pushing and jostling. We felt like monkeys in a cage, as the other patrons of the nightclub clustered around, pointing and laughing.

With the arrival of Sammy Davis, Jr., and Julio Iglesias all hell broke loose. By now there were at least twenty-five photographers, and we were blinded by the flashbulbs. Luisa Moore, in her volatile Italian way, threatened to hit one of the photographers if he didn't leave us alone. They had even followed me onto the floor to get a picture of me dancing. This appeared in a tabloid some weeks later with the caption "Joan's New Guy." Since rumbles about my marital rift abounded, this was probably the reason. The irony was that I had never met the gentleman before!

At eleven o'clock the following morning Judy and I arrived at Radio City Music Hall for the rehearsal of the "Lovers of the Silver Screen" segment.

I was assigned a dressing room. It was rather full. In it were Bette Davis, Janet Leigh, Lillian Gish, Ruth Gordon, Ginger Rogers, Anne Jeffreys and Jane Russell. Jane Powell, Brooke Shields and Diane Keaton were also supposed to be there. Every one of these ladies had an entourage of at least two. Managers, agents, press agents, hairdressers, husbands, lovers and friends. The air was thick with cigarette smoke and gossip. Judy and I escaped to the sanity of the auditorium. Grace Kelly was rehearsing her speech and lighting one of the one hundred candles on the enormous birthday cake. I remembered when I had first met her, before her marriage to Prince Rainier. Sitting around looking bored were Liza Minnelli in a black minidress, and no makeup, Paul Newman, blue-jeaned and blue-eyed, Brooke Shields in her Calvin Kleins, and Henry Winkler, who had brought a home-movie sound camera and was happily photographing everything and everyone. As I walked up to the front of the house to sign the official poster, which was to be reproduced and auctioned for charity, I marveled at the artillery of names that had accepted the invitation of Alexander Cohen, the producer and entrepreneur who had had the *chutzpah* to organize this event that everyone had said couldn't take place.

I was honored to have been included. It seemed I was having yet another renaissance. So many of these names had played important roles in my life and in my career. Warren Beatty, Gregory Peck, Farley Granger, Roger Moore, Linda Evans, John Forsythe. . . .

Farley arrived. He looked great and we congratulated each other on how well we looked considering the movie clip they'd be showing of us was twenty-seven years old!

I said hello to Bette Davis. We hadn't met since my first Hollywood movie, *The Virgin Queen*. She had intimidated me then. She still did.

We watched "One" from *A Chorus Line* being rehearsed. The most staggering array of leading men, past and present, from theater, movies and TV strutted on stage, each flanked by a Rockette. Robert De Niro, Al Pacino, James Caan, Richard Chamberlain, Dudley Moore, Christopher Reeve, Roger Moore, Larry Hagman, Jose Ferrer, Gregory Peck, Tony Perkins, Donald Sutherland, Gene Kelly, Burt Lancaster, Douglas Fairbanks, Jr.—and Lee Strasberg, not to mention ex-Mayor Lindsay—high-kicked and moved like veteran hoofers. It was quite enthralling. We rehearsed the finale. We were all told to get up on stage to face a vast set of bleachers which were numbered from 1 to 218. It wasn't the Night of 100 Stars after all—218 stars were shining!

I stood on stage next to Elizabeth Taylor and Liza Minnelli. We waited like disgruntled beauty contenders while Alexander Cohen called out our names and then a number. The top rows of the bleachers filled up. Finally I was called. Number 168. Next to Farley Granger and behind Ethel Merman and Warren Beatty.

"It is imperative you remember your number and the people who are next to you, behind you and in front of you," boomed out Mr. Cohen to his captive audience of fidgety celebrities.

I marveled at how disciplined and well-behaved everyone was. The public could never believe such a lack of temperament could exist. We all stood, including even the older actors, some of whom were well into their seventies and eighties, for over forty-five minutes while Mr. Cohen barked instructions. "No running backstage. There are likely to be holes in it due to the many film changes. No visitors backstage after six-thirty." Where to go, what to do, how to get there. A five-star general giving commands to his troops before battle. All paid attention. Brooke Shields passed along her autograph book for signatures. At four-thirty it was off to the hotel for a quick bath and makeup, and by 6 P.M. we were back again.

The crowds outside the hotel and lining the route all the way to Radio City Music Hall were mind-boggling in their enthusiasm. Two security men led me into the car. Hundreds of fans lined the hotel lobby and were outside the Music Hall brandishing autograph books and snapping Instamatic cameras.

"Alexis!" they screamed. "We love you, Alexis." Roger Moore patted my cheek. "Fame at last, Joanie. It's more intense on TV than anywhere else." The fans went crazy for me. It was all rather incredible to realize what had happened to me in such a short time. Altogether one of the most staggering evenings I have ever experienced.

Steve Allen summed it up when he said, "If a bomb dropped on Radio City Music Hall tonight, Pia Zadora would become the biggest star in the world!"

After appearing in only three episodes of "Dynasty" I began receiving an avalanche of fan mail. Although I had been an actress for nearly thirty years, the amount of attention I was receiving from people in the street, in stores, and especially from the media, was overwhelming. After "Dynasty" had been airing for five or six weeks I finally stopped going to supermarkets other than in disguise as my recognizability quotient was so high that it took me twice as long to shop, having to stop to answer the questions that the avid "Dynasty" watchers would fire at me.

The scene that really put the "Dynasty" ratings through the roof was the one in which Alexis Carrington, using every ounce of her feminine wiles, lures her fiancé, Cecil Colby, played by Lloyd Bochner, to her boudoir where, in the last throes of passionate lovemaking, Cecil suffers a major heart attack. Horrified, Alexis in her usual charming and delightful way starts slapping the hapless Cecil about the face in a frenzy of rage and frustration because now she might not inherit the Colby billions. "Don't you dare die on me, Cecil!" she screams at him. "We're getting married tomorrow. You can't die on me—I need you to get Blake!"

The filming of this scene was considered so daring and sexy for network TV that all kinds of precautions were necessary to satisfy the ever vigilant censors.

Network TV was not allowed to show any nudity other than an occasional chaste back or leg. Certainly simulated copulation culminating in a heart seizure for the male was excessively adventurous, even in 1982.

Care was taken that no hint of nakedness would show on the screen. I eschewed the flesh-colored leotard Breezy Brooks from wardrobe produced and instead wore a purple strapless bathing suit with matching tights and leg warmers. If Bobby Dawes, our camera operator, caught so much as a sliver of purple during our thrashing about he would have to call "Cut."

I was fairly keyed up and nervous. There had been so much secrecy, talk and preparation about this scene that I just wanted to get it over with. Not one but *two* censors had to be on the set to observe Lloyd and me as we did our heavy-breathing act.

One of them, particularly eager, insisted on sitting right *under* the camera at all times, gazing expectantly at the border of the satin sheets that just covered my purple Lurex. Whether he hoped it would slip or not I do not know. He smiled a lot though, all flashing teeth and wide expectant eyes. Every one of our producers except Aaron Spelling and Doug Cramer was on the set looking anxious.

If this scene went too far and looked too sexy, the network would refuse to use it, thus necessitating a reshoot—an expensive proposition. If the scene was too tame, it would disappoint the network, as this was to be *the* cliffhanger of the '82–'83 season.

Does Cecil die or *not?* All America would wait with bated breath for nearly six months for the truth to be revealed the following October.

Lloyd Bochner looked rueful as we tried to get comfortable in the slippery satin sheets preparatory to huffing and puffing.

"Do you die, Lloyd?" I asked, ever eager to know what was hap-

335

pening in our series. Our scripts usually arrived just a week or so before we shot, and therefore I was as curious as the public to know what the future held.

"I suppose so," said Lloyd somewhat bitterly. "My agents were informed I won't be back next season, so I suppose this is my swan song."

"Put us on a bell."

"Quiet on the set," called Bobby della Santini, the first assistant director. "Rolling."

"Speed," called the soundman. Joe Valdez, the camera assistant, snapped the clapperboard in front of our noses and called out crisply, "Thirty-three apple, take one."

"Action!" called Jerome Courtland, the director.

Lloyd and I went to it.

"Cut—I can see her suit," said Bobby Dawes quietly.

The wrecking crew of makeup men, hairdressers, wardrobe and body makeup rushed to me to repair the ravages of a fast twenty-five seconds of television smooching.

"What are you *doing* to yourself?" tut-tutted Andi Sidell, the body-makeup girl. "What's all this orange stuff all over your neck and shoulders?" She busied herself with a sponge and makeup while Breezy tried to tuck a bit of satin sheet down the front of my purple bathing suit so it wouldn't show.

"It's Lloyd's body makeup," I whispered to Andi. "It comes off all over me, and the sheets, too." I noticed the orange pancake that the prop man was trying to wipe off the satin.

Painted, powdered and perfect again, we started our ritual writhing once more.

"Aaahh aaahh, oooh!" yelled Lloyd-Cecil, clutching his chest. "It *hurts*, Alexis."

"Don't you *dare* die on me, Cecil," I yelled, and hauled back and slapped him mightily three times on each cheek.

"Cut, cut, cut!" called Jerome Courtland. "We can't see your face, Joan. Your hair's all over it."

Resignedly I was "touched up" by the "wrecking crew" again. And again. And again.

After seven takes from various angles, my voice was hoarse from screaming "Don't you dare die on me, Cecil," and my chin was raw from rubbing against Lloyd's. Out of the corner of my eye throughout the whole performance I observed the censor's teeth gleaming eagerly as he watched us with more than a hint of professional interest, I thought.

Finally it was time for Lloyd's close-up. We had finished the master shot, the two-shot, two over-the-shoulder shots and every other conceivable angle. That scene was over at last. Now I sat next to Richard Rawlings, our cinematographer. I was in Lloyd's eyeline, and I gave him the appropriate moans, groans, slapping motions and dialogue.

"Action!" called Jerome.

"Aaahh! Ooohh! Oh-oh!" screamed Lloyd, giving many readings and interpretations of these noises. He had no dialogue other than sexy moans, which then had to become heart-attack moans. He writhed around believably.

I clutched Richard Rawlings, trying hard not to giggle. Love scenes always make me laugh, and Jerry seemed to be letting this close-up on Lloyd go on forever. Finally "Cut!" yelled Jerry, and added quietly "Did you come yet, Lloyd?" The crew and the censor broke up, and Lloyd, good sport that he is, did too. The scene turned out to be everything the network and Aaron Spelling Productions had hoped for, and we zoomed to number one the following season.

As "Dynasty" started to gallop up the ratings, and the popularity of both the show and myself increased, so did my personal life plummet. I was desperately anxious to remain married to Ron for Katy's sake; at the same time I knew how destructive it was for her to hear our bickering.

"Don't *fight*, Mummy and Daddy," she pleaded. "Please stop being so *angry* with each other!"

Biting my tongue, I would hide in the bathroom or the tiny patio of this far-too-small apartment to give vent to my anger, hurt and frustration—frustration at being bound into a marriage that was no longer happy. Only my concern for Katy and my guilt at failing once again in marriage had been keeping me in it up to now.

It was now eighteen months since her accident, and my major concern was for her welfare and complete physical and mental recovery. I knew that her recovery up to now had been miraculous. Her efforts with the various physiotherapists, tutors, piano teachers and counselors to bring her back to the perfect child that she had been before, and that I *knew* she would become again, were outstanding. She was brave and indomitable. Her school work was excellent in most subjects, but her short-term memory was still not functioning as it should, and this was giving her some problems with retention of certain subject matter. She still dragged her left foot slightly, had slight shakiness in her left hand, and her speech was a bit slow. But her diligence and hard work were paying off, and every month showed an improvement. If ever a human being deserved an A for effort, she did. In spades.

"Promise me you'll never divorce Daddy like you did Tara and Sacha's daddy," she whispered as she snuggled up to me while I lay on the bed staring blankly at the TV screen after another battle with Ron.

"I can't promise you that, baby, but I'll do my best. I'll really *try*." I hugged her with despair in my heart. I believed in trying to be honest with my children, but this was a difficult time for Katy, and I desperately wanted not to upset her or interfere with her improvement in any way.

My closest friends saw the marriage crumbling even if I refused to acknowledge it openly. During the day I went to work on "Dynasty," to all intents and purposes hard-working and full of jokes and *joie de vivre*. At night, in the hateful Century City apartment, I called on all my acting skills to convince Katy that all was well between Daddy and Mummy.

I knew I should be taking charge of my own destiny. I knew I should end the marriage, but, as throughout all my life, a decision of such magnitude was incredibly hard for me to make. I agonized.

I vacillated. I convinced myself that Ron would eventually change. He'd get another job. He'd lose weight. He'd get himself together and work really hard. He'd become the man he used to be—the man I'd married who had been so wonderful. But I was fooling myself and making no one happy. Burying my head in the sand. Joan the ostrich.

In December of 1982 I was asked to be the mistress of ceremonies at a concert at the Royal Albert Hall in London before Her Majesty Queen Elizabeth and His Royal Highness Prince Philip. The Royal Philharmonic Orchestra was to perform the music of the Beatles. It was to be in aid of one of their favorite charities, the Royal Society for the Protection of Birds, and I was honored to be chosen to be the narrator at this wonderful event.

The Royal Albert Hall is an extraordinary building with a fascinating history. Some of the most renowned performers in the world have played there ever since Queen Victoria had it built in memory of her husband, Prince Albert.

I was even more thrilled that the organizers of the charity concert requested that Katy present a bouquet to Her Majesty after the performance.

Katy was overjoyed; she was a staunch Royalist, as was I. We debated at length about what to wear. Eventually Nolan Miller made a beautiful pink velvet gown with an antique lace collar for Katy, and a ruby velvet gown for me, with which I wore some of my more majestic "Dynasty Diamonds"—ruby-and-diamond fabulous fakes. Only the Queen would know the difference!

The "Dynasty" producers, also Royal Family fans, gave me a few days off to enable me to fly to London. In recent months the English press had been having a go at me. Rumors of our marital discord abounded, and although we continued staunchly denying it, it was hard for me to lie so blatantly. At the same time, we were not completely clear on how to break the news to Katy about our problems. Our marriage counselor had advised us at this moment to "do nothing and deny all." So be it.

I felt like a total hypocrite. Although I knew my personal life wasn't anybody's bloody business except my own, I thought it was wrong to be such an out-and-out liar. I was lying to everyone: to Katy, pretending all was well; to the press, who hounded me for "the Truth," which I constantly denied; to the "Dynasty" cast and crew, who knew nothing of my problems; but most of all to myself. I *wouldn't* face reality, *couldn't* admit the truth, the unbearable fact that marriage number three was on the rocks. I rushed around patching up little cracks, hoping the dam wouldn't burst.

The week before I arrived in London, headlines screamed that my electricity supply had been cut off in the South Street house because of nonpayment. "She ignored our requests for payment," sniffed the London Electricity Board. "She is making thousands, yet she's refused to pay the £350 she's owed us for over a year."

They had repossessed the meter from the South Street house—a house I had not lived in for two years. Naturally, this was front page news in the tabloids both in England and in the States.

Tearfully I confronted Ron. I knew *nothing* of it. The house wasn't my responsibility. He was supposed to be in charge, but obviously he wasn't anymore.

Hoping things would have simmered down, I arrived at the Albert Hall with Ron and Allan Tinkley, the manager of the concert, for rehearsals on December 13. I was excited, as I had just heard I'd been voted "Female Star of the Year" by the Hollywood Women's Press Club. Tom Selleck was voted top male star. As I stepped out of the car, a man jumped from the shadows. "Joan Collins?" he barked.

"Yes," I said charmingly, extending my hand to sign the autograph he so obviously desired.

"You are hereby served with a writ of . . ." I didn't hear the rest. I pulled my hand away and fled into the sanctuary of the Albert Hall.

The front-of-house manager arrived with the writ, which of course it was. It was for the nonreturn of a car loaned to me three years before by British Leyland in return for promotional work I was doing for them to publicize their new model, the Mini Metro. I'd been told the car had been returned months ago. It hadn't.

The newspapers had a field day. The following day, alongside lovely photographs of a delightful Queen, a demure Katy and an overawed me, were banner headlines, all along the lines of "Royal Star Joan Gets Writ"; "A Writ on Joan's Big Night"; "Bill Row, Joan Blows a Fuse"; etc. etc.

I was humiliated and embarrassed, not only for myself but for the Queen, who I'm sure was not amused by the tackiness of the whole situation.

Ron and I had another raging row, he absolving himself of most of the responsibility and me feeling abused, misused and terribly unhappy. I discovered a huge number of unpaid bills that had been virtually ignored for the past few years.

Ron's excuses that due to Katy's accident he had been unable to cope didn't wash with creditors now. The press were gleeful. I was in financial hot water. It made headlines, whether or not *I* was to blame. "They've Cut Off Joan's Electricity" sold a lot more newspapers than "Ron Kass Fails to Pay Bill."

The final marital crunch came on the day Linda Evans and I were to shoot a fight scene between Krystle and Alexis. The rivalry between the two women for Blake Carrington's affections had been building all season. The bitchy, hostile scenes between the two of us, who were of such physical and emotional contrast, had caught the viewers' imaginations and contributed to "Dynasty's" soaring success. This scene was to be a high point. A knockdown, drag-out cat fight, no holds barred. Scratching, biting and feathers flying. Claws out. The cat fight to end all cat fights. ABC was gleefully anticipating huge ratings.

I, however, was filled with trepidation. I loathed physical violence. I hated fighting, and, after watching the stunt double go through the extremely complicated and choreographed fight in rehearsal, I was nervous. Linda was two or three inches taller than me and very sportive. She actually preferred doing the physical fighting scenes to the verbal ones. With me it was vice versa.

Gene Kelly had told me during the time I was going through the rigors and fears of learning to horseback ride for *The Virgin Queen*, "Never do anything dangerous on film, kid. People get paid for that. Stunt people. Don't put 'em out of work." I totally agreed.

As the day of the fight approached I became more and more apprehensive. Things between Ron and me were bad. Katy was aware of it, and so was Daphne Clinch, a friend from Chichester who had come to look after Katy for the six or seven months I had thought the "Dynasty" gig would last. She was a kind woman who reminded me greatly of my own lovely mother, and she was constantly chiding me about working too hard, having too much responsibility and not getting enough support from Ron.

The morning of the fight scene I arrived on the set nervous and slightly queasy after a restless night. As I drove to the studio, I tried not to think of the day ahead.

Alice brought a cup of coffee to the trailer while I began shakily applying my makeup. The third assistant director came in and called me over for a rehearsal. I watched the stunt doubles throw their bodies about and flail their fists with expert agility.

A spasm of searing pain racked through me. A strange, unusual feeling. I doubled over in agony. "Appendix," said someone briskly. "Heartburn," surmised another expert. "Ulcer," said another. Whatever it was, I couldn't stand up straight. I was whisked off to the nurse's office on the lot, where they examined me and advised immediate admission to Cedars Sinai emergency.

Judy came with me, and, after a thorough examination in the emergency room, punctuated by beefy policemen barging in and reporting that there was "a cadaver" in the corridor, I lay bare from the waist up, electrodes attached to my chest, trying to cover that up as well as my by now famous face.

Dr. Al Sellers, who had saved my life when I had the shrimp allergy, said I appeared to have gastroenteritis, a condition exacerbated by extreme pressure, tension, exhaustion and nerves.

Judy called our apartment several times from the hospital to tell Ron of the situation, but Daphne reported she could not wake him up.

A few hours later, released from the hospital, I stood over our bed and beseeched Ron to rouse himself. I told him I was ill and had to go to bed. He continued sleeping and would not budge. I went into Katy's bed. I realized hollowly I had to escape. There was no longer any point in continuing with a situation that was causing so much pain to both of us, and was now affecting Katy.

A few weeks later when my first "Dynasty" season had ended, I flew to London with Katy. I had accepted a mediocre film called *Nutcracker* and was relieved to be leaving Ron in L.A. We decided to try a trial separation, going to great lengths to keep the truth from Katy, the press and everyone except our closest friends. We hoped that in some magical way, being separated by a continent and an ocean would do something for our marriage. But it had disintegrated too much. After endless talks, discussions, sessions with a marriage counselor, pathetic attempts at living together amicably, and enormous emotional strain, we finally came to the conclusion that there was no other choice for the three of us but for Ron and me to separate for good.

• • •

With a long career behind me, I had never received any awards of particular significance. Not that anything I had done had been particularly meritorious, but it would have been nice. I had been voted in 1956 "Star of Tomorrow" and "Most Prom ising Young Actress," and in 1957 "Most Outstanding Young Actress"—and in 1977 I got a best actress award for—believe it or not—*Empire of the Ants!*—but with my usual objectivity I realized I actually did not deserve any acting awards for the body of work I had done. When in 1982 the Hollywood Foreign Press Association nominated me for their coveted Golden Globe award for Best Actress in a TV drama series, I was pleased. I didn't win—but I didn't really expect to. In 1983 I was again nominated in the same category, up against Linda Evans in "Dynasty," Stefanie Powers in "Hart to Hart," Jane Wyman in "Falcon Crest." Heavy competition. Again, I did not feel that I had much of a chance. Flattered to be nominated, I agreed to be a master of ceremonies with Wayne Rogers. When the nominees for Best Actress were being announced I stood backstage stoically, prepared for rejection.

"And the winner is—Joan Collins."

Stunned, I stood there for a second, then dashed on stage to raise my arm in a victorious gesture and hear my green chiffon Nolan Miller dress rip under the arms. I had no speech prepared— just "I would like to thank Sophia Loren for turning down the part, and everyone on 'Dynasty' from Aaron Spelling on *up!*"

Ron escorted me to the Golden Globes. We had been separated for several months but were seeing each other in a friendly way. He was more thrilled than I was. But with all the joy of winning this award I was still very sad that my marriage was dead.

Ever eager to get away from the image of being just another pretty face, I jumped at the opportunity when director Jim Frawley offered me the dual role of the wicked stepmother and the wicked witch in "Hansel and Gretel."

"Hansel and Gretel" was being produced by the actress Shelley Duvall for Showtime cable TV. They were making a series of fairy tales called "Faerie Tale Theatre" and were able to tempt some fairly important stars into appearing. Robin Williams had just starred as the Frog Prince, and Mick Jagger, Christopher Reeve, Liza Minnelli, Malcolm McDowell, Vanessa Redgrave, Tom Conti and Tatum O'Neal had been signed. It was an interesting project with which to become involved.

Certainly it was no stretch for me to play the evil stepmother who sends the two innocent young children into the forest to their doom. With a curly red wig, scrubbed face and frumpy period clothes, I easily fitted into that role. The Wicked Witch, however, was another kettle of fish completely. My makeup for this part took over four hours to apply. Thick greenish paste was applied all over my face. A false hooked nose, false chin with a wart on it, brown, snaggly false teeth, a matted long gray wig, filthy curled false nails, thick straggly black eyebrows and a large hump on my back transformed me totally. On top of this went the classic witches' gear of black dress and pointed hat. I changed my voice and my walk completely. When Katy walked onto the set she came face to face with me and said, "Where's Mummy?" This was the most challenging and difficult part I had ever performed. We shot in 100-degree weather in Griffith Park. It was so hot that my nose and chin kept on getting detached from my face because of the sweat pouring down. The makeup girl spent hours pushing and prodding it back onto my face with surgical adhesive and a sharp instrument.

I had very long speeches. Since we were shooting on video, and fast—the whole episode was shot in six days—time waited for no one. It was nonstop and extremely exhausting, but very rewarding professionally for me. Particularly so when a year later I was nominated for Best Actress for this part by the National Cable TV Association.

In my third season on "Dynasty" we went to Denver, the city where "Dynasty" is set, to shoot at the Carousel Ball. This is an annual event to aid the Children's Diabetes Foundation, and it is hosted magnificently by Barbara and Marvin Davis. Marvin, one of the world's richest men, does not do things by halves, and to guest at the ball he had flown in some of the biggest names in films, TV and politics. Cary Grant, Lucille Ball, James Stewart, Raquel Welch, Lee Majors, Dolly Parton, Robert Wagner, Diana Ross, Merv Griffin, Stefanie Powers, Henry Kissinger and ex-President Gerald Ford were just some of the famous faces on the glittering dais, along with John, Linda, John James, Kathleen Beller and Michael Nader (two new faces on "Dynasty") and me. We had already shot John and Linda arriving by limo at the ball, and then Alexis with Dex, her new lover, played by Michael Nader, driving up in a white vintage Rolls-Royce.

It was amusing to hear the vast crowd in the street outside the ballroom screaming out our names with fanlike frenzy. How would that match our normal characters in "Dynasty"?

Our crew mingled inconspicuously with the gorgeously gowned and bejeweled women, the cream of Denver society. The crew embarrassedly all wore black tie and evening dress as they scurried around trying to shoot as much footage as possible before, during and after the dinner and ball.

I was seated at the dais between my escort, Peter Holm, and Dr. Henry Kissinger. I had met Dr. Kissinger the previous year at the ball and had found him a lively and scintillating dinner companion. I was draped in a two thousand dollar gold lamé Nolan Miller gown and wearing about a million dollars' worth of Harry Winston diamonds and emeralds. Suddenly a brilliant idea hit me. Why couldn't we do a little scene between Dr. Kissinger and Alexis? Why not, indeed? John and Linda had had some dialogue with Barbara and Marvin Davis, and Marvin had introduced "Blake" and "Krystle" to Dr. Kissinger at the ball, and also to ex-President and Mrs. Gerald Ford.

Elaine Rich, our line producer, was lurking in the auditorium with the camera crew shooting all and sundry. I beckoned to Elaine and whispered my idea to her.

"Will he do it?" she said eagerly. "It would be *dynamite!*"

"One can but ask," I said, boldly approaching him. "How would you like to do a scene with Alexis, Henry?" I batted my lashes and leaned close so that a hint of Scoundrel would engulf him.

"Vot vould ve do?" He twinkled conspiratorially. "I'm not an actor, you know."

"Oh, yes you *are*, Henry. Anyone who can make the wonderful speeches that you do all over the world—and convince people that you are so *right* in what you say—has got to be a *brilliant* actor. Let's do it—it'll be fun."

Reluctantly the good doctor agreed, and after the ball we went to the VIP room where the "Dynasty" crew, led by an excited Elaine Rich, were ready for us, surrounded by a multitude of sightseers.

"Now all you have to do, Doctor," explained Phil Leacock, our director, "is cross the room and meet Joan coming from the opposite direction, and just greet each other. It won't be difficult, Dr. Kissinger. It'll just take a second—Joan will help you."

And so Dr. Henry Kissinger, ex-Secretary of State genius-in-exile—his own phrase—and statesman supreme, found himself playing a scene with TV's naughtiest villainess, after I showed him how to hit his marks.

Dr. Kissinger: Alexis—how are you?

Alexis: I'm fine, Henry, how are you?

Dr. Kissinger: I'm vonderful, Alexis, good to see you.

Alexis: It's good to see you too, Henry. Yes, we haven't met since Portofino . . . wasn't it fun!

The crew collapsed at this ad lib, and another moment of television history was captured forever on film.

Ever since *Land of the Pharaohs* I have a couple of times been so convulsed with giggles while in the midst of shooting a scene that I have been unable to continue.

One such incident happened at the end of my second season of "Dynasty" when Alexis, Krystle and Mark Jennings (Geoffrey Scott) had just escaped from the burning cabin in which someone had tried to kill Krystle and/or Alexis.

Irving Moore, who was our resident director and usually directed every alternate show, was shooting this episode. He had a wonderful sense of humor, and I was very fond of him.

We were shooting inside the studio on a synthetic grass verge next to the back projection of the burning cabin. "Mark" carried me out to where "Krystle" lay panting and coughing, gazing fearfully at the flames. I was supposed to be unconscious. I was wearing a beige jodhpur suit and a large cap that kept falling off my head whenever Geoff placed me on the ground. Although my hairdresser, Linda Sharp, had attached it to my hair with forty-three hairpins and bobby pins, it still fell over my eyes each time Geoff put me down, giving me the look of a demented ventriloquist's dummy.

Elaine Rich decided I looked much too clean for someone having been almost asphyxiated by smoke, so Melanie Levitt, the makeup girl, liberally applied black pancake to my face and hands. A little too liberally. "*Cut,* cut!" yelled Irving exasperatedly. "She looks like Al Jolson, for Christ's sake. Wipe some of it off."

By the time Melanie wiped my face down, which then became an even gray, and Linda attached my cap even more firmly with more pins, I felt the whole thing was ludicrous. I "corpsed" every time Geoffrey set me down and spoke the immortal lines, "Krystle, that cabin was locked from the *outside*—somebody *deliberately* set that fire." I laughed so much that this started Geoff and Linda laughing too. Each take, the more I called on all my willpower—not to mention fiercely biting my tongue until it hurt—to refrain from laughing, the more I found it impossible to stop. Eventually we got the scene in the can, and I tottered off, still hysterical with laughter, to the shower, where it took me half an hour to remove all the fuller's earth and black pancake makeup with which I was covered. Ah, the glamour of show business!

One of the most dastardly deeds Alexis Carrington ever perpetrated was to cause saintly Krystle to lose her unborn baby by firing a shotgun into the air near where Krystle was taking a gentle ride on a horse. I wasn't too pleased about having to do this. Alexis, though mean and evil and Machiavellian in her plots and plans, would not deliberately kill or physically hurt someone, and I felt that this was a pretty low thing even for her to do. Nevertheless, do it I must, so one fine fall day I found myself traipsing up a hill next to my massively tall son, Steven (Al Corley), to go for a little skeet-shooting session, at which Alexis is supposed to be an expert—according to the script.

I had informed the writers that I was hopeless at all forms of sport and *anything* to do with horses ("Alexis *cannot* ride!" I had said to the producers loudly and clearly from the beginning), but nevertheless they decided that Alexis, *femme du monde*, jet-setter and social butterfly that she was, was an expert at all manner of sports.

It was a freezing November morning and we were shooting at a ranch in Hidden Valley. I had persuaded the wardrobe department, albeit reluctantly on their part, to let me wear a Scottish red-and-green-plaid kilt, a long plaid scarf and a beret. They in turn talked me into wearing a red angora turtleneck sweater, which I hated. Thus unsuitably attired, and carrying a huge shotgun of which I was extremely wary, I tottered up the hill, next to Al, the six-foot-four hulk.

"You must remember, Steven," I said crisply, expertly cocking my gun to shoot a skeet, "that you are a Carrington and a Carrington does *everything* well. We swim well, ride well, play tennis well and skeet-shoot well." With this I cocked my gun into space and let off a round, and the bullet went straight through the scrim surrounding an arc lamp, which promptly exploded!

Somewhat ruffled by this, and with my fear of guns still intact, I watched as the electricians replaced the lamp bulb, and then we started another take. By this time the sun had risen high in the sky, as is its wont in Southern California. The temperature had now crept up to the mid-seventies. Bits of red angora fluff had attached themselves to my eyelashes, making everything a faint reddish blurr, and some had floated up my nose, which caused me to sneeze uncontrollably at the end of each take.

Because of this I now started blowing my lines, which I rarely do. Alf Kjellin, our Swedish-born director, was patient with me, but with the heat, the angora fluff everywhere, the *ghastly* gun over which I seemed to have no control, and the "apple box" I was balanced on to get close to Al Corley's height, I was, to say the least, frazzled.

"Thirty-eight baker take nine!" called Joe Valdez, clapping the board in front of my nose and causing me to stifle another sneeze. Take nine—oh, God, how awful. I, who usually get it in one. I concentrated hard. The heat had brought out many insects, and, attracted to my hairspray, they started buzzing around and taking little nips at me.

"Action," called Alf in his calm Swedish way.

"You must remember, Steven, that a Carrington does *everything* well. We swim well, ride well, play tennis well and skeet-shoot well."

Thrilled that I had said the entire line without a fluff, I was about to raise my gun with studied nonchalance when the butt of the gun caught in my hanging plaid scarf and I inadvertently pulled the trigger, shooting myself in the foot! Luckily the gun was loaded only with blanks, but it still stung madly and I hopped around on one foot cursing wildly.

"OK— that's a print," said Alf "Now let's move over to the tree and have Joan shoot Linda."

Disheveled, sweaty, limping and humiliated, I put on my most evil Alexis look, and with angora fluff and insects floating like an aura around me, I raised the shotgun and shot the two blasts that caused Krystle's horse to bolt, throwing her to the ground and causing her to lose the baby. For which she and thousands of viewers never forgave me!

"*Playboy* layout!" What did these words mean to everyone? Some cute little nymphet taking off her all for a thousand dollars? It was pretty meaningless in that respect. As far as I was concerned, it had farther-reaching consequences. Women had been exploited for years, whether by themselves or others made no difference. The women I saw in *Playboy* and other men's magazines were young girls doing their erotic or sexy "thing." I certainly didn't consider myself to be in that category any more. I didn't even consider the possibilities or ramifications of what it meant. I was never prudish—selective nudity per se did not bother me. But Middle America, to whom all Hollywood bowed, was a different problem.

Being a woman of "a certain age," I felt that revealing what I did in *Playboy* was a definite plus for women. "A significant step for feminism," I lightly announced. I was exploiting myself—yes, indeed. But in doing so I felt I was breaking the ageism taboo that so many women feared and dreaded. Be that as it may, the December 1983 issue of *Playboy* became a sellout issue and a collector's item. I realized that it was because of me—Joan Collins—not Alexis. I hoped to prove that a woman can definitely be attractive and sexy over thirty-five, or even over forty-five, and I didn't get as much flak from this layout as I had expected. I had had reservations about it, but the admiration that I received, from *women* particularly, for doing it, was well worth the minimum amount of negativity I received. "Well, Brickman," I said to Leslie Bricusse at a party the night *Playboy* hit the stands, "I think I'm about to become notorious." "What do you mean 'about,' " joked he. "You already are, Joanie!"

My life has changed radically since I started "Dynasty." The stardom that I never tried to attain as a young actress I have now. How long it will last—who knows? This is the toughest of professions. Very tough. Flavor of the month changes rapidly. Only the strongest, the cleverest and the most resilient survive—but survival is not the only objective. To live as normal a life as possible without letting the enormous pressures that one faces change one's attitudes and sense of reality, without giving in to drugs, booze, sex, flattery, the "woodwork people"—to keep one's sense of balance—is an art in itself.

If my success ended tomorrow and I no longer had the attention, the money, the magazine covers, the media interest, the fan frenzy, the paparazzi, the scripts plopping onto my doorstep, I know that I could survive and still be a happy person.

Success is not enough. Money and material possessions are not enough. Nor beauty—nor men—nor love nor lust or whatever it's called these days. The truly important things in my life now are the health and love of my children—particularly Katy, with whom I have an irrevocable bond—and the love and loyalty of my close friends who have remained by me throughout the years.

To me, a good, loving relationship is one in which two secure and mature individuals are committed to *wanting* and needing to be with one another. Unfortunately, one's needs change with the years, and couples must acknowledge this and try to change too—otherwise love can only end in disappointment. The quest for true love can take many forms, as I have discovered. The acid tests of a relationship are time and growing together toward a mutual goal that is satisfying to both parties.

My life has been full of surprises, excitement, many highs and several lows. Hard work. Many relationships. Some pain, and a lot of fun. Most of the time I have enjoyed it completely. "Life is a banquet and most poor suckers are starving to death," said W. C. Fields. I agree.

Today I must contend with the public's disparate image of me as the manipulative and bitchy Alexis. Sometimes it can be amusing, like the day Judy Bryer and I were driving down Benedict Canyon about four months after I started appearing on "Dynasty." A station wagon full of little kids about seven or eight years old drew up as we stopped at the traffic lights, and they all began waving excitedly.

"Your junior fan club," joked Judy.

I smiled generously at the sweet little things and lowered my window to bestow a wide smile and my "Queen Mum" wave on them.

"Alexis," they shouted joyfully, "we hate you! we HATE you!!!"

They jumped up and down with glee and I turned, stunned, to Judy, who was shaking with laughter. "You're the woman America loves to hate," she said. "May as well face it and go for it. It's a compliment, really."

I realize there is a side to my character a tiny bit like Alexis. Often I wish I were more like her in her strength and positivity in business relationships. However, I feel it is ironic that the bitch-goddess label will probably live with me forever, like it or not.

There is a man in my life now. He came into it unexpectedly last summer at a time when the last thing in the world I felt I wanted or needed was another relationship. After so many mistakes, I am wary and careful of involvement. What the future holds for us I cannot possibly predict. As I realize, there are no guarantees in life, and the only constant is change.

My past was not perfect—whose is?—but it certainly wasn't dull. Hopefully I have learned much from my mistakes and have paved the way for a happier and more peaceful future. *Onward!*

Filmography

LADY GODIVA RIDES AGAIN
GB 1951 / D: Frank Launder / with Pauline Stroud, Dennis Price, Stanley Holloway, Kay Kendall, John McCallum, Diana Dors.

THE WOMAN'S ANGLE
GB 1952 / D: Leslie Arliss / with Edward Underdown, Cathy O'Donnell, Lois Maxwell.

JUDGMENT DEFERRED
GB 1952 / D: John Baxter / with Hugh Sinclair, Helen Shingler.

I BELIEVE IN YOU
GB 1952 / D: Basil Dearden / with Cecil Parker, Celia Johnson, Laurence Harvey, Harry Fowler, Ursula Howells, Godfrey Tearle.

DECAMERON NIGHTS
GB 1952 / D: Hugo Fregonese / with Louis Jourdan, Joan Fontaine, Binnie Barnes, Mara Lane.

COSH BOY (US: THE SLASHER)
GB 1953 / D: Lewis Gilbert / with James Kenney, Hermione Gingold, Hermione Baddeley, Betty Ann Davies.

THE SQUARE RING
GB 1953 / D: Basil Dearden / with Jack Warner, Robert Beatty, Maxwell Reed, Kay Kendall, Bernadette O'Farrell.

353

TURN THE KEY SOFTLY
GB 1953 / D: Jack Lee / with Yvonne Mitchell, Kathleen Harrison, Terence Morgan, Glyn Houston, Geoffrey Keen, Thora Hird.

OUR GIRL FRIDAY (US: ADVENTURES OF SADIE)
GB 1953 / D: Noel Langley / with George Cole, Kenneth More, Robertson Hare, Hermione Gingold, Hattie Jacques.

THE GOOD DIE YOUNG
GB 1954 / D: Lewis Gilbert / with Laurence Harvey, Richard Basehart, Gloria Grahame, Stanley Baker, Margaret Leighton.

LAND OF THE PHARAOHS
US 1954 / D: Howard Hawks / with Jack Hawkins, Sydney Chaplin, James Robertson Justice, Alexis Minotis, Kerima, Dewey Martin.

THE VIRGIN QUEEN
US 1955 / D: Henry Koster / with Bette Davis, Richard Todd, Herbert Marshall, Jay Robinson, Dan O'Herlihy, Lisa Daniels.

THE GIRL IN THE RED VELVET SWING
US 1955 / D: Richard Fleischer / with Ray Milland, Farley Granger, Glenda Farrell, Luther Adler, Gale Robbins.

THE OPPOSITE SEX
US 1956 / D: David Miller / with June Allyson, Ann Sheridan, Ann Miller, Dolores Gray, Joan Blondell, Agnes Moorehead, Leslie Nielsen, Dick Shawn.

SEAWIFE
GB 1956 / D: Bob McNaught / with Richard Burton, Cy Grant.

ISLAND IN THE SUN
GB 1956 / D: Robert Rossen / with James Mason, Joan Fontaine, Harry Belafonte, Patricia Owens, Stephen Boyd, Dorothy Dandridge, John Justin.

THE WAYWARD BUS
US 1957 / D: Victor Vicas / with Jayne Mansfield, Dan Dailey, Rick Jason, Dolores Michaels, Betty Lou Keim, Larry Keating.

STOPOVER TOKYO
US 1957 / D: Richard L. Breen / with Robert Wagner, Edmond O'Brien, Ken Scott, Larry Keating.

THE BRAVADOS
US 1958 / D: Henry King / with Gregory Peck, Stephen Boyd, Albert Salmi, Lee Van Cleef, Henry Silva, Kathleen Gallant.

RALLY ROUND THE FLAG, BOYS
US 1958 / D: Leo McCarey / with Paul Newman, Joanne Woodward, Jack Carson, Tuesday Weld, Gale Gordon, Dwayne Hickman.

SEVEN THIEVES
US 1959 / D: Henry Hathaway / with Rod Steiger, Eli Wallach, Edward G. Robinson, Michael Dante, Berry Kroeger.

ESTHER AND THE KING
US/ITALIAN 1960 / D: Raoul Walsh / with Richard Egan, Denis O'Dea, Sergio Fantoni, Rik Battaglia, Gabriele Tinti.

THE ROAD TO HONG KONG
GB 1962 / D: Norman Panama / with Bob Hope, Bing Crosby, Dorothy Lamour, Robert Morley, Frank Sinatra, Dean Martin.

LA CONGUINTURA
ITALIAN 1964 / D: Ettore Scola / with Vittorio Gassman, Jacques Bergerac.

WARNING SHOT
US 1966 / D: Buzz Kulik / with David Janssen, Eleanor Parker, George Sanders, Stefanie Powers, Lillian Gish, Walter Pidgeon.

SUBTERFUGE
GB 1968 / D: Peter Graham-Scott / with Gene Barry, Tom Adams, Suzanna Leigh, Richard Todd, Michael Rennie.

CAN HIERONYMUS MERKIN EVER FORGET
   MERCY HUMPPE AND FIND TRUE HAPPINESS?
GB 1969 / D: Anthony Newley / with Anthony Newley, Milton Berle, Connie Kreski, Bruce Forsyth, Tara Newley, Sacha Newley.

IF IT'S TUESDAY, THIS MUST BE BELGIUM
US 1969 / D: Mel Stuart / with Suzanne Pleshette, Ian McShane.

STATE OF SIEGE
ITALIAN 1969 / D: Romano Scavolini / with Mathieu Carrière, Faith Domergue, Michael Coby.

THE EXECUTIONER
GB 1970 / D: Sam Wanamaker / with George Peppard, Judy Geeson, Nigel Patrick, Keith Michell, George Baker, Charles Gray.

DRIVE HARD, DRIVE FAST
US-TV 1970 / D: Douglas Heyes / with Brian Kelly, Henry Silva, Karen Houston, Joseph Campanella.

UP IN THE CELLAR (THREE IN THE CELLAR)
US 1970 / D: Theodore J. Flicker / with Larry Hagman, Wes Stern.

QUEST FOR LOVE
GB 1971 / D: Ralph Thomas / with Tom Bell, Laurence Naismith, Denholm Elliott, Juliet Harmer, Lyn Ashley.

REVENGE (US: INN OF THE FRIGHTENED PEOPLE or TERROR FROM UNDER THE HOUSE)
GB 1971 / D: Sidney Hayers / with James Booth, Sinead Cusack, Kenneth Griffith, Tom Marshall, Ray Barrett, Zuleka Robson.

FEAR IN THE NIGHT
GB 1971 / D: Jimmy Sangster / with Judy Geeson, Ralph Bates, Peter Cushing, Gillian Lind, James Cossins.

TALES FROM THE CRYPT
GB 1972 / D: Freddie Francis / with Ralph Richardson, Peter Cushing, Nigel Patrick, Richard Greene, Martin Boddey.

DARK PLACES
GB 1973 / D: Don Sharp / with Christopher Lee, Robert Hardy, Jane Birkin, Herbert Lom, Jean Marsh.

TALES THAT WITNESS MADNESS
GB 1973 / D: Freddie Francis / with Michael Jayston, Kim Novak, Jack Hawkins, Donald Pleasence, Georgia Brown, Peter McEnery.

L'ARBITRO (US: THE REFEREE)
ITALIAN 1973 / D: Louis Phillipo D'Amico / with Lando Buzzanca.

ALFIE DARLING (US: OH! ALFIE!)
GB 1974 / D: Ken Hughes / with Alan Price, Jill Townsend, Hannah Gordon, Rula Lenska, Annie Ross.

CALL OF THE WOLF (US: THE GREAT
  ADVENTURE)
SPANISH 1975 / D: Paul Elliotts / with Jack Palance, Fred Romer.

THE BAWDY ADVENTURES OF TOM JONES
GB 1975 / D: Cliff Owen / with Nicky Henson, Geraldine McEwan, Georgia Brown, Trevor Howard, Madeline Smith, Terry-Thomas.

I DON'T WANT TO BE BORN
  (US: THE DEVIL WITHIN HER)
GB 1975 / D: Peter Sasdy / with Ralph Bates, Donald Pleasence, Eileen Atkins, Caroline Munro, John Steiner, George Claydon.

THE MONEYCHANGERS
US-TV 1976 / D: Boris Segal / with Kirk Douglas, Christopher Plummer, Anne Baxter, Lorne Greene, Susan Flannery, Jean Peters.

EMPIRE OF THE ANTS
US 1976 / D: Bert I. Gordon / with Robert Lansing, John David Carson, Pamela Shoop, Jacqueline Scott, Albert Salmi.

THE BIG SLEEP
GB 1977 / D: Michael Winner / with Robert Mitchum, Sarah Miles, Edward Fox, Oliver Reed, Candy Clark, James Stewart, John Mills.

POLIZIOTTO SENZA PAURA
ITALIAN 1977 / D: Selvio Massi / with Maurizio Merli, Franco Ressel, Gastone Moschin, Jasmine Maimone, Alexander Trojan.

THE STUD
GB 1978 / D: Quentin Masters / with Oliver Tobias, Sue Lloyd, Mark Burns, Emma Jacobs, Walter Gotell, Doug Fisher.

ZERO TO 60
US 1978 / D: Darren McGavin / with Darren McGavin, Sylvia Miles, Denise Nickerson, Dick Martin.

GAME FOR VULTURES
US 1979 / D: James Fargo / with Richard Harris, Ray Milland, Richard Roundtree, Sven Bertil-Taube, Denholm Elliott.

THE BITCH
GB 1979 / D: Gerry O'Hara / with Michael Coby, Carolyn Seymour, Sue Lloyd, Mark Burns, Pamela Salem, Kenneth Haigh.

SUNBURN
US 1979 / D: Richard Sarafian / with Farrah Fawcett, Charles Grodin, Art Carney, Eleanor Parker, Alejandro Rey.

PAPER DOLLS
US-TV 1982 / D: Edward Zwick / with Joan Hackett, Marc Singer, Jennifer Warren, Darryl Hannah, Alexandra Paul.

NUTCRACKER
GB 1982 / D: Anwar Kawadri / with Finola Hughes, Paul Nicholas, Carol White, William Franklyn, Leslie Ash, Geraldine Gardner.

THE WILD WOMEN OF CHASTITY GULCH
US-TV 1982 / D: Philip Leacock / with Priscilla Barnes, Pamela Bellwood, Lee Horsley, Howard Duff, Morgan Brittany.

HANSEL AND GRETEL FAERIE TALE THEATRE
US-TV 1982 / D: James Frawley / with Ricky Schroeder

THE MAKING OF A MALE MODEL
US-TV 1983 / D: Irving J. Moore / with Jon-Erik Hexum, Roxie Roker, Jeff Conaway, Kevin McCarthy, Arte Johnson, Ted McGinley.

MY LIFE AS A MAN
US-TV 1984 / D: Robert Ellis Miller / with Robert Culp, Marc Singer, Robin Douglas.